CO-CONSPIRATOR FOR JUSTICE

CO-CONSPIRATOR FOR JUSTICE

THE REVOLUTIONARY LIFE OF DR. ALAN BERKMAN

Susan M. Reverby

THE UNIVERSITY OF NORTH CAROLINA PRESS

Chapel Hill

This book was published with the assistance of the
Thornton H. Brooks Fund of the University of North Carolina Press.

Designed by Jamison Cockerham
Set in Arno, Scala Sans, Irby, Cutright
by Tseng Information Systems, Inc.

Cover illustrations (left to right): Berkman's Columbia University Medical
School orientation photograph (courtesy of Columbia University Health
Sciences Library); FBI's wanted poster for Berkman, August 10, 1983;
Berkman speaking at a demonstration (photograph by Barbara Zeller)

Manufactured in the United States of America

The University of North Carolina Press has been a member
of the Green Press Initiative since 2003.

Cataloging-in-Publication data for this title is available at the
Library of Congress, https://lccn.loc.gov/2019049812
978-1-4696-5625-0 (cloth: alk. paper)
978-1-4696-5626-7 (ebook)

To Alan and Barbara's grandchildren,

Gabriel and Amelle,

and my former students who become activists

The thing I don't like about the word *ally* is that it is so wrought with guilt and shame and grief that it prevents people from doing what they ought to do. . . . Co-conspiracy is about what we do in action, not just in language.

ALICIA GARZA, cofounder of Black Lives Matter

CONTENTS

ILLUSTRATIONS

KEY NAMES

MARION BANZHAF, *leader in the John Brown Anti-Klan Committee and AIDS activist*

SILVIA BARALDINI, *key figure from May 19th*

JERRY, LARRY, *and* STEVEN BERKMAN, *Alan's brothers*

LOU BERKMAN, *Alan's uncle*

MONA *and* SAM BERKMAN, *Alan's parents*

SARAH M. ZELLER-BERKMAN, *Alan's daughter*

DANA BIBERMAN, *Alan's lover and comrade*

TERRY BISSON, *key figure from May 19th*

TIM BLUNK, *resistance conspiracy codefendant*

DONNA BORUP, *key figure from May 19th*

MARILYN BUCK, *resistance conspiracy codefendant*

DIANE GILLMAN CHARNEY, *Alan's high school and college girlfriend*

RICHARD CLAPP, *Alan's medical school and longtime friend*

HARRIET CLARK, *Alan's daughter*

JUDY CLARK, *key figure from May 19th*

BETTY ANN DUKE, *key figure from May 19th*

LINDA EVANS, *resistance conspiracy codefendant*

LAURA FONER, *Alan's friend from Weather and Washington Heights*

TOM GARRETT, *physician friend from Alan's internship
who also became one of Alan's doctors*

LIZ HOROWITZ, *key figure from May 19th*

RON KUBY, *one of Alan's lawyers who became a close friend*

BOB LEDERER, *Alan's comrade and AIDS activist*

SHELLEY MILLER, *key figure from May 19th*

ANN MORRIS, *Quaker friend of Alan's*

HANK NEWMAN, *Alan's high school drama teacher and friend*

SHARON NEWMAN, *wife and then ex-wife of Hank Newman*

ANNE NOSWORTHY FISHER, *high school friend who also went to
Cornell and stayed in contact with Alan when he was in prison*

EVE ROSAHN, *key figure from May 19th*

SUSAN ROSENBERG, *resistance conspiracy codefendant*

BRUCE TAUB, *Alan's friend*

STEVEN WANGH, *Alan's friend*

LAURA WHITEHORN, *resistance conspiracy codefendant*

BARBARA C. ZELLER, *Alan's wife and comrade*

CO-CONSPIRATOR FOR JUSTICE

Alan Berkman, "Boy Most Likely to Succeed," Middletown High School yearbook, class of 1963, p. 60. *Author's collection.*

CHILDREN OF THE HOLOCAUST
AND COLD WAR

A very few — as heroes, patriots, martyrs, reformers in
the great sense, and men — serve the state with their
consciences also, and so necessarily resist it for the most
part; and they are commonly treated as enemies by it.

HENRY DAVID THOREAU, "Resistance to Civil Government," 1849

I never thought I would know an American revolutionary. Yet my brilliant
childhood friend Alan Berkman became one, and then a political prisoner of
the United States as well as a global health activist.[1] The man whose bar mitzvah I attended, and whom we voted the boy "most likely to succeed" in high
school in 1963, found inspiration in John Brown, Vladimir Lenin, Che Guevara,
and the poorest of the poor. He was an ally to Native American, African American, and Puerto Rican radicals and other revolutionaries around the world. Although never a killer, he believed for years that through "armed propaganda"
he could change America. And later he would do more than that, much more,
to transform policies and save lives across the globe.

Alan kept missing our high school reunions for none of the usual reasons.
By the time of our tenth gathering, he had become a successful physician. He
was absent because he had just crawled under the guns of law enforcement, illegally, to provide medical care to American Indian Movement stalwarts at the
siege of Wounded Knee, or because he was busy caring for those the government labeled terrorists in New York City. It was only the beginning of efforts
that brought him to attention of the police and the Federal Bureau of Investigation (FBI). In 1983, he missed our twentieth reunion, having skipped out

on bail to go into the "underground" and become a bomber of political sites. Once he was caught and convicted, he survived nearly eight years in some of our country's worst dungeons. By our thirtieth class get-together in 1993 he was a working physician again, in New York fighting acquired immunodeficiency syndrome (AIDS) at the height of the epidemic; by the fortieth he was transforming how life-saving drugs were made available worldwide. And when our fiftieth came in 2013, he was already four years gone, felled by the treatment for his *sixth* round of cancer.

Growing up during the Cold War in Middletown, our upstate New York community, no one at our high school imagined being wanted by the FBI, or receiving an indictment for conspiracy to resist the policies of the U.S. government. Many of us only thought about becoming adults and leaving for somewhere, and something, bigger. Cornell University accepted both of us in 1963, but after orientation our college worlds drifted apart: his to the rigors of premed and mine to labor history and the antiwar and civil rights movements. He and I symbolized the many divides of the 1960s. Alan loved being a fraternity boy who played football. I organized men to burn their draft cards in protest against the Vietnam War and was almost thrown out of the university. As my friends and I considered the possibility of prison time for civil disobedience, Alan dreamed of a successful medical career.[2]

After graduation in 1967, we saw one another from time to time in New York City. I worked for grassroots organizations committed to social change in education and health care before heading off later to graduate school in history. Alan entered a prestigious medical school, won prizes, and launched his medical career. We remained distant friends.

Even now, Alan's next move was startling: he quit after his internship that could have led to a promising academic medical career to become a community doctor, committed to solidarity with the most radical elements in the African American, Puerto Rican, and Native American political movements. He and his white comrades were condemned by the government, forced into the political underground, labeled terrorists, did bombings, and were finally caught and convicted during the 1980s. He spent his middle age in the depths of prisons, often in solitary confinement, fighting off two serious cancers that nearly killed him.

Alan survived the gulag and his illnesses. Miraculously, he was allowed to keep his medical license after he emerged. Eschewing the tactics of his earlier politics, he devoted himself to caring for very poor people with human immunodeficiency virus (HIV)/AIDS. Through Columbia University's Public Health School and the AIDS organization he helped to found, Alan became a world-renowned and respected HIV/AIDS global researcher and activist. He trained a generation of public health practitioners to fight the disease and galvanized political actions to make available generics of the antiretroviral drugs that likely saved millions of lives around the world. In his life after prison, Alan fought the U.S. government and international indifference to suffering in a wholly new way. When he died in 2009 at sixty-three, not everyone who admired his courage and humanity for his AIDS work knew how he had balanced his revolutionary beliefs with his professional positions throughout his life.

This biography is about Alan's unique journey into differing forms of political action. As others abandoned their youthful radicalism for professions, working-class lives, or wallowed in the illusions of acid-formed consciousness, Alan became a self-described revolutionary. One of his close friends described Alan as "the closest person I ever knew to an avatar in Hinduism" — that is, the incarnation of the god Vishnu, who returns to Earth to restore the balance of good over evil.[3] Others in the revolutionary movements of Native Americans, Puerto Ricans, and African Americans considered him a comrade who took personal risks, courted death, and repeatedly refused the FBI's promise of freedom and witness protection if he gave information on his allies.

I really knew Alan only as a boy and young man, and after that we drifted in and out of touch. I wrote him only once when he was incarcerated. I was not sure what to say to him because I did not agree with his political tactics, even when we shared basic beliefs. I did tell his story in our twenty-fifth Cornell reunion book, with the encouragement of another Middletown friend, when he was still in prison in 1992. I thought our classmates should know what had happened to him, and I, too, was trying to figure it out.[4] I saw him briefly once after he served his prison time, spoke to him a few times on the phone, and he granted my request to speak at our thirty-fifth Cornell reunion on how the Vietnam War had affected our class. I realized then that he was a stranger whose life I did not understand. I had my stem cells tested to see if I matched when he needed a transplant to fight his cancers (I did not), and burst into tears when I learned he had died — because, somehow, I always expected him to recover.

When I was asked to give a plenary lecture at a professional history of medicine meeting in 2012, I thought I could use Alan's story to focus on how historians judge "infamous" doctors.[5] It was only then that I met his widow, the physician Barbara Zeller, and she gave me his unpublished prison memoir, hundreds of letters, pages of legal papers, and linked me to friends willing to talk. His story intrigued me for its complexities, insights into political resistance, and health activism. I suspect above all I was fascinated because part of his journey was the path I, and others of my generation, had imagined at one time we would take, but ultimately did not. After all, a survey of college students showed that in the late 1960s "350,000 considered themselves revolutionaries," although I only thought of myself as a radical.[6]

The self-centered, sports-oriented, smart, and arrogant boy who chafed under the pressures of conformity in Cold War America became a compassionate physician and impassioned organizer. The doctor who pledged "to do no harm" was willing to take a gun with a silencer into a robbery at a pharmacy with a faked Food and Drug Administration (FDA) badge, wig, and glued-on mustache to fund his underground life. The high school actor would stage incendiary political theatrics with bombs signifying that the U.S. government's racist and imperial acts could not take place without consequences. And then after all the prison years he changed his tactics by taking on U.S. trade policy to save the lives of those in the Global South with HIV/AIDS who needed treatment, not just prevention. Once a fraternity president, then a revolutionary and political prisoner, in his later years he was a brilliant diagnostician and consummate listener, adored by patients, friends, colleagues, and students.

I am riveted, too, by Alan's story as it reflects the perennial American questions of what role white allies can play in the struggles for equality and justice, especially as the Black Lives Matter movement has brought these essential political questions back to the forefront in the face of the police killings of black men, women, and children. I remembered him when contemporary black activists called for "allies" and then really "co-conspirators." He had been this. I wondered what Alan would have thought of members of the antiracist group Redneck Revolt, who took their AR-15s to a Nazi and white supremacist rally in Charlottesville, Virginia, to protect protestors, or the actions of other Anti-Fascists (Antifa) activists. At a time when Americans wonder about our place in the world, Alan thought deeply about global responsibility. He understood the connections between the struggles for liberation at home and abroad. Unlike those in law enforcement who assumed American radicals conspired with revolutionaries abroad, Alan was inspired, sometimes naively, by the latter's bravery and commitments.

To understand Alan's life, I also thought about his masculinity as it intersected with race, sexuality, and class. Raised under Cold War dictates of manliness, in reaction to the murders of European Jewry and from a family in which prowess tied to intelligence mattered, Alan came to manhood with the expectations that he meld his character and physicality together.[7] He sharpened his manly bearing in his family of all boys, and when he became an Eagle scout, and then a fraternity president and a football player in college. While he never proved his gender in the military, he did so in a different kind of war, as he took on his own government with retaliatory violence and then political demands.[8] And under the pressures of his anti-imperialist and antiracist women comrades, he struggled to find a way to balance his learned masculinity with his feminism.

His life embodied a form of solidarity that crossed all the usual lines as he continually negotiated the use, and negation, of the privileges his gender, class, sexuality, and race gave him. His strength and fearlessness combined with an extraordinary compassion for people with the very least, whom others shunned. At a time now when shooters and terrorists claim righteousness for their actions, Alan's passage from small-town Eagle Scout, to self-absorbed college student, to medical-school radical and beyond is worth understanding, even if each of us is changed by our times tied to our psychodynamics. His ability to imagine what could lead to political and social change, and then to fail at it, and then make it happen marked his extraordinary tale. His life epitomizes the possibilities of health activism to change what seem like intransigent government and corporate policies.

"Brother Doc," his prison moniker, best symbolizes Alan's efforts to shed his privileges and yet to use them to organize for those whose lives could not have been more different from what his *might* have been. There were really four parts to his journey: conventional upbringing, move toward political extremism, imprisonment of the worst kind, and recommitment to meaningful global political actions. The quote from James Joyce's *Ulysses* our high school yearbook's editors put under his name was both right and very wrong: "A man of genius makes no mistakes. His errors are volitional and are portals of discovery."[9] Alan did indeed lead a remarkable life of discovery driven by love. His life was, in the end, a white American man's story like, and unlike, any others.

EAGLE SCOUT, FRATERNITY PRESIDENT, DOCTOR

REMEMBERING

It was the fall of 1970, and Bobby Seale, the leader of the Black Panthers, was about to go on trial in New Haven, Connecticut. He was accused of conspiring to murder a fellow Panther, an act he had neither committed nor ordered. Yet as the jury's voir dire went on for months, it grew obvious to everyone, from radicals like me to Yale College's president, that there could be no fair trial. The President's Commission on Civil Unrest released a report warning of violence stemming from "divisions in American society as deep as any since the Civil War." The fear of disorder in New Haven, after bombs had exploded months earlier, was palpable.[1]

Alan and I were both in New York City: he was in his last year of medical school and I was working for a left health policy think tank. A few months into 1971, as the trial began, Alan came to see me. We shared a deep anger over what was happening, but our strategic visions were diverging. Just how far became clear when he asked in all seriousness, "Would you be willing to take up arms if Bobby is convicted?"

In an instant, I knew that my childhood friend and I had crossed lines. He was ready to consider violence, and I was terrified—too aware intellectually as a historian of what happened to the left when it confronted state power with weaponry, and too scared emotionally to participate, even though I knew how to handle a rifle. "We will be outgunned," I remember telling him, sounding more sure than I felt. "We always are, and the consequences will be terrible." I don't remember if we argued, but I think he accepted my position with grace.

When Seale was acquitted, the threat of a major street action with guns, or at the very least an effort to free him, became moot. Still, I wondered then what allowed Alan to imagine that this plan made sense. I used to tell this story to my students, long before I ever thought about writing about Alan, to illustrate the kinds of decisions radicals were making then. It would take me nearly half a century finally to understand why Alan thought he had to act, and what it would mean for his life. It began with his family, but not because they were on the left.

BORN STRONG WITHOUT FEAR

TOUGH JEWS

Alan came from a long line of men who were taught how to respond when confronted with danger. His remembered stories, as with most American Jews, started in Eastern Europe.[2] Not all of the Berkmans recollected, or even heard, the tales of Grandpa Moische exactly in the same way. Not all of them knew, or acknowledged, whether or not Grandpa Moische had been a killer.

Alan knew the legacy. His was not a family of *yeshiva bochers* but of manual laborers in Europe and America. They were tough men who knew how to work and fight.[3] Moische, the family stories attested, had gone to work in the old country as a farrier's apprentice when he was eight to help support the family.[4] He was also a member, maybe even the key organizer, of a "gang of Jewish youths . . . the Horse Heads." They saw themselves as responsible for retaliation against those who perpetuated the pogroms that sent Eastern European Jews fleeing, fighting, or dying. When one "Cossack" raised his voice to Moische's mother, Moische threw "one fist to the forehead" and the man had died. Now "wanted for murder," Moische had to flee with his family from their shtetl in the Jewish Pale of Settlement between Poland and Russia.[5]

The American government did not know the history of this Jewish avenger when twenty-six-year-old Moische Berkman and his wife, Minnie, arrived to join other family on August 7, 1911, on New York's Lower East Side. A year later he was in the junk business in Brooklyn.[6] There was another tale, about a knife, a fight, and Moische coming out ahead against a Nazi sympathizer on New York's Upper East Side sometime in the 1930s, maybe even dodging a murder charge with a plea of self-defense. By the 1940s, the family had three sons and one daughter, all living at home in tight quarters.[7]

Moische was a "bull of a man," his grandson remembered. He stood his ground and taught his family to do the same.[8] In the junk business, Moische and his crew raced to fires and demolitions, found old buildings where they stripped the copper and lead pipes, got paid to take the stuff away, and then again when they sold it. So there was always the need to be tough, to be the strongest, fastest, and "to scare other junkmen away," even to outsmart those with Mob connections.[9] Moische's toughness did not make him the easiest man to live with.[10] Still, he passed his abilities down through the Berkman family, teaching the business to his two oldest sons, Sam (Alan's father) and Lou (Alan's uncle), as he maintained strict control.[11]

The Berkmans fascinated Brooklyn-born novelist Joseph Heller, best known for his World War II novel, *Catch-22*. He grew up near them and fictionalized the family in his 1995 novel *Closing Time*. Moische's physicality in Heller's words fit the family stories: "a short man with the biggest, thickest shoulders . . . and small blue eyes in a face that reminded people of a torpedo or artillery shell. With his freckles and hard lines and liver spots, he looked like an iron ingot, an anvil five and a half feet tall."[12]

For Heller the key character in the family was his childhood friend Lou, Alan's uncle. Lou's chapter of Heller's novel starts, "I was born strong and without fear."[13] Lou's brilliance at pinochle made it into the novel, as did his willingness to use his high school German to his advantage during the war, while still showing off the "H" for Jew on his army dog tags.[14] Heller recalled Lou, like Moische, as "a strong, physical man who rarely backed away from a fight . . . also a charmer—what is known in Yiddish as a *tummler*, a big talker with a big heart."[15]

Heller's jealousy of the Berkman men's strength was clear: "Lou and his brothers were huge. They'd take an automobile motor and pick it up and just throw it up into something. They came from a strong, muscular family. It was genetic." In his stories, they could take on those bigger or older than they were, or younger as they got older, because their verbal banter was always backed up by their physical menace. Lou was built like a wrestler, but Sam was nearly six foot four, and powerful.

Old enough to be drafted, Moische's oldest sons went to war. Lou saw action in Germany, survived a prison camp, and left the service a captain.[16] Sam, by now married to Alan's mother, Mona Osit, and with a young son (Alan's older brother Jerry), managed to postpone his enlistment till March 1945.[17] He spent the short remainder of the war as a private at Ft. Tilden at the tip of Rockaway Beach, not far from his young family in Brooklyn. On September 4, six months after his father's enlistment, Alan was born. Sam moved his family to Ft. Tilden at war's end and stayed on the base for three more years of service while Mona took care of her boys.[18] When they mustered out, Sam and Lou went back to work for Moische.

In those years, the New York junk business played a critical role in the arming of Israel as the new state emerged between 1945 and 1948 from its status as a British protectorate (the "Mandate for Palestine"), with no legal way to prepare itself for war. The German American Jews had the money, but it was some of the Eastern European immigrant junk dealers who collected the munitions and snuck them out through New York harbor.[19] There is no historical evidence of the Berkmans' involvement, but there is a family story that Alan and some of his brothers recall. The tale is of their father Sam and Uncle Lou getting stopped by a cop as they sped toward the Brooklyn docks to get the guns in their car trunk to a ship bound for what would become Israel. The policeman was Irish American and understood what it meant to fight the British state. The guns passed and no one was arrested. Another brother says this never happened, and yet it is plausible.[20]

By the early postwar years, Alan's father Sam and Uncle Lou had decided that working under the "tyrant" had become too difficult and they needed their own chances.[21] Lou had friends in the farming and rolling hills of Middletown, New York, at the foot of the Catskill Mountains, more than three hours upstate.[22] It was still close to family in the City, but far enough to require a deliberative trip for a visit.

While Sam finally finished his time in the army, Lou moved up first in 1948, scouting for business opportunities. Within a year he convinced Sam and his growing family to join him to begin a secondhand plumbing and building supply company.[23] Moische provided the $10,000 to buy the building they needed. He charged more interest than the banks, but then again, the banks had not been willing to give the loan.[24] The Berkmans soon joined a very small Jewish community, becoming deeply involved in its cultural and religious life.

IN THE MIDDLE AND UPSTATE

Middletown was literally in the middle, halfway between the towns of Mount Hope and Montgomery, whose borders were west of the Hudson River by about twenty miles in New York's Orange County. When the Berkmans arrived in 1949, residents of the thriving summer colonies in the "mountains," surrounding farming communities, and nearby hamlets came into the city of Middletown (with 22,586 inhabitants, a fifth of whom were in the local state mental hospital) to shop, see their doctors, and go to the movies.[25] Small drug and hardware stores, bakeries, banks, groceries, and clothing stores for rich and poor lined North, South, East, and West Main streets near the junction of Franklin Square in the center of town.

Sam, Mona, Jerry, and Alan, then four years old, joined by a baby brother, Larry, moved first to a small house on Little Avenue, in a white, working-class neighborhood only a few blocks over from Fulton Street, the center of Middletown's small black community.[26]At least the Berkman family had running water: segregation and enforced poverty consigned black families to outhouses and wells even within the city limits.[27] Migrant labor farmed the black dirt acres in nearby rural districts, harvesting onions in season and then disappearing. Alan's older brother remembered "very little racism," but it would have been largely invisible to Middletown's white families.[28]

Middletown had its own smells and sounds. A Dutch immigrant family that also kept a factory in Holland made chemical flavors for the food and perfume industries in the large Polak's Frutal Works.[29] A different odor would waft through the city every morning, depending on what was being made. The Erie and Ontario and Western railroads ran their trains through town, their horns, engines, and railcars providing the soundtrack for daily life, as did the roar of stock cars in the summer at the Orange County Fair. And every year there was the firemen's parade through the main streets, as the visiting fire companies showed off their latest shiny trucks, and the brass bands and bagpipe contingents marched by the crowds. It was vintage small-town America.

Politically, Republicans led the town as in the rest of upstate New York, except for the Democrats in the Italian American wards.[30] There was also an ugly side to the politics. The Ku Klux Klan operated in the area by the turn of the twentieth century, and in the 1920s large rallies, with "10,000 members of the Ku Klux and its affiliated orders," were held in Peekskill, just thirty miles away. The year the Berkmans moved in, the Klan and the American Legion attacked singer and actor Paul Robeson's concert in Peekskill.[31] Even twenty years later, known Klan members were on the school board in Pine Bush, just ten miles from Middletown.[32]

The sense of being different yet wanting to belong seeped into the Jewish children. The schools had everyone sing Christmas carols, even the "Jesus Christ our Lord" lines. Anti-Semitism was always there, if hardly mentioned. Swastikas on occasion showed up on the houses of the Middletown Jews, and almost every Jewish family counted a relation murdered by either the Cossacks or the Nazis.[33]

Still, there was little to do, and proximity meant that the adventures of childhood were shared across these divisions. Middletown kids learned to sneak over the fence into the Japanese garden on land owned by the richest family to play together, roam the woods around the local state hospital in joyful fear of meeting the insane, swim in the nearby lakes and sun on man-made beaches, hunt in the hilly countryside, or shoot the rats at the local dump. "It could have been the Midwest," Alan's older brother recalled, "with conservative values."[34] One of Alan's grammar school classmates agreed: "It was safe, secure, and we wanted to get out."[35]

The Berkmans slowly made their way into Middletown's middle class as their business, home, and family expanded. When the building boom called more for supplies than secondhand materials, the family's business became Middletown Plumbing Supply, and then just Middletown Supply. Moische's loan was paid back. A modern split-level ranch in a nicer neighborhood replaced the house on Little Avenue as the family grew to four boys after Alan's youngest brother, Steven, was born. Five men outnumbered Mona in the family.

Alan's baby pictures show a slightly rotund young kid whose nose would grow faster than his body. By adolescence, we whispered behind his back that he looked like the Lebanese American TV star Danny Thomas, from *Make Room for Daddy*. Alan was well aware. Campaigning for high school student government president, his slogan was "The Nose Knows." His then girlfriend said her hope for him was "Berkman wins by a nose."[36] He lost by a little to another Jewish boy.

Much of Alan's early life focused on family, sports, and religious activities. The Catholic students got released early from school once a week to go to their religious training. The Jewish kids schlepped to the synagogue *after* school twice a week for the endless Hebrew lessons and went back on Saturday mornings for services at Junior Congregation, and Sunday morning to hear the parables from Rabbi Goldblum.[37] Alan absorbed the moral lessons of Judaism, but not the need to carry on the religious tradition so important to his parents. Their communalism was profound, and they explained to their son "that you can only trust your own, that you always had to be aware of what the gentiles could do to you."[38]

Like many of his contemporaries, Alan grew apart from his family's religiosity. Once while playing ping-pong with friends at the synagogue social hall, the congregation was short two men for their *minyan*. Alan and his best friend, Jeff Millman, were asked to participate, but both refused. When Alan's father heard about it, he was "livid . . . [and] there was some punishment . . . and he felt the family name had been disgraced."[39] By high school, Alan was questioning Jewish exceptionalism, and felt what he called "the drive to integrate" into American life.[40]

Alan found his athleticism early even though Sam had no interest in sports and barely managed to toss a ball around in his backyard to his four boys. There were enough Berkman brothers to form a small team, and to engage in rough and tumble play and physical back and forth. To his younger siblings, Alan was the big brother, their superhero, while Jerry was so much older and studious he might as well have been another parent. Alan excelled at baseball, and the family often went to his Little League games, where he befriended both black

Alan's formal bar mitzvah photograph, 1958, Temple Sinai, Middletown, New York. *Courtesy of Barbara Zeller.*

and Latino boys, not always to his family's approval.[41] By high school he was running cross-country, on the tennis team, and became sports editor of our high school paper.[42] He wanted to try out for the football team, the center of the high school's life and identity, but his mother wouldn't hear of it.

Sam and Mona taught their children to be civic and support their own. Sam supported his mother-in-law and his mother after Grandpa Moische passed away.[43] Uncle Lou served for many years on the Middletown School Committee, and his children would go on to high local political offices as well. Alan's parents were much more focused on the Jewish community and believed deeply in the dangers of the gentile world and in Jewish specialness in the world.[44] Sam became president of the Jewish congregation and Mona the head of its sisterhood, where she handed out the personal prayer books to all those who made it through bar and bat mitzvahs. Alan was active in the Jewish boys scouting experience, went to the scout camps, made it to Eagle Scout (where he was "cited for citizenship in the nation"), and represented his troop at a national jamboree.[45] His scoutmaster made Alan the "assistant junior scout master" for his skills and leadership abilities.[46]

The belief in civic virtue was reinforced through Cold War rituals of preparedness. Duck-and-cover drills were mandatory in elementary school. Children assembled in lines against the inner walls holding newspapers over their heads, which were supposed to offer some kind of protection from bombs.[47] When the Cuban missile crisis occurred in October 1962, Middletown High School responded by staging an overnight shelter drill in the subbasement. It made national news.[48] Doing well then was a responsibility not just to self but also to one's family, as well as a national duty as part of the Cold War script.

Racism, when it was discussed at all among the white kids, was spoken of in the context of how bad it made America look in the world's eyes, a problem that seemed far away.[49] When the synagogue's rabbi went to the March on Washington with several of his congregants in August 1963, Alan did not go, and my mother wouldn't let me because of the "crowds." One liberal family brought some of the Little Rock Nine to Middletown for an evening.[50] Alan was not there, but I was, and I left impressed by their bravery. Racism was seen primarily as a problem of the South.

Work, hard and manual, and success were built into the Berkman family's expectations. Alan had a paper route when he was seven and eight. He remembered the regularity of his father's work routine: up early every morning and into his truck by 7:15 while the rest of the family was just awakening.[51] All the boys worked for Sam and Lou hauling and driving on the weekends after they turned sixteen, and one summer Alan drove a meat truck filled with pastrami and brisket for a kosher butcher; another summer it was dry cleaning delivery or construction.[52] Physical labor and those who did it were never looked down upon even as the family did better, going on to invest and build the first garden apartments in Middletown, ironically on land the city's richest family had once controlled.[53] The financial rewards for the family were visible in Mona's Fontana Rosé–colored Cadillac with huge fins, the modern *tchotchkes* that she bought for the house, and the bad toupee Sam wore to cover his bald spot.[54]

Sexual adventures for us started in about sixth grade with "spin the bottle" parties.[55] The dances for teenagers in junior high were held in church basements that were open to everyone white, with the implicit understanding that the black kids would never dare to participate. Once everyone was old enough to drive, there was the place literally called "Farmer Brown's" or else the movie drive-in where the introduction to sexual foreplay or more could occur outside parental control in the borrowed family car.

Alan's knowledge of where to "park," as it was called, was noted in the high school yearbook's "last will and testimony." He would, his classmates wrote, "leave his map of the outskirts of Middletown to the highest bidder."[56] His house's family room with its wood-paneled walls and banquettes was the site of parties for slow dancing to Johnny Mathis and making out in the dark corners. By high school, the Jewish community made sure there were socials with the other Jewish kids from the nearby cities and towns, but there was a lot of dating across religious and, on occasion, racial lines, although this was mostly seen as dangerous.[57]

Alan had various adventures with numerous shiksa goddesses attracted to his wit, intellect, and strength. It was said that he climbed out of one young woman's bedroom window ahead of parental notice. He told his girlfriend that he had lost his virginity while driving as a deliveryman for Hymie's Kosher Butcher the summer before his last high school year, when he met "a gang of lusty women in the Catskills. Bored waiting for their hubbies to come up for the weekend, they attacked him! At first he tried to fend them off, but then he said to himself, 'what the heck?'"[58]

Diane Gillman, a year younger, who caught his eye and whom his brother Jerry dared him to ask out, was Jewish, thin, and blonde. She was a very bright doctor's daughter, served on the high school color guard, and her French was better than his. After several months during his senior year observing his obvious crush, she finally found Alan's smarts appealing, while his Jewishness pleased her parents after her many years of dating a Catholic boy. She responded to Alan's kindness and understanding of her personal stories and his excellent kissing abilities.[59] They would develop a private world of secrets, special coded words (his mother became Monalagoon, and they sometimes wrote with pretend stutters to make fun of a friend), and typical adolescent gossip about others in their crowd. Their relationship would last for seven years, all through college.[60]

As much as sports and dating, Alan's love was theater and the amateur theatrics that were almost as important to high school life as football. He starred in the senior class productions and was in the chorus for another. As he waited to leave for college in 1963, he was part of the summer theater presentation of *Li'l Abner*, while spending more than a little time with the play's hot ticket "Daisy Mae" while his girlfriend was away. He was as concerned about his acting as he was his schoolwork, and was much relieved when the shows came together and proved to be successes.[61] Most of all that year he became close friends with Hank Newman, the high school's handsome and sophisticated new drama teacher, and their connections to one another would extend for years.[62] Acting provided Alan with a way to imagine himself into someone else's reality, and to know how a wig, makeup, and theatricality could transform him into another being. These would prove useful skills in the years to come.

As with many Jewish men, Alan feared most of all being seen as a schlemiel or schlimazel. As the joke goes, "A *schlemiel* is somebody who often spills his soup and a *schlimazel* is the person it lands on."[63] With his pal Jeff Millman they went riding one day. Alan fell off the horse, had it step on his foot, and then was almost stung by a bee. Alan was mortified, his friend remembered, out of proportion to the accidents.[64] No man raised in the sports-centered and Cold

War milieu of the time, in a physically strong family like Alan's, or as the brother who was supposed to be a superhero to his younger siblings and still beat his older brother at everything, could afford to be so labeled. Becoming tough was part of the script of becoming a man.

THE REALLY, REALLY GOOD STUDENT

"We were smart," his classmate and future fellow physician Elihu Sussman recalled, "but Alan was really really smart." The family knew he was quicker and brighter than other kids. It meant he was expected to work hard to make good on his promise. He had the best grades consistently, getting the highest marks in the county on the state exams his senior year. "Tops in test," as the local paper put it next to his photograph and a National Merit Scholarship that proclaimed the recognition of his accomplishments.[65] He even won the prizes for driver's education and typing.

All of us just knew he was going to do well and without the kind of effort we needed to put in.[66] He seemed to be able to visualize and remember a page of text at first glance, and then to reproduce the answer in a multiple-choice test, or analyze a text in his neat, rounded, and readable cursive. He could listen intently and give well-developed responses, often to complicated questions. The only trouble I remember him having was squeamishness when we had to dissect a frog in biology. The teachers, of course, loved him.

Everyone expected Alan to emerge as the class valedictorian and at first, he was. Then the scores were recalculated and a girl beat him to first place by tenths of a percentage point. She had done better in music theory, where the girls had been sent, than he had, ironically, in the all-boy shop class. Mona and Sam were livid that this top honor was taken from him and lodged a complaint to no avail. It seemingly hampered Alan in one way: the girl went on to Radcliffe, while Harvard turned him down. It made him very angry. Yale promised him money, but Cornell University's College of Arts and Sciences offered him more combined with the Regents Scholarship for New York State universities. At the last minute he decided to join his brother, then in law school, farther upstate in Ithaca.

At the high school graduation held on the football field in June 1963, prize after prize came his way. In his program he wrote his name "Alan B" on all the awards he garnered: "First Scholarship Award, Salutatorian's Award, American History Prize, and the McQuoid Americanism Award."[67] He won a third of all the prizes given.

Yet Alan carried a certain amount of anger about him. His family valued the success they assumed his intelligence would gain him, but Middletown expected conformity. The messages from the family were there: use your brains

Alan's informal photograph in the Middletown High School yearbook, class of 1963, p. 47. *Author's collection.*

to menace, compete, and win, and your strength when needed to support your family and your tribe. His Jewishness became both a badge of difference and a source of pressure to conform. His family's physicality linked him to the working class, and his maleness and love of sports gave him a place to seem equal. For all his efforts to contain himself as he navigated these paradoxes, there was something in Alan that smoldered beneath the surface.

Alan's awareness of his own talents made him consider what he would do with them. His girlfriend suggested to him he might want to become a governor of the Federal Reserve Bank, one of the best jobs they could imagine.[68] His brother Jerry was already in law school. His best friend Jeff's father was one of the few local pediatricians, and his girlfriend Diane's father was a dermatologist. Alan spent much time discussing medicine with these men, who took him in as another son in their families; none of their other children expressed an interest in the profession. The combination of caring, science, intellectualism, and the ability to control one's life with the money to be made appealed to him.[69] By the time he left for college, he was sure he would be a premed. He would leave Middletown and his family behind, but not the lessons about how to be in the world.

THE OTHER 1960S STUDENT

In 1963 Alan arrived at Cornell, an institution on the cusp of change, yet mired in the past. Nearly 10,000 undergraduate students, almost all white, gave Cornell nearly half the population of Middletown, while in area it was even larger, set atop steep hills that overlooked glacier-carved Lake Cayuga.[1] Cornell was always coeducational, but male students outnumbered the women 3.5 to 1. The differences were clear: women students had to live in the dorms or sororities with stricter curfews, while the men lived more freely in fraternities or apartments after their first year. Everything about the university told its young men that they were in charge.[2]

Cornell, despite the millions poured into faculty research and its membership in the Ivy League, was in many ways a party school with a focus on practicality. Nearly half the students came for a bachelor of science degree for their vocational-focused studies, not the liberal arts.[3] With a drinking age of eighteen, nearly everyone could legally imbibe to oblivion at bars or the endless parties that the sixty-four fraternities staged, though they could not yet vote. Mescaline, lysergic acid diethylamide (LSD), and other drugs circulated widely, too, and "grass," as marijuana was then called, became fairly ubiquitous.

The conformity of the early 1960s meant everyone was supposed to know, or learn, their place. The religious and cultural divisions were clear enough that the middle section in the student union's dining area was jokingly called the Gaza Strip (then under Arab control), separating the Jews and Gentiles. There was a "beatnik" crowd, varying political groups from left to right, intellectual nerds, and the Greek life.

Alan lived with nearly 2,000 other men in the concrete barracks of the freshmen dorms known as the "pig pen." He seemed disgusted by the disorder. Writing to his girlfriend Diane back in Middletown, he described the "puke patrols," organized after his dorm advisor slipped on vomit, or the time that a shower flooded his floor, or another when the social lounge was covered in shaving cream.[4] Still, Alan could embrace the fun of it, throwing eggs at a guy who walked into his room one night in an uproar of adolescent humor.[5]

Alan still maintained a connection to home, continuing to get the local paper and the synagogue newsletter. He knew he did not want to be back in Middletown, but he needed Diane. Half kiddingly he told her, "Would you like to get married—NOW?" He was struggling to allow her to enjoy her last year in high school but terrified she would abandon him. He even sent her clippings about a student report on the need for birth control services, "whether or not [students] were married," that would "not injure campus morals."[6] His warmth and concern for her, and his willingness to listen deeply to her worries, continued to characterize their almost daily letters.[7]

It did not take long for him to adjust to the demands of the premed major and his own desires. Without his parents to hold him back, he got on Cornell's lightweight (sprint) football team, and the athletics and starchy food bulked him up to 163 pounds.[8] Only a broken wrist later in the season after a scrimmage seemed to slow him down.[9] He told Diane that he wanted to bring her up so that he could "(1) . . . show you off (2) you'll see what it is like."[10]

He styled himself straight and pre-professional, wearing a sports jacket to class when few other men did. He also took up a pipe but only for "affect," he admitted. As for the other students, "About 1 out of 10 don't wear socks; 5 out of 10 wear real tight white Levis. What shlups(?)," he added in a plaintive letter.[11] Later in the year he commented on students at another university, arguing "they should stop with marijuana and beatnikism, & start some kind of normal life."[12]

He found comfort in his studies. "I've decided to study every night, even when I don't have a test," he confided to Diane. "I understand it's the only way to do well."[13] His first grade in an English composition, a 75, was sobering, and he knew he'd have to work harder. "I'm learning things right & left," he promised his girlfriend.[14] A friend down the hall taught him how to use a slide rule, and as dedicated studying took effect his grades rose to the highest in his classes. He seemed to relax a bit, but almost every letter reported his worry about the next exam and how well he was doing.[15] He would have slept more, he complained, if he had not been spending a lot of time "helping everyone else on the corridor."[16]

Still, he was taking advantage of what Cornell had to offer, attending a debate between conservative William Buckley and then progressive Cornell history professor Donald Kagan on "The Welfare State," enjoying Buckley's ability to demolish the professor. Meanwhile the thousands of books shelved in the massive Uris Library, with its metal stairwells and garret corners, beckoned and filled his reading needs outside of class.

His insensitivities reflected his small-town upbringing and the casual racism of white everyday language he was steeped in. Trying to provide jokes for Diane he told her, "Maybe these will help keep you laughing, altho they're not very good: (1) I have nothing against Negroes—I think everyone should own one. (2) Hire the handicapped—they're fun to watch."[17] Joking about an albino woman who was getting married, he quipped, "the poor sucker is probably a Negro who thinks his kids will turn out flesh-colored that way."[18] When Diane expressed an appreciation for social critic and novelist James Baldwin, Alan disagreed. "If he weren't a Negro," he argued, "he would be considered a third-rate novelist. In my opinion, all he is a poor potboiler. If you want to appreciate the guy, I'm afraid I can't help you, because I can't even tolerate him."[19] When Diane described a visit to New York City when she could not get a cab in Harlem, Alan told her, "The idea of walking through Negro and Spanish Harlem at twilight petrifies me, no matter how much 'sang froide' [sic] I may have. Don't you realize what a temptation a beautiful white girl offers to most of the 'gang' there? . . . It's just not funny & it could be tragic."[20]

Alan found his place socially when he "rushed" the Jewish Tau Delta Phi fraternity. Pledging involved being paddled, wearing an onion around his neck, and bringing "a bucket of cow manure, a goldfish and several unmentionables" to the fraternity house.[21] One of his fraternity brothers remembered that Alan had picked this house because "they were intellectual, funny kids who didn't really care about the fraternity stuff and just wanted to have fun."[22]

It was not all fun. I caught a ride with Alan and his brother back home for Thanksgiving break, just a few days after the murder of President John F. Kennedy, and there was much talk in the car about what the assassination meant for America. Nothing had prepared us for this kind of national mourning, and the conspiracy theories had not yet taken hold. We sensed that a different world shimmered nearby, and our bewilderment deepened.[23] Then we were back from the break, and we focused on our work as our first-year exams loomed.

Alan's fears of doing badly abated when he was inducted second semester into Phi Eta Sigma, the men's freshmen honor society.[24] He castigated himself for forgetting a twenty-point question on a chemistry exam and promised Diane, "Never again will I do something out of stupidity—ignorance, yes, but stupidity never."[25] He even bragged to her about getting the highest grade out of 550 students in his literature course. "I want to be a record breaker," he wrote.[26] When he did badly, he felt terrible. When Diane received a low mark, he empathetically wrote how he felt when it happened to him: "Your stomach seems to contract all at once, & your eyes even seem to get a little misty. You tell yourself that it can't be true, & you go over the paper half-hysterically. It's a disgusting feeling."[27] He also tried to remind her he was often helpful to others after a high school senior stayed in his room and wrote Alan a thank-you note.

"I just wanted to show you that I'm not nasty *all* the time & that I sometimes do help people."[28]

He was well aware of how hard his parents had worked to make his life at Cornell possible. "My father makes $15,000 dollars a year," he confessed to Diane. "He spends more than $4,000 dollar a year on Jerry and I. He also contributes $2,000 to his mother's support. He also gives $1,200 a year to my mother's mother . . . and he supports 6 people."[29] At the same time, however, he made jokes about his own egoism and position. Heading out of a dorm bathroom and down the hall, he reported to her, "I kept saying, 'the King is coming, the King is coming.' Everyone opened their door, & when they saw me, bowed down. I've got them well trained, no es verdad?"[30]

Alan's early casual racism appeared to be receding. He had gone to hear Roy Wilkins, head of the National Association for the Advancement of Colored People, and thought he was a "very persuasive & emotional speaker . . . by far the best Negro leader in the country at this time."[31] He befriended one of the few African American men in our class, and noted that his room at the fraternity house the next year was going to be what he called "a minority group room: two Jews & a Negro."[32]

As the semester drew to an end, he tired of studying and competing. He looked forward to the return to Middletown, where the summer meant driving a delivery truck for Gilman's Dry Cleaners, playing tennis, going out with his friends to the movies, and more time with Diane till she began her first year at the University of Rochester. He had not yet let go of his small-town life.

RADICAL POLITICS, FRATERNITY MAN

After the summer of 1964, Alan returned to a Cornell that was already a different place politically from the year before. He knew now, too, that he could handle the work. After the first-year rankings came out he wrote Diane, "I was 35th in my class of 871. That's the top 4%. I'll try to do better this year."[33] Many of his fellow students had broader concerns. As a contemporary activist put it, "It felt like the whole world was exploding."[34]

When Alan had first arrived at college, the newly formed Cornell Liberal Union had bemoaned the students' "political apathy," but the civil rights movement and then the Vietnam War would change that.[35] His African American roommate, John Haywood, began to get him to understand racism and its consequences.[36] Civil rights work by Cornell students and faculty began in Fayette County, Tennessee, close to the Mississippi border. Students returned from the project to campus to report on what they had seen, but Alan made no mention of this in his letters. The murder of three civil rights workers in the summer of 1964 hit Cornell hard because Mickey Schwerner, one of those killed, was a 1961 alumnus. A rally held in November 1964 featured Schwerner's father, Congress of Racial Equality head James Farmer, and Cornell students and faculty who had worked in both Tennessee and Mississippi. I remember how moving the event was, but Alan was not there.

The year 1964 was also when the Free Speech Movement exploded on the Berkeley campus of the University of California. In fiery speeches and demonstrations that were covered by the *Cornell Daily Sun*, Berkeley students' campaign for the right to hand out literature about the civil rights movement morphed into a national debate on the role of the university and the creation of its students as cogs in the machinery of an advanced capitalist country. It ignited tensions that would later explode into what one author calls the "campus wars."[37]

By December, as the demonstrations at Berkeley mounted, the Cornell faculty passed a resolution in support of the Berkeley faculty and students formed a Friends of the Free Speech Movement chapter.[38] Alan never discussed any of this in his letters to Diane, nor do his roommates recall any real political conversations. The only politics he mentioned to her in a year of writing was around the time of the November elections, commenting on the U.S. Senate race that would give Robert Kennedy the seat from New York, but expressing his ambivalence about Kennedy's win, and his pleasure that Lyndon Johnson would beat Barry Goldwater for the presidency.[39]

Alan was a typical student of the 1960s, just not the one lodged in historical memory. He wasn't a beatnik, hippie, or political activist; he was fraternity man. He wanted to be a doctor, to make his parents proud, and to be part of the liberal state. He wanted his girlfriend to love him and support him on his climb to the medical pantheon. Nothing could distract him from those goals, it seemed.

PREMED PRESSURES, LOVE, AND FRATERNITY LIFE

The work was getting harder. He kept reassuring Diane, now a freshman at the University of Rochester, less than two hours away, that she was going to do well. He, however, seemed to have hit the sophomore slump. "All I discovered is what I already knew: organic [chemistry] is impossible; history is boring; zoology I like, & English I couldn't care less."[40] Organic was a killer, but Alan assured Diane, evoking the civil rights movement, "I shall overcome some day-y-y-y."[41]

They agreed to date others, but their bond and the sense of something special between them continued. "I LOVE YOU," he wrote to her one day in giant capital letters.[42] "God, I really miss you," he told her plaintively in late October after asking her who got the other two points when she received a 98 on a quiz, "Why aren't you here to help me, huh?"[43] He often made suggestions to her on how to write her papers, but their assumed sexual division of labor reflected the times: he bemoaned her washing his T-shirt with her clothes that made it pink, and now felt he could not wear it, since he was "a future famous doctor."[44] Mostly he wrote about how much he loved her and wanted her, his attempts at erotica subdued but unmistakable.[45]

Their fights often left him forlorn.[46] He was learning that it was possible to be mad at someone you cared for, extremely mad, but still want the connection to continue. In his romanticism, he told her the pain he felt when she was not there only meant his love was deeper.[47] He also understood the need for others. When Winston Churchill died, he wrote Diane to say he didn't mean to be "overdone, but I almost started crying when I saw Lady Churchill throwing the dirt on her husband's casket."[48]

Alan's focus was not just on himself and his love life. A compassion for others was sometimes hidden in braggadocio that was not mere puffery. As a former fraternity brother recalled, he had a "Rasputin-like ability to capture people's attention and their credibility, their beliefs. . . . He would listen in a way that most people didn't know how to listen, so we would all love to talk to him and I always found him to be great fun to be with. He always understood me."[49] He was also already practicing his doctor skills, helping a roommate with his ills, driving him to the infirmary, and then describing in detail student accident victims (two of whom died) who were triaged ahead of them.[50]

Though sympathetic to others, Alan had also absorbed his family's standards about hard work as the means to achievement. He was angry with a roommate who faked an illness to get out of an exam, and annoyed that another friend lacked initiative to work harder.[51] Mostly, he focused on the pressures he felt to do well. The exams were killers: organic was curved, so that getting 50 percent of the questions right gave you a grade in the 90s, while the government exam included numerous "picky quotes and chronological order," as well as long essays.[52] He admitted to a "natural inertia" and "struggling with my good intentions to work really hard."[53] He relied on what would become a hallmark of his later life, his photographic and aural memory, telling Diane he never took a note in his English course.[54] Getting only three hours of sleep during exam weeks and still committed to working intensely, he channeled his family's standards and expectations.

His empathy for others came out during fraternity rush. The sophomore members of a house were tasked with telling freshmen when they had been "flushed," or not accepted. It had to be done in person, and Alan hated it. One guy he told "burst out crying," Alan reported. "You can't take an 18 year old boy in your arms & console him no matter how immature he is (& he was immature). I could empathize with him, & I tried to reassure him, but he wouldn't stop. . . . Some of the other kids I spoke to were almost like that."[55] During a pledge raid he twisted a freshmen's finger and dislocated it during a friendly tussle. "He claims it doesn't even hurt," he promised Diane. "Well, at least the pledges will leave me alone during the pledge raids now."[56] He intertwined physical strength with tenderness, as he projected his particular brand of masculinity.

Though still very much a straight fraternity guy, Alan's interests were expanding. Even though French existentialist philosopher Jean-Paul Sartre refused to come to Cornell to give lectures because of the U.S. war in Vietnam, Alan was reading his *The Age of Reason*. Still, rowdy protests annoyed him for the disorder they engendered. When Cornell was celebrating its 100th birthday, Governor Nelson Rockefeller was invited to speak. "In the middle of his speech," Alan reported to Diane, "about a hundred kids got up and started yelling about ending the war in Vietnam & all that crap. A fine display by the Young Socialists of Cornell."[57]

Much more was going on at Cornell, but Alan never mentioned it. When the national Students for a Democratic Society (SDS) organized one of the first major Washington, D.C., demonstrations against the Vietnam War, Cornell sent busloads of students to participate and the faculty coordinated a major teach-in on May 7, 1965.[58] Four days later W. Averill Harriman, former American ambassador to Vietnam, gave a speech on the war. According to the *Cornell Daily Sun* reporter, he was "repeatedly hissed and booed" leading to a "demonstration shortly after Harriman left when approximately 100 students sat-in on the Bailey Hall stage."[59] There was a sit-in to protest the Vietnam War at the cavernous Barton Hall a few days later (when the college president reviewed the Reserve Officer Training Corps cadets). The scene grew ugly as 2,500 "shouting and booing" students condemned the 76 students who had tried to stop the review.[60] It would be a prelude to the tensions that would split both the campus and the country in the coming years.

Alan's only other mention of the war came when a student from the Middletown area who was doing well at Cornell was reclassified as "1A" and became draftable. "I only hope that was a bad mistake," he told Diane.[61] As with most of the Cornell students, despite the continued protest, Alan generally became concerned about the war only when it became personal. In the meantime, Alan kept his focus on his studies, while making time to visit his dying grandmother as her cancer led to kidney failure. Ignoring campus politics, he finished his courses and went home to a summer job on a construction crew.

When he returned he no longer lived on campus, but he did go back to football and the expected injuries from the games. He had inherited his brother's apartment on the lake and shared it with two fraternity brothers. He had a room to himself that was really a barely reconstructed porch, and the freezing temperatures in the winter were awful. He still had multiple eight o'clock classes that required getting up really early to drive to campus. Now outside the dorms and fraternity house, he and his housemates had to learn to cook, efforts that sometimes filled their house with smoke.[62]

His letters to Diane were gradually replaced by phone calls and visits. Alan's workload of physics, comparative anatomy, English, an honors English course in representational fiction, and the constant football kept him busy enough, as he was also weight lifting to see if he could get up to 172 pounds. His exhaustion led to an incomplete in the honors course, but he finished it up within the deadlines with a B+ that left his grade averages unharmed. Sharing a house with two other fraternity men also meant enjoying their antics with girl-friends and bad driving.[63] He had found a way to balance his studying, sports, and social life. While antiwar protests escalated across the country, Alan spent the rest of the academic year taking more science courses and getting ready to spend a summer in Europe.

THE WANDERING JEW IN EUROPE

The almost requisite undergraduate trip by himself to Europe proved to be the manhood-making adventure he wanted. Separated from both his family and Diane, he was wandering on his own, happily commenting on cultures he explored. He found the British dull and "obedient," the result, he declared, "of centuries of class discrimination." His pronouncement was clear: "They are tired and limp, & it's no wonder we took the world away from them."[64] There were the bedbugs in a hotel in Calais, drivers' universal disinterest in picking up hitchhiking Americans, the exhaustion from lugging his suitcase, and long train rides. He was happy to find that his high school French seemed to suffice. "The rooms are crappy, & the bathrooms worse, but it's all part of the experience, I guess." He described himself as "the wandering Jew."[65]

He managed to hitch to Spain and met up with his high school buddy Jeff. They went to bullfights and then Pamplona for the running of the bulls.[66] They slept on the beaches in southern Spain, absorbing the beauty and warmth.[67] He was keeping up his end of the bargain by writing to Diane faithfully, though disappointed when he would show up at the American Express office in a new city to find no letter from her to greet him.[68]

He missed Diane but not his life in Middletown. He appreciated the sights but even more the generosity of strangers who shared space and meals with him in cars and trains.[69] Beholding art and antiquities, he admitted, "many times . . . I had goose pimples looking at something I had previously only seen in books or heard about."[70] Along the way, however, the slovenly and disrespectful actions of his fellow Americans on the trains offended him and pushed him to think about his own position in the world. "Here I am, a rich American, grubbing from these poor people." As the world opened up to him, his sensitivity to class was deepening.[71]

A FUTURE IN MEDICINE

When he returned, Alan was not happy to be back in Ithaca. He lamented Diane's decision to spend her junior year abroad, and he wrote her even before her ship had landed in France.[72] He was beginning to get the medical school applications and already bemoaning the work it would take to fill them all out.[73] His workload was heavy: nearly eight hours a day of classes and labs, and an additional three hours on Saturday. He admitted to thinking he had to get off the football team. Instead of studying his histology (where he ended up with a C), he wrote Diane suggesting that he should give her his fraternity pin ("pinning" was considered a precursor to engagement).[74]

Even with all his busyness and exhaustion (including four days in the college infirmary with a fever of 103°F), he managed to do more than others. He was now also president of his fraternity, although not living there, responsible for making it run financially, keeping the parties worth coming to, and separating feuding roommates.[75] He was about to be inducted early into Phi Beta Kappa with his 3.77 average and his place as 23rd out of 807 seniors in Cornell's College of Arts and Sciences.[76] He even had time to attend High Holiday services, although instead of atoning he left early to fill out his medical school applications.[77] And he finally stopped playing football when he broke his right hand in a game, making note-taking and writing nearly impossible.[78] He hated wearing the cast: "I'm just not made to be cooped up, I guess."[79]

His high grades and scores were beginning to get him the interviews he needed for prestigious medical schools. He was constantly driving up and down the East Coast: Harvard in Cambridge one day, New York City two days later, Rochester the next. The physicians who kept him waiting at his interviews annoyed him immensely. He described in detail being taken around the halls of Johns Hopkins by a Southern gentleman doctor who told him "how all the 'Nigrahs' and 'po-white trash' come into the hospital for every little bellyache because of Medicare." Alan was outraged but kept quiet, telling Diane, "It's a good thing he didn't ask me my opinions."[80] He seemed to have forgotten his own racist jokes from three years before. Soon enough acceptances began pouring in. Having received the third-highest score on the New York State Regents Medical Scholarship exam taken by 6,000 others, he learned he would receive financial support if he went to medical school in New York State.[81] School after school wanted to admit him.

Trying to explain how difficult all of this was even as he was excelling, he came across as conceited and arrogant, angering Diane and forcing him to apologize frequently to her. Although he had expected Diane to understand when he wrote about his brilliance, he still felt pressured to deny its existence. "You know damned well," he wrote her, "that my biggest asset is I cheat well. We've got a lot better things to talk about than my intelligence."[82] Mostly he was tiring of the endless pressure, even though he was having fun, too, and wishing that his college days were over.[83]

He made his decision about the future. Despite Diane's still being in Rochester the next year, he turned down their medical school, as the idea of spending four more years in upstate New York was clearly not compensated by her presence. Harvard made him an offer, but he decided to accept Columbia. "I really hate turning Harvard down," he admitted, "but the difference isn't enough to compensate for the money."[84] There was also a pleasure in revenging Harvard's decision not to admit him as an undergraduate, in nurturing his need to be the best and in control.[85]

By February, just as his plans for a brilliant future were set, he sank into a short depression. He poured out his worries in a letter to Diane, explaining that he was "pretty concerned about what happens to other people." The help he gave others both academically and emotionally left him exhausted. "Basically, I think I'm just about drained totally empty. For a while, I just have nothing left of myself to give to other people; in fact, I barely have myself left." His insight into his sense of self deepened. "I've been evading my responsibilities," he admitted, "& I've been lying to people just to get them off my back. But mentally I can't accept that, because I've spent my whole life trying not to be that kind of person. I cannot believe in evading responsibilities and problems; I've been brought [up] to face them and fight them."[86]

Ten days later his misery cleared. He promised he could "take on the world again." He was still professing his love to Diane, reminding her of their first lovemaking and how much they were meant to be.[87] At the same time, he understood that getting married so soon did not make sense.[88] As his education at Cornell wound down, he described himself as having "a rather mundane existence, *malheureusement*," although one with comical interludes, as when he watched one of his roommates sail off on a LSD trip.[89] Alan knew, despite the pressures he had felt at the beginning, that he had not worked that hard at Cornell but had a lot of fun in the end. "The closest I've ever come to testing myself is something stupid like trying to do a whole semester's studying the night before the final," he admitted.[90]

Alan weighed what he should do with his talents. "I think in a way I have a yearning to have my name down in a book next to Salk's polio vaccine perhaps, or DeBakey's heart-pump operation," he told Diane. "I know that great-

ness isn't a planned thing, but I also think that you can enter a field w/ an attitude that opens up your eyes to opportunities that you might otherwise gloss
over." He was aware he was telling his perhaps-future wife that he would not be
making money in private practice, asking her to wait for years while he did extra
training, and primarily expecting her to be supportive and take care of him. "All
non-existent modesty aside," he admitted, "I don't think I could be a bad doctor if I tried, but I have my doubts if you can be a great one & still do everything
else you want to do." He also accepted he liked to "spend time with my family,
& to be relatively free. It's a completely different way of fulfillment, but I think
it's just as valid as the dedicated way."[91] Just to make it clear, he signed his last
college letter to Diane, "Alan Berkman, B.A., M.S., M.D., Ph.D."[92]

ANTIWAR

While Alan was planning his life in medical school, other students at Cornell
were becoming deeply imbedded in the antiwar movement. I was one of them.
After returning from my junior year in London totally politicized, I joined a
group that helped raise money for North Vietnamese medical supplies by not
eating for a week, stalled FBI investigators as a draft evader fled to Canada,
and picketed the nearby Syracuse Army Center where preinduction physicals were held.[93] Our SDS chapter, led by Alan's former fraternity-mate-for-
a-few-months Bruce Dancis, formed one of the first "We Won't Go" chapters
and urged other draft-age men to burn their draft cards. Dancis had dramati-
cally torn up his own card in December and would eventually spend nineteen
months in a federal youth detention prison for his actions. Student activists,
including me, called upon men to burn their cards at the major antiwar demonstration scheduled for April 15, 1967, in New York City, set up a table in the student union to solicit pledges for card-burning. We were "cited" by the university
for violating a minor ruling, given a short "trial," and essentially told to never
do it again. Dancis later found out the FBI was thinking about prosecuting us
for treason.[94]

Though these actions were not Alan's style, he and his roommates did join
thousands of other Cornell students on buses to New York for the April 15 demonstration.[95] Writing to Diane, he was sure there were nearly 400,000 others
there, nearly three-quarters of whom, he noted, "were dressed in sport coats,
but television would only interview beatnik types & tried to give the impression
that everyone was like that." He seemed not to notice that half the people in
the crowd were women. In the only comment that might at all hint at his future
views, he concluded, "The amount of willful distortion [in the media coverage]
was terrifying."[96]

Alan's own political memories of this period are different. Though he had not been an activist at Cornell, he would later recall times he took stands or was deeply affected by what was happening. He remembered a memorial on campus to the girls killed at the church in Birmingham, or the time he went to downtown Ithaca with his roommate John Haywood to organize to change the local Elks' policy of having separate white and black clubs.[97] He told numerous interviewers about a debate staged in the Middletown Hebrew Association his freshman year with another student about the Vietnam War, in which he took the antigovernment side to ask "what right did we have to tell their country what kind of system they should have."[98] His father was aghast that his son had taken a position against the U.S. government. After the debate, Alan's father distanced himself from his son's position, and their verbal fight reverberated within the family. The same argument was repeated in many households across the country as sons and daughters challenged their families about the war.

Above all, Alan remembered when his views on the war and racism changed. At the end of his fall semester senior year, when Bruce Dancis became one of the first college students to destroy his draft card, Alan began to believe that actions against the war would be necessary. Early in the spring semester, the Inter-fraternity Council, chaired by Sandy Berger (later the national security advisor to President Bill Clinton), organized a "Soul of Blackness" week. Stokely Carmichael, then head of the Student Nonviolent Coordinating Committee (SNCC), came to campus and gave an impassioned speech linking the need for "black power" with criticism of the war in Vietnam.[99] There are only "two choices," the charismatic and eloquent Carmichael told his 2,000-person audience mostly made up of white fraternity men, "to inflict suffering or to suffer." His point was not to denounce the civil rights efforts of whites but rather to define the problem as white supremacy, which white people could not stand by passively and expect black activists to solve for them.

Carmichael's argument cracked through to Alan's emotional center. His "flashbulb memory" of that night resonated forever, as he told and retold the story in interviews and memoirs. He left the lecture, he would recall again and again, wandering into the freezing cold Ithaca night to work through what Carmichael had said. "How did I see myself.... Who would I identify with," he tried to reason.[100] It was not the reaction of a guilty liberal, and he did not immediately compensate for previous inaction by joining SDS or fund-raising for the Black Panthers. Something deeper was happening inside him, as his emotive abilities linked with his intellectual understanding of what was immoral about the country's actions. It was the beginning of a fundamental shift in his beliefs, dedication, and thinking.

Alan as fraternity president with unnamed woman in *The Cornellian*,
Cornell class of 1967 yearbook, pp. 20–21. *Author's collection.*

Except that he never told Diane or his roommates that any of this happened.[101] The same young man who wrote letter after letter to his girlfriend
about everything never wrote her a word about Carmichael's speech. It is certainly likely that as his fraternity's president he would have attended the event.
There is also little doubt that Carmichael affected him deeply. This straitlaced
fraternity president, who started his college years amused by William F. Buckley
and racist jokes, may not have left Cornell a convert to antiracist radicalism, but
his views were changing. The Carmichael event must have affected him deeply,
even if this did not happen exactly as he remembered it. Alan headed to Columbia dreaming of a career as a brilliant doctor and researcher. Carmichael's arguments would shape the rest of his life.

3

DR. SALK OR DR. LENIN

In the hot months of 1967, psychedelics and politics exploded across the country. Thousands of hippies descended on San Francisco to be part of the Summer of Love, while their more conventionally political brethren fanned out across the country to do "teach-ins" during "Vietnam Summer." Others planned for an October antiwar march and confrontation at the Pentagon. So-called riots, or rebellions, in major cities led to conflagrations, deaths, and National Guard occupations, making manifest Carmichael's message about the anger simmering in African American communities. Whatever gradual effect Carmichael's speech might have on him, Alan wasn't in the streets. Still focused on beginning his brilliant career, he spent the summer working in a cytology lab at Columbia to learn about tumor suppressor genes.[1]

P&S, as Columbia's College of Physicians and Surgeons was called, stood on a rocky parapet in New York City with commanding views of the George Washington Bridge and the Hudson River. Fifty blocks north of Columbia's main campus, it was located in the Washington Heights neighborhood increasingly dominated by families from Puerto Rico and the Dominican Republic. As America's oldest medical school, founded in 1767, P&S was long considered a patrician bastion focused on research, not the medical needs of its community. It had a track record of rejecting Jews and rarely taking women or people of color.[2] The school accepted 120 students in Alan's class, including only 10 women and 2 black men, 1 of whom was from Nigeria.[3]

Not all the students arrived planning to devote themselves to study alone. At least a handful of P&S's class of 1971 and students in the adjacent nursing school had been civil rights and antiwar activists in college.[4] They did not lose their political perspectives or suspicion of those in power just because they were now in professional schools. Even as Alan began to cram his brain with the specifics of medical science, he would find that his classmates and friends had much more to teach him.

Alan Berkman, Columbia University Medical School orientation photograph, September 1971, Student File. *Courtesy of Archives & Special Collections, Columbia University Health Sciences Library.*

LEARNING THE SCIENCE, JOCKEYING FOR POSITION

"Berkman, A," reads the placard Alan holds in the mandatory orientation photo. He has a somewhat sardonic glare, slight mustache, close-cropped haircut, suit jacket, tie, and college ring. Perhaps unintentionally, Alan's middle finger pokes out slightly, in what bears more than passing resemblance to a mug shot.[5]

Alan staked out his position among his classmates fairly early. One nurse friend labeled him an "intellectual jock," and another found him "pretty square."[6] Alan told Diane he was voted "the most valuable player" at a get-to-know-you football game between the first- and second-year students that left "a lot of 2nd year students whose aching ribs will remember me from that game." With his characteristic acerbic self-deprecation, he promised Diane, "If I can't be famous, at least I can be notorious, n'est-ce-pas?"[7]

In admitting him, the medical school student dean had a sense of his physical prowess and leadership. On his record after his application and interview, the dean wrote "homely, medical breadth, mature, athlete (150 lb. varsity football), scholar, fraternity president, excellent self-starter and leader."[8] Alan, in turn, emphasized on his application how little money his family had. He declared there were no doctors among his relations, and "my summer employment has been exclusively manual labor."[9] The dean must have thought he was admitting the Jewish version of an All-American boy who would be grateful for the education.

Once classes began, Alan figured out quickly he had to rely on his own judgment and time-management skills. He was shocked to discover that medical students were left with little guidance from their faculty members: "No assigned reading, no indication of what or how much you should know, and damn few exams. I guess the idea is leaving the student in the dark forces him to do more work voluntarily than would have otherwise been assigned." Having chosen to live in an apartment rather than the medical school dorm, "I have so little contact w/ the other students that I don't get to compare ideas on what's important. It's going to be me against the world," he told Diane. "Want to join the fight?"[10]

Despite his bluster, he acknowledged the fear of failure everyone shared. In addition to the dreaded shame of flunking out, the ever-present military draft haunted male students, whose deferments would disappear if their schooling ended. By November of his first year, one-third of the class had received a note that they had flunked the biochemistry test with scores below the curved 40.[11] Not Alan. He had also gone back to work in the genetics lab two hours a day, in addition to the endless time that was supposed to be spent on the basics: anatomy, biostatistics, biochemistry, microbiology, and pathology in lectures and labs.[12]

Dick Clapp, a fellow medical student who would become a lifelong friend, watched Alan from the next table over in the gross anatomy lab. Alan nimbly went through the motions of the dissections, then stopped coming once he figured out he could learn the material on his own. He abandoned the stench, grease, and emotional cost of taking apart cadavers day after day, opting to cease violating the privacy of the dead.[13] His failure to attend was not mere arrogance. With a ratio of one instructor to fifty students in the anatomy lab, many of his classmates despaired about the lack of guidance and had to find knowledge through their "cadaver mates" (four medical students to a body) rather than their professors.[14]

To balance all the science being stuffed into his mind, by second semester Alan had taken out a public library card and stayed up after studying till two or three in the morning to read novels.[15] This habit meant he often fell asleep in class, he confessed. His grades were not, despite his bravado, all As, and professors reported that he was "average, not outstanding in any respect," or "industrious, average," as they gave him a B in physiology and a B– in clinical pathology.[16] He never gave up reading the *New York Times* and often could be found outside of class in the medical center's coffee shop, a cup on the table, a cigarette in his hand, and the pen for the crossword puzzles in the other.[17]

He seemed to have figured out quickly what he needed to do and assumed that his research prowess and memorization skills would carry him through well enough. Many attested to his ability to just look at a text and remember it, or "zone" into the lecturer, almost "self-hypnotize" himself to listen, and recall what had been said without taking notes.[18] One classmate seemed amazed that he would "not show up to class a lot and then he'd ace the exams."[19] He believed his degree was never in doubt, signing his first letters to Diane from New York as "Alan Berkman, M.D."[20]

In addition to the novel-reading, he escaped by playing contract bridge, as he had in his fraternity, and began to enter tournaments with a doctor colleague. He kept it up throughout his medical school years, even taking various friends with him to watch him play. He was good enough at poker as well to consider, at least for a few moments, whether he should drop out of medical school to become a card shark.[21]

He was learning something else even more important to his future. Through reconnecting with Lynn Johnson Rosen, a high school friend who was a nurse and in a left political organization called Progressive Labor, he participated in a study group reading Marx.[22] "Intellectually," he admitted to an interviewer years later as he tried to make sense of his own trajectory, "I began to realize that not only were there different realities about the nature of the system, but I began to feel that the reality that my life was proceeding along was in fact that other people were disenfranchised, [not just in the sense of the vote . . . and] what was I going to do about that?"[23] He was linking his hometown connections and familial sense of masculine responsibility to Stokely Carmichael's dictums by beginning where many would-be leftist intellectuals began: with learning about Marx.

PRACTICING EMPATHY

After two years of basic science courses, Alan was happier when his training moved into more clinical care. He still did not impress all his supervisors.[24] His surgery professor commented that he was a "capable student" without much interest in this field, and the orthopedic surgery clinician thought he laughed too much, had an "underlying personality security deficit," and showed more interest in the "laboratory and medical facets." In contrast, the psychiatry instructor reported that he was "very bright . . . good rapport with his patients. His insight was greater than the average student [and he] was open to supervision and criticism." Alan clearly annoyed many of his professors, with one preceptor in pediatrics calling him "a combative, bright, argumentative student" and yet another, in obstetrics, lacing his comments with the alliterative "sullen, self-assured, sarcastic, supercilious" (this professor gave him a B).

Invisible to some of his teachers was Alan's compassion, which emerged when clinical rotations exposed him to the men, women, and children of the surrounding neighborhood in need of his care. He recalled that his parents had felt disrespected by professionals because they had not gone to college. With that in mind, he began to see in his poorer patients a kind of dignity and perseverance that he appreciated, and it shaped his sense of the privilege of being a doctor and entering other people's lives.[25]

In the medical care clinics, Alan found he excelled when he linked his knowledge of disease to the needs of a patient. Those professors who understood his humor called him "superior to many 4th year students" and emphasized his "comprehension of clinical diseases," as well as his ability to "synthes[ize] clinical cases and [be] articulate in presentations." He was, one professor concluded, "possible intern material if he matures."

His medical school buddy Dick Clapp had a more mystical view of this, suggesting that Alan could see the "auras" around patients and intuit their ills. Not usually taken to spiritual views, Clapp had a sense that there was just something about Alan's abilities that could not be explained by intelligence and commitment alone. The house staff who supervised Alan in the Vanderbilt Clinic, Columbia's outpatient department, must have seen something, too, because at the year-end party they voted him an honorary screener for having the best diagnostic skills and ability to triage those in the need of most immediate care.[26] As he continued his laboratory investigations, his teachers named him the best researcher in the fourth year.[27]

Despite his expanding skills, Alan became skeptical about what he could do within the confines of medicine. I remember a discussion with him about medical care as we shared a ride to Middletown from New York City for Thanksgiving in 1970. As a doctor's daughter, I had much respect for what a skilled medical practitioner could do and, from my father's stories, understanding of the tragedies that could occur when a patient got the wrong doctor. Alan told me he sometimes felt as if he were being taught "voodoo" and that it made little difference. I recall how shocked I was that he was this disillusioned with what Western medicine could provide. Alan, however, was already thinking about what was next, and it would not be a turn to Chinese herbs, exercise regimes, self-help, and acupuncture.

Alan would tell the same story over and over of how he came to understand medicine's limits. It involved an African American woman, although sometimes the tale was about a man, whom he treated for congestive heart failure but who was released from the hospital to an apartment that required her (or him) to walk up five flights of stairs. All Alan's skill in diagnosis and treatment could not save the patient from realities like these that made recovery doubtful. Those hearing this story remarked on Alan's empathy and heart, not just that he could intellectually explain the patient's disease.[28] It was as if he realized, as one of his classmates put it, that even with his "enormous empathy and enormous anger, his accurate adjusting of his patient's digoxin levels" would not be enough.[29] If he were going to be able to keep someone alive, more than medicine would be necessary.

CONTESTING THE HIDDEN CURRICULUM
AND COLUMBIA'S PRIORITIES

Slowly over his medical school years, Alan became part of a core group of students angry over the hidden curriculum that taught them doctor power and conformity. They were to learn a kind of "brutality and flippancy" as a way to protect themselves from what they had to do. "You had to project a kind of objectivity," a lack of caring, "even if you did not feel it," a classmate recalled.[30]

Despite their somewhat liberal dean of students, Alan and his friends started to rebel. P&S's administration insisted that male students have no more than a very trimmed mustache and no other facial hair. Twelve of Alan's classmates showed up at orientation in violation of this rule, and the dean threatened their recommendations for internships four years later if they did not shave. Most complied, but not everyone. As Alan would tell an interviewer later, "There was something behind the demand to grow mustaches—because we saw medicine in a different way. It was all about what was happening in the society."[31] Alan was growing closer to his more radical classmates Dick Clapp and Franklin Apfel, who had been antiwar leaders at Dartmouth and Swarthmore, respectively. They in turn were starting to consult with him about teach-ins and protest events they were planning. They accepted his strategic insights, which came from his ability to think in terms of both tactics and long-term goals.[32]

The fights with P&S's administration continued. A short sit-in in the dean of student's office in the spring of Alan's first year led to demands for affirmative action to increase the number of women and blacks in the school, a pass-fail system to decrease "the competitiveness among students," the right *not* to wear their white jackets unless they were seeing patients, and permission to grow a beard.[33] They were publishing a newsletter called *Iatrogenia* that critiqued what they were learning and called for "educational counter-insurgency."[34]

Led by Dick Clapp, several students created an Issues in Health course that met weekly to discuss concerns ranging from medical school socialization and Columbia's affiliation with Harlem Hospital to double standards in health care and Marxist theories of accumulation and oppression. Clapp remembers Alan attending, though his name is not on the sign-in sheet. "He was a listener," Clapp recollected, "not a leader."[35]

Alan loved how Clapp's critique of a racist parasitology course, in the form of a fake exam: "Working with Firestone in Liberia was an example of: a. imperialism, b. colonialism, c. neo-colonialism, d. an elective at Columbia medical school, or e. all of the above."[36] Alan also helped Clapp stage sociopathological conferences to counter the solely body-focused clinical pathological conferences that were required.[37]

Alan's first real confrontation with state authority came with the spring 1968 strike at the downtown college campus in protest of Columbia's student policies, hidden war-related research used to support U.S. military operations, and expansion into the Harlem community. It involved building takeovers and police confrontations that garnered international media attention, part of the "Long March, Short Spring" of student activism worldwide.[38]

When the sit-in was violently ended, students hurt by police nightsticks needed first aid. Those who showed up at a nearby hospital to be patched up were being pulled out and handed over to the waiting police for arrest. Rather than let the students get caught this way, Alan's classmate Franklin Apfel quickly organized a number of medical students, including Alan, to set up a first aid station in a nearby dorm. "It was," Alan asserted, "my first exposure to police violence."[39]

Later, he would argue it was the beginning of his sense that he would have to abandon his liberal perspective that things could be fixed, and that there was "more wrong with the United States than I had previously thought."[40] It also meant that he was not only seeing the violence but also actively seeking to thwart police actions by intervening to protect those harmed. He was still afraid, he admitted, of what this kind of activity might do to his future medical career.[41]

The Columbia strike provided, as strike participant and future screenwriter Lewis Cole recalled forty years later, "an incandescent moment" of "participatory democracy." For in that instant, he concluded, "'Columbia' mattered not just because of what we did. It mattered because of what we believed. That this was a moment of real internationalism. The Blacks and whites getting together was a moment of international solidarity. Our saying that we would stand with the Vietnamese people was a moment of international solidarity.... This is how you really do make the world. These ideals really do give you power."[42] It was this articulation, however romantic, of ideals that provided the political energy for what would come next in Alan's life.

Alan and his classmates began to articulate this concept of solidarity at the medical school, too. The university had long failed to provide community mental health services, drug detoxification, and other programs to the surrounding Latinx/black communities, while continuing its building expansionism. Those communities were demanding change. Activist health workers and community members sought assistance in their struggle from the students. Organizers of a union drive at the medical center also appealed for their support. Students worked with community residents to set up the Ad Hoc Committee for a Better Vanderbilt (P&S's primary care clinic) and leafleted with demands for a real appointment system, hospital-based interpreters, and a community board.[43]

At the core, the students were trying to challenge the "values they were being taught at Columbia."[44] Alan remembered he and his group tried to buy an old ambulance. "We were going to paint it up, fix it up . . . and make it into a little local jitney bus — that we could give free rides to all the people. . . . We were challenging capitalist values by trying to get our free little bus, so that people would have access to services that they need without paying too much."[45]

Alan was now reading more Marx and other theorists with a group of his classmates, trying to connect the inequalities in health they could see around them to larger theory. He liked the scientific nature of the Marxist literature, with its promise of a method for concretely analyzing political power. His classmate Franklin Apfel recalled that Alan "took some pride in identifying ways to apply theory — explain current politics with theoretical frames — to make links. And he had convincing raps to deliver."[46] Alan continued to spend time with Lynn Johnson Rosen, his Middletown classmate, and to go to lectures by members of Progressive Labor, but he was increasingly seeing his politics as separate from theirs.[47] While being asked to decide between obstetrics, surgery, or internal medicine for his professional future, he was also beginning to make choices about his political affiliations.

Outside Alan's world at Columbia much else was happening that might trouble the assumption that liberal reforms could cure America's ills. The January 1968 Tet Offensive in Vietnam made it clear the United States could not win the war. Assassins' bullets felled both Martin Luther King Jr. and Robert Kennedy by the end of Alan's first year. All hell broke loose across the country after King's death, including burned buildings along New York's Lenox Avenue near Columbia's medical center.[48] In the summer of 1968, the police riot at the Democratic convention left hundreds of peaceful protestors bloodied in the streets of Chicago. In New York, a contentious school strike in the fall pitted communities of color against the teachers' union. Violence was in the air.

Alan could hardly avoid listening and reading the critiques from many sides that linked the war in Vietnam to what was being called on the left the medical "empires" and their priorities and power.[49] What medical students were exactly to *do* about this was the subject of endless discussion and actions. The politicization of health issues, within an expanding women's health movement and groups such as the Young Lords Organization and the Black Panther Party, led these organizations to appeal to medical and nursing students. These students were being asked to put their own bodies on the line. They could always refuse to take action, but the pressures were there. If you could talk the antiracism and anti-imperialism line, what would you actually do when called upon to act?

Like-minded students and young professionals held meetings to figure out their responses to such questions. Dick Clapp and others at Columbia were part of the Student Health Organization, which exposed health professional students to community organizing and differing perspectives on health care.[50] The Health Policy Advisory Center (Health/PAC), a New York–based think tank critical of the health system, analyzed health politics in its monthly bulletins and the need for institutional organizing for change, controlled by community members and health workers.[51] It served as the intellectual and propaganda arm of the various health movement struggles or, as its critics labeled it, "the ideological ministry of the radical movement."[52] During the three years that I worked at Health/PAC in the early 1970s, Alan and I would meet on occasion at various events.[53]

Part of what was changing him was just being a student in an institution like Columbia, whose expansionism and paternalism made it an easy target in an increasingly polarized time. Yet the majority of medical students did not respond in the way Alan and his friends did. Instead, they kept their heads in their books, attended their labs, learned to detach, and went on to their medical practices. Some were moved to do an action or two, to work in an antiwar candidate's political campaign, or to attend a meeting or demonstration. Years later they might recall their "war" stories as an amusing reminder of their braver and younger selves from the vantage point of their professional lives, often in social medicine or public health because of what they had experienced in those medical school days.[54] Alan's class as a whole, for example, refused to do a yearbook and donated the money instead to social causes.

Others were going further in their actions. Alan's friend Dick Clapp was finally overwhelmed by the limitations of clinical medicine. In his second year he was continually raising the connections between corporate money and medical teaching in their tropical medicine course. It would be the coup de grâce for him, and by the end of the year he dropped out. He went on to become an epidemiologist and to change health policy, but he continued to live for a number of years in the Washington Heights community.[55] Alan and his friend Franklin Apfel just kept trying to do really well, aware that if they didn't keep their grades up this might give the administration an excuse to throw them out.[56]

But what should they do? The reality of violence by police and the FBI was everywhere. Examples included Black Panther cases that were really due to prosecutorial misconduct and provocation by undercover police (a P&S biochemist Alan knew became part of what was known as the Panther 21) and the execution of Panthers Fred Hampton and Mark Clark in their beds by the Chicago police.[57] Among the white left, SDS had split and a faction called the Weatherman, then Weathermen, then the Weather Underground Organization, had begun bombings from their clandestine locations.[58] Many of them had ties to Columbia, both at the downtown campus and the medical school, and Alan was increasingly drawn into their circles.

Militancy in communities and colleges reverberated especially among African American activists, who asked, and many times demanded, that whites of conscience consider what they would do in response. The power of the state seemed to be increasing, and the idea that this violence would have to be met with equal force was discussed in meetings across the country. Knowledge that FBI and police red squads had infiltrated political groups heightened the paranoia, leading to more tightly organized groups and a belief in the need for clandestine action.[59]

By the spring of 1970, and in Alan's third year, student strikes over the expanding war in Southeast Asia closed many universities, including P&S. There was an increasing sense of the country being in real crisis. Bombings in public buildings became the new normal. The need for martial law, with expanded police power and restriction of civil liberties, was openly discussed at the White House.[60]

As this was going on in the broader society, in medical schools students had to be taught how not only to prevent death but also to accept that sometimes they would *cause* it. The questions of differing forms of death were never far away. In the netherworld of medicine, where day and night merged and illness and death were ever present, medical students had to learn to make hard decisions and difficult choices.

As protests in the streets mounted and he learned to manage deaths, Alan was moving much more seriously toward believing in the need for action, even illegal action. It was during this time that he and I had our fateful discussion about taking up arms. At heart, Alan and those around him were considering how to put political theory into practice. They were influenced by theorist Franz Fanon, who reasoned that violence was necessary for revolutionary change and the creation of a decolonized position. French political theorist Régis Debray's arguments for "focoism," based on the physician and revolutionary Ernesto "Che" Guevara's view that small insurrectionary cadres could spark a revolution, were being enacted by American self-defined urban guerrillas.[61] Along with others reading SDS's *New Left Notes* and these theorists, Alan was part of discussions about what actions they would all take. He had to consider what it meant to risk everything, and whether he was willing to do this.[62]

Raised to believe they would all have power someday, Alan and his friends began to assess what that would mean now.[63] They called their group the Little Red Lighthouse, after the signal tower just below the nearby George Washington Bridge as well as their political leanings. At the start, their efforts mostly consisted of supporting one another as an affinity group at demonstrations, staying together to avoid getting arrested for stopping traffic in the streets, spray-painting "Bring the War Home" on buildings, and leaving burning Molotov cocktails outside military recruiting offices. Another time a Vietnamese National Liberation Front flag was secretly hung from a very high pole on the roof of the medical school, while an American flag was hung upside down as a distress symbol.[64]

They were taking their role in street actions seriously, reading a pamphlet called "Medical Cadre" that explained what kind of procedures to take to assist those harmed by police clubs, tear gas, and even bullets.[65] "Vote with your feats," Dick Clapp remembered they would chant as a pun but also to spur one another on to action.[66]

They also were learning to protect one another. When Franklin Apfel was caught spray-painting a denunciation of the dean on a medical school building just weeks before graduation, Alan was the chair of the Student Affairs Committee that let him off with a slap on the wrist.[67] Alan did not tell the committee that he had been the "look-out for the spray-painting but had not been caught."[68]

Mostly Alan was thinking through what it meant to move beyond protest politics and to take seriously the Black Panthers' slogan of "Serve the People."[69] He knew that he and others who shared his concerns had a responsibility to stop the racism at home and the war in Vietnam, that "the motivation was solidarity and wanting to stop the killing," as he put it bluntly. Looking back on his thinking two decades later he remembered, "It was a way of figuring out, of being led almost inevitably to violence but trying not to kill while running the risk we might kill somebody. . . . That radical opposition seems to lead toward at least symbolic violent protest. What we used to call 'armed propaganda.'"[70]

For him at the time, it was a way to think of himself as more than just a "radical," a term that described a tradition that he increasingly saw as too limited and too focused on single issues. He was beginning to define himself as an "anti-imperialist," though, as in many other groups, that term had a tendency to slip into "revolutionary." He was developing a sophisticated understanding of the "dilemma of trying to be a revolutionary in a non-revolutionary country."[71] When Che Guevara stopped practicing medicine, he at least worked in countries on the verge of revolution. Alan had a different kind of problem here.

He was beginning to take a long view. He had skipped the rebellions of college. He had seen the limitations of demonstrations, petitions, and negotiations with those in power. The "roots" of his outrage were at first moral and theoretical. It was, he believed, "much more about a fundamental sense of fairness, injustice and wanting to do the right thing, wanting to stop the wrong thing, and we were trying to almost impose on ourselves, you know, how do we steel ourselves as revolutionaries."[72] His approach, as in much of his life to that point, was, according to his friend Franklin Apfel, "cool and analytic."[73]

Picking up the traditions of masculinity that were rooted deep in his family, Alan was not afraid of action, or of the use of some kinds of violence.[74] He never condoned terrorism or killing, but he was learning to accept the possibility that in a war there might be losses, and he knew that those on his side were already being killed daily. He was becoming open to a strategy that would "bring the war home," making the costs of injustice too high, and he was becoming ready to use his own physical and mental strength to make this happen.

Only two dozen years out from the Holocaust, Alan, along with many other Jews in the student movements, thought, as Columbia's SDS leader Mark Rudd put it, "about the moral imperative to not be Good Germans. . . . Morally and emotionally we could not fit into the civilized world of the racist, defense-oriented modern university. Such was our ordeal of civility."[75] Alan was becoming a secular Jewish male avenger, true to his grandfather Moishe.[76]

The words Alan had used are telling: "trying not to kill while running the risk we might kill somebody" could also describe what medical students might learn: to trust their judgment, to act to save lives, but at the risk that someone might die. Learning to be a doctor, taking risks to stop war and racism, neither becoming a Good German nor a Jew easily led to slaughter, all came together for him.

Police and FBI investigations became common, straining family relationships and driving Alan's friends into the secrecy of their own groups as the Columbia-based connections to other radicals exposed them to questioning.[77] Dick Clapp's FBI file revealed that FBI agents had gone through his trash, tracked the radical publications he subscribed to, and lifted fingerprints from his mail without warrants to see if he was hiding any wanted person from the Weather Underground. Clapp refused to speak to agents in July 1970 looking for an ex-girlfriend. When Clapp proved uncooperative, the FBI talked to his surgeon father and homemaker mother in Lewiston, Maine.[78] Others in their circle had their apartments broken into and their mail read. Alan escaped this kind of surveillance. He was not yet on the FBI's radar.

A year after the FBI went through Clapp's mail, Alan was asked by individuals in the political underground connected to his Columbia friends "if I would be willing to help out people who were formally in Weatherman."[79] Alan quietly said yes, telling almost no one what he was doing.[80] "I would see people in clandestine circumstances who had been injured and didn't want to go to a hospital for a variety of reasons," he would admit decades later. "I was asked to train people in first aid who were underground so they could have more of a capacity to take care of themselves."[81]

By the time Alan graduated he was learning more than medical care. He was beginning to have two lives. On the surface, he was winning awards and was a marshal at the medical school graduation. Beneath it, he was helping those in the underground and beginning to think about what else he was willing to do. He was getting into, in the vernacular of the time, "heavy" politics, that is, a willingness to step over the legal line. It seemed logical.

FALLING IN LOVE, FINDING A COMRADE

Medical school was for Alan a dive into endless classes, long labs, and complicated politics. But drugs, especially marijuana, mescaline, and acid also flowed. Even for medical students, serious parties could interrupt serious studying. Sexual freedom, and the expanding women's movement, led to experimentation, an emphasis on "smashing monogamy" and a kind of sexual abandon that would have been unlikely a decade before. "We were," Dick Clapp remembered chuckling, "always talking politics or falling in love with each other."[82] It was for many a world upended, a chance to create a culture outside bourgeois norms and values.

Alan's bond to Diane did not survive past his second year in medical school. They had always agreed to date others, but Diane assumed their special relationship would eventually lead to the marriage Alan had hinted at in his endless college letters. When he decided to go to Columbia, and not to join her in Rochester for her last year of college and his medical training, it was clear his relationship to her would not define his future. When she graduated from Rochester in 1968, she took the larger scholarship given to her by Duke University for a PhD in French, though Columbia had accepted her too. She remembered hoping that maybe Alan would miss her if she were even farther away.

As it looked less and less likely that Alan would become either a small-town doctor like Diane's father or a famous medical academic, their relationship unraveled. Having begun too soon and lasted too long, it finally could not accommodate his political changes or her needs.[83] They finally broke up.

Alan dated a number of women who formed part of his political circle. The political bonds and ability to spur one another to action were shared in bed and in intimate circles. As Franklin Apfel remembered, Alan's "newly acquired radical theoretical knowledge [allowed him to] impress a whole new set of folks/ some of whom were interesting/desirable women."[84] His sexism, so much a part of the environment and times he was raised in, was beginning to be challenged as the women's movement gave a language of protest and rebuttal to the women he was meeting and bedding. Then he met Barbara.

Barbara Carol Zeller, daughter of a suburban Connecticut psychiatrist and homemaker, was also in Alan's medical school class. A beautiful Mount Holyoke College graduate with springy brown curls in her long hair, she had an almost preternatural calm, a warm and welcoming smile, and an abiding concern for patient care. She was at first interested in being a veterinarian, until her doctor father introduced her to women physicians. The support of her women's college made the process of being a woman premed student less difficult than if she had been somewhere where her interests might have been thwarted.

Because so much of the organization at Columbia's medical school class was by the alphabet, Berkman met Apfel and Clapp before Zeller. He noticed her doing the crossword and smoking in the medical school coffee shop. He began to chat with her and share hints of "crosswordese" so they both could complete the puzzles. She had been attending many of the same meetings as he had, although she listened more than she spoke. Barbara was a match for Alan in her intellectual inquisitiveness and medical acumen, and she worked harder than he did to get things done. She found her voice through the expanding women's movement. Its teaching would be a revelation to her, showing how she might have become more than the "honorary" woman tolerated in so many male-dominated situations.

At the time, Barbara was still involved with a long-term boyfriend. She found Alan's attentions, intellectual curiosity, extraordinary compassion, and ironic humor underneath his seriousness appealing as they talked, but she was not yet searching for another man. Although not Jewish herself, she had grown up in suburbs with lots of Jewish kids, and Alan had a kind of familiarity. She was taken with how well he dressed (once in a pink oxford shirt, she recalled with a smile) to match her snappy miniskirts, lipstick, and eye makeup. After a breakup with the old boyfriend and some dating around, she was very much on the rebound when Alan's constant entreaties and flirtations proved effective by the summer of 1970. At a time when newly minted feminists made many men wary, Barbara was attracted to his confidence and search for a partner, not a plaything. His acceptance of her as a professional woman was alluring. In turn, Alan seems to have appreciated her warmth, intelligence, sexual attractiveness, social commitments, and political savvy.[85]

Barbara Carol Zeller, Columbia University Medical School application photograph, September 1971, Student File. *Courtesy of Archives & Special Collections, Columbia University Health Sciences Library.*

Like Alan, Barbara was from a deeply religious family that taught their children about the compassion and altruistic responsibilities toward others that marked adulthood. Barbara's looks made her seem Jewish, and her German-sounding last name added to the assumptions people made about her cultural origins. She was raised Presbyterian, however, in an apolitical family where politics were not discussed, and where going to church and "charity, prayer and good works" mattered.[86] Her parents stressed humanitarianism, and her mother was given a Martin Luther King award by the Hartford black community because of her church work and caring. Her father did pastoral counseling before it existed as a real field, and her parents' friendships were within their church, rather than in the medical community.[87] She grew up in solid middle-class neighborhoods that were what she called "100% white."

In her telling, as in Alan's about his own conversion, it was her chance attendance at a lecture that began her political transformation. One day in 1963, during her senior year of high school, she picked up a leaflet advertising a lecture by Malcolm X. With a friend, she joined a thousand others in a big church in downtown Hartford. There were, she recalled, maybe three or four other whites in the hall. Expecting Malcolm X to be antiwhite, she was moved by his eloquence and thoughtfulness: "I was transfixed. It was like hearing truth. . . . It was turning my world upside down in terms of perspective."[88] When he was murdered two years later, it was as if she had lost someone she knew. Hearing Malcolm X did not cause a sudden transformation but an opening, as the words and presence of Stokely Carmichael had for Alan in his own account.

She, too, began to see the world through nonwhite eyes, in part because it was her nature to look beyond what she already knew. "I didn't have a rebellious streak," she maintained, "but I had an adventurous streak." Although the Mount Holyoke students she knew were not particularly radical or involved in antiwar or civil rights movements, Barbara, and the high school friend who had gone with her to hear Malcolm X, made plans to do work through an organization called Crossroads Africa in the summer of 1965. Sent to Sierra Leone to participate in a building project, she met other American students who had worked in the South, as well as activists from South Africa and pan-Africanists.[89] It taught her to think about issues of race and imperialism beyond a charity mindset, and she began to develop a sense of "outrage" about the United States and anger that she had been lied to about American policy. She thought she might eventually work as a doctor in an African country.

She and Alan were alike in many ways. They had not been college rebels; neither belonged to SDS. They had done all the right things, been the second good child in four-child families, gone to elite colleges, made it through the premed gauntlet, gotten into a prestigious medical school, and were on their way to successful careers as doctors. Yet because they both also had a sense of responsibility to others, and an ability to imagine themselves within someone else's world, they could no longer just pretend there was nothing wrong. As Barbara would put it, "I was a college graduate with no politics but then I came to New York City in 1967 to Columbia."[90]

Unlike Alan, who was aware that his intelligence, maleness, and synthetic mind marked his leadership abilities, Barbara was more hesitant to do what Alan was willing to consider. She was then "afraid of crossing too many lines, becoming too radical and endangering her medical career."[91] Because she was endlessly curious, she was willing to venture into doing some things, to see the world anew, to provide first aid during the Columbia strike, to go to demonstrations. She learned from Alan's growing ideological leanings and those of their friends, but she was reluctant to be as outspoken yet, and less certain than he became about what needed to be done. Even when they graduated, she recalled, "I was still very protective of my world as a doctor."[92]

By the end of their third medical school year, as they took their dating more seriously, some of Alan's nursing and political friends took Barbara aside and in "sisterly" fashion told her he was trying to end a relationship with someone else to really be with her. They suggested she might want to stop wearing makeup and join them in a women's group. Barbara gave up her apartment and moved in with one of his women friends in a more collective household. By their last year in school Alan and Barbara had moved together into another apartment collective. He took some flak from friends who thought Barbara was neither serious enough nor political enough for him. By their last year in medical school, they were beginning to imagine their personal, professional, and political lives in tandem.[93]

As their last year of medical school training was ending, Alan and Barbara began the harrowing process of applying for internship spots, and hoping they would "match," as it is still called, to their top choices. They could have chosen to go with some of their other friends to the growing radical program at Lincoln Hospital in the heart of the Puerto Rican and black barrio in the South Bronx.[94] Despite Alan's political work, the lure of science still held him in its thrall, and Barbara wanted more intense internal medicine training. Deciding to stay in New York, Barbara chose the mid-Manhattan location of Roosevelt Hospital, and Alan picked the more research-oriented Presbyterian Hospital program at Columbia. They both "matched."

Their involvement in political actions continued. A Mayday coalition (playing on the date and the distress call) organized for antiwar actions for May 1, 1971. This was to be more than the usual demonstration in the nation's capital. Instead attendees were urged to form "affinity" groups, to be mobilized for street events at particular points in the city, and to prepare to be arrested. The slogan for the demonstration was "If the government won't stop the war, we'll stop the government." Unlike the bombings that the Weather Underground had been doing, this was a different kind of public disobedience, a form of "armed propaganda" that put your body, not your bomb or spray paint, on the line.

Many of the differing collectives who lived in Washington Heights went together. There was a sense of importance, and danger, as they roamed together into the Washington, D.C., traffic on streets and bridges, trying to shut down the machinery of government by snarling traffic completely. It was to be "action rather than congregation, disruption rather than display." They used the small groups as support, to keep out police spies, and to maneuver tactically in the streets.[95]

The government never shut down. However, as activist L. A. Kaufmann assessed, "a force of more than 14,000 police and National Guardsmen were mobilized to remove the radicals from the streets, and a staggering 13,500 people were placed under arrest."[96] While they were stopping traffic, the Washington Heights groups managed to avoid arrest. It would be, however, the last major antiwar demonstration in the nation's capital. Demonstrations, and now mass arrests and traffic disruption, did not seem to stop the war, although the disruptions and arrests frightened the Nixon White House. Alan had to consider more seriously what he was willing to do next to force change.

He was now a doctor. He was responsible for doing something. Alan's final high standing, and presumed maturity despite his doubts, earned him the next step into a career in academic medicine through his internship at Columbia's

Presbyterian Hospital. His national medical board scores put him in the ninety-eighth percentile of all American medical students at the time.[97] He continued to teeter between the demands of a supposedly objective science and his belief, buttressed by anger, that society had to change to make decent health possible. Learning to be a doctor, he was learning to be in charge. Of what was the question he had yet to resolve.

POLITICAL MEDICINE

Alan's yearlong internship in 1971 taught him more than he expected. On an intern's twenty-four-hour-or-more on/off schedule came sleep deprivation, exhaustion, panic, and the dreaded scut work of blood draws, patient transport, coffee runs, and anything that the doctors above him demanded.[1] Time did not really exist except as a warp through which the newly minted intern had to travel.

Time was not the only thing that fractured during the year Alan was an intern. Less than three weeks before he began this grueling schedule, the *New York Times* released its report on the supposedly top secret Pentagon Papers on the wars in Southeast Asia. These 7,000 pages exposed decades of official administration lies to Congress and the public about the reasons for the wars and their continuation. Everything that the nation's antiwar activist children had been telling their parents for nearly a decade had the imprimatur of truth, and from the highest levels.[2] Just months before, an antiwar group's burglary of an FBI office made public the agency's counterintelligence program, labeled COINTELPRO, detailing extensive spying on law-abiding citizens.[3] Senate hearings would later reveal details even the most paranoid leftists had not imagined.

Alan was now facing what it really meant to take responsibility for American modernity and its hidden truths. He did this as the economic and social welfare expansions of the 1960s were giving way to the stagflation, deindustrialization, fiscal crisis of the state, and rising cries for law and order that were hallmarks of the 1970s.[4] While the language of markets and individual accountability for social and economic success expanded, so did the radical demands and actions of various identity groups.[5] In the face of such fractures, illegalities on multiple sides, and violence, the move into more clandestine actions began to make even more sense to those, like Alan, who were trying to stop the juggernaut of American power. Still, before he could be truly useful to the cause, he first needed to make it through his internship and learn to be a doctor.

Alan had decided to stay at Columbia to train at its massive Presbyterian Hospital because it would give him access to a wide range of cases, responsibility for patient care, research possibilities, and world-class specialists who might teach him.[6] While he was focused on learning more medical science, he also looked more and more the part of the radical. His hair had gotten longer in the back as the male pattern baldness began, exposing more of his forehead, and a thick dark beard and mustache now framed his face, thinner than in his athletic days.

On his first day in the emergency department on July 1, 1971, Alan worked on a case that would become infamous. Just a few days earlier in northern Westchester County outside New York City, Grace Cochran served herself, and her husband, a sixty-one-year-old bank vice president, vichyssoise soup from a can, prepared cold as the directions indicated. A day later Samuel Cochran was dead from botulism, and his wife was transferred, completely paralyzed, from a local hospital to Columbia Presbyterian. Alan was on her medical team.[7] As he learned to care for a victim of botulism and administer antitoxins, the story became well-covered news.[8] By the end of July, after government investigations, suspicious lots of the soup were recalled nationwide and its manufacturer, the Bon Vivant Company, filed for bankruptcy.[9] Grace Cochran spent more than three months in Presbyterian's intensive care unit, in part under Alan's care, as the antitoxins did their work. She lived to testify against the soup company two years later.[10]

Alan could not forget the extraordinary treatment that made it possible for his patient to survive one of the world's deadliest bacteria.[11] It was a perfect summary of the two-class health system, which spent so much to save a white, upper-class woman who had eaten a fancy soup and so little on others. He would tell the story years later, pairing the suburban matron who did not die with an "impoverished . . . black widowed domestic worker with four children . . . struck down in her middle years by heart disease and high blood pressure," whom he cared for in the same hospital's back wards.[12] Nothing seemed to symbolize more perfectly the injustices in a health system he increasingly could not accept and was unwilling to shore up.

Two months after his work to save Cochran, Alan was introduced to political militancy and a different kind of medical need when a supposed prisoner escape attempt at Soledad prison in California ended in death. Killed in the prison yard was the not-yet-thirty-year-old George Jackson, a left celebrity whose prison letters had just been published in his highly acclaimed book *Soledad Brother*.[13] Incarcerated in 1961 for a seventy-dollar robbery that gave him a sentence of one year to life, Jackson used his time in prison to cement his standing as a charismatic and muscular convict hustler and gang leader. Self-education and study groups led him to become a militant theoretician of Marx,

Lenin, and Mao to explain what had happened to him and other prisoners. He was beginning to mobilize others incarcerated for a "revolutionary mentality," not a criminal one.[14] In 1970, he and two other prisoners were charged with murder in the death of a prison guard following a fight.

On August 21, 1971, guards shot Jackson to death after what remains a confused confrontation. Other corrections officers were murdered with their throats cut, and Jackson was accused of sneaking a gun into the prison, somewhat preposterously, under an Afro wig after a visit from his lawyer before the shootings.[15] Bob Dylan would croon mournfully in a song he wrote almost immediately after what he considered to be Jackson's murder.[16] Even the pacifist author James Baldwin would claim, "No Black person will ever believe that George Jackson died the way they tell us he did."[17]

Alan remembered that he was "outraged" over Jackson's murder, as was everyone else in left and liberal political circles.[18] Coming after the New York Panther trials, the police murders in Chicago of Panther leaders, the death of antiwar students, and the invasion of Cambodia, Jackson's death was perceived as another extralegal "execution."[19] It led those in deep solidarity with the black power struggle to see the threat of state violence all around them.

Three weeks after Jackson's death, the prison uprising at the Attica Correctional Facility in upstate New York would be even more shocking, and critical to Alan's politicization. After continued worsening conditions and unmet demands for change from politicized prisoners, a rebellion began that left four guards murdered, others taken hostage, and the prison's control ceded to the imprisoned. The state's governor, Nelson Rockefeller, refused to find a nonlethal way out of the rebellion, despite the presence of an outside negotiating team and a desire from the prisoners to end their siege. Rockefeller instead ordered the prison to be stormed, guns blazing.[20]

Four days after the Attica takeover started, and in less than an hour, 39 men lay dead in the prison yard. They had been killed in the state-ordered firestorm of tear gas sprayed from helicopters, followed by a military-style invasion with machine guns and rifles where "over 2,500 hollow tipped and deer-slug bullets [rained] down into the confines of the 50-by-50 yard enclosure where inmates and hostages alike had congregated."[21] Armed troopers and guards murdered 29 prisoners and 10 guards in the initial prison retaking, while immediate rumors and news accounts blamed those incarcerated for the deaths. Nearly another 400 prisoners were wounded.[22] Most had started to surrender once the gas was dropped, but the shooting erupted anyway.[23]

The public revulsion, toward the prisoners rather than the state's use of force, was magnified when the first news reported that the guards killed in the initial takeover had been castrated.[24] This turned out to be untrue. Instead, the troopers "forced the survivors to strip naked and crawl through mud as state photographers captured their humiliation from helicopters above. Guards beat the naked captives with clubs, burned them with cigarettes, and hurled racial epithets at them along with threats of castration, torture and murder."[25] Later reports showed that 63 percent of those involved in the uprising had physical injuries, and many more who were quickly shipped off to other prisons were not counted.[26] Attica became the most shocking prison debacle in U.S. history, and the worst mass killing to date between Americans since the Civil War, "except for Indian massacres in the late 19th century," the authors of the official state report declared.[27]

Central to the prisoners' revolt was the need for decent medical care. The rebellion itself had started in solidarity and reaction to Jackson's murder.[28] Their first demand was for better legal representation and procedures for parole, but the second was for "a change in medical staff and medical policy and procedure," and another for "periodical check-ups . . . and sufficient licensed practitioners available twenty-four hours a day."[29] Once the prison had been retaken, it became clear that no provision had been made to treat a mass casualty situation in a rural community forty miles from a major hospital, where there were only two doctors on the prison staff and a handful of state trooper medics.

As the rebellion was ongoing, a group of doctors, medical students, and nurses organized by psychiatrist Eli Messinger from the Medical Committee for Human Rights (MCHR) tried to get into the prison to help. The group had been organized quickly, and Alan was not part of it. As the mop-up and retaliation continued inside, this rag-tag group of doctors, medical students, and nurses stood outside the facility's massive concrete walls unable to make it inside, although they were able to put pressure on some, but not all, medical personnel going in and out. "People died that night and we stood out in the rain," nurse Donna Karl recalled with great sadness, regret, and a sense of impotence.[30] In contrast, physician Howard Levy thought that it was not exactly clear what the MCHR team was there to do: witness, provide care, or something else.[31] They could do little as prisoners were left to bleed out, writhe in pain, or suffer new injuries and beatings from the conquering state forces.[32]

Though he had not been there, "the Attica Rebellion changed my life," Alan would later write.[33] He saw the Attica events in political terms, more as "a continuation of African American slave rebellions than simple uprisings. The passion and politics of national liberation and personal dignity seemed to be the motivating force behind it." He could imagine that "they were in a no win situation. Yet they fought because it would have been worse not to."[34] From what he had seen at Attica, MCHR's Messinger had argued, "there is no politically neutral medicine, only politically unaware medical people."[35] As with the prisoners' manifesto and Messinger's impassioned point, Alan was trying to parse how to stand up to the oppression he saw around him as a politicized physician.

A few weeks after the rebellion ended the Attica experience became even more personal for him. The Fortune Society, an organization created in 1967 to help formerly incarcerated persons reintegrate into society, asked Alan to use his doctor credentials to visit former Attica prisoners who had been shipped to high security prisons across New York State.[36] Many of them still had wounds from the assault and were subjected to the notoriously poor medical care that was the norm in prisons.[37]

Alan had never been in a prison before, and the visits connected his theoretical rumblings and medical school efforts at "armed propaganda" to his emotional core. "The fall of 1971 became a blur of bars, massive concrete walls, broken and bruised bodies housed in strip cells that had a hole in the floor as the only furniture," he would write two decades later. "The prison doctors were sometimes openly hostile & sometimes cloyingly friendly—never were they competent or concerned about the prisoner's demand."[38] It became possible for him to imagine that he might make a difference in such a setting. He also understood how much his own privilege had kept him from this fate.[39] In these senses he was right: Attica did change his life.

MOVING TO THE COMMUNITY

The rest of the internship year flew by in a blur of sleeplessness and patient demands. In addition, there were the requests from the political underground for Alan's services. These experiences led Alan to a difficult decision that surprised his mentors and many of his classmates: he refused to continue into the residency program and quit his medical training.

"It was just too far from what was happening," he later recollected.[40] Although the lure of fascinating medical cases might keep him intellectually engaged, he would be politically inert. "I was afraid I'd never leave it, that I'd find an excuse."[41] Seeing no way to specialize and politicize at the same time, he decided he would make his living as some kind of community doctor, and continue his political work.

Alan wanted a kind of post–medical school education that Columbia's hospital could not provide. As health activist Dr. Quentin Young wrote in 1970, "It is a painful truth that . . . medical students . . . complete . . . their education to levels of exquisite specialization only to enter a complex, crisis-ridden system of health care with the naiveté of a newborn."[42] Alan had no intention of being naive. Barbara joined Alan in ending her training. As part of a generation in search for community, authenticity, and, in their case, real medical service, Alan and Barbara took the leap together.[43]

Like so many others, they were making political decisions that moved them away from their natal families to create a new one with shared political beliefs.[44] It was difficult for Alan's parents, especially his mother, Mona, to watch their brilliant and talented son seemingly throw away his potential in academic medicine and scientific research, and to be involved with a "shiksa goddess." The struggles with his parents that had begun with his talk on Vietnam at the synagogue when he was in college continued as his commitment to social change deepened. They suggested to him that he could be "concerned" but still have his professional career.[45] He could not, he explained. They were "bewildered by his choices," so outside their ken of experience or expectations.[46] Nor did they understand why Barbara, his choice as a partner, was doing this too.

Alan's friend Dick Clapp, now the deputy director of the Prison Health Project at the New York City Health and Hospitals Corporation, solved part of the problem of what Alan would do next. Clapp hired him and his medical school buddy Franklin Apfel, who had also dropped out of advanced training, to share a position as physicians in the Bronx House of Detention as the city's health department was attempting to improve prison health services. It was a first step in bringing decent medical care with politicized doctors into the prison system, and to put into practice what Alan felt he had to do.

This was not enough to meet Alan's political needs, however. The rest of his time he volunteered at the Black Panther–sponsored People's Health Center in the South Bronx, part of the Panthers' community service efforts to provide primary care.[47] In the burned-out and rotting slums of the 1970s Bronx, he made house calls. He was impressed, in particular, by the strength of the women of color who attempted to hold health and home together amid poverty, violence, and drugs.[48] It was community medicine he was practicing, not guerrilla warfare, in keeping with the Panthers' focus at that time.[49] Barbara joined him in this medical community effort, working part-time as an emergency department physician at Harlem Hospital and in one of New York's newly legalized abortion clinics.[50]

Alan and Barbara would end their first year as community doctors with their first arrests. In the summer of 1972, as the Paris peace negotiations to end the war in Vietnam dragged on, the Democrats were about to nominate antiwar senator George McGovern for the presidency and the Republicans were set to renominate Richard Nixon for what would be a truncated second term. At the Democratic Convention, McGovern presided over a party whose delegates, for the first time, were nearly a third women, a party that was openly discussing feminist and gay issues, even if in the end key concerns never made it into the platform.

Opposition at the Republican convention in Miami was different. Organizers like New Left stalwart Rennie Davis sent out a call to a wide variety of groups to mass in protest against the war there. Along with the Vietnam Veterans Against the War (who staged a "last patrol" drive from across the country that would be immortalized in Oliver Stone's film *Born on the Fourth of July*), the 4,500 protesters included feminists, gay groups, hippies, zippies (those who believe in doing things for free), students, retirees who lived along Miami Beach's Collins Avenue, and Alan and Barbara's affinity group from Washington Heights.[51]

The demonstrators provided the kind of disorganized protest that law-and-order Republicans railed against. Protesters with red bloody hands or white death masks painted on their bodies pushed against a metal fence and corralled into a place called Flamingo Park, where they faced helmeted Miami police wielding batons, tear gas, guns, and gas masks. Demonstrators chanted "Ho Ho, Ho Chi Minh. The NLF is gonna win!" and "Attica means—fight back!" as the veterans yelled "Murder, murder, murder!" at the delegates.[52] The veterans' silent march to the convention center offered a rare moment of dignity.[53]

Expecting to provide rudimentary first aid, Alan and Barbara instead became witnesses to violence as the police waded into the crowds with batons and tear gas. The couple's medic armbands proved little protection as they were arrested, spending four days in jail, along with 1,400 others, before being released without charge.[54] Mostly Miami had been a disaster, as everybody soon realized when McGovern lost by a landslide that November. The war would drag on for another three years.

To make all of this even more surreal, Alan and Barbara, along with several friends, flew directly from Miami after the demonstrations and jail to the Caribbean island of St. Maarten for a short vacation at the home of Alan's uncle and aunt. "Mostly Alan's idea of relaxing was just to read and read," his friend Franklin remembered.[55] At some point during those days, however, he stopped reading long enough to take the hallucinogen mescaline with Barbara. She has a vivid memory of standing with Alan in the shining blue water, with the waves about them, as he pronounced that he had two choices: to win a Nobel Prize, if he went back into medicine, or become a revolutionary, if he continued his politics.[56]

NEW YORK TO WOUNDED KNEE

Alan and Barbara continued their daytime medical work, once back in New York, but they were increasingly looking for something more meaningful. Their friend Franklin, and others from their medical school class, became part of a politicized group of doctors working at the run-down, desperately overcrowded Lincoln Hospital in the South Bronx that served a primarily Latinx and black, very poor population.[57] Politicized health activists and health care practitioners were reading pamphlets such as "The Opium Trail: Heroin and Imperialism" and discussing the social and economic basis for disease, and especially the links connecting drugs, capitalism, addiction, and pacification of the ghettos.[58] Radical health activists organized a group called Think Lincoln and began to take over aspects of the care structure in the hospital, much to the consternation of those opposed to the radical changes they proposed.[59]

Alan, Barbara, and their friends were trying to answer the critique of radicalism offered by a medical school classmate: "As for Vietnam and the Ghetto — what am I, personally supposed to do? It seems that we should all break out of complacency and clean up the slums and stop the war. Fine. Any suggestions where to begin?"[60] Their first response had been to work in communities of color, to treat their patients with the decency and care that had not been available, and to attempt to protect prisoners and those in the underground. But was this enough?

Alan and Barbara would find another answer 1,600 miles away after February 27, 1973, when 200 American Indian Movement (AIM) activists and a small number of Oglala Lakota took over the trading post and tiny town of Wounded Knee, South Dakota, site of the 1890 massacre. They acted to protest corruption by the tribal leader and his Guardians of the Oglala Nation (GOONS), as well as centuries of violence and broken treaties. As the FBI cordoned off the area in response, sniper fire was exchanged, electricity and water were cut off, food and medical supplies were restricted, and violence led to two deaths. The standoff would last for seventy-one days. The AIM activists' supporters included actor Marlon Brando, who declined his Oscar for *The Godfather* and instead sent to the stage Sacheen Littlefeather, an Apache actress.[61] Two U.S. senators tried unsuccessfully to mediate the siege, and supporters arrived, from unknowns eager to be part of a real cowboys-and-Indians drama to activist Angela Davis, but they failed to get past the FBI lines.[62]

Rumors of caches of weapons and imminent confrontations spread wildly, and the *New York Times* decried the possibility of another "senseless slaughter" as at Attica.[63] Firefights between the sides and the blizzards of the harsh South Dakota winter became part of the daily experience.[64] Inside the encampment, the AIM supporters had one AK-47 brought back from Vietnam by a veteran, but their primary weapons were hunting rifles and materials to make Molotov cocktails. Stockpiled against them by the government were "phantom jets, 17 armored personnel carriers, M-16 rifles with 50,000 rounds of ammunition, 11,760 rounds of M-16 tracer ammunition, 8,200 rounds of M-1 ball ammunition, 20 sniper rifles, 2,500 star parachute flares, M-79 tear-gas grenade launchers and infrared lights."[65]

A month into the takeover, nearly 4,000 people attended a meeting at the St. John the Divine cathedral on New York's Upper West Side to hear what was happening and requests for aid. One of the key problems became the lack of medical care and supplies. With the government blockade, supporters trying to get into Wounded Knee risked being shot or arrested. Mostly they did not get through, or had to wait till night to sneak through miles of back trails to bring food in backpacks in the winter cold and snowdrifts.[66] Word began to get out that limits on supplies were leading to serious illnesses and early stages of malnutrition in children. Supporters followed up the St. John the Divine meeting by asking that doctors and nurses go to Wounded Knee.[67]

It would become another powerful, emotional, and pivotal moment in Alan and Barbara's lives. Asked to bring supplies and their skills, they had to decide whether they were really willing to risk their lives and futures, whether they were ready to put their bodies where their politics had led them. They had to decide as well whether they would gain in return a sense of what political theorist Hannah Arendt termed "public happiness," as in the Declaration of Independence's "life, liberty and the pursuit of happiness," that is "the exhilaration of acting in such a way as to make a difference in the world."[68] It required measuring the romanticism that infected everyone on the left about Native American struggles against the reality that they might be killed by the FBI, raped or robbed by the reservation GOONS and local ranchers who supported the government, or even harmed by AIM and Lakota protesters who had become increasingly suspicious, sometimes violently so, of anyone showing up to "help" who might instead be an undercover agent.

With bravado, Alan claimed the decision was easy, although "getting in . . . [would be] harder."[69] After flying to Rapid City, South Dakota, with their political friend nurse Phyllis Prentice, they drove the ninety-two miles to the outskirts of the encampment. Their medical credentials and a week of negotiating with the Justice Department and the Bureau of Indian Affairs did not get them past the FBI lines. AIM militants outside the encampment asked if they would be willing to sneak in at very high risk. Alan worried too of what might happen to Barbara or Phyllis if they were caught. But the only answer for all of them at that point was yes. For the next forty-eight hours, they trekked more than twenty miles, moving with their AIM guide only at night, sleeping in tree-lined gullies during the day and evading the patrols of ranchers on horseback.[70]

Their guide was not from the reservation, and they got lost. Drawing upon his astronomy skills from the Boy Scouts, Alan looked to the stars for direction and took over as guide.[71]After wandering in at least the right direction, they finally "crested a hill and looked down on a scene more reminiscent of South Vietnam than South Dakota," he wrote later. He described "rings of fire — dry grass ignited by the flares . . . government bunkers and armored personnel carriers," and still smoldering rocks. They had "to crawl past those machine guns only to end up in the little town that sat like a bulls eye on a target." As the dawn broke, out of "commitment, anger at the government's actions, stubbornness, [and] exhaustion," they decided to run across a small creek and into Wounded

Knee.[72] They made it undetected. "Okay I was an adventurist," Alan would admit decades later, "but we're talking about the soul of a nation here."[73]

The welcome Alan, Barbara, and Phyllis received was not warm. The AIM activists and Lakota were suspicious about why they were there, even though they brought in medical supplies and explained their credentials. The most difficult personal and political challenge came the very first day, when they were told that a woman was in obstructed labor. "Which one of you is the doctor?" her husband finally asked Barbara and Alan. They both raised their hands. The husband stared down at them, a rifle in his hand . . . and picked Alan.[74]

Taken to the laboring woman, Alan quickly determined that without a caesarian section, neither she nor her fetus would survive. The delivery could not be done in the camp. Alan was adamant, but very scared, when he had to deliver this diagnosis to the armed husband. At first the pregnant woman refused to consider leaving, fearful of being arrested, or not being allowed to return to the encampment, and accepted the possibility of death. Alan finally prevailed upon the family that negotiating with the FBI for an ambulance was the only option. The mother's willingness to die for freedom, and to take her potential infant with her, was something he would never forget. "Any day's a good day to die," he would tell an interviewer, was one of the lessons he learned from those taking this stand.[75]

After this experience, Alan, Barbara, and Phyllis spent eight more days providing rudimentary care, eating only two meals a day like everyone else, a little oatmeal for breakfast and beans for dinner. Alan treated a young boy who had been scorched by a steam iron his family had tried to use to provide heat in the old trailers they lived in, and he cared for those with flu and bronchitis. He worried about a potential outbreak of scurvy, and that the drinking water could become contaminated by overflowing latrines.

Finally Alan, Barbara, and Phyllis were able to walk out. For reasons they did not understand, they were not arrested when they crossed back over the FBI lines, nor did their names appear in the FBI files. Barbara and Phyllis returned to New York for work, but Alan went on to give medical testimony at the South Dakota state capitol about the horrendous conditions, possible starvation, and medical dangers. "If the blockade isn't lifted," he warned, "the people will die from hunger, and the government will simply take over."[76] Once back in New York, he, Barbara, and AIM cofounder Clyde Bellecourt gave a news conference to national media about the life-threatening health hazards confronting those in the encampment.

The differences between Barbara and Alan became clear in the televised news conference. With her natural curls flattened to hang below her shoulders and a macramé necklace over her black turtleneck, Barbara looked beautiful and serious, much like the then-popular Native American singer Buffy Sainte-

Alan Berkman, Barbara Zeller, and Clyde Bellecourt from the American Indian Movement (AIM) at a press conference on conditions at Wounded Knee during the AIM takeover and government standoff, New York City, March 1974. *Courtesy of the Associated Press.*

Marie. She spoke after Bellecourt in measured terms about the dire medical situation they had found. "The nutrition is a major problem," she explained in detail. She described the emergency delivery, leaving out the way they had been questioned and the father with the rifle in hand. She came across as a thoughtful doctor giving the facts of a serious situation. Filmed much more in close-up, Alan said very little, but his glowering countenance spoke volumes.[77]

On May 8, the food shortage, medical needs, exhaustion, and increasing bad publicity for the U.S. government brought the confrontation to an end.[78] Despite assurances to the contrary, the tribal government's reign of terror would only deepen, and the demanded investigation of the treaty of 1868 never happened.[79] Senate hearings criticized the FBI's handling of the takeover and the tribal leadership's corruption, but little improved.[80] Debates still rage over the events that followed, between the mass arrests and the killing over the next two years of more than sixty people who had supported AIM and its allies on the reservation. The aftermath also brought mistrials, prosecutorial misconduct, the FBI's withholding of evidence, shootouts that left two more FBI agents dead, and a controversial conviction and life sentence for AIM leader Leonard Peltier. Others, including the FBI, got away with murder.[81]

Alan was now twenty-eight years old. He had seen in person what the power of the state could do and the willingness of activists at Attica and Wounded Knee to stand up and fight it, even at the cost of their lives. He gave an interview to our hometown newspaper before the Wounded Knee siege ended urging a letter-writing campaign to President Nixon and Congress, but it was clear that he had other plans for his own activism.[82] These experiences had added an emotional depth to his analysis of what was wrong with America. How he and Barbara would turn this into action was not yet clear.

PART
TWO

INTO THE STRUGGLE

THE FUTURE

On the night of October 20, 1981, Alan made a house call that changed his life forever. For more than a decade, he had been both a practicing community physician and a doctor to those in the political underground. He had joined a hidden economy filled with typewriter repairmen servicing stolen machines, health department workers providing blank birth certificates, doctors not reporting their patients' wounds to the police, political movements commandeering city-owned x-ray vans, and nurses and others using made-up names and birth information to get certain "patients" into hospitals.[1]

This house call would be different — after that night, he would become the second doctor in American history to be charged with accessory to murder after the fact. The first was Samuel Mudd, the nineteenth-century physician who treated John Wilkes Booth after the Lincoln assassination.[2] That night, however, he could not think about the legal consequences — he had a job to do.

The October day had started like many others. In forty-degree weather that already felt like winter, Alan left his Brooklyn apartment and took the D train as it wended through Manhattan to the South Bronx. When he tired of people-watching on the hour-long ride, he read the *New York Times* and did the cross-word puzzle, as always in pen.

He spent the day seeing his patients. They came to him suffering from heart failure, diabetes, asthma, and the range of diseases that ravage the primarily black and Latinx patients who crowded into the clinics of Lincoln Hospital. He treated them all as individuals, listening to their complaints, searching for ways to explain what they had and what they could do to get better. He warmed his stethoscope before the cold metal touched a chest and spoke fluent (not just medical) Spanish when needed. He would order all the tests he thought required to make the appropriate diagnosis, "always driven for the facts and more data."[3] He always tried after that to make sure that social service, not just abrupt medical treatment, was made available.

Work did not finish when the clinic closed. At the end of a long day, he was back on the subway into Manhattan for a meeting of a support group for various revolutions in Africa, providing aid at the time to Robert Mugabe's party in the newly independent Zimbabwe. Well into the meeting, the apartment phone rang and a political comrade asked for him urgently: he had to come now and should tell no one why.[4] When he got downstairs to the waiting car, his friend's visible worry and her shaking belied her usual toughness. As he recalled the exchange in his memoir:

"Do you know what happened? Did you hear?" she asked in rushed and breathless tones.

"No. What's the matter?"

"Judy's dead. I don't know for sure, but I know her car crashed."

"Wait. Wait. Please slow down. What are you talking about?"

"Everything's fucked up. We tried to take off this armored car. It was fucked. There was a shootout. People were shot and captured. We barely escaped. It was terrible. I think Judy's dead."

"Holy shit. What's happening now?"

"Somebody else was shot pretty bad. We got her away but she's still bleeding. You've got to help us."[5]

Years of medical training had taught him to think about what would be required. "There could be bits of clothing, bullet fragments and dead tissue to clean out," he went over in his mind. The first stop was his apartment for the antibiotics and painkillers he stashed at home for this kind of emergency. Next they headed back north to Lincoln Hospital as, looking calm and appropriate, he made his way through the emergency room, surreptitiously collecting the intravenous setup, intravenous therapy (IV) tubing, splints, gauze, bandages, needles, and sterile saline necessary to treat bullet wounds.

Alan's friend drove them back onto the highway toward what he would later learn was suburban Mount Vernon. "Close your eyes," she told him. "We're going to a safe house and you don't need to know where it is." Even those who were trusted were told little, as much for their own security as anyone else's. Behind his closed eyes, fear started to take over as his friend flipped on the radio news. A Brink's truck had been robbed, two policemen and an armored guard were dead, and there had been arrests and an intense manhunt for the others while some were already in jail, including his friend, whose car had crashed.

The car stopped. They waited. Alan kept his eyes shut until he was told, "Come on out now. It's OK. Just follow me." Up the stairs of a darkened apartment building, there was silence. Then a door opened and he remembered:

As we walked into the dim room I heard the metallic sound of cocked hammers being released. Three black men wearing bulletproof vests and carrying a variety of weapons stood around the room. Another man in a vest, and a woman seated together, on a couch directly in front of me. A white woman lay on a day bed along the right hand wall and was being ministered to by someone crouching near her head. Her right pant leg had been torn open and a large pool of blood stained the bed around it. The woman seemed in shock. Her complexion was pale and her eyes didn't focus as I came near. I recognized the familiar figure crouched by her side placing acupuncture needles in her ears and face.

The puckered entrance wound was a few inches above the knee and the surrounding skin was speckled with gunpowder. The knee joint and lower thigh [was] massively swollen. I first thought . . . it was a large collection of blood, but then noticed her right leg was much shorter than her left and realized the femur was shattered and the powerful thigh muscles were forcing the lower segment of bone to slide over the upper. Without even seeing the exit wound or touching the leg, I knew I was out of my depth. I also knew there was no one else we knew who could deal with it.[6]

5

REVOLUTIONARY ROAD

In 1973, almost a decade before the Brink's events, what Alan and Barbara would do following Wounded Knee was uncertain. They needed time and a different space to consider their options. They knew comrades in New York were increasingly coming under state surveillance, their movements tracked and apartments broken into in warrantless searches.[7] They were fortunate that their own actions had not yet made them visible to the enforcement power of the state.

To consider what was next, they left New York City in May 1973 for a planned four-month road trip across America to get some rest and meet like-minded friends elsewhere. They were not seeking an escape, as many others did in the drugs and rural communes of the 1970s, but a meaningful way to deepen their political principles in actual practice.[8] Their car's backseat held Alan's books — Marx, Engels, Fanon, Hegel, and Mao — not camping equipment and bongs.[9] Along the way to the West Coast, they stopped to visit friends doing political work, especially those connected surreptitiously to the Weather Underground Organization, which included Weather's leadership. Barbara hoped that the awe of the landscape and a chance to hike in the West would renew them too. But Alan hardly looked up from his Marx as they drove along the Snake River in Wyoming with the vast Teton Mountains above them.[10]

Their experiences months earlier on the plains of the Oglala Sioux reservation at Wounded Knee had been life-altering. As their medical school friend Franklin Apfel recalled, "I got the impression when [Alan] was talking about Wounded Knee there was more an emotional edge to his rap. He was always so cool and analytic. There was something that got him and that affected the way he was communicating. It was quite a bit different Alan."[11] Both Barbara and Alan knew that the risks they had been taking for several years, seeing patients in the underground, were minor compared to those of comrades taking more dangerous actions. Now that Wounded Knee had shown them the kind of power they were up against, they had to decide how far they were willing to go.

Looking back on his 1973 self years later, Alan described realizing at the time that "if we thought, as we did and felt, that hundreds of thousands of lives, if not millions ultimately, were at stake, then we had to figure out some way of developing a politic inside the United States that had at its core solidarity with other people and a desire that we had to stop the killing."[12] He was not wrong that there was a war of sorts being fought in America's streets and across the world. Those who met with the Vietnamese or Cubans, or spent time with various Puerto Rican leftists, black power advocates, or members of the American Indian Movement, began to understand what solidarity in a worldwide struggle really meant.[13]

Alan and Barbara were serious people looking to do serious political work, while remaining good friends to others as well as one another. As one member of the groups they became allied with put it, "People always ask why I did what I did, and I tell them I was a soldier in a war. And they always say, 'what war?'"[14] To Barbara and Alan it was clear this was a war for freedom. To win it, they became increasingly tied to a part of the left building clandestine cadres alongside more mass and public movements for political change. Neither Alan nor Barbara could have predicted how far the commitments they were about to make would lead them.

THE MOVE TO BOSTON

American society's fractures grew deeper and more overt in the 1970s. The Watergate congressional hearings in May 1973 became the soundtrack to Barbara and Alan's cross-country drive.[15] The New York City they left behind was staggering toward what looked like bankruptcy, while draconian drug laws and violence escalated.[16] The Yom Kippur war between Israel and Egypt and Syria, and the subsequent oil crisis, was still a few months away, but the Middle East was again heating up. The recession of the mid-1970s was coming, as the ease (at least for some) of finding decent jobs that the post–World War II expansion made possible was ending. Nixon's southern strategy was bringing conservative working-class whites into the Republican circle, exploiting the increasing backlash against civil rights gains and the women's movement.[17] The hopes that Salvador Allende's socialist revolution in Chile would add another liberated anticapitalist country to the world's nations crashed on September 11, 1973, when his regime was overthrown with the support of the Central Intelligence Agency (CIA).[18]

Alan and Barbara's friends, in the collectives across the country that they visited in the summer of 1973, all faced the age-old revolutionary question:

What is to be done?[19] In the face of political breakdowns, economic crises, the moral bankruptcy of powerful elites, and continued U.S. involvement in imperial wars, what response made sense? Alan knew that "the goal of revolution is to seize power" but that "realistically," and "subjectively," he and those who shared his politics were nowhere "near that ballpark and yet . . ."[20] He, Barbara, and his comrades faced the dilemma of trying to be "revolutionar[ies] in a non-revolutionary country."[21]

Even if more could be done, the right and most revolutionary thing to do was not at all obvious, especially to a thinker as analytic and synthetic as Alan. As he would tell an interviewer years later, "We weren't just going to go off and do our own thing. I think that was part of being a 'revolutionary' doctor and not just a doctor or a radical doctor."[22] He was making a different kind of commitment, and as one of his brothers put it, in part "organized himself" into revolutionary beliefs and actions.[23]

Even in light of the ebbing rebellion in the United States, Alan still wanted to be in a larger movement that saw itself as part of worldwide revolutionary efforts. As he would remember, "I needed to define myself as a revolutionary, it seemed like it was the ultimate conclusion. . . . And . . . the more rebellion died down inside the United States . . . the more I tended to substitute the sort of revolutionary dogma and spend more and more of my time in organizations worried about the correct line and having less and less of a relationship to mass rebellion."[24] Like many other radicals and revolutionaries of his day, Alan was looking for something more organized than endless demonstrations and meetings.[25]

Given these central beliefs, Alan was perfectly situated to deepen his involvement with support for the Weather Underground Organization. Many of those who identified with Weather continued their public political lives.[26] Fewer than 100 individuals ever went underground to take more clandestine positions, to continue the occasional bombings in response to U.S. or corporate policies, while avoiding for a time criminal charges against them.[27] Despite the romanticism and "armed struggle" rhetoric of Weather, and the frantic fervor with which the FBI tried to track them, their bombings were all against property (both governmental and corporate). Their efforts to make bombs in both New York and Detroit in 1970 that could have led to mass casualties ended, in one case, in their own destruction and, in the other, grand jury indictments eventually dropped because of illegal government surveillance.[28]

What Weather most needed was an above-ground apparatus to articulate its politics and financially and materially support those underground. Alan was a perfect ally in this endeavor. As he noted later, "My politics supported it, because I'd already done some actions of my own within the context of my collective [in Washington Heights] and because I wasn't very well known as far as I could tell to the government apparatus."[29] No other political organization made more sense for him at the time. The only question that remained was, where?

Boston beckoned as he and Barbara drove back east. Alan's family was still in upstate New York, four hours from Boston. Barbara's family was in Connecticut, and her mother had developed an illness that would need attention.[30] Their medical school friend Dick Clapp, then in public health school part-time at Harvard, lived in Boston, where he also continued his work in prison health. Barbara and Alan's doctor's licenses gave them a way to make a living, and other Weather allies they knew from New York were now in Boston.

In the fall of 1973, they settled in with Dick Clapp and his girlfriend in the working-class Boston neighborhood of Dorchester, accepting part-time medical jobs at two local community health centers.[31] With Clapp's connections, they also supervised prisoners making blood donations at Walpole State Prison on Saturdays.[32] Though doctoring would pay the bills, exactly how they might be part of Weather's above-ground politics still needed working out.

They arrived in Boston as the city's long history of racial, class, and religious segregation was about to spasm into the open.[33] While the worst of the violence would come a year later, in September 1974, with mandatory busing to desegregate the schools, the increasingly racial rhetoric of violent opposition coming from Boston's all-white school committee and its supporters was palpable. They experienced the building Northern version of white populist racial rage, coupled with class and ethnic resentment.

Alan, along with others, tried to take seriously what it meant to build a political organization that could challenge American imperial power and the ever-present racism visible daily in their Boston life. Alan was ready to become what Weather called, in a weirdly mixed metaphor, part of the above-ground "ocean," separate from the clandestine leadership's underground "forest."[34]

Despite some misgivings, Alan had come around to Weather's strategy, such as it was.[35] His reading of the histories of other revolutionary movements suggested that hidden cadres had to be supported by secret collectives above ground while other kinds of public organizing went on.[36] He accepted the Weather's leadership statement that "revolutionaries must make a profound commitment to the future of humanity, apply our limited knowledge and experience to understand an ever-changing situation, organize the masses of people and build the fight. It means that struggle and risk and hard work and adversity will become a way of life, that the only certainty will be constant change, that the only possibilities are victory or death."[37] He read more on the history of American and left politics, learning the deep history of white supremacy that had not been part of his formal education.

He was also writing more political theory. Dick Clapp remembered a representative story about Alan at the time. He happened on Alan working one day. "I'm writing Lenin," Alan said quickly, then corrected himself: "I meant I am reading Lenin." Clapp was not so certain which statement was true.[38] Nevertheless, Alan's belief in the need for a leader of politicized cadres with the "right" line to lead the masses seems to have filled his thinking, lit up his imagination, and became part of his mission.

The work of being a doctor or thinking about what it meant to be a revolutionary together did not take up all of Alan's time. His seriousness, occasional quickness to anger, faith in his own intellect, and commitment to analytic precision were still coupled with playfulness, an ironic sense of humor, and an interest in the theater. He played pickup basketball, went to visit friends in Maine and Vermont, hung out, saw movies sometimes even in the afternoon, cooked dinners with his friends and their partners, and talked politics and sports. He did not think getting stoned was antirevolutionary.

Close to his natal and then fraternity brothers as a younger man, Alan continued to seek bonds with other men. His friends in Boston, in addition to Dick Clapp, included actor and director Stephen Wangh, who had been doing street theater for years and pioneered a kind of physical and psychological theatricality. Steven Krugman, a psychologist Alan had known in Washington Heights, was now working in a prison diversion program, trying to write a book on police informants he was calling "Best Friends." Through Krugman, Alan befriended Bruce Taub, from a Bronx working-class family not unlike Alan's and an anthropology graduate school dropout, who was living in a commune that Alan visited in Vermont. Taub had just moved to Boston for work and to start law school. All of them were swayed by Alan's brilliance, camaraderie, and his ability to talk deeply about the most crucial ways to fight for justice.[39]

All these men were committed to understanding a way to critique male power and to become better comrades to their women partners as feminism's demands were part of the left gestalt. Despite this, Alan's selfishness was sometimes a point of concern. Once while packing for a group picnic, Alan split open a large watermelon, then cut a large triangle out of the red, richest part of the fruit, and ate it before he packed the rest. That simple act led to an effort by his male buddies to point out his emotional and, to them, political immaturity.[40] Alan was challenged to apply his politics even on the most basic level, and he took seriously his need to change as part of becoming a real revolutionary.

As Alan's friends struggled with what their political commitments meant for their careers, relationships, and emotional lives, they were struck by Alan's certainty. All of them remembered a men's weekend when they hung out at Stephen Wangh's father's Connecticut home and dropped LSD together. As all the men admitted to one another their own emotional ups and downs, Alan amazed them by reporting that he had never felt depressed.[41] It was not that he did not have an emotional life; it was that his ability to intellectualize and compartmentalize seemed to have overwhelmed everything else.

Even if he did not know what the right way was, he would tell his friends, the point was to make a commitment to force real revolutionary change and to do the things that seemed very hard. "He was always so steadfast," Steven Krugman recalled. Alan's intellect was capable of questioning, but not giving up. Fear, he thought, was something to be conquered, not something to stop you.[42] The obligation to listen to others, not just act alone, became his cardinal belief. Once he had defined himself as a revolutionary, he worked to make his practice fit his tenets.

STARTING A PRAIRIE FIRE

To make his beliefs into deeds, Alan became one of those in the Weather "ocean" who read and rewrote the drafts of what became Weather's bold statement about America's past and its vision for the future: *Prairie Fire: The Politics of Revolutionary Anti-imperialism.*[43] Alan may have been doing this when Dick Clapp caught him in his "Lenin" moment. Not all of this drafting was done alone. Alan in all probability attended at least one of the cadre meetings where Weather's blueprint for revolution was debated.[44]

By July 1974, the result of that effort would become a nearly 200-page book, with thousands of copies clandestinely published (by printers wearing gloves to leave no fingerprints) and delivered to bookstores, newspapers, organization offices, and communes across the country.[45] Getting it written, printed, bound, and delivered in secret was a monumental task in an era without faxes, home computers, or an internet. Eventually, nearly 40,000 copies would be printed and sent out.

The book was a brief on American history that acknowledged the centrality of racism and imperialism, and the efforts to counter them, while pointing the way to revolutionary change. It linked Weather's previous political actions back to John Brown and other historical figures in the struggles against white racial power. It became a critical reminder of what one literary critic has called the centrality of "righteous violence" to the American experience.[46]

The title *Prairie Fire* drew upon a Mao aphorism that "a single spark can start a prairie fire," assuming that the book and discussion of its ideas would beget a revolutionary moment set in an international perspective.[47] It tried to do many things: analyze the impact Weather's leaders thought their bombings had, critique some of their past mistakes, examine the consequences of the Watergate debacle, and provide examples of antiracist and anti-imperial struggles in America's past. It ended with a call for continued organizing in a multigendered and multiracial working class. It declared the necessity for both continued long-term organizing in the working class and recognition of the importance of national liberation struggles in the United States and abroad.

Alan was critical of *Prairie Fire*'s final draft and its politics, and presumably still held to whatever positions he had himself advocated. In the spring of 1974, just before the book appeared, he made comments about its failure to really see both racism and imperialism as what Mao would have called the "primary contradictions," that is the most important focus of struggle.[48] He would admit years later that he "wasn't very happy with the direction my old SDS friends were taking."[49] He did not plan to be part of what was being called the Prairie Fire Distribution Committee. He was looking for a real revolution.

IN SOLIDARITY

Alan convinced himself that he had to become some kind of guerrilla fighter. Clearly influenced by his experiences at Wounded Knee, "I decided I wanted to participate directly in a struggle where people were actually fighting in a liberation war & where there were attempts to build new social relations in the course of the liberation process."[50] Yet his years of urban doctoring had brought him face to face with the physical consequences of bullet fragments, stab wounds, and broken bodies. He was not considering putting on fatigues and picking up an AK-47 in the fight against imperialism. Having given up his plans to be a leading medical researcher, he redirected his diligent work ethic and intellectual power to his political world.[51]

The crucial question was his distinction between action and support. His readings on imperialism, and his efforts to continue to discuss Weather's politics with his friends and others, led him to consider what he could do to *support* anti-imperialist movements and armed struggles. His first turn was toward Africa. Contacts were already in place between American radicals and the forces in many African countries, especially Guinea-Bissau and Mozambique, then fighting wars against the colonial power, Portugal.[52] There, he thought, "I could make a contribution, learn firsthand what a revolution was like, and stand a reasonable chance of coming out alive."[53] Through his networks that were providing material, money, and political support for these independence movements, Alan began preliminary inquiries about whether he could go to Mozambique to work for the Front for the Liberation of Mozambique (Frelimo).[54]

Alan was hoping that his medical skills would prove useful in the various military encampments for two years. He was not volunteering as a soldier; he was going to be a doctor. As he negotiated the details with Frelimo officials, he expected that "I would spend the first 6 months at a small hospital in Tanzania used by Frelimo learning surgery, & then I would go with Frelimo combatants into northern Mozambique where liberated zones would be set up & a clinic established."[55]

The Mozambique liberation struggle ended, however, before he could depart. On April 24, 1974, a military coup in Portugal overthrew that country's right-wing second republic. The new government promised independence to Portugal's remaining African colonies, including Mozambique. Alan's chance to be a doctor in a guerrilla war for independence disappeared, as Frelimo prepared to take power, not staff military base camps with foreign doctors. He was told to stay home.

The idea of an American physician going to aid a foreign anticolonial struggle was not completely idiosyncratic. Other doctors over the course of the twentieth century had taken their commitment to internationalism and anti-imperialism to countries across the globe, some staffing, for example, the medical facilities for the American Abraham Lincoln Brigade in the war against fascism in 1930s Spain.[56] Most of the American health left had been reading English surgeon Joshua Horn's 1970 book *Away with All Pests* on the changes in medicine and public health in China after the revolution, or listening to his lectures when he came through the United States on tour. Practitioners in social medicine were beginning to make trips to China openly after 1972 and to Chile to support the Allende regime before it fell in 1973, and more clandestinely to Cuba.[57] Other health professionals Alan knew would make the commitment to Mozambique several years later, after Frelimo took power.[58]

Barbara had more practical concerns about deepening her own medical skills. She never lost her focus on medicine as the best place to use her talents. To develop them, she knew she needed to return to complete her residency in internal medicine. As Alan continued to consider what made revolutionary sense, Barbara made plans to return to New York on July 1, 1974, to continue her training at Roosevelt Hospital.[59] Though deeply committed to one another, Alan and Barbara's feminism and critiques of traditional couples also made it crucial for them to allow one another the freedom to do what they each thought necessary.

ALABAMA NOT MOZAMBIQUE

When it appeared working for Frelimo would not work out, Alan found something else meaningful to do in the United States.[60] Contacted by a health group as part of the Quakers' social action–focused American Friends Service Committee, he agreed to spend several months over the summer of 1974 at the Lowndes County Community Health Clinic in Hayneville, Alabama. The town was the county seat of what was known as "bloody Lowndes," for all the violence that occurred there during the 1960s civil rights struggles. It was also there that the local freedom organization, along with Stokely Carmichael and others from SNCC, had fought to register black voters. For a mostly illiterate electorate, the civil rights workers picked a drawing of a black panther to differentiate their freedom party from the white rooster of the Democratic Party.[61] The symbol would make its way west and north to become the avatar for the Black Panther Party. For Alan, it must have seemed like he was going back to the start of it all, a chance to work in the South that he had missed during his college years, and in the place that had produced the very symbol of antiracist militancy and black self-defense.

Lowndes was a deeply economically depressed county. It was 75 percent African American, with more than 60 percent of its people living in poverty, and only three white doctors for a population of approximately 13,000.[62] It suffered all the ills that plagued the rural Black Belt South: "lack of doctors, failure to educate people in public health, missed appointments, unplanned pregnancies, lack of routine screening and tooth decay," and no money to pay for any of it.[63]

A federal Office for Economic Opportunity clinic run by the white health department had failed, and a local black community group was trying to start it up again.[64] Alan was focused on seeing patients and writing a successful grant to the Ford Foundation to study the nutritional impact of the food made possible by the Women, Infants, and Children program, which gave coupons for basic foodstuffs to pregnant and nursing mothers and their at-risk children up to the age of five, as well as health care referrals and nutritional counseling.[65] While he had worked with the urban poor, this would be his chance to see what rural and Southern black poverty really looked like.

Lowndes County proved more dangerous than Alan expected. Two years before he arrived, tensions around the health center had soared to the point that one of the federal health staff members received death threats and had to be whisked away.[66] Alan's work there would reinforce his sense that health meant improving housing, creating jobs, ending discrimination, and empowering communities, not just providing access to medical care for individuals.

Alan met people who were willing to struggle to make this happen. He heard their stories about their community experiences and not just their ills. Hayneville was only sixty miles southwest of Tuskegee, and the scandal of the government's forty-year syphilis study among African American men that left them untreated had broken only two years earlier. Alan cared for one of the men from the study and listened to him explain what it meant to have been lied to by the government for this unethical research.[67] Primarily what Alan saw were the health consequences of racism, poor education, and economic inequality in its rural form: untreated preventable ills and nutritional deficits of those who lived in homes with no running water, proper wells, or sewers.[68]

Listening to the stories of civil rights veterans, he learned that the vaunted nonviolence of political movements past had in fact been backed up by guns, used primarily in self-defense and, as one man he befriended told him, "to intimidate the Klan."[69] Such stories confirmed what he already knew from the rhetoric and actions of the Black Panther Party he had supported while at Columbia.[70]

Alan's time in Alabama helped give him a better sense of his own commitments, though it could not answer the question of how best to use his leadership skills, synthetic intellect, and fearlessness. He knew he needed to be part of a larger group that was trying to parse through these questions and make tactical decisions based on a theoretical understanding of how to move forward, and with whom. With Barbara back in New York, the city beckoned again.

JOINING PRAIRIE FIRE

After his work in Alabama and failure to join the struggle in Mozambique, Alan rejoined Barbara in Brooklyn's Park Slope, where he hoped to find another way to revolution. Despite some of his misgivings about the politics of Weather's *Prairie Fire*, he became deeply involved in the effort to use the book to build a revolutionary movement. Recruited by what the Weather leadership now called the Prairie Fire Organizing Committee, or PFOC (which one of its more disenchanted members suggested should have been pronounced "fuck"), Alan was asked to take on a leadership role in the Northeast.[71] "I let myself be convinced," he recalled, "in part, through a political argument about not being able to be effective as an individual, but [at] a deeper level, I think I was attracted by the idea of being a 'leader.' Yes, like so many before & after me, I think I wanted to be a big fish in a little pond & taste a little power."[72]

For the next year and a half, this commitment meant seemingly endless meetings, writing and rewriting leaflets, talking to people at demonstrations or at community or work events, and setting up study groups to read left classics. While so much of what he was doing was ideologically driven, he never seemed to lose either his willingness to ask hard questions or his concern for individuals and their needs.[73]

Alan's zeal for the anticolonial struggles in Africa did not wane either. He became part of the anticolonial and antiapartheid American Committee on Africa, raising money, writing news reports, hosting African independence leaders when they came to New York for UN meetings, and sending supplies. His medical skills were called upon when various visiting revolutionary dignitaries needed such care.[74]

And most of this is what Alan and others did *after* work. Like so many of their friends, Alan and Barbara lived in a communal household where people split rent, tasks, and even incomes to allow them to arrange their lives around their political commitments. Shelley Miller, one of Barbara and Alan's closest friends, worked as a day care teacher but spent her lunch hour making calls from a phone booth to organize people to attend meetings and demonstrations.[75] Housemate Dana Biberman took secretarial positions in left organizations but mostly worked to support demonstrations and major public events for various Puerto Rican leftist groups.[76] In an effort to break from traditional family structures, their household pooled money, with those who could contributing more. Only Barbara and Alan had positions that paid somewhat decently.[77]

While Barbara was still in residency training, Alan used his basic medical credentials to find work in neighborhood health centers.[78] He became a community doctor primarily to black and Puerto Rican patients on Manhattan's Lower East Side, first at the Northeast Neighborhood Association (NENA) clinic and then the Betances Health Center. These efforts at community-based care were set up to meet local health priorities and to make "community-worker control" a reality.[79] Facing overwhelming unmet medical needs and limited funds, however, these centers often ended up providing either "tiny band aids for everyone or continuity of care for a few."[80]

Alan struggled as he worked to support the community-based health workers. After much debate, he quit NENA over political differences with the center's administration. At Betances, he became a leader of staff workers, a role that led to conflict with the administration over layoffs and unionization in the face of needed financial retrenchment.

When Alan initiated what became a "heated" confrontation with the Betances administration, a strike followed and Alan was fired along with several others. Those dismissed filed for a hearing on unfair labor practices with the National Labor Relations Board, but the board judge found that even if Alan had been justified in angering the director with his style and organizing, financial exigencies made his dismissal and that of the others legal.[81] Alan's political positions and ease to outrage did not endear him to beleaguered clinic administrators, who had to balance conflicting exigencies and were not driven by revolutionary beliefs. His experiences seemed to demonstrate the difficulties of creating a revolutionary world within the pressures of the capitalist system and a state budget with scant funds for health care. These lessons would haunt him.

LOVE AND HARD TIMES

By the fall of 1975, both Barbara and Alan had turned thirty and had been a serious couple for five years. They quietly began to discuss using what was seen in their political world as the "heterosexual privilege" of getting married and

Alan and Barbara wedding
photograph, October 25, 1975.
Courtesy of Barbara Zeller.

having children. Barbara recalls that even thinking about it made her feel that she was "abandoning the women's movement," especially at the height of discussions about the view that "if feminism is the theory, lesbianism is the practice" and at a time when the struggle for marriage equality for gays and lesbians had not yet begun.[82]

Barbara and Alan nevertheless made the decision to wed. On October 25, 1975, they asked someone they barely knew in their household to be their witness. They took the subway into Manhattan, went to the Washington Square Methodist Church, and had the progressive minister administer their vows. Their wedding photograph does not show the usual wedding garb, but they do look very happy. Rather than just go back home, they spent the afternoon seeing Sidney Lumet's film *Dog Day Afternoon*. In this fictionalized account of a real Brooklyn bank robbery gone awry, Al Pacino's character yells "Attica, Attica!" to gain crowd support against the police. A week later they had a small party with their families, but it was all very low key.

Around the same time, the Weather leadership asked Alan and his friend Shelley Miller to be two of the five national organizers for what would be called the "Hard Times Are Fighting Times" conference, bringing various left organizations together to plan more above-ground political work.[83] While the purpose of the conference, and its politics, was supposed to be coming from the PFOC, in fact the underground Weather leaders orchestrated most of it behind the scenes.

Alan and Shelley Miller proved to be good organizers. The conference was both an organizing success and a political disaster. Nearly 2,000 people showed up at the University of Illinois–Chicago campus from January 30 to February 1, 1976, at the height of 1970s recession, to settle on a strategy for great change. But nothing was settled.

Anger exploded as women's groups and organizations of people of color, especially black nationalists, condemned Alan and the other conference organizers for failing to allow separate caucuses and for the ways the Weather leaders, in hidden ways, positioned themselves as masters of the revolution.[84] Shouting matches erupted, denunciations cracked the alliances, and solidarity dissolved into fury. The black nationalists led particularly devastating criticisms of the conference leadership.[85] As a conference-goer remembered, "In an organization where . . . 'you'd rather die than be characterized as racist and sexist,' the criticisms at Hard Times had a shattering effect."[86] A united left proved impossible to establish, and Alan's political hopes and leadership position were dashed.

One good thing came out of "Hard Times." Barbara had been ovulating during the conference. While everyone was crashing with multiple others and sleeping on floors, Barbara and Alan found a private space.[87] Their efforts proved successful: Barbara became pregnant.

THE ACT OF RECTIFICATION

After "Hard Times," Alan faced a set of political dilemmas that haunted many white political progressives, especially men: How might he express his solidarity without being arrogant or exerting too much control? How could his politics demonstrate the relationships linking class, sexuality, race, and gender?[88] As a white male straight doctor, Alan even admitted to himself that in making his political practice fit his principles, his loving side and his intellectual and competitive prowess were often in tension. There was the Alan who seemed to know everything, and who could make others feel belittled, especially if they were women. Yet there was also the Alan who was a "wonderfully loving human being," as one of his friends recalled.[89]

After the fiasco of "Hard Times," Alan and those in his political organization in both New York and San Francisco attempted to understand what they had done wrong. To do so they put everyone through a process labeled "rectification," used by Mao to consolidate power in 1940s China, where individuals renounced their mistakes and accepted the proper political line. A kind of secular confessional, it was an intensification of the kinds of criticism and self-criticism that had been going on in the left women's movement for nearly a decade.

In a classic form of initiation into a political and cultural cadre, those who made political mistakes had to be torn down through this kind of verbal inquisition, then rebuilt and perhaps reaccepted into new groupings to find "salvation."[90] The political badgering and demand for self-renunciation in Alan's political group was withering.[91] Under the assault of being frozen out and denounced, longtime friendships dissolved and skilled organizers lost faith in their own abilities.

Never one to quit when things got hard, Alan acknowledged his mistakes and submitted to "rectification" to make himself a better revolutionary: "I increasingly substituted the collective ideology—the 'we'—for my own judgment, & once having convinced myself, would work hard to convince others."[92] His written responses to the criticism in the required left jargon acknowledged that he had filled the "Hard Times" program with "national chauvinist and male supremacist politics" while using his "intellect to intimidate." His "bourgeois leadership," he confessed, kept his comrades from theoretical understanding and political struggle.[93]

Others would fault him for not listening to women's criticism of his leadership and political positions, even for downplaying their ideas.[94] As one woman member of the New York group charged in words that seemed particularly aimed at either Alan or his friend Russell Neufeld, "Leadership was seen as a thing 'smart' people do. Lack of study meant that peoples' ability to articulate questions, doubts, etc. were undermined. We often felt powerless. . . . People were left to find books on our own, or call a friend who might have an answer."[95] The group, especially several of the women, was determined to fix this by focusing on those who had felt shut down by "the various manifestations of sexism."[96] Alan was also censured for not realizing that separate black nationhood was needed to end racism. It meant accepting the position of the small but articulate Republic of New Afrika (RNA) with its demand, as reparations for slavery and racism, for a separate black country made out of five southern states.[97]

As the rectification took hold, Alan and his comrades regrouped. A number of the PFOC women organized study groups to reread Lenin (especially on the need for vanguard political groups). They sought to understand why whites had to be under the leadership of people of color, and to make many of the men listen to why many women had felt demeaned by male intellectualism and rhetorical power.[98]

The criticisms focused on how lives were lived, not just public political positions. Pressure was beginning to be put on some of the remaining straight women to consider becoming lesbians, and some of the men to admit they were gay, even if they only had relationships with women.[99] Friendships that had been formed for years began to fall apart.[100] There were the continued debates about monogamy and the revolutionary possibility of family life.[101] It was becoming very difficult, as one of their comrades recalled, "to figure out how to live as a revolutionary and to make your personal life in line with your political life."[102]

The men, in turn, began to discuss how much they had seen themselves as warriors and intellectuals, while trying to figure out what it meant to accept revolutionary discipline and admit their own arrogance. There were no easy answers. "If I said something I would get criticized," Alan's friend Russell Neufeld remembered, "and if I didn't say something I would get criticized." Even though Neufeld believed those trying to have correct political positions were turning into sectarians with rigid views, he was required to denounce this analysis as well.[103] By the summer of 1976, Neufeld had enough, especially after his partner, Phyllis Prentice, who had been with Alan and Barbara at Wounded Knee, quit over what she increasingly saw as unreasonable demands. Neufeld spent the next two years driving his cab, hanging out with his dog, and editing the National Lawyers Guild *Midnight Special* newsletter on prison issues.[104]

Alan did not give up. He was willing to think through his power as a white intellectual, man, heterosexual, and doctor. His consideration was not just out of guilt, even if his "rectification" statements sound this way. While working in community medicine on New York's Lower East Side, he became increasingly impressed with the strengths and resilience of his black and Puerto Rican patients, and many of the women health aides. He and Barbara discussed this often.

Above all, Alan took seriously his need to increase his listening skills, to especially appreciate the life experiences of women and to accept their leadership.[105] It was not always simple to make these changes. His closest political ally and friend, Laura Whitehorn, described him as struggling to understand why his relationships with women were easier, perhaps because he did not "compete with women in the way that he did with men. And it came from a lack of respect, somewhere." Even as Alan sought to change these deeply rooted behaviors, his anger when his women comrades "made mistakes," Whitehorn recalled, "tinged with this [sense of being] patriarchal." But, she added, "What I love him so much for is that he struggled . . . with it his whole life."[106]

Alan's decision to stay within this political frame built on an urgent sense that he had to do something.[107] His political ally and friend Susan Rosenberg would admit much later, "the intensity of that period, it's very hard to convey. So I think the combination between the fact that there was so much repression, that we really were committed to revolution, and we were also wrong. All those things moved us one step at a time down that road."[108] As one of Alan's colleagues admitted, our "worldview was very self-perpetuated, [and we were] caught up in self-criticism which made it hard to see the outside world."[109]

Once the rectification ended after several months, Alan and his comrades were ready to build coalitions for anti-imperialist and antiracist work. One of the central alliances they formed was with various Puerto Rican groups denouncing the island's internal colonial status and demanding independence. Other relationships included ones with Iranian students fighting the U.S.-backed Shah then in power and continued connections with militant black organizations.[110] Feeling stronger about their political ideas and personal behavior, there was now much new work to do.

THE LEFT OF THE LEFT

After Alan and his comrades finished the rectification process, they renewed their work in various coalitions as they began to sort out their own political organization and direction. It was not as if Alan, or Barbara, did this full time. They may have been revolutionaries, but they were still physicians, applying their medical skills to the needs they found in the world around them. As Alan's comrade Nancy Ryan put it, Alan "was a doctor in order to take care of people and to change the balance of forces in health care and for social justice. His medical work and career grounded him. He was committed to social justice, but also led a full life outside of his activism."[1] Both he and Barbara were continually trying to balance their caregiving, family, and political actions. For each of them this would take a different form, and the decisions made would affect the rest of their lives as they moved from being allies of militant black and Puerto Rican groups to what the government would see as co-conspirators.

BICENTENNIAL CELEBRATION AND PARENTHOOD

After his rectification, Alan saw his task as continuing to support anti-imperialism and antiracism work in a nonsexist manner, but now in coalitions. Whites would be responsible for organizing one another and, in his words, for "avoid[ing] an arrogant and national chauvinist attitude toward the Third World organizations in the coalition."[2] He joined with individuals from the Puerto Rican Socialist Party and the American Indian Movement in a broad coalition to prepare for a major antibicentennial demonstration on July 4, 1976, in Philadelphia. He became part of the national board that hammered out the acceptable slogans on self-determination and support for gay rights. He made efforts to thread through the political difficulties fairly, while trying to both lead and follow.

The July Fourth coalition was broad-based enough to attract 30,000–40,000 participants from multiple racial and political groups to a series of peaceful demonstrations with many marching through the mostly black parts of North Philadelphia under the banner "For a Bicentennial without Colonies."[3] While Alan's work ended in July, other coalitions continued to raise concerns about urban redevelopment, unfair housing practices, and police violence for several years.[4] He had organized a successful action, but it was still unclear what those outside of Philadelphia would do next. Alan also now faced his impending fatherhood.

Barbara was more focused on her immediate future, as her medical residency training was ending in June 1976 and their baby was due in October. When her contractions started, Barbara wanted to stay home, but their comrade and midwife Jennifer Dohrn insisted it was time to go to the hospital.[5] Ever the doctor and trying to be a supportive spouse, Alan said, "Are you sure?" Dohrn recalled replying, "You're not supposed to be the doctor, don't examine her. You are just a man having a baby." Their friend Russell Neufeld would rush them in his cab over the Brooklyn Bridge to Roosevelt Hospital in Manhattan.[6]

On October 16, 1976, Sarah Machel Zeller-Berkman was born. She was named after the Mozambican independence leader Samora Machel. Had she been a boy she would have been Robert, after Zimbabwe's Robert Mugabe.[7] A little jaundiced, the baby was kept under the lights in the hospital nursery for a few days and then brought home to her parents' collective household in Brooklyn.

As new parents, Alan and Barbara faced the exhaustion of caring for an infant and the exhilaration of falling in love with their daughter. Alan was "incredibly happy" after Sarah's birth and played Stevie Wonder's "Isn't She Lovely" over and over on the record player as he danced her around their apartment.[8] Barbara, too, was trying to determine how to have time for her child and what medical and political work now made sense. They sang political songs along with traditional lullabies to integrate their daughter into their world. They now had to determine what it meant to be both political revolutionaries and parents.[9]

MAY 19TH

Alan and his comrades were not just going to be allies to others. They needed their own political grouping as well. Out of the debates over the failures of "Hard Times" and splits within the national PFOC, those who remained in New York formed the above-ground group they called the May 19th Communist Organization. The name, drawn from the birth dates of both Vietnamese leader

Ho Chi Minh and black power internationalist Malcolm X, as well as the anniversary of the death of Cuban independence leader José Martí, signaled a commitment to anti-imperialism, internationalism, and antiracism.[10]

Although not a name likely to attract a mass membership, it would make members visible to other like-minded organizations.[11] Inspired by lessons they had learned from reading revolutionary leaders and committed to women's leadership, members of May 19th thought of themselves as a cadre of white people in an above-ground political group whose purpose was to support the self-defense and, if necessary, armed struggle of revolutionary people of color in the United States and around the world.

It was 1977, the year that Jimmy Carter became president, ending nearly a decade of Republican rule. That same year in South Africa, Stephen Biko, a leader of the Black Consciousness Movement and a socialist, was murdered by the apartheid regime. The violence toward communities of color in the United States was continuing and rising inflation was wiping out the economic gains of a generation. Seeing the growth of the New Right and the rebirth of the Ku Klux Klan, members of May 19th believed America's commitment to white supremacy and imperial control was not abating. Alan and Barbara believed their new political grouping was supporting the revolutionary struggle at home and across the globe.

Although the organization was led at first by a mix of men and women, many, but not all, of the men eventually left. In the end, three strong anti-imperialist and antiracist activist women — Susan Rosenberg, Silvia Baraldini, and Judy Clark — became its central leaders. As May 19th member Nancy Ryan recalled, "So gradually the balance shifted as women's leadership was promoted as really crucial to the struggle. . . . Being an out lesbian and experiencing that kind of oppression put you [as a white person] more in line with the black people and the oppression they were facing."[12] Or so it was assumed as more of the leadership went to lesbians. The FBI, which began to track the group, noticed this too and described May 19th as having many members who "display homosexual tendencies."[13]

Alan, as one of the few men who remained in May 19th, indicated his willingness to put his body where his belief in a critique of male power demanded. As his longtime friend and comrade Laura Whitehorn explained, "Alan and I both had a lot of respect for people who put their bodies where their mouths are."[14] And the group's leadership believed his rectification had worked. Although once he was briefly told to leave for smoking weed with Susan Rosenberg, they were both readmitted to the group and Rosenberg was in leadership again.[15]

It was not an easy decision for Alan to stay within what was becoming a small cadre. In his own chronology of his political life, he was not sure what to do, writing, "For a brief period after Sarah's birth, I thought about leaving the whole political scene (10/76) but I wasn't sure Barbara wanted to and wasn't sure I could bring myself to do it. So, instead, I stayed and once more made politics primary."[16]

It was a difficult time for these new parents, and Alan never wrote much about it except to say he accepted the need for the "collective ideology."[17] His political circle was rejecting nuclear families, and even children for a while, making their own family an outlier. When Barbara and Alan visited their natal families with Sarah, it would be a reminder that their marriage and child made them "normal" in the eyes of most of the world. Yet in their political nexus, their normal was not as accepted.[18] "Men are pigs," one of her friends told Barbara as she was pressured to leave Alan, a decision she was not willing to make.[19] Alan, in turn, stayed because he wanted to keep Barbara and Sarah in his life, fearful that if he left May 19th he would somehow lose them.[20]

Barbara continued to work with May 19th, and to focus on her medical position. She spent her days as a physician, now at Lincoln Hospital, often "bearing witness," as she put it, to the "daily intense struggle" of her patients to just survive. When needed, she continued to answer the call to provide medical care to those in the political underground. She was increasingly drawn to work on women's issues and was considering where this might lead, while caring for Sarah. Because she also decided to continue primarily in medicine, she often attended May 19th's open meetings but not the "smaller internal ones."[21] There was still much collective work, except when connections were made to the concealed cadres in other liberation groups on a need-to-know basis.[22]

To join May 19th was to become part of an all-encompassing world. Because everyone was living together in various collective households, if you left the organization you would lose your friends, home, and connections. When one May 19th member had enough, she remembered she was "purged," lost her place in her apartment, and had her notes and files ransacked by other members.[23] Barbara and Alan also shunned some of the people who left, and yet Alan seemed to be the one whom at least two of his comrades talked to honestly before they quit. They found his compassion much different from the harder dismissal they received from others.[24] Whatever their possible doubt, Alan and Barbara still believed and suppressed their criticisms. Indeed, Alan helped write May 19th's fourteen-page "principles of unity" statement for worldwide "national liberation struggles for proletarian power."[25]

The group's romanticism about violence and inability to see the possibility of the coming corruption in various struggles was on clear display in its hopeful statement. In Zimbabwe, the "What We Believe" statement supported the victory of Robert Mugabe's forces as the first step toward ending white domination in all of southern Africa. They cheered the Iranian revolution that overthrew the U.S.-backed Shah, believing that it had "advanced the struggle for socialism." They backed the liberation struggles of the former Portuguese colonies and the Palestinians against what was labeled Israeli Zionism. They expected that the "armed clandestine front" in Puerto Rico would mean a "full peoples' war." They believed the victory of the communist forces in Vietnam would be repeated elsewhere around the world, especially within the "second front" led by black, Puerto Rican, Chicano/a, and Native American communities in the United States. All of these efforts were linked to the struggles against racism in the United States and for "revolutionary nationalism."[26]

In sum, May 19th members promised they would "commit [them]selves to the strategy of revolutionary anti-imperialism under the leadership of national liberation struggles." They articulated their support for "armed struggle" both in the United States and around the world as they denounced male supremacy, national chauvinism, heterosexual power, and white privilege, and accepted that the leadership of political movements in the United States had to come from progressives of color. And they linked women's and lesbian liberation to this work. They followed through on their revolutionary coalition-building when Susan Rosenberg met with communist leaders in Cuba, Silvia Baraldini with heads of the Zimbabwe African National Union (ZANU), and Judy Clark with Palestinians in Lebanon.[27]

Yet those in May 19th had to explain what they were willing to do. The "What We Do" section of their "Principles of Unity" statement only took up three pages in part because they were uncertain, and in part because of what they could not say in print. Most of what they did declare was fairly defensive: a lawsuit against the FBI for its illegal raids on their homes and support for what were called political prisoners who had been part of the U.S.-based revolutionary groups. The group promised to raise money for a "Dollars for Bullets" campaign to support revolutionary forces in southern Africa.

They also worked out of their Brooklyn office in the Park Slope neighborhood, then rapidly gentrifying. They opened the Moncada Library, named after the military barracks where the Cuban Revolution began. Members taught Spanish, showed movies on revolutionary actions, started a young people's mural project, loaned out books and pamphlets, demonstrated against police repression, and taught classes on black history and other liberation struggles among Native Americans and Puerto Ricans, and had a special focus on women's issues presented from an anti-imperialist perspective.[28]

They also took on local issues to try to make other whites aware of how much their privilege depended upon the oppression of others. Young white and middle- to upper-class families were pushing black and Puerto Rican residents out of the neighborhood that had once been described as a "blighted backwater."[29] When an anticrime taskforce campaigns focused on the "dangers" of the neighborhood, in barely veiled racist language, the May 19th members worked hard to explain the limits of this "law and order" approach.[30] The "moralism," as one member of the group remembered, was linked to shaming. As Mary Patten recalled, "Picture a small cadre of community activists stationed outside the neighborhood food co-op, hawking tract-like leaflets with the message: 'the brownstone movement and the Ku Klux Klan: fight urban genocide.'"[31]

These committed revolutionaries, as they saw themselves, were also very much taken up with cultural issues and art. A number of the members were skilled artists "who existed on the fringes of the art world and on the fringes of the left," as Mary Patten described herself and her comrades.[32] Together they formed the Madame Binh Graphics Collective, named after the Vietnamese woman who had led the "Provisional Revolutionary Government of South Vietnam's delegation to the Paris Peace talks in the early 1970s."[33] Following the Cuban Revolution's posters, street muralists, and pop art, they produced "countless flyers, stickers, pamphlets, buttons, offset posters, T-shirts, and other propaganda, which were wheat-pasted and distributed in New York City and other parts of the east coast."[34] Their direct but elegant posters, filled with fierce faces, clenched fists, and rifles, offered another way to announce meetings in the pre-internet age and created a graphic vocabulary for the left.[35] Alan, with no visible artistic talent, was not part of this subgroup.

The May 19th members were always busy, always trying to figure out what to do next. There was so much to do, especially for a group of probably fewer than 100 people.[36] And each was expected to give everything she or he had. Nancy Ryan and Shelley Miller recalled that when illnesses and deaths in their natal families took them away, they were criticized for not returning soon enough to fulfill their political obligations.[37] Nothing else mattered, not even dying parents.

FIGHTING THE KLAN AND CRITIQUING INCARCERATION: THE JOHN BROWN ANTI-KLAN COMMITTEE

From its very beginnings, May 19th linked prison issues, internal colonization of people of color, and revolutionary change. The issues of incarceration were crucial to the group's efforts: from critiques of the use of psychotropic drugs to quell political organizing within prison walls, to the lack of medical care that could translate an inmate's sentence into death, to deep concerns about the reach of Ku Klux Klan membership into northern prison guard systems.[38] Their newsletters reported on problems within the prisons and linked them to other national and international struggles. Long before the terms *mass incar-*

ceration or *the New Jim Crow* came into usage, May 19th members understood the racism embedded in a growing carceral state.[39]

In 1975, black prisoners in the Eastern Correctional Institute in Napanoch, New York, filed a lawsuit charging that the Klan was organizing both prison guards and white prisoners to harass political black prisoners.[40] Concern about the Klan's infiltration of the prison system's power structures, as well as of disgruntled and unemployed white communities, led to organizing across the country on these issues over the next few years.[41]

May 19th members took the lead in creating what they named first the Anti-Klan Commission and then the John Brown Anti-Klan Committee (JBAKC).[42] It would be an obvious way to link their actions to militant white support for antiracism and to other prison organizing. Alan became deeply involved with the JBAKC, writing for its newsletters and publications and providing its political direction.[43]

The JBAKC attracted adherents and grew into small cohorts across the country in New York; Chicago; San Francisco; Los Angeles; Washington, D.C.; Austin, Texas; western Massachusetts; Bowling Green, Kentucky; and Portland, Oregon. The use of John Brown's name hinted at violence, even if this was never made explicit. "John Brown, live like him, dare to struggle, dare to win," they would say at their meetings and in their written work, using the words from Weather.[44]

Brown's move to violence was implicit in their newsletter's title—*Death to the Klan*—whose first issue appeared in November 1979.[45] The JBAKC's purpose was to organize against white supremacy ideas, counter groups that expressed such views, and fight state power. Reporting on the killing of four anti-Klan organizers from a parallel political grouping in Greensboro, North Carolina (two of whom were doctors Alan knew from New York), the threat to both black prisoners and whites opposed to racism was stark.[46] As the principles of unity stated, "Fight White Supremacy in All Its Forms, Follow Black and other Third World Leadership, and Support the Struggle of Third World People for Human Rights."[47]

For those looking for a way to talk to other whites and fight racism, the JBAKC had appeal. In Portland, Oregon, acupuncturist Beth Sommers joined because she thought it would offer ways to discuss white privilege and do something about racism. She remembered, however, that the slogan "Death to the Klan" was not a particularly useful organizing term and "turned people off" as the JBAKC tried to explain the Klan's spread.[48] The group's members put out newsletters, staffed tables at colleges or political events, and spread the word for support for prisoners as much as they could. Their intention was to make whites in particular aware of the most overt antiblack violence perpetuated by those in power. In many cases, however, alliances with black communities fell apart, or led to mere criticisms rather than actions.[49] As local organizing gave way to centralized command from New York, some of the groups seemed to falter, while others became more autonomous.

Because there was overlap between the leadership in May 19th and the John Brown groups, their efforts were as much about anti-imperialism as about antiracism at home. This connection prompted the concerns of the FBI, which linked militant American groups to what it saw as international terrorism.[50] Members made alliances with the most militant, pro–African power groups in Namibia and South Africa. Alan, who cared deeply about what was happening in southern Africa, continued to organize meetings within May 19th and with other supportive organizations in New York on the African independence struggles.

By 1982, the FBI was watching the organization closely and had identified both Alan and Chicago-based May 19th member Susie Waysdorf as the national coordinators.[51] Washington, D.C.-based JBAKC member Marion Banzhaf, also part of the national leadership, remembered Alan's crucial position in setting strategic direction and talking about how to form coalitions with people of color, fighting police brutality, and why raising money for African liberation struggles mattered.[52] Banzhaf herself was willing to take more direct actions and to travel, as when JBAKC members confronted both Klan members and the Austin police in Texas. Banzhaf and her comrades came ready to fight, with lead pipes in their boots and wood sticks holding their placards. But they outnumbered the Klansmen, and "defensive actions were not necessary."[53] As Susan Rosenberg had told Banzhaf when they met, they were becoming "dangerous people," even if Banzhaf was not exactly sure what this meant.[54] Alan and Barbara were about to find out.

ACUPUNCTURE AND EXPROPRIATIONS

Barbara's connections also would change Alan's life. In the late 1970s, while Alan was working both in community medicine on the Lower East Side and within the JBAKC, Barbara expanded her interest in alternative forms of medicine, especially acupuncture. During the Vietnam War era, connections between the rise of heroin trafficking from Southeast Asia, the CIA's role in bringing in the drugs, and the genocidal impact of drugs in creating ghettoes as internal colonies circulated on the left.[55] This worry also extended to the rise of government-sponsored clinics that used methadone, the synthetic opioid, to wean those addicted. Methadone, many feared, was yet another form of state and drug control.

Activists mounted their confrontational efforts to change treatment priorities. Acupuncture, with its links to Chinese medicine, was seen as a possibly different form of drug detoxification.[56] Partly in response to the growing drug problem in their community, the Puerto Rican political group the Young Lords worked with an organization called the Health Revolutionary Unity Movement to take over a floor of Lincoln Hospital in the South Bronx in 1970, demanding changes at Lincoln, including a new approach to drug treatment.[57] Out of these efforts, they created what was known as the People's Program at Lincoln Hospital, Lincoln Detox, or Lincoln Recovery, to provide methadone at first, and then a new form of auricular (ear) acupuncture to stave off the symptoms of detoxification without drugs.[58]

The political men and women who staffed Lincoln Detox helped addicts while also educating and recruiting for their political organizations. Alan and Barbara's friends Franklin Apfel, Jennifer Dohrn, and Susan Rosenberg all worked in Lincoln Detox because of its political stances and discussed the use of alternative treatment modalities with them.[59] Hospital administrators and public authorities expressed increasing concern, however, about what was really happening at the Detox program. The police often came by looking for political fugitives, and the FBI tapped the program's phones and sought personnel records.

In one of the most frightening episodes, an unaccounted death occurred. Physician Richard Taft (great nephew of President William Howard Taft) had learned acupuncture in China and brought it to Lincoln, but in 1974 he was murdered, or overdosed. Just before he was supposed to meet with a federal drug official, his body turned up in a closet in a Lincoln hallway. Authorities never determined the reasons for his demise.[60] Amid the dangers, political fights, enormous cutbacks in public funding during New York's fiscal crisis, and overwhelming need, even many committed doctors found it difficult to work at Lincoln.[61]

Alan was not taken with acupuncture or drug detoxification, but Barbara was intrigued by alternatives to Western medicine. The year she came back to New York in 1974 she took a course and was certified as an acupuncture practitioner. She then volunteered as a medical consultant at Lincoln Detox. To gain more skills, she took more courses long distance from the Quebec Association of Acupuncture and received her license as a doctor of acupuncture by 1980.[62] Supported by Alan and others in her household, she became the unpaid medical director of the women-run Chelsea Women's Health Center in Manhattan for the next two years and was one of the first physicians to provide alternative fertilization services to lesbians.

The Detox program would have consequences for Alan and Barbara, particularly after an investigation and police raid in 1978 led to the firing of political staff, including the Detox program's charismatic leader, Mutulu Shakur.[63] Born Jeral Wayne Williams in Baltimore in 1950, Shakur had been raised by a legally blind mother on the teachings of Malcolm X with an emphasis on the right to self-defense. By the time Shakur was eighteen, he had joined the Detroit-based Republic of New Afrika (RNA), which believed in self-determination and argued for making five Southern states a "separate nation for Black people."[64] RNA members, who had led the criticism of racism at the "Hard Times" conference, now became closer allies of May 19th.

Shakur considered himself a "New Afrikan," not an African American.[65] After starting as a volunteer at Lincoln, he received a doctor of acupuncture degree and rose into leadership in the Detox program. Known as "Doc" for his education and acumen, Shakur traveled to China and became well known in the alternative medicine community. He was also the partner of former Panther 21 defendant Afeni Shakur and stepfather of future rapper Tupac Shakur, with whom he would later write the code of "Thug Life."[66]

After his firing by hospital officials in 1978, Shakur began a clinic and teaching program in Harlem called the Black Acupuncture Advisory Association of North America (BAAANA). His efforts led to many being treated with acupuncture for addiction, and others training to become skilled acupuncturists themselves. BAAANA was able to open in part because Barbara allowed it to use her doctor's license to provide the legitimacy the city required of a medical facility, and as many of her and Alan's friends who were skilled acupuncturists moved there from Lincoln.[67] Barbara's work to help build this clinic was much applauded by those in May 19th as a "tangible" representation of her politics.[68] And Mutulu Shakur was becoming her "mentor . . . and teacher of life and revolution."[69]

BAAANA needed more than an acupuncture service to support its staff, and Shakur was concerned with more than just alternative medicine. By the late 1970s he was part of small group, the New African Freedom Fighters, that considered itself part of the Black Liberation Army (BLA). BLA was an umbrella term used to describe loosely connected clandestine groups that began operating in the 1960s, some from within the Black Panthers, others not, determined to use self-defense and violence to fight police brutality.[70] Having experienced racism, police harassment, prison abuse, many of BLA members considered preemptive violence against police as a form of self-defense.[71] BLA groups, always a small number in their cities, became involved over the years in about a dozen shoot-outs or murders of police.[72] Raids against drug dealers financed their initial operations and seemingly revolutionary lives. They then moved on to bank and armored truck robberies they described as "expropriations," meaning a rightful recovery of money taken by ruling-class interests through the exploitation of the poor and working classes.

The police branded them "terrorists" whenever policemen were killed and treated them as criminals.[73] Still, it was difficult many times to determine what were actual BLA actions. The police, out of moral panic and horror at the murder of their own, often labeled robberies or police shootings by black men as BLA actions.[74] In turn, the BLA robberies often looked like just that — robberies — especially when no manifesto was left behind and no statement was phoned in to the media to declare their revolutionary intent.[75]

Underground and armed black militants had been in the *imaginary* of white America since slavery, and part of the *reality* of black history even during the seemingly nonviolent era of the civil rights movement, as Alan had learned when he was in Alabama.[76] Many who joined the Panthers or the BLA had started out in street gangs, served prison time, and were converted from "gangster mentality to revolutionary consciousness," leading them into the Nation of Islam, or militant groups, or both.[77] At the same time, the FBI's continued use of undercover agents exacerbated paranoia and splits in the organizations.[78] The formation of clandestine groups was supposed to at least make state infiltration more difficult, but it also meant that the openness of early groupings was exchanged for tighter cadres where dissent was unwelcome.[79]

At BAAANA, Shakur surrounded himself with political individuals recovering from drug addiction or learning to be healers, as well as those who were still part of the drug scene in some fashion. Others he recruited shared his political commitments, or else were willing to mouth the rhetoric while bringing street skills and hustle to their political actions. As a lawyer in one of the BLA cases put it, the cause needed "the kind of street brother who provides the backbone to the movement."[80]

All of these men, and some women, were willing to participate in self-defense and retaliation in the face of what they believed were genocidal attacks from police and unknown others.[81] Taking the words from Malcolm X at his most angry, BLA member Sekou Odinga declared, "Malcolm said, 'When a snake bites you, you don't go running into the woods with blood running all down your jaws looking for that particular snake . . . any snake will do. And if enough snakes get moved on, then snakes would stop biting Black people.'"[82] Many saw themselves as warriors and wrote poetry to channel their anger and despair toward revolutionary love.[83] "By Way of Introduction," wrote BLA member Albert Nuh Qayyum Washington in 1975,

Who are you, I am asked
If I give a name
It only tells what I am called
Having had many names
It still does not say
Who nor what I am
To the oppressed I am the angel of deliverance

To the oppressor I am the anger of destruction
So who I am /
depends on who you are." [84]

BAAANA became the site that brought May 19th and BLA members together. While several May 19th leaders were working at BAAANA, the connections were cemented through white activist Marilyn Jean Buck, a Texan deeply involved with SDS and then with underground groups. She had been providing logistical support, buying guns and ammunition, and driving cars for others associated with the BLA since the early 1970s. In December 1977 she was on furlough from the federal Alderson Prison in West Virginia, to which she had been sentenced for these actions. [85]

Having come to New York to be with her lawyer, Susan Tipograph, Buck met a number of the women in May 19th at a party. Buck decided she was going into the underground rather than finish her prison time and asked for support. The May 19th leadership agreed to help her find places to live, a way to survive, and above all connections to others who could help her continue her political life. Never a member of May 19th, Buck would be drawn more into the group's circles and its members into hers.

This association would culminate in more dramatic actions. [86] Much of this began in the early 1970s. In 1973, the police had been hunting for a woman known to them as Joanne Chesimard, and to others by her chosen African name, Assata Shakur. Shakur had been in the Black Panther Party, and then the BLA, and was purported to have been involved in a number of the "expropriations," as police assumed she was the only black woman involved in these events, many of which they later could not substantiate. [87] In May 1973, state police stopped her and two BLA members, Zayd Shakur and Sundiata Acoli, in her car for a broken tail light on the New Jersey Turnpike. The confrontation turned bloody quickly. In the subsequent shootout, Zayd Shakur and officer Werner Foerster were killed, and Assata Shakur was badly wounded and captured along with Acoli.

Over the next seven years she would be tried in multiple criminal trials. She received only one conviction, as an accomplice in the state policeman's death on the turnpike; the medical evidence of her arm wounds suggested it would have been impossible for her to fire a gun that killed the officer. [88] Held in extremely harsh conditions even though pregnant, sometimes in men's prisons, Shakur was forced by authorities to give birth behind bars. There was growing fear among her comrades that she was not holding up well, and she sent word she needed to get out.

Members of the BLA connected with BAAANA worked with Marilyn Buck and women from May 19th to pull off an audacious escape on November 2, 1979. Without harming any guards although holding them at gunpoint, the armed team sprang Shakur from her New Jersey prison and hid her in safe houses for the next five years until 1984, when she was able to get to Cuba.[89] While she was still in the United States, the FBI and police were looking for her everywhere, but especially in Harlem.

May 19th's Madame Binh Collective was asked by their comrades in the Republic of New Afrika to make a poster of Shakur that was put up throughout New York black communities. The "Assata Is Welcome Here" poster, which gives the name of the Republic of New Afrika, not the BLA or May 19th, would be seen throughout the city.[90] Shakur still lives in Cuba and remains on the FBI's most wanted list.[91]

Shakur's successful escape revived the BLA, which had been decimated by deaths and imprisonment, and renewed its members' sense of invincibility. It was a high mark in practice for the May 19th leadership's theoretical belief in the need for revolutionary action. As May 19th's Silva Baraldini claimed, "When a movement takes responsibility for freeing one of its captured freedom fighters, it is always significant because it communicates to the people the depth of the commitment to liberation."[92]

It was this kind of appeal, and the sense of the need to do something now that would mean something forever, that pulled some of the May 19th leaders toward the BLA as they developed a way they might provide support for self-defense and armed struggle. Neither Barbara and Alan, nor most of those in May 19th, had been involved in Shakur's escape or knew about the growing connections with the BLA. The sense, however, that some in their group were actually doing revolutionary work kept them engaged.

Another action, more in keeping with other kinds of civil disobedience, demonstrated May 19th's practice of antiracism in a global connected context. Despite UN resolutions against sports exchanges with South Africa during the apartheid era, the Springboks, the all-white South African rugby team, was on tour and being protested throughout the world in 1981.[93] May 19th members attended a demonstration against the team in Albany, New York, and on September 26, 1981, joined about 60–100 demonstrators from differing antiapartheid groups at New York's John F. Kennedy airport, from which it was thought the team would be flying to South Africa. In the planning for this protest, May 19th members decided who could afford to be arrested if they did confront the team, and who might be involved in a fight with the South African athletes if this happened. Alan, it was decided, should stay home.[94]

The airport protest became a melee, as some in the protest group tried to enter a security area and raced up a ramp toward a gate.[95] The story of what happened next varied depending on who told it. The police claimed that May 19th member and artist Donna Borup "hurled a caustic solution" of "battery

Republic of New Afrika

"Assata Shakur Is Welcome Here" poster created by May 19th's Madame Binh Graphics Collective, November 1979. *Courtesy of Mary Patten.*

acid, mace, vinegar and ammonia" at one of the officers trying to stop her.[96] However, what the group had brought with them were mason jars filled with the much less dangerous butyric acid, better known as "stink bombs."[97] Mostly very smelly, the substance is also slippery and can harm eye and other human tissue with which it comes in contact. In the chaos, as police, airline officials, or protestors pushed one another, the jars were dropped, and some of the demonstrators skidded on the oily mess. One officer, police claimed, was partially blinded by the solution, although a private detective later discovered that he recovered enough to be able to drive.[98]

Five of the May 19th demonstrators, including Borup, were arrested immediately for assault on a police officer and other felonies and roughed up or beaten on the way to jail. Eve Rosahn, a May 19th member, still carries scars from the substances that also splashed on her.[99] The five were imprisoned for weeks as officials demanded names of those in the antiapartheid movement, but the five never gave them up. Four of them would serve more than a year of jail time for the action, but Borup, a talented artist and activist, jumped bail in the spring of 1982 and disappeared into the underground.[100] She has yet to be found decades later.[101]

Coverage of the jailing of May 19th members added to the group's growing reputation for action. Their "Anti-Springbok 5 Defense Committee" continued to put out newsletters for months in their support.[102] May 19th members were proving they were willing to put their bodies where their ideology and commitments led them.

HOSPITAL ESCAPE

Clandestine efforts were never discussed in the open and were very much on a need-to-know basis within May 19th. Alan always made clear that he was unwilling to take a life, and Barbara participated primarily in the public organizing efforts. The question of what solidarity really meant with a variety of militant black and Puerto Rican groups, and what actions to take, continued to drive May 19th internal discussions.[103]

Alan's next steps brought him under the ever-watchful eyes of the FBI. At the request of radical lawyer Susan Tipograph, he had become the attending physician for imprisoned Puerto Rican militant William Guillermo Morales. Morales was the major bomb-maker for the Fuerzas Armadas de Liberación Nacional (Armed Forces of National Liberation, or FALN), the clandestine pro–Puerto Rican independence cadre. He was linked to, but never indicted for, the group's 1975 lunchtime bombing that killed four diners near Wall Street at the eighteenth-century Fraunces Tavern.[104]

While in his apartment on July 12, 1978, Morales accidently touched some wires together in a bomb he was making, and it blew up. In the explosion he lost his fingers, leaving just "a thumb and a palm," sustained serious eye and facial damage, and lost some teeth. He later claimed that the police intentionally made it impossible for his hands to be reattached by dumping them in formaldehyde, and left the burns on his face as a message.[105] A hospital nurse who watched over Morales later testified that the police were roughing him up by putting pressure on his hand stubs, even as he was recovering from the anesthesia from surgery.[106] Alan, who had first seen Morales when he was in the jail on Rikers Island, was horrified by his treatment.

Convicted on various state and federal charges, Morales faced a sentence of up to ninety-nine years. Just before he was to be sent to state prison, his lawyer was able to get him moved to the third-floor prison ward at Manhattan's Bellevue Hospital to have his hands evaluated for prosthetics and to get surgery on his eye. "We were in the operating room with heavily armed FBI agents with all their weapons," Alan recalled. "[It] gave me a sense of what the police agencies will do with political prisoners."[107]

What happened next on May 22, 1979, has never been proved in a court of law and became a great victory for the FALN. Though she was never charged, the FBI claimed that Morales's lawyer Susan Tipograph snuck fourteen-inch wire cutters to Morales by taping them to her leg. With the wire cutters, however obtained, the small but muscled Morales is presumed to have cut a one-foot hole in the metal gate on his Bellevue window and pushed through a second set of wires.[108]

Morales was still forty feet above the ground, however. According to the police, he then used ten feet of wetted elastic bandage (which will stretch another five feet) and sheets tied to his bed and "possibly looped around his waist" to shimmy himself out, dropping part of the way into the waiting arms of those who had arranged to catch him.[109] Footprints under the window made this analysis seem plausible. From there he made his way to Mexico. Though captured again in a shoot-out a few years later, tortured, and jailed, he was nevertheless eventually allowed by Mexican authorities to flee to Cuba, where he remains.[110]

After this, the FBI began to realize that Alan might be important. Alan noticed an FBI van nearby as he worked at Betances, the Lower East Side health clinic where Dylcia Pagan, Morales's partner, was a patient.[111] The police could never determine if Alan had anything to do with the escape. The FBI agent in charge of the case alleged that Alan told Morales about the layout in the Bellevue ward and provided the extra bandages. This was never proved, and Alan was never charged. "There was a grand jury," he remembered, "and I was not called." But the FBI van became more ubiquitous in his life.[112] Other Bellevue prison guards were thought to have been bribed, or merely asleep and incompetent, and lost their positions.[113] The FBI believed Marilyn Buck, and members of the BLA and May 19th, made Morales's escape to Mexico possible.

Alan did learn firsthand from Morales's experience why the Puerto Rican militants, when captured, called themselves "prisoners of war," the term Puerto Rican revolutionaries used for themselves as soldiers in an anticolonial struggle against an imperial power. This was a way, Alan understood, that Morales and others separated themselves from the state's labeling of them as criminals. What they were doing, as Alan put it, was "not a matter of innocence or guilt, or level of involvement; it [was] a matter of principle."[114]

Morales's importance for Alan's evolving political positions is clear in a letter the former wrote from his Bellevue prison cell a month before his escape — a letter Morales dictated to and was likely penned by his companion Dylcia Pagan.[115] "Dear Alan," it read, "When I first met you at Riker's, I thought that this was an action by a guilt-ridden liberal, but I was wrong. You turned out to be a revolutionary." Commenting on the care Alan provided to him and others, Morales expressed gratitude that Alan had given up a career that could have supported the "status quo, but instead you decided to dedicate yourself to helping the oppress [sic] and exploited. A noble deed in every sense of the world [sic]." His final sentences were the most encouraging: "In short, Alan, your [sic] my hero, and above all you will be my brother no matter what the damn consequences are. Some day I'll be coming out of jail, and when I do, we will have a lot to talk about. Until victory is ours! Your Brother Comrade, Guillermo Morales."[116] Alan kept the letter for the rest of his life.

Four years before, Alan had decided to make "politics primary." The letter from Morales must have confirmed that decision, and the memory of Morales's courage and the way he was treated would affect Alan forever.[117] The letter symbolically welcomed him into the revolutionary brotherhood. He would get to prove his courage again soon.

CREATING LIFE, CHOOSING LOVE

For those involved with May 19th, there was always more to do: more meetings, more discussions, and more efforts to define what being an American revolutionary meant in practice. Whether they succeeded or failed, it was vital that this work be done together. "The very essence of liberation is social participation," Alan mused years later to Barbara. "The fact that we all *felt* better during the May 19th days even though there were many bad things — is that we were all participating in a political process. We more than most people really do need that political realm to be happy."[1]

The political realm they were in by late 1979 and the early 1980s had grown much more complicated. The election of Republican Ronald Reagan as president in November 1980 forced many aging radicals to acknowledge that their 1960s and 1970s were over. Reagan's "revolution," with its emphasis on limited government, military interventions, corporate power, and backlash against the gains of feminists and people of color, was antithetical to everything liberals to the far left wanted. The murder of the Beatles' John Lennon a month later in December seemed to confirm the feeling that the radicals' promising past was dead, too.[2]

May 19th's members were not so ready to mourn. For them, the last years of the 1970s had been successful: Assata Shakur and William Morales had been freed, alliances with black and Puerto Rican revolutionaries were cemented, and they had been part of a coalition that brought a Black Human Rights Campaign to the United Nations.[3] FBI agents and administrators involved in illegal surveillance of above-ground members of Weather like Judy Clark and Dana Biberman were convicted, even though their fines were minimal and pardons soon erased any punishments.[4]

On the international level, anti-imperialism was ascendant, at least briefly. The Sandinista National Liberation Front had overthrown the Somoza dictatorship in Nicaragua, while a coalition of communists, left radicals, and Shiite clerics had expelled the Shah from Iran. Zimbabwe had become independent from white colonial rule.[5] The U.S.-backed wars in Central America, the creation of an Islamic Republic in Iran, and Zimbabwe's long struggle with corruption still lay ahead.

Those in May 19th believed that the path forward was clear: they had to follow the leadership of their most militant comrades of color.[6] As Alan acknowledged sarcastically later, but *not* at the time, "The May 19th line was easier—let the TW [Third World] comrades figure it out."[7] Such a rigid position left those in May 19th without standing for moral or political objections. They were bound to do what was asked, and offer firm support once actions had been taken.[8]

This stance also led to accepting not just the possibility but the necessity of violence to counter violence perpetuated by the state. As Alan admitted years later, "We had an increasingly narrow focus of making revolution and armed struggle synonymous. And which was a potentially real mistake. Because the armed struggle is a manifestation of a radical drive to change society, but it is not synonymous with revolution itself."[9] Alan and his comrades increasingly did see armed struggle as the revolution.

While there was mass left organizing in the early 1980s first around nuclear disarmament and then about the wars in Central America, May 19th members saw themselves as preserving a linkage between the most militant political sectors of the United States and around the world. Lacking a mass movement with their perspective, Alan admitted years later, we "hunkered down ourselves and became more clear about our militancy." All the while, as Alan put it, they did "the best we could to keep alive a tradition of the right to struggle."[10]

To be sure, Barbara and Alan did not live every moment in politics or work. Their sense of happiness, as with most of us, meant that their private lives mattered, too. They had a child to raise, a collie to walk, natal families to visit, and friends with whom to spend relaxed time. Despite this, the political and private often meshed in unexpected ways.

CREATING HARRIET

This tie between family life and politics was clearest in Barbara and Alan's relationship to Judy Clark, one of May 19th's leaders.[11] When she turned thirty, Clark wanted very much to have a child. The vivid, bright blue poster of an African woman freedom fighter cradling both a rifle and a baby, which hung on the walls of many radicals' homes, seemed to sum up her desire: love and power united.[12] A red diaper baby herself, she had been drawn to the most action-oriented left groups as an adult when she was in Weather and then May 19th leadership.[13] She was, by her own admission, a "good soldier" who could cut off any fears or feelings in order to do what was deemed necessary, and who never put herself first.[14] She had long been on the FBI's radar—in one unlawful raid agents burned down her apartment.[15] It led to the lawsuit against the government that she and others in May 19th won in 1980.[16] While still a May 19th leader, she also wanted to have a child. As a lesbian, she faced the dilemma of finding the sperm she needed to get pregnant.[17]

By the late 1970s, queer women often asked gay male friends to donate sperm rather than turn to the more expensive sperm banks.[18] Those who could find donors then inseminated themselves, taking a condom full of sperm and transferring it to a syringe or turkey baster, and doing the rest either alone or with the help of friends.[19] At various women's health clinics there were physicians who did the procedure more formally if no friend's sperm was available. At the Chelsea clinic, where Barbara served as the volunteer medical director, if a woman had the money she could buy three vials or "straws" of sperm from a local sperm bank for seventy-five dollars each, after which Barbara would do the placement when the wanting-to-be-a-mother was ovulating.[20]

Clark thought she had found a friend as her donor. While working briefly at a bookstore to support her political actions, she had become friends with a coworker, a gay Cuban American dancer. His skin coloring reminded her of her father's olive complexion, and his joy warmed her soul. Meeting him again accidently on the street during the time she wanted to conceive, she realized they could have been siblings. She asked if he would be willing to donate sperm. He considered it at first, but at the last moment said he would be unwilling to do this unless he could really be in the child's life.[21]

Clark had planned to raise her child within the collective of May 19th women and not with a donor father. She resolved to buy the seventy-five-dollar anonymous sperm straws, but her money ran out. Barbara suggested asking Alan to provide the sperm.[22] Clark wanted the sperm for the conception, not Alan as her child's father.

A father already to the four year-old Sarah, Alan thought of his physical contribution to Clark at the time, too, as more political than personal. The usual problems of such donations by a straight married man—objections from his wife—were not an issue. As Barbara put it years later, she was in some physical way the "father" herself, as she did the insemination. Clark only told a few people in May 19th's leadership who had donated the sperm. Almost no one knew.

As with much of what Alan and Barbara did medically, this effort worked. Right after Ronald Reagan's 1980 election and before his inauguration, dark-haired Harriet was born to Clark, at home among her comrades. Any of

Harriet's physical similarities to Alan as she grew were left unmentioned, even when comrades began to notice them.[23] At that point, she was just Clark's infant daughter, raised by a collective of women in their joint household.

CHOOSING CHICAGO

For Barbara, the decision to ask Alan for his sperm was an index not only of their shared political understanding of what being a comrade truly meant but also of their increasing distance from one another. The pressures not to be an insular nuclear couple were taking its toll. "We were mostly silent," she remembers about their relationship at the time. They were feeling incredibly busy with work, political demands, and their daughter, Sarah. They were also wrestling with the critique of monogamy, and one of their comrades remembers Alan arguing that it was bad for them both, and even for Sarah. There seemed to be nowhere in these political discussions to consider the positive emotional aspects of a family's intimacy or the consistent caring needs of a child.[24]

Political demands continued. Feeling the necessity to expand their support work for Puerto Rican revolutionary groups, the May 19th leaders asked Alan, around the same time as Judy's daughter, Harriet, was conceived, if he was willing to leave Barbara and Sarah behind for a few months to work in Chicago to continue the solidarity efforts.[25] In Chicago, as in New York, a politicized Puerto Rican population had been fighting for the independence of their island for decades. May 19th and the JBAKC also had a presence in Chicago doing political work with them and other anti-imperialist groups.[26]

Anyone doing this support would attract increased state attention. The FBI focused much of its domestic surveillance in the late 1970s on these various Puerto Rican groups, especially after bombings and deaths in retaliation for police killings and other governmental violence led the groups and the FBI into a warring pas de deux.[27]

After much consideration, Alan declined, fearing the separation's effects on his family, but Barbara does not remember his even telling her he had been asked till months later. He may also have known the work in Chicago was becoming a failure trap, given the multiple factions and fights within the Puerto Rican organizations and the frequent burnout of other May 19th members who tried to help.[28]

After Alan turned the move down, the leadership made the same request of Barbara. Uncertain about her own political strengths and, as she recalled, "somewhat flattered that someone would give me the chore, really the challenge, to work in Chicago for a few months," Barbara said yes. It gave her the chance to prove herself separately from Alan and everything he had done successfully.[29]

Alan did not think he could dissuade her or articulate a reason that would stop her from going, even though he was sure this was a mistake.[30] They made arrangements for continued collective households: four-year old Sarah would go initially with Barbara and then return to New York to be with Alan for part of the summer. Barbara saw her move to Chicago as a step toward political growth, not an end to her marriage.[31]

Barbara landed in Chicago on April 2, 1980, at a chaotic time among those supporting Puerto Rican independence through armed struggle.[32] Two days after she arrived, police in the Chicago suburb of Evanston arrested six men and five women because someone noticed people near a van in parkas and fake mustaches who were supposedly "jogging" in the warm spring weather.

Thinking they had "something big" because they found firearms in the van, the police called in the FBI, which had just begun to set up a national terrorism taskforce. The federal officials identified the suspects as long-sought members of the FALN (the same group for which William Morales was the bomber in New York), on their way to a bank "expropriation."[33]

The FBI linked the suspects to over 100 bombings or attempted bombings on the mainland and in Puerto Rico. Bail was set at $22 million dollars. Those captured called themselves "prisoners of war" and refused to cooperate with any of the legal proceedings.[34] The police and the FBI continued to search for a "bomb factory" and found evidence in apartments in Milwaukee and Jersey City of other planned actions.[35] The search for more suspects and bomb-making equipment went on for weeks in homes, and even cemeteries, making regular headlines in Chicago papers, which especially savored the melees and screaming in the courtrooms.[36]

If Barbara had little knowledge of the FALN's plans, she had no doubts about what kind of support they needed. Solidarity with prisoners in a colonial struggle for freedom against the United States meant defense work.[37] For the next months she visited them in jail, helping get the word out about how they saw their position and planning demonstrations as the trials began.[38] The police were carefully watching who showed up for support, even taking names and addresses of those who entered the courtrooms, and FBI surveillance followed.[39] The risks of her support were becoming clearer.

In between all this political work Barbara needed an actual job. She worked as a physician part-time at Cook County Hospital's Outpatient Department, did some insurance physicals, and volunteered at a clinic in Uptown.[40] Others who were part of the May 19th family in Chicago helped with Sarah, while also lending their solidarity efforts not just to the FALN but also to Palestinian and Iranian groups, and raising money for ZANU in Zimbabwe. There was also the effort to support what became known as the Pontiac Brothers case, a trial of black prisoners accused of killing guards but acquitted.[41]

Sarah moved back and forth between Chicago and New York over the next year and a half as the "just a few months" expanded. While trying to meet Sarah's needs, Alan and Barbara found their relationship on hold and transforming into a trial separation. "Only after I got there did I realize that our relationship disintegrated," Barbara related. "I was heartbroken. It was the change and he understood it on a deeper level."[42]

Alan's situation was different. Having been fired from his job at the Betances clinic, he needed another position. His decision to quit his medical training after his internship, and not go on to a residency in internal medicine, made him a "general practitioner" in the medical hierarchy. It was a hindrance to his getting another position, despite his decade of experience and obvious skills.[43] It took a few months to finally get hired in the community medicine department where all his friends had gone before: Lincoln Hospital in the South Bronx.

With Barbara and Sarah away, Alan grew emotionally closer to Dana Biberman, his friend, comrade, and former housemate.[44] Younger than Alan and Barbara by six years, she had been part of Columbia SDS, worked at the National Lawyers Guild on support actions for the Black Panthers and on Puerto Rican political issues, and, after being part of Weather, had agreed to join Prairie Fire. She was a sophisticated organizer with a long political history.

Dana always had her doubts about some of her comrades' more adventurist actions. In 1969, she had chosen to help plan a major demonstration at the U.S. Army's Fort Dix in New Jersey rather than join Weather during its Chicago Days of Rage. She knew where violence could lead: a close friend had died after being hit in the head by the police at the 1971 Mayday march in Washington.[45]

In the late 1970s, she had lived collectively with Barbara and Alan, along with her then-partner, and had helped raise Sarah until she was three. Dana and Barbara became close friends who understood one another, especially amid the criticism of straight women's privileges within May 19th.[46] Dana, because of the work she did to support the Puerto Rican nationalist organizations, was often a target of FBI scrutiny, and she had been one of the plaintiffs in Judy Clark's suit against the Bureau for its illegal surveillance.[47] When Barbara and Alan became part of May 19th, Dana disagreed and moved out. But by 1980 she was back in the organization, living as a roommate with Jackie Haught, an acupuncturist who was also in May 19th.[48]

Dana and Alan stayed connected, even when she was outside May 19th. Over the years they had spent hours arguing over differing political positions at the dining room table, gone running together in Brooklyn's Prospect Park, and shared thoughtful critiques of everything they were involved in. Like Barbara, Dana was known as a rock, a person who could be counted on to be "stable and politically astute."[49] A pretty blond with a round face, she looked like a cross between Diane (Alan's high school and college love) and Barbara. Her intellect, warmth, and support were important to Alan, while his ability to listen carefully to another person's pain, among his sharpest clinical skills, made for a great platonic friendship. That is, until it became something more.

In the summer of 1980, they began what in any other circumstance would just be seen as an affair, not an experiment in new emotional arrangements. Alan tried very hard to keep it quiet, knowing that Barbara would see it as a betrayal and the leadership of May 19th would disapprove of his actions as male privilege, not an attack on monogamy.[50] As he would admit to a friend years later, "Although I did avoid overt lying, I was definitely not what you would call forthcoming about it."

He was conflicted. His love for Barbara had not abated and, in many ways, despite their distance, she was still his "soul mate."[51] The passion of a new relationship with an old friend, however, and the necessity to sneak around the May 19th hierarchy, kindled desires and bonded Alan and Dana's lives. They both felt a little bit like teenagers disobeying family orders.[52] Their relationship would last then for more than a year.[53]

When Dana expressed an interest in having a child in the fall of 1981, however, she was told directly by the May 19th leadership that Alan could not be the father. No one at the time, including Judy Clark, had told her Alan was Harriet Clark's biological father. Dana was not willing to wait any longer. While doing political work in Texas, she would become pregnant, and not by Alan.[54]

In turn, Barbara felt everything was "pushing away, burning bridges."[55] After she learned of Alan and Dana's relationship, she looked elsewhere for emotional comfort: she began a relationship with Susie Waysdorf, a community organizer and May 19th member in Chicago. While the FBI did not know about the nature of her relationship to Waysdorf, they were still watching them, keeping track of their activities, even when Waysdorf set up a lemonade stand outside Wrigley Field, where she also offered flyers expressing support for various militant groups.[56]

It was a tumultuous time for both Alan and Barbara. And then the violence escalated.

8

VIOLENCE, DEATH, AND
THEIR CONSEQUENCES

On October 20, 1981, everything that May 19th had built began to unravel in a burst of violence in New York. It was not supposed to happen this way. Though "the revolution will not be televised," as jazz poet Gil Scott-Heron had famously declared in 1970, it had to be funded.[1] As New York BLA member Kuwasi Balagoon explained, "Expropriation is an act of war carried out by every revolutionary army in history."[2] The BLA was no different. Its members, who operated out of Mutulu Shakur's Harlem acupuncture center, had to support themselves and their families, and procure weaponry and the other equipment needed for their actions.

The BLA needed an auxiliary for its efforts in multiple forms. Most of the support work done by May 19th members for their allies was in public: fundraising, leafleting, educating, and organizing spectators for their trials, all protected First Amendment speech of differing kinds despite all the FBI surveillance. The effort to aid the expropriations by BLA members had to be done clandestinely.

Most May 19th members had no idea about the concealed actions, although they may have suspected.[3] A very small number of the women in leadership worked with Marilyn Buck to rent cars, scout locations, find safe houses, print false identification with specially bought cameras and printers, and drive getaway cars to confuse police looking only for black men.[4]

Where the money from the expropriations would eventually go was left to BLA leaders to determine. Despite the emphasis on treatment for drug addiction and the need for weapons, some of those surrounding Shakur admitted later to their own cocaine use, and police wiretaps confirmed that calls for drugs were coming out of BAAANA's building by some of the men.[5] Those supporting the actions within May 19th either did not know or did not want to know about the drug use.[6]

Years later, May 19th leader Silvia Baraldini claimed that the potential for violence had really frightened her group's leadership, and that they sought to discuss it with their black comrades. It is impossible to know if these concerns were really voiced or not.[7] Others would identify May 19th leaders as taking part in target practice for the robberies/expropriations.[8] Either this leadership rationalized the violence inherent in what might happen or they blinded themselves to it. As Dana Biberman recalled, "You don't want to see things and you don't want to believe it."[9] With their sense that police or FBI surveillance or violence might happen at any time, they accepted on some level that this was part of being a revolutionary.

During the fall of 1981, the BLA leadership around Shakur requested specific assistance for a very big planned expropriation. To find their own soldiers, the May 19th leadership turned to one another, and to old friends still hidden from authorities. They chose old former Weather comrades David Gilbert, who began his radical career as a thoughtful leader of the Columbia SDS strikes, and Kathy Boudin, who had survived the townhouse bomb explosions on Eleventh Street in Greenwich Village in 1970. Both had been underground for more than a decade even after Weather collapsed, although Gilbert had surfaced briefly, before going back underground. Then a couple raising their fourteen-month-old son, Chesa, they were already making peace with surfacing and facing whatever legal charges might come, as most of their Weather comrades had already.

They agreed, as a last act, to support what the BLA members were planning, one more chance to act as revolutionaries.[10] Neither Gilbert nor Boudin knew about what political differences existed within the BLA group, or what role white people willing to assist were expected to play.[11] What was different now was that white people were going *to* the event, not just, as one May 19th leader put it later in explaining the action and the previous freeing of Assata Shakur, "show[ing] up after the event and express[ing] their solidarity."[12]

Tempting the BLA planners was a Brink's armored truck pickup at the Nanuet Mall in Nyack, a suburban part of Rockland County just north of New York City. The plan was to rob the truck, drive to a nearby parking lot, and switch into several cars and a U-Haul van driven by the white supporters to get away. The BLA men around Shakur believed that this expropriation would be worth the considerable risks, although others like the BLA's Sekou Odinga thought the location was too dangerous and did not participate.[13]

No one who agreed to be involved seems to have imagined it would go wrong, or if they did, they repressed their objections and fears. Gilbert and Boudin said goodbye to their child at his daycare that morning and made no plans for anyone else to pick him up. Judy Clark from May 19th had done the same with Harriet, leaving her with one of her other comrade mothers to go do what she thought of then as her political work. Fearful and nervous, she still felt she had to do this.[14] Everyone seems to have expected the operation to go as planned, with a rendezvous at a safe house (apartment) in the nearby West-chester County town of Mount Vernon.

Late in the afternoon on October 20, 1981, a red Chevy van pulled into the mall near a Brink's truck that had just picked up $1.6 million. After that, almost nothing went as planned. The BLA men in their van supposedly came out shoot-ing, according to the police and trial reports. Unlike in other robberies/expro-priations where they waved their guns, demanded money, and were handed the cash, this time the guards either did not cooperate immediately or did not have the chance.[15] Joe Trombino, one of the guards, had his arm nearly severed by bullets as he sought to close the truck door. Guard Peter Paige died instantly when M-16 automatic rifle fire hit his body.[16]

Within two minutes, the BLA men had scooped up the cash. Fleeing with the moneybags, they drove their van toward the switch-up point down the road, only to face new complications and errors. Instead of being in the predeter-mined spot, Gilbert backed into a space just a few yards off, but visible from a house nearby. A woman looking out the window of the house observed the BLA men transferring the bags of cash into the getaway truck as another car drove up and other cars hung back. She called the police, who now knew their suspects were no longer driving the abandoned red van.

The violence escalated. Officers set up roadblocks along the entrance to the highway in nearby Nyack to try to catch the U-Haul and stopped the one they saw driven by Gilbert with Boudin as the passenger. The police had no idea who they were, since they had not been told to look for anyone white. They were stopping U-Hauls. Assured by Kathy Boudin when she came out of the truck with her hands up that they were doing nothing, the police put away their guns.

In her panic, Boudin hoped this would be enough to get the police to leave as she stood outside the truck. But then the police went around to the back of the U-Haul. The BLA men in the truck's back saw the police lights flashing be-hind them and came out shooting. As the police tried to respond, three of them were hit in the crossfire. Waverly Brown, the city's only black officer, died at the scene. White officer Edward O'Grady died at the hospital ninety minutes later.

In the mayhem, Kathy Boudin could not escape, as the U-Haul took off without her. Two BLA men on foot commandeered cars from terrified motor-ists at the roadblocks. Another stashed his M-16 rifle and another firearm in the nearby woods, hiding out for another day and a half till he could be picked up. Judy Clark sped away in a car with David Gilbert in the passenger seat and the BLA's Samuel Brown in the back. The road made a sharp turn, and they crashed first into a pole and then a concrete wall as the police closed in. The three other cars raced away.

After the crash, the police hauled Clark, Boudin, Gilbert, and Brown off to the Rockland County jail. Police gunfire had grazed BLA soldier Mtayari Sundiata's chest but did not penetrate his bulletproof vest as he escaped. Marilyn Buck had also been driven away, but while pulling her gun out of her boot she shot herself in the leg, tearing through bone and muscle. She was bleeding heavily and needed treatment fast.

Buck's comrades rushed her to the Mount Vernon safe house, where the BLA's Kamau Bayette applied his first aid and acupuncture skills to her wounds. What they didn't have were the tools to remove the bullet, clean and suture the wound, and set her leg. An emergency room was not possible since bullet wounds have to be reported to the police.

It was then that Alan made his fateful house call, where he had "to figure out how, with little equipment and amid the clanging of guns and intense whispered voices and a palpable threat of a police raid to staunch the bleeding and stabilize the patient and immobilize a severely fragmented bone well enough to move the patient out."[17] Acting as a doctor comrade, he saved Marilyn Buck's life.

THE IMMEDIATE AFTERMATH

The police moved quickly. The BLA and May 19th members had no way to know what evidence officials had, or what had happened to those captured. With a partial license plate number of one of the fleeing cars, the police were able to trace the vehicle registered to Marilyn Buck under an assumed name to an apartment in New Jersey.

When that apartment was raided, the police found that Buck, as the BLA's supply and logistics officer, left behind maps, guns, ammunition, plans for bomb-making, walkie-talkies, and names and locations of police stations and businesses. There was more: the names of the judge in the Assata Shakur case and that of a white police officer who had been acquitted of shooting an unarmed black teenager, as well as addresses of safe houses.[18] The next morning, armed with warrants, the police raided another apartment and the Mount Vernon safe house. They found the bloody bandages and other detritus left behind after Buck was stabilized. By now, the authorities thought they knew who had rented the U-Haul, had identified the owner of the crashed car, and had begun to put together who was involved.

Because the attack had killed or wounded officers as well as the Brink's guard, the response mobilized hundreds of police and FBI throughout the New York area. The government desperately searched for anyone else involved, as the state sought criminal charges and the FBI looked into conspiracies. As court and crime reporter John Castellucci wrote, within a few days, "the cops believed they were the target of terrorists," but for the moment they had no idea who they were or where they were.[19]

The violence was not over. When Samuel Brown was taken into custody, David Gilbert described him as "unable to sit up, moaning in pain."[20] He was given a neck brace and diagnosed with a small abrasion. The next day Gilbert could hear the Rockland County jailors beating him over and over, especially around the brace. This continued for days.[21] The prosecutors claimed he had been injured in the car crash.[22] However, Brown was diagnosed later with a broken neck that was not treated properly for months. He often showed up for legal proceedings moaning, delirious, falling over, and in intense pain while he was denied care.[23] Gilbert had a loaded shotgun held to his head when he was caught and appeared at his preliminary hearings beaten with swollen eyes.[24]

Two days later more death would occur. Following a tip on a license plate, the police tracked yet another vehicle that held two black men: the BLA's Sekou Odinga, who was driving, and Brink's participant Mtayari Sundiata, his passenger. A chase ensued in New York City in a scene out of *The French Connection*. Sundiata fired out the car window; Odinga sped up, and the police raced behind them. When the tires blew out, the car careened, and it all ended on a dead end street. Odinga and Sundiata jumped out and started to run. Cornered by the police, Sundiata was "shot in the neck and head as he tried to scramble up a stack of concrete sewer pipes and over a fence." He died there, although whether he could have been arrested rather than killed is unclear.[25] Odinga gave himself up rather than die shooting or kill anyone, although police sources claim his gun jammed.[26]

By the time Odinga's lawyer saw him the next day, the bruises and cigarette burns on his body were glaring. Odinga reported his head had been put into a toilet as it was flushed and a gun repeatedly held to his head. His toenails had been removed and the beatings he received left his pancreas punctured. It took him three months in a hospital prison ward to recover.[27]

The media could not get enough of the terrorism angle, a term until then mostly applied either outside the country or against Middle Easterners like Sirhan Sirhan, who had murdered Robert Kennedy in 1968.[28] Stories filled newspaper front pages and led television newscasts for weeks.[29] The authorities and the media were transfixed by the recognition that fragments of the repressed violence-bent left of the 1960s and 1970s had reunited, in what they saw as a gruesome racial pairing. "Secret Network behind the Brink's Massacres" and "Armies of Hate," the *New York Post* declared, with a drawing of a black man holding a gun, while standing very close to a white woman.[30]

Retaliatory and seemingly arbitrary violence against authorities was labeled as terrorism. Most of the public did not think of Brink's guards or policemen as supporters of white supremacy or soldiers of an occupying army. The Brink's action was a made-to-order American melodrama about a new form of terrorism in the Reagan era: middle-class white women, street-tough black men, remains of the New Left, and a dangerous underground erupting in violence on the street. It would become a pivotal moment in the fears of terrorism that would only be surpassed by the Oklahoma City bombing and then September 11th.

Much of the news focused on Kathy Boudin, the daughter of a poet and noted radical civil rights lawyer, last seen fleeing the bomb-making deadly explosion of her unlucky Weather comrades in the Greenwich Village townhouse in 1970.[31] David Gilbert, as a white man, was ignored, and May 19th was hardly mentioned. Instead, it became a story of the resurrection of Weather (which did not exist), now married to the BLA. The story was written as an almost Freudian return of the not-repressed, told in psychological and family terms of dysfunction and white guilt coupled with black criminality. Left unmentioned was the political motivation behind the alliance: the participants' opposition to state violence.[32]

With the newspapers continually referring to everyone as members of a "gang," the "hysteria," as one lawyer put it, was palpable. Famed radical lawyer William Kunstler called it a government "'frenzy'" to "attack 'progressive organizations' and 'stifle dissent.'"[33] The Rockland County district attorney charged Gilbert, Clark, and Boudin with felony murder, even though they had been drivers only. Under this rule, if there is a death during a dangerous felony all those involved can be charged with murder, not the just the person or persons who did the killing.

The FBI refocused its examination of radical political groups, one that had been curtailed after the exposure of COINTELPRO a decade before.[34] As former FBI special agent William E. Dyson Jr. recalled, "In fact, the Bureau's willing to do this now, because now the whole nation is saying, 'What the hell! What are you doing about this? We've got a clandestine black-white group doing terrorist attacks and so forth. They've got the Puerto Ricans blowing up buildings all over the place.... The Bureau's willing to support it and now terrorism is okay to investigate."[35] In response, the FBI began to ramp up its Joint Terrorism Taskforce that enabled it to coordinate with local police departments.

The left response to the action and its violent loss of life was swift. Some on the older left saw these as their children gone awry. Antiwar activist and feminist writer Grace Paley knew the Boudins. She understood the passion behind the actions, if not the outcome. In one of her short stories, her main character laments about her child, "What if history should seize him as it had actually taken Ruth's daughter Rachel ...; a moment in history, the expensive moment when everyone his age is called but just a few are chosen by conscience or passion or even love of one's own age-mates."[36] *New York Post* columnist Murray Kempton, who had written the definitive book on the Panther 21 trial a decade earlier, was not as kind. In his usual florid prose, he claimed, "The suddenly blazing funeral pyre of the revolution of the sixties has made ruffians of once-principled people and principled people of formerly simple ruffians. A very few of the affluent have joined a very few of the indigent in a coalition of common destructive passions."[37]

Even those who still thought of themselves as radicals or anti-imperialists were aghast, both at the violence and the prospect of ramped-up state repression of their own political work. Brink's had created what one activist called without hyperbole "problems for leftists."[38] As one of the lawyers for those caught said, "Most left forces didn't want to have any association with the defendants. And, in the name of wanting to disassociate, many progressive Movement people refused to protest."[39] Very few were willing to support the claims that this was political action by enemy combatants in a war the United States was raging against black militancy.

DEFENSE, CONSPIRACIES, AND THE GRAND JURY

Everyone in May 19th and the group around BAAANA scrambled to cover their tracks. Debates were held quietly, but the public actions were clear. As a JBAKC leader put it, "After the oh shit oh fuck . . . then there was also this was righteous . . . we need to rally around the troops now. They all said it was war and it really was war, and rally around the troops."[40]

Alan later wrote that at the time "I most certainly did not know the damn robbery was going down before it happened and I most certain [*sic*] did think it was a hare brained, adventurist, misdirection."[41] But these were his comrades, his fellow soldiers. Marilyn Buck was his continued concern, since it was clear she would need somewhere safe to recover where the police could not find her.

Another May 19th member joined Alan in moving Buck to safety before the state could find her, or them. They wrapped her leg in an air cast. They agreed on a skiing-accident story that would seem probable for a young white woman, if anyone asked. They whisked her out of the New York area and met up with other supporters near the Mexican border. Buck would recover in safety, but she would have a limp for the rest of her life.[42]

Alan's medical work was not yet done. The lawyers for the BLA's Samuel Brown and Sekou Odinga knew to ask for him. After legal fights, Alan would see them both in jail and in the hospital, and testify to the severity of their wounds. Using Brown's hospital records, Alan was able to claim to authorities that he could "expose the facts of his torture." Regarding Odinga, Alan told a reporter,

"If my medical intervention helped him in any way to survive intact, I believe it is a contribution to the Black liberation struggle and to all progressive movements in this country." The state took note of his role, watching every moment that he was with either Brown or Odinga.[43]

There was still more to do. May 19th leaders called Dana Biberman back from her work in Texas. She had the unenviable task of telephoning Judy Clark's parents to explain what had happened to her.[44] Shelley Miller continued to care for Clark's daughter, while Kathy Boudin's parents took her son in.[45] Barbara came back from Chicago on and off to coordinate support actions.[46] Lawyers came from New York, Detroit, Los Angeles, and Washington to work on the cases.[47]

May 19th members were sent to scrub apartments of documents, flyers, letters, posters, and anything else, no matter how public, that might help authorities build a conspiracy case. Soon two defense committees formed: the Coalition to Defend the October 20th Freedom Fighters and the National Committee to Defend the Afrikan Freedom Fighters.

The police moved quickly to determine who was involved with the suspects, even in open political groups. Sometimes they made little differentiation. Eve Rosahn, under indictment for the Springboks demonstration and the owner of a car driven at Brink's, was arrested and charged with criminal facilitation for providing both the car and renting one of the vans used. She had not known other May 19th members had taken her shared car and had not rented the van, but it took time to prove this.[48] Two former Weather Underground members still in hiding, Eleanor Stein and Jeff Jones, were arrested even as they were negotiating with the FBI to face other outstanding charges. It did not seem to matter that they had nothing to do with Brink's or May 19th.[49]

The state response came not just in New York. FBI and local police swooped down on Republic of New Afrika leader Fulani Sunni Ali outside Jackson, Mississippi, with tanks, guns and helicopters. Falsely accused by a mistaken eyewitness of cleaning out the safe house apartment, she had been in New Orleans at the time of the Brink's action.[50] Even after she was let out of solitary, she was subpoenaed before a New York grand jury and kept from having her chosen lawyer.[51]

Other arrests would follow in the next few months of almost everyone who had been in the red van, except Mutulu Shakur, who would evade authorities for another four years.[52] Phone taps monitored the BAAANA offices, while Barbara, as one of the acupuncture center's medical advisors, in an interview with the *New York Times*, "denied that it had served as an underground revolutionary center."[53]

May 19th's members mobilized to try to rebrand the crime in political terms.[54] In a local Brooklyn newspaper, Dana Biberman argued against the term *robbery*. Instead, as the reporter quoted her, she termed it an "'attempted expropriation' . . . [of] the 'people's money'" and said "the three men killed 'were defending imperialism.'" [55] To many, this came across as a heartless statement in the face of the deaths. Still, the left hyperbole of "expropriation," with its political implications, became the language used in leaflets, demonstrations, and interviews. No one on the May 19th side was *publicly* calling it a robbery, although there was debate on the terminology. [56] However critical individuals might have been of the action, there really was not much choice about what to say in public if they were to maintain revolutionary solidarity.

The district attorney's office in Rockland County scoffed at the idea of "expropriation" and filed robbery and murder charges. The federal government had already set up a grand jury to look into the BLA two weeks before Brink's even happened. [57] The Racketeer Influenced and Corrupt Organizations (RICO) Act from 1970 had been used against the Mob to prosecute people in the same organization for crimes other members had done, had assisted in doing, or had ordered. The grand jury prepared to use it in the Brink's case.

In the course of the various trials at the state and federal level, the revolutionary solidarity that Alan had expected fell away, at least on the BLA side. Three men from the BLA turned into government witnesses. Together with another woman, who had been diagnosed as paranoid schizophrenic and had been in and out of mental institutions, they provided evidence of who was involved. [58] Whatever revolutionary fervor they had expressed did not withstand fear, pain, threats, or the chance to make the best deal possible to escape decades in prison. [59]

While the state trials geared up, the federal grand jury continued to meet in New York for the next two and a half years probing links to other robberies/expropriations. Even after Eve Rosahn proved she had not given up her car, or rented a truck, or been in Nanuet, she was called before the grand jury and asked for handwriting and hair samples. When she refused, she was jailed for seventeen months until the grand jury's work was finished. Thirteen more men and women from the BLA, May 19th, and the remains of Weather would also be jailed for refusing to cooperate. Most had done nothing except be friends or in political groups with those who had been at Brink's, or sheltered them afterward. Under RICO, this would be enough to go after them.

ALAN, THE FBI, AND THE STATE

Government witnesses began telling the prosecutors who had been involved both in Brink's and in the cleanup. With this information, the authorities had a clear link to Alan but less certainty about how to charge him. Not reporting a gunshot wound was a Class A misdemeanor under New York State's penal law, punishable by a maximum of one year in jail, probation, and fines, but he might also be protected by the principle of patient confidentiality, so that under other circumstances he could have gotten off with a wrist slap.[60] Authorities suspected, but could not prove, that he had helped move Marilyn Buck. As he would claim, seeing both Samuel Brown and Sekou Odinga as a physician was not "illegal." In fact, prison or police officials accompanied him whenever he was examining the BLA men.[61] In the end, the state passed Alan over to federal prosecutors as they tried to cast a wide net to find whoever was involved, and to instill fear in those who might support them.

Four months after Brink's, the authorities showed up at Alan's Lincoln Hospital office. FBI special agent Tom Terjeson and New York police officer Elmer Turo, whom Alan described as "two guys in the cheap suits and the brown shoes," presented themselves at Alan's door while he was with a patient. Standing in the busy hospital hallway, they demanded that he "give them Marilyn Buck."[62]

They wanted information about everyone involved in Brink's and its aftermath. As Alan recollected, "One [was] saying, 'If you don't cooperate we will destroy you . . . make sure you never practice medicine again . . . and put you in prison.'" The other promised, "'We'll give you $50,000 . . . arrange for you and your family in the witness protection program.'" When Alan said he had no interest in speaking to them, they handed him a subpoena for the grand jury. "I have no interest in speaking to them either," Alan replied.[63]

Rudy Giuliani, then the U.S. attorney for the Southern District of New York, began to center his case on Mutulu Shakur and the activities surrounding BAAANA, not, as the state had, on the events surrounding Brink's.[64] From the acupuncture center, the grand jury branched its inquiries into the links connecting the BLA, May 19th, and the FALN.[65] To many on the left, the grand jury, used to squelch dissent and activism for decades, harkened back to the medieval Star Chamber as an instrument of political power.[66] "Non-collaboration," as one pamphlet put it, was "the only answer to political investigations."[67] Eve Rosahn argued that there was already "a good 10-year struggle in the Catholic Left, the lesbian community and in the Puerto Rican movement to establish a tradition of non-collaboration with the Grand Jury." Others noted that this tradition went back to the end of the nineteenth century and the early struggles over Puerto Rico's independence.[68] As novelist and May 19th member Terry Bisson wrote in his poem "RSVP to the FBI," "Thank you for handing me this invitation to talk to you / But I am otherwise engaged."[69] He, too, went to jail rather than testify before a grand jury.

Alan was less poetic but just as adamant. His politics and sense of self-respect meant no collaboration: no giving over the handwriting or hair samples demanded, and above all no talking.[70] He admitted to no criminal wrong but acknowledged he had become an "enemy of the U.S. government . . . because I refuse to collaborate with their strategy to use health care and torture to attack revolutionaries."[71] Whatever his feelings about armed struggle, or even what had happened at Brink's, he stood on principle: he could not collaborate with the government's investigations.[72]

The government had threatened to come after him, and come after him they did for his refusals. For the seven months between May and November 1982 when the grand jury was in session, he wore the khaki prison clothing of the Metropolitan Correctional Center (MCC) adjacent to the federal courthouse in downtown New York. It was the first time he spent more than overnight in jail.[73]

In jail there was time to think, if nothing else. Even if his comrades were in separate cells and wings of the institution, Alan had opportunities to speak to them as they sat at tables with their lawyers to discuss the legal next steps, or met with visiting friends and family. Barbara, while still in Chicago, came back frequently to provide support.[74] They had the chance to discuss what had happened between Alan and Dana, and Alan took the time to apologize to Barbara and discuss the future. Otherwise, he felt useless: cut off from his work, he was no longer a doctor, or a revolutionary.

In conversations with comrades, Alan was beginning to raise criticisms that were circulating among others too. He critiqued the actions, the leaders, and their unquestioned support for whatever the BLA had planned. Such statements had to be carefully situated within an anti-imperialist stance that accepted the reality of a "war" and did not compromise anyone's legal cases.[75]

In an interview with the hometown paper in Middletown some five months after he was put into MCC, Alan's bravado was evident, but so was the tension between violence and political education. "There is a going to be a price exacted in blood," he promised. Yet he immediately added a critical flourish, "It's not just about picking up guns, but it's also profoundly about changing people's consciences where people are willing to fight for their own liberation."[76]

The government was less interested in such revolutionary explanations. Soon after the grand jury session ended and Alan was out, he was indicted again on different federal charges, along with members of the BLA. The federal prosecutor charged him with being an accessory after the fact to robbery and murder, racketeering conspiracy, and obstruction of justice.

When he was in the courthouse bathroom trying after the booking "to wash the ink off from the finger printing," he found himself confronted by the same two government agents who had come after him at Lincoln Hospital. This time the threat was stronger and uglier: "Ok now you are looking at 12 years in prison," they said. "Now would you like to talk to us?" Even more ominously, he claimed they threatened "to charge me with helping William Morales escape."[77]

Ignoring them, Alan went up to the urinal, unzipped, and began to pee. "I can proudly say my urinary stream never faltered," Alan recalled to a friend. As the FBI special agent moved in next to him and unzipped as well, Alan noticed. "I finished, washed my hands & as I was leaving, went over to him, looked down & noticed that nothing was coming out, & said, 'Take some medical advice — you should see a urologist about that inability to piss.' And laughed & laughed."[78] His boldness was evident, but underneath he must have known how serious things were now.

Alan was not about to settle his future in the courthouse men's room. He again said no to collaboration, although, as he wrote a friend a few years later, if he had given the hair and handwriting samples the government would not have had a case, since he had not been at the "expropriation."[79]

Unable to come up with the $25,000 for bail to stay out of jail this time, he reluctantly asked his family to help. His Uncle Abe, his mother's brother for whom Alan had always been a favorite, put up his own house as collateral. Alan would have to show up in court to face his charges, but at least for now he was not in prison.

As the media maelstrom over the Brink's case mounted during the legal proceedings, Alan became increasingly certain he could not receive a fair trial. At his arraignment, the judge connected him to history by declaring that Alan had become the first doctor since Dr. Samuel Mudd treated Lincoln assassin John Wilkes Booth in 1865 to be charged as an accessory to murder.[80] Alan's lack of a history of violence or connection to the actual event, or even his judgment of it, would become irrelevant, and probably not even discussed because it would compromise his comrades' cases. Others in May 19th agreed. The need not to collaborate transformed into the imperative not even to participate, or at the very least to try to turn the proceedings into a political statement.[81]

ONE MORE STEP

Out of jail by late November 1982, Alan continued to organize demonstrations of support for his comrades. He had plenty of time now. Lincoln Hospital had fired him after he was given the subpoena, and even before he refused to speak to the grand jury. Despite the tensions, he and Barbara both showed up at a hospital when Dana Biberman's daughter was deathly ill and used their doctor connections to get her baby to the right specialist. Her other comrades had not been as supportive. With her daughter's life on the line and doubts now about everything, Dana made a new choice: to leave May 19th. Alan listened to her reasoning as he had for others and supported her decision, but he could not bring himself to do the same. He was too far in.[82]

There was also the question of who would take care of Judy Clark's daughter Harriet, given the likelihood of Clark's long prison sentence. In January 1983, Alan finally went to see Clark's parents to tell them he was the biological father of their granddaughter, a fact they had not known. He reassured them that he would be around, and that Shelley Miller, Barbara, and he would be able to raise Harriet. He didn't mention that Miller was also being investigated by yet another grand jury about her support for the FALN, and Barbara at the time was mostly in Chicago.[83] Alan probably thought he would, as always, be able to step up.[84]

With their organization in shambles, some in May 19th felt they could no longer wait for the government to determine their fates. Following the tradition of other revolutionaries in the United States and around the world, several May 19th members made the decision to go underground to carry on their political work in a different way.[85] All that had happened had made them want to fight back, not give up.[86]

Alan now had decisions to make about his own life as he held very serious discussions with his closest comrades.[87] He knew this latest grand jury wanted his handwriting and hair samples, which he had previously refused to provide.[88] He expected his bail would be revoked when he did not cooperate again. If convicted of the accessory charges he might face imprisonment for decades. If the government could make good on its speculations about Alan's role in Morales's escape, it could mean the rest of his life. He did not know yet that one of the government witnesses in the Brink's cases would be caught in multiple lies on the stand, and that a straightforward criminal defense might get him off, or limit his sentence, as it would for some of those, but not all, who went on trial.[89]

With many of his closest comrades now either in jail, awaiting trial, expecting to be picked up by the government, or underground, Alan later wrote to a friend that he "decided that I shouldn't risk the time in prison. My decision was not based in personal fear but an assessment that I as a doctor had skills useful to a variety of political forces inside and outside this country."[90] He saw the options as a question of putting "his body on the line" and making a choice between "the desire to be an exemplary revolutionary and the desire to be a bourgeois beneficiary of the capitalist system."[91]

He still had a wife and two small children, whose needs tugged at his emotions and paternal feelings, not to mention his uncle's bail money that would be lost if he did not turn himself in. He considered that other revolutionaries, especially women, left their children for the battles they were part of, and he knew there were comrades who could love and care for both Sarah and Harriet. He and Barbara, and a few others, had serious discussions about what it might mean for him as they weighed his political and personal responsibilities.[92] He went to Chicago in early January to express his love for Barbara and to analyze what had to happen next.[93]

Back in New York the night before he was due in federal court, he called Barbara and Sarah again. He had wanted to see them a last time, but Sarah was just getting the chicken pox and "sounded sick and miserable," so now he could not go. He struggled with his conflicting identities, at once a father and a doctor, and yet also a revolutionary. He felt "guilt and sadness."[94] But he had made his decision.

The next day he vanished. On February 3, 1983, Judge Kevin T. Duffy issued a bench warrant in USA v. Alan Berkman for his arrest for "failure to appear in U.S. District Court as required."[95] When Barbara told six-year-old Sarah her father was now in the underground, she believed he was like Sesame Street's Oscar the Grouch, living in a garbage can. She began to watch all the cans as they walked along the streets, waiting for her father to "pop up."[96]

CLANDESTINE ACTIONS

Alan's descent into the political underground began on February 4, 1983, with a subway ride to New York's Grand Central Station. In the men's room he changed his clothes. He was following what his comrades called a "trajectory."[1] After he had done several evasions (changing subway lines, ducking into differing buildings) and before a comrade went to meet him while he was still a "public person," he had to make sure that he was not followed. His "observer" had to double check, too, and notice his maneuvers. After watching his reversals and becoming relatively sure there was no one following, the "observer" would meet the "public person."[2]

Alan's trajectory next would take him a lot farther than Grand Central. He used fake identification to register at a hotel. He went to the Metropolitan Museum of Art, then to a parking garage where a car was waiting. Scrunched down in the back seat, he was whisked away.[3] His May 19th comrade Linda Evans greeted him on the other end in Austin, Texas. Breaking the underground rules of engagement that required as much anonymity and normality as possible, Evans handed him a bouquet. The gesture could have been dangerous because it enacted a reversal of a gendered ritual.[4] It was the first time anyone had given him flowers — it was her way of signaling he was wanted by his friends.

Alan's comrades had appealed to him to join them in the political underground. "We needed his brains and we needed his strategic thinking," said his comrade and close friend Laura Whitehorn.[5] Under pressure from possible prosecution, his comrades had also disappeared from their public lives: Susan Rosenberg skipped out on a subpoena that would have led to grand jury questions about her purported role in the Brink's action and Assata Shakur's escape. Others, like Laura Whitehorn, Linda Evans, and Betty Ann Duke, slipped away before the federal government came looking for them, although Duke and Evans had been under surveillance in Austin.[6] Tim Blunk, after nine months in New York City's Rikers Island jail for his role in the Springboks demonstration, was afraid he too would be called to testify. Despite having married May 19th's Italian-born leader Silvia Baraldini as a way to keep her in the country before she was indicted, he told his family of liberal Presbyterians in New Jersey that he was headed for medical support in Central America, then disappeared.[7] Marilyn Buck remained hidden as her wounds healed.

Alan joined them to build "a cadre for armed propaganda" against the government's "war machine."[8] It had already started. Five days before he jumped bail, United Press International received a call after a small bomb went off at night at the FBI office in New York. It caused damage by exploding some water pipes, causing minor flooding. It meant, however, that the FBI could be attacked. The message from the self-named Revolutionary Fighting Group, at that point unknown to the authorities, declared, "We bombed the FBI office on Staten Island. They are responsible for attacks in the United States and around the world. Death to traitors! Free political prisoners!"[9]

It foreshadowed the underground work of Alan and his comrades both in its target and its overstated claims.[10] The action and the communiqué were not some fantasy based on another country's revolutions, although the May 19th cadre did think of themselves as internationalists involved in a worldwide revolt. They declared themselves as American revolutionaries through violence that would be powerful and symbolic, but not lethal. And they realized the FBI's fears since the early 1970s that it would be the target of bombings by the left.[11]

May 19th had named their public anti-Klan organization after John Brown, and in the underground those in this cadre continued to think of Brown and his actions as exemplars for whites struggling against racism, as did many others on the left over the years.[12] In a declaration he would later publish about his actions, Alan paraphrased black abolitionist Frederick Douglass, avowing, "*If we are not yet strong enough to be a definitive part of the solution, let us at least be part of the problem.* Perhaps today's North American armed clandestine groups can best be seen as the descendants of John Brown, who took Frederick Douglass seriously and gave the slavocracy the problem of white resistance as well as Black rebellion."[13]

Alan's memory of this dictum, however, neglected Douglass's actual actions. When asked by Brown to join his raid on the military depot at Harpers Ferry, Douglass declined, seeing it as futile. He later fled to Canada and then England, fearing he would be caught up in the government reprisals that followed Brown's capture. After Brown's death, many other abolitionists joined Douglass, who eulogized his fallen friend, supported the North in the Civil War, and never stopped railing against the immorality of slavery and its accompanying racism.[14] Douglass and Brown may have agreed on a moral and political position against slavery, but they did not agree on Brown's tactics to end it. Alan ignored the fact that Douglass had rejected Brown's actions as political and personal suicide.[15]

Over the next two and a half years, Alan and his comrades would work very hard to determine what it meant to be a clandestine revolutionary group in 1980s America. Alan was clear on where he stood at the time: "I believed violence was necessary. I was equally convinced that revolutionary change must be an assertion of life, optimism, and respect for humanity and not primarily an act of destruction." They wanted to be revolutionaries, but they also refused to kill.

The effort to reconcile these beliefs became central to Alan's life.[16] The group, now made up of former May 19th members and Marilyn Buck, had serious discussions about the differences between symbolic property bombings and the accidental killing of civilians, or the targeting of the powerful. Alan really did believe, as he told a reporter from his hometown paper just before he went underground, that "there has to be a real strategy, and a serious revolutionary strategy . . . , a protracted ongoing struggle that involves, educates and mobilizes peoples on many different levels, but also involves building up an army and a military capacity . . . we're definitely early in that stage."[17]

In the underground, Alan understood himself as a guerrilla and revolutionary. He would write autobiographically nearly two decades later, "I no longer had to ask myself why I wasn't doing anything to put my money where my mouth was. . . . I became a guerrilla because I was frustrated with the failure of the left to move the country. It was also very romantic to think of myself as a guerrilla. But more than that it was exceptionally compelling and very hard work, intellectually and politically hard work, and I liked that. A lot."[18] He really did differentiate between terrorism and revolutionary actions, though he did not object to the considered use of arms and bombs. Now there were new skills to learn, risks to take, relationships to be formed. Those underground had to learn how to develop contacts with other groups with similar politics as they shared advice, experiences, and matériel that would help them make their revolutionary rhetoric a reality.[19]

What Alan and his comrades failed to see or admit was the extent to which they were *not* building a revolutionary movement. They were looking forward, but they did not see how few were either next to them or behind them. And unlike in Brown's case, there was no Civil War to follow their clandestine acts, no abolitionist equivalents in the remains of the left, no large community of people of color in any kind of military action, and above all no clear political direction or party of support. Alan did not seem to consider that this work did not lead others to join them but rather triggered even more government reprisals.[20]

The cadre underground believed that they had to stop American state violence with violence. As the Reagan administration's foreign policy led to support for Israeli incursions into Lebanon to attack the Palestinians, the U.S. invasion of the Caribbean island of Grenada after the murder of its Marxist president Maurice Bishop, illegal administration funding of the contra rebels to sustain their counterrevolutionary war in Nicaragua, and continued support for the apartheid regime in South Africa, Alan and his comrades would respond accordingly, picking targets for retaliation against American power. Their politics linked trying to stop these kinds of imperial actions abroad to the racism and police actions they saw growing at home. As Alan's comrade Susan Rosenberg would admit years later, "All the signs that I was moving in the wrong direction didn't stop me."[21] Nor did they stop Alan, who knew he was now acting on his principles. Rosenberg's reflections suggest they knew they had few with them, and that the country was in no mood to support this kind of revolutionary action. Yet they carried on.

THE SCIENCE OF CLANDESTINITY

There was a method to life underground. It began with the creation of a new identity. At a time before chips in credit cards and cross-checked electronic lists, assuming a new identity took ingenuity, time, and paper. Friends who worked in hospitals obtained blank birth certificates, and a small special Polaroid camera and laminating machine could be either stolen or bought in the still-thriving hidden economy in fake driver's licenses and other "official" documents. Silk-screening equipment could forge motor vehicle inspection stickers, blank social security cards, and licenses of various kinds. Comrades who worked in car rental offices or retail stores compiled names and information from licenses, checks, and credit cards to reuse someone else's identity, and others whose jobs involved typesetting did the printing.[22] Libraries held old newspapers where the obituaries of dead babies of the "right" age could be used to create the identity of someone who did not exist. Claims of a "lost" license were replaced fairly routinely at government offices with a "new" one from the name and birth date on a newly obtained birth certificate. Then a road test could be taken under a new name.

Anyone who watched the hundreds of spy films that came out during the Cold War years, or read the stories on the underground printed in multiple alternative newspapers, or talked to other clandestine comrades would know in general what to do to disappear.[23] Alan's comrades passed around, or memorized, packets of information of how to "go under."[24] While he never wrote about the details, he did later tell a hometown reporter, "When I first went underground, I was more nervous. And then I understood there's a science to being clandestine. In some ways Big Brother was not everywhere, if I was careful. I became less nervous."[25] Both his medical school training and his experience in high school theater proved useful in lessening that anxiety.

The actions of Linda Evans, his then-Austin-based comrade, reveal some of what they did in the underground to get what they needed. Six days after Alan disappeared, she was more than 500 miles away from Austin in Arabi, Louisiana. Using one of her invented identifications as Louise Robinett, she went to the St. Bernard Indoor Shooting Center, where she bought an Israeli-built Uzi submachine gun for cash. The FBI later reported that she told the clerk she "wanted to buy the Uzi for her daddy, and [the clerk] recalled that Robinett talked about her dad liking the Uzi and that he may turn it into an automatic. Robinett told her this in front of an unknown white man who accompanied her. [The clerk] described the white man as being tall, with a slim build and having average dress (no further specifics)." A day later she was in Norco, Louisiana, thirty miles away, buying a Mini-14 .223 caliber rifle and a Browning Hi-Power 9 mm pistol from the Sportsman's Center. This time a "shorter unknown black man" accompanied her.[26] Over time others in Alan's cadre acquired other guns, much ammunition, bombing equipment, and the instructions on how to use it all. Given the prevalence of gun ownership in the United States, none of this was unusual or concerning, especially given that there was no way to know they were using false identification and there were few background checks.

New to the life of a clandestine revolutionary, they all had to figure out how to live and survive undetected. This required a simple disguise, since the money for plastic surgery was not available. With dark hair and a male-pattern balding Alan had two choices: dyes and wigs. Without a beautician comrade, the drug-store dyes took their toll. The first time Alan tried to make his dark hair lighter, his baldness contrasted with his bleached and brassy Donald Trump–like hair. Even his comrades "rolled on the floor laughing" at how ridiculous he appeared in hair covered in what was known, at least in their circles, as "underground orange."[27] Others in their group "straightened their curls" or wore makeup for the first time since they were teenagers, if they had ever worn it at all.[28]

After the disaster of the hair dye, Alan had to settle for cheap brown and black wigs that barely stayed on his head but at least made him appear less bald. Gone too were his characteristic mustache and short beard.[29] His comrade Laura Whitehorn recalled with amusement sitting with Alan in a coffee shop in a Hasidic neighborhood in their wigs. Laura looked appropriate as an Orthodox Jewish woman, but they got sympathetic stares and comments from fellow customers who assumed that Alan had cancer.[30]

Those who tried to sustain them from the above-ground took their own evasive actions to deter any government agents who might follow them. When they met to plan together they never did so in a public place, JBAKC organizer Marion Banzhaf recounted. "We found secure meeting places where we would all go independently. We took subway lines that had tunnels we could switch trains from, and made sure no one was following. . . . We'd change clothes in the toilets in Grand Central Station, put on makeup and wigs, wear something different, get on a suburban train and meet up at a new rendezvous spot, always checking to make sure no one was following us."[31] They were not just being paranoid. Seven months after Alan disappeared, FBI agents set themselves up in an "observation post" across from Barbara's apartment to monitor who came and went.[32]

For those underground, finding a place to live and paying for it was essential. If they had not all come from the financially precarious working class, they were certainly part of it now. "Every resource, everything that is taken for granted in daily life under normal conditions had to be painstakingly acquired, often at considerable risk," Alan would relate.[33] Clothes were mainly found in thrift shops and Salvation Army stores. The grocery chain Stop and Shop was jokingly referred to as "Stop and Grab" or "Stop and Steal."[34] Cars were shared, often in need of repair, and the bane of their existence when they broke down repeatedly.[35] Apartments in working-class and poor neighborhoods could be paid for monthly or weekly, with money orders or cash. In such areas, where transience was more common and households more fluid, fewer questions were asked. To draw less attention to themselves, they often lived alone or in pairs, but they met up frequently for meals. They invented kin and became cousins to one another. After a short time in Texas, Alan spent most of his next few years in the working-class Connecticut town of Bridgeport, in the poorer sections of nearby New Haven and Hamden, and other places in parts of Pennsylvania, Baltimore, and the Washington, D.C., area.[36]

In the 1970s, those who fled government authorities often hid with friends or in communes.[37] In such communities, sharing, without asking questions, was common. Refusing to give information when the police came calling was a matter of course. In those years, government authorities learned to look for their suspects in rural hippie communes, feminist collectives, or in the college and dropout havens of a Northampton, Ithaca, and Berkeley, though they rarely got the information they wanted.[38]

It had been easier to find financial support for those in the underground when politicized violence threatened property, not people, and a war was still raging in Southeast Asia.[39] As underground cadre member Susan Rosenberg realized, "By the time I fled . . . whatever underground had existed as a result of the antiwar movement, the antidraft movement, and the movement to give illegal immigrants sanctuary had all but disappeared."[40] Her statement was a bit hyperbolic since the sanctuary movement to shelter Central Americans fleeing the U.S.-backed wars in their countries was at its height then.[41] The situation of those close to Brink's did not have the same moral cachet, however, as that of the Central Americans, who were housed primarily in churches and synagogues.

The difficulties for the underground cadre was reflected in an angry article that radical feminist Janis Kelly wrote for the Washington, D.C., women's paper *off our backs* two months after Brink's: "I am tired of women from male-dominated, gun-slinging 'vanguards' who stop off for a little R & R in the women's community before going back to plotting bloodshed," she declared. "If you still hold those values, find some other place to rest up."[42] While readers wrote back to critique Kelly's views, and to offer principled criticism paired with support of those involved at Brink's, Kelly's disgust reflected a real problem.[43]

Alan and his comrades knew they were primarily on their own, or would have to make contact with other small groups of revolutionaries in their hidden settings. It became paramount to develop ways to keep themselves together, yet separate enough so that not everyone could be picked off after a single arrest. Communication had to happen without faxes, cell phones, internet, thumb drives or cloud computing, none of which yet existed. Instructions, surveillance notes, and position papers had to be written by hand or typed, then filed. Yet there was no way to make their thinking clear, or connect to others, except by writing down their more analytic reflection. This is exactly how a well-timed police raid had turned Marilyn Buck's careful record keeping into a trail for the authorities to follow.[44]

What was not written down was transmitted verbally and individually, since conference calls were not an option. The key to much of their connecting was public pay phones, since these were much more anonymous than landlines, and less likely to be subject to what the police and FBI called "trap and trace," a system of listening devices that told the authorities who was being called and from where.[45] To avoid the possibility of the pay phones being caught in this web, they had to be found on safe corners, and hours were spent driving to phone locations far from where cadre members lived or worked. Calls had to be made to set up calls, and often they failed. Alan sometimes got angry when no one picked up at the other end. It never seemed to cross his mind that maybe he had gotten the times or numbers wrong.[46]

Some of the cadre members were less known to the police and not yet fugitives from legal charges, or they had skills that could more easily translate into jobs. Linda Evans, although under surveillance before she went underground, was a printer and worked under an assumed name in a number of small printing shops, wearing a wig (which accidently came off once when she went horseback riding with her shop mates and a branch lifted her "hair" up). Sometimes she lived in collective households with her other comrades, other times alone.[47] Marilyn Buck, who had come back from Mexico to join them, had a limp that could not be easily disguised (although she wore lifts in one shoe to try), and her work usually did not involve paid labor.

For Alan, paid work, as any kind of health worker, was impossible. The FBI had sent out what they labeled a "fugitive circular letter" to over 60,000 "convalescent, nursing and rest homes, telephone answering services, ambulance services, medical laboratories, hospitals and medical clinics nationwide" to make sure they could find him if he tried to work.[48] It was one thing to fake a driver's license, but doing this for a medical license and an easily checked work history would have been impossible. It did not keep a concerned citizen doctor in New Mexico from imagining that he had almost hired Alan, and reporting this to the FBI.[49] Instead Alan spent much time trying to keep up with his medicine, reading every medical journal he could obtain from his friends or in libraries. He had become his comrades' doctor, able to diagnose and treat small ills, when he was not preparing for their various actions.

Sustaining the group's spirits and lives in the underground required new kinds of family life. Everything was shared, and individuals were given "allowances" from collective monies.[50] Eating out was too obvious and expensive. Alan, who had never cooked much, learned to be a chef. Practice improved his skills, but his comrades recalled disastrous early efforts, such as his infamous clams, spaghetti sauce, and cream cheese. He and Marilyn Buck became closer friends, even lovers for a time. They cooked together to the dismay of their colleagues as they endured Marilyn's culinary imagination, which led to a good deal of kale before its hipster time. They had to pretend they lived straighter than they had before, trying desperately to blend in and not be noticed.[51] Like everyone else in America, they went to the movies. There were lots of "jokes," Susan Rosenberg recalled, "to cope with the loneliness and pain."[52]

They spent a good deal of time driving around, talking in the liminal space of the cars about their actions, pasts, and hopes, while learning to trust and love one another. Sometimes there was just silence, most difficult for one-time activists and organizers.[53] And yet, as Susan Rosenberg remembered, "although living in obscurity was difficult and tedious, there was a feeling of power that came from invisibility. Anonymity was often invigorating and chilling at the same time."[54] There were also those moments of magical connection. Rosenberg recalled a cold drive late at night with Alan. The roads had turned icy, snowy, and dangerous. As they considered whether they should turn back, the moon shone brightly and a giant blue heron flew across their windshield. "We looked at each other," she remembered, "and said we should stop. We got off the road."[55]

There were rules to invent and learn, as they lived in what Rosenberg described as a "hyperaroused state" of constant carefulness and commitment. As Alan put it, "Every movement [was] filled with paranoia and [a] heightened sense of alertness."[56] Simple mistakes, leaving a photo in a print-shop camera at work, or touching a newly made license without gloves and thereby leaving fingerprints, could easily bring disaster. They also demanded enormous honesty from one another, digging deep into their own commitments and admissions of failure.[57]

Training in various skills took time, as books were bought or borrowed on the actions of Latin American guerrillas, or as they reflected on the disastrous errors friends had made that led them to blow themselves up or get caught. There was a "Security and Clandestinity Seminar" and a "Rules of Security and Operations" document. In addition, they read a "Welcome to the U.S. Ordnance Museum" pamphlet that came from their surveillance actions, the infamous *Anarchists' Cookbook*, with its guide to making simple bombs, and numerous other books on making and using weapons and explosives.[58] They knew that according to law enforcement they "should be considered armed and extremely dangerous."[59]

The cadre members also knew they were smart people. They could read, challenge one another, and learn. Alan was clear: "We were concerned with development of revolutionary morality or character. This was not an abstraction. Problems with character affected our ability to perform as exemplary and effective revolutionary cadre. . . . The real test of character, however, was in having the strength to move from theoretical understanding to practice, to more effective practice."[60] There was much to do to build what Linda Evans called "clandestine capacity."[61] They were a very small group against a very strong and powerful state.

Knowing that their natal and chosen family members would be visited and watched by the police and federal agents, they separated themselves, or reached out to them only with great difficulty and enormous care. When one comrade's parent died while she was underground and could not visit, Alan shared his tears with her.[62] Susan Rosenberg found a way to meet up just a few times with her parents after precautions which made her mother comment that it all felt "right out of a John Le Carré novel." [63]

Alan found the separation from Sarah particularly difficult. Several times, after going through many diversions and a foul-up that made him furious, Laura Whitehorn was able to help make arrangements for Alan to see Sarah that kept them both safe. Sarah would at least know her father was not living on Sesame Street, although Alan was bemused that his Upper West Side New York and "achingly beautiful" daughter asked for quiche in a working-class diner. She liked pretending that she was named Cyndi (after her favorite pop star, Cyndi Lauper) and her daddy was "David Cohen," but that they could still talk about the "before" time. Alan tried to keep up with his daughter's life, telling Barbara through convoluted connections how he thought she ought to be raised.[64]

Some of Alan's old, nonpolitical friends worried that they were being watched. His high school best buddy Jeff Millman, an architect in Cambridge, Massachusetts, who did not share his politics, was sure that he had seen Alan in

Boston's "T," and that the government had agents sitting in cars watching his house in his cul-de-sac or taping his phone.[65] Millman may have imagined it all, but others with closer connections did have the FBI, if not a grand jury summons, on their doorsteps. And Millman was partially right: one of the aliases Alan must have chuckled when he created it was that of Jeffrey Millman, MD.[66]

THE POWER OF THE GOVERNMENT ON TRIAL

The cadre went underground to send reminders to those in power that they could not operate with impunity. At the same time, the government's control was fully on display as the trials of others involved in the Brink's action began. The existence of clandestine cadres who had broken others out of prison only added to the concerns of law enforcement, as they shuttled the Brink's defendants between jails and courthouses. Alan and his comrades kept up with the news of their comrades but did not try to get them out, despite the government's fears.

Recalling the trial of Brink's codefendants Judith Clark, Kuwasi Balagoon, and David Gilbert in Goshen, New York, one lawyer said she had never seen such militarization of the courts in her life.[67] The state was clearly worried about a possible escape attempt. As Kenneth Gribetz, the Rockland County district attorney, sought three life sentences for the defendants for each of the men killed, the state spent $5.4 million on extra security, requiring a tax increase on all Rockland County property owners. The money paid for additional guards, fortified offices for court officials, armored truck caravans, troopers with rifles, helicopters, and cars with screaming sirens as the defendants were shuttled between jail and court.[68]

To counter this show of force, multiple demonstrations were held outside the courthouse, and those who got into the trials frequently signaled their support for their comrades by refusing to stand when the judge entered. As police officers walked down the center aisle at the opening of the Goshen trial, using their billy clubs to make people get up, JBAKC organizer Marion Banzhaf lunged to protect the Republic of New Afrika's Ahmed Obafemi, sitting on the other side of the aisle, from being hit. In the subsequent melee she lost her glasses and was hauled off to the county jail. It took a day for her lawyer to get her out, while officials checked her glasses prescription, thinking she might be the equally myopic and tall Marilyn Buck, whom they had not caught. It gave Banzhaf political credibility in her circles even to be mistaken for Buck, while also demonstrating the state's eagerness to use its power even though someone in the underground was unlikely to show up for a comrade's trial.[69]

News of what was happening was passed on to Alan and his comrades by those above ground or could be tracked in the local and New York City papers.

Alan already knew much about the physical and emotional violence directed at his comrades: the beatings of Brown and Odinga he had testified to were known, as was the government's refusal to let either Clark or Boudin touch their babies during jail visits for fear that there were "weapons in their Pampers."[70] Clark would testify that on her way to a medical appointment before her conviction, "as we reached the highway, the trooper in the front seat turned around and pointed his rifle at me. Then he screamed, 'If we so much as go over a stone in the road, I will shoot you!' He appeared to chamber a bullet and put his finger on the trigger. At one point, he ordered the caravan to stop along the roadside, where we sat for what felt like an eternity. The entire time he repeated to me, 'You are as close to dead as you will ever be.'"[71]

Alan had to know what he might have to do if caught, and what he would face in custody. He could not have missed the irony that the Brink's jury, drawn from the voting pool in New York's Orange County, was composed of people who could have been his former classmates or Little League teammates. In turn, Balagoon, Clark, and Gilbert, seeing themselves as prisoners of war and not criminals, refused to participate in most of the trial's proceedings, which they watched instead on a video feed in the courthouse basement. "We are neither terrorists [nor] criminals," Gilbert wrote in a statement. "It is precisely because of our love of life, because we revel in the human spirit, that we became freedom fighters against this racist and deadly imperialist system."[72]

The contradictions of Alan's life played out in the streets before the Goshen courthouse. Defense committees brought supporters to the trial, held public meetings, and continued the antigovernment rhetoric.[73] They chanted their ire at Kenneth Gribetz, the Orthodox Jewish Rockland County district attorney, jeering, "Gribetz, Gribetz, Gribetz, you can't hide; we charge you with genocide." Orange County supporters of law enforcement countered, "The USA is here to stay; if you don't like it, go away."[74] The outcome was a foregone conclusion. On September 23, 1983, the jury returned a guilty verdict. Without a criminal defense, they were all given sentences of seventy-five years to life.[75]

There would be many more trials. Kathy Boudin and Samuel Brown were tried separately in a trial moved to Westchester County beginning on October 12, 1983, eight months after Alan went underground and nearly two years to the date after the Brink's action. Boudin, convinced by her parents that she should at least attempt a criminal defense, eventually agreed to plead guilty, and received a sentence of twenty years to life with the possibility of parole. Samuel Brown gave state's evidence, then reneged on it, and received a life sentence.[76] Meanwhile, in New York City, the federal government went after six others in a federal conspiracy trial that encompassed Brink's, "several other armored-car robberies, four murders and a prison escape," even though connections to the Brink's case could not always be proved.[77]

What the trials did show were the differing ways juries vetted their charges and how solidarity held or did not hold. Two men who had been May 19th's allies as BLA soldiers, and one man's girlfriend (the one with documented mental illness), made deals with the government after being pressured. The BLA's Sekou Odinga labeled them "traitors." Revolutionary fervor had its limits. Others had lawyers who offered a criminal defense, pointing out the contradictions and outright lies of the government's witnesses and the errors in the eyewitness accounts, which confused several of the BLA soldiers for one another.[78] In September 1983, and seven months after Alan went underground, some of the defendants would get off, receive shorter sentences for aiding and abetting after the fact, or, like May 19th's Silvia Baraldini and the BLA's Sekou Odinga, be given decades of time for their participation in what the government labeled robberies (although not in Brink's) and for their roles in Assata Shakur's prison break.[79]

None of this would stop Alan and his comrades. They doubled down on their reading and training. After fifteen months underground, Alan offered a report that sounded almost like a corporate manager's end-of-the-year review: "Overall, the military level of the cadre is higher than it was last year. This is true at the very practical level of physical training, competence with small arms, ability to build a device. We have grown in our collective ability to do surveillance & make a plan of action." Assessing the failures of Brink's, he understood they had not linked their political position to their training. He argued that "the weakness in the plan resulted in more shooting than necessary. For the white people it meant being realistic about how little they had learned about certain aspects of the work, & how poorly trained they were as combatants."[80] To resist the government's power through armed struggle, they would need to learn new skills.

EIGHT BOMBINGS AND A ROBBERY/EXPROPRIATION

Against the backdrop of the trials of their comrades, the former May 19th members in the cadre was determined to make something happen. They talked about and debated what had gone wrong in the Brink's action.[81] Alan was adamant that no innocent civilian should be killed. For Laura Whitehorn, because he had confronted death nearly daily in his medical work, and held patients' lives in his hands, "he was the one who understood, on some level, something about violence and death that escaped the rest of us, and he had a better understanding of the sanctity of life."[82]

As a physician, Alan, like all his medical colleagues, could have or had "kill[ed] somebody" through medical errors.[83] Such unintentional mistakes were accepted as part of the profession, errors to be learned from. That is why physicians in medical institutions hold mortality and morbidity conferences to assess mistakes in patient care, or insist on autopsies, to learn to prevent such errors in the future. The underground cadre held the political equivalent, as they discussed mistakes in actions and personal failings. As with medical errors, there were lessons to be learned and practices to improve.

Alan's position on this need to avoid killing innocent civilians was long-standing, dating back to at least 1970. He was horrified that year when the bombing of the University of Wisconsin Math Building by antiwar protestors led inadvertently to the death of graduate student Robert Fassnacht and the serious injuries sustained by three others. He abhorred the accidental bomb explosion at the Weather townhouse in Greenwich Village that same year. The Weather members had been making antipersonnel bombs that could have killed soldiers and their dates at Fort Dix. He knew the Weather leadership had understood what might happen in this kind of bombing, and he objected to it. Some of his old friends in Weather rationalized such deaths as "aberrations," or the costs of war. For him, there was no excuse.[84]

He thought his position through in deliberative fashion with his cadre. If there were to be expropriations, he reasoned, "they must always be approached from a revolutionary & not criminal perspective: . . . we [must] do everything to maximize our chance of success & minimize the chance of violence — if such a plan can't be developed, don't do the action. Unlike criminals, we don't take 50-50 propositions."[85] After Brink's, Alan knew that they would have to make sure no one was killed deliberately and that they controlled their own actions. His statement made this clear: "We cannot develop a view that in any way places our interests as revolutionaries above those of the people — to do so leads to gangsterism and terrorism."[86] Reading Lenin had clearly affected Alan's thinking about "what was to be done" and why terrorism was not the right political action, although he clearly ignored how revolutionary actions could be seen as terrorism. That those he allied with had done such actions that led to deaths did not figure into his written position statements.

Alan and his comrades reasoned their way into accepting the *possibility* of killing by considering the difference between the innocent and the police, or other representatives of governmental power. In writing, and presumably when arguing with his comrades, Alan at least tried to consider what visiting this kind of death might mean and why they should have the right to make these decisions. He knew that his white comrades at Brink's were unprepared and mostly "froze." At least on paper, he declared that they "had to be willing to take the offensive, act decisively, and get away. To help us, we got some combat training & began to transform ourselves from target shooters to combat shooters." Here he would express their most violent, and perhaps fanciful, thoughts, since none of this was attempted or happened:

Should we have killed the NATO general staff if we could have; should we kill naval officers; should we assassinate individuals? There is no hard & fast answer but we did begin to develop some guidelines to apply:

1) Revolutionaries must demonstrate a deep respect for human life and not be afraid to take that of the enemy if it is appropriate,

2) the decision must be made in the context of an evaluation of the overall struggle, our long-term strategy, our organizational capacity to withstand the repression,

3) it must be very clean; we don't want to promote the view that a system can be reduced to individuals or small groups, or that the war is between the state & the revolutionaries with the people as passive spectators,

4) individuals should be killed only if their crimes are very clear (judge, prosecutor, cop, etc.) or they are truly strategic (Kissinger, e.g.). . . . Do we kill a racist & reactionary judge in retaliation for long prison sentences?[87]

No such actions ever materialized. As Alan realized decades later, "We hid behind our fear, our repulsion, our lack of unity, and our desire not to escalate the violence beyond that of the enemy."[88]

Instead, they learned to make bombs and to use them against symbolic political targets. They amassed the equipment they would need for this, much of it stolen in Austin, Texas, in 1980, and some of it having been used by the FALN in its bombings: detonating cords, electric wires and blasting caps, explosives such as Hercules Unigel Tamptite dynamite, DuPont Tovex water gel explosives, and Atlas Gelodyn blasting powder.[89] They taught themselves, or were taught by others, how to make and detonate bombs without killing anyone else, or themselves, using a type of timing device that had been popular in the Weather bombings.

Between April 26, 1983, and February 23, 1985, the cadre decided on targets, surveyed locations, and made sure no one would be around when the blasts went off. They sent communiqués by voice and then tape to the media after the explosions. They used a variety of names for their group, starting with the Revolutionary Fighting Group at the first bombing on Staten Island to the Armed Revolutionary Unit and the Red Guerrilla Resistance, to confuse law enforcement and to make it seem as if there were many groups. They saw their actions as retribution for the U.S. invasion of Grenada and support for those fighting the contras in El Salvador and Guatemala. They bombed to confront Israeli and South African power. They linked these actions to racist police killings of innocents.

All their targets were either in the Washington, D.C., area or in New York City. On April 26, 1983, a five-to-ten-pound bomb was planted in a concrete flowerpot outside the main entrance to the National War College building at Fort Lesley McNair in southwest Washington. The bomb went off at night, taking out some windows. The message declared the bombing's motive to be protesting the U.S. role in training soldiers for counterinsurgency in Central America.[90] Another bombing followed in August outside the Washington Navy Yard computer complex, and then another on the Senate side of the U.S. Capitol building in November, right after the U.S. invasion of Grenada in late October. The group's carefulness paid off as no one was harmed. They were also lucky no janitor was staying late, and no pedestrian was passing by who could have been injured or killed by the glass shards from a window.

The FBI had no idea who the group or groups were, and what, if any, relationship they had to the FALN or other militant groups. The Capitol bombing came just two weeks after large dump trucks driven by "Islamic Jihad" suicide bombers struck at the U.S. Marine and French military buildings in Beirut, Lebanon, killing 299 servicemen and women. While the Beirut operation involved an estimated 12,000 pounds of TNT and led to hundreds of deaths, the one at the Capitol did little damage and entailed only 3 to 4 pounds of explosive.

The FBI director, William Webster, was careful as he related details of both events in response to reporters' queries, but the "foreign" connection to the bombings on American soil was still raised as a possibility. Soviet or Cuban involvement in the U.S. bombings could not "be ruled out," he said.[91] It was an index of the government's imagination: how little the authorities knew, and how much they feared an international terrorist conspiracy. The underground cadre did see itself as connected to a global retaliation to U.S. power, but there was no link between them and Hezbollah or governments supporting such organizations.

For the next year and a half into early 1985, the Red Guerrilla Resistance struck four more times: at the Washington Navy Yard officers' club and in New York City at an Israeli Aircraft Industry office, the South African consulate, and a New York Patrolman's Benevolent Association building. Each time phone calls warned the bomb was coming, then the cadre sent out their statements, denouncing differing forms of U.S. militarism aligned with what they saw as outlaw nation-states. The police building bombing was retaliation, they claimed, for the police union's support for officers indicted in the killing of two innocent African American civilians and linked the police as an institution to an "imperialist strategy . . . to terrorize."[92]

The FBI, still trying to identify the group or groups, was willing to wait them out. "Sooner or later, we'll get lucky," said Kenneth P. Walton, deputy assistant FBI director in charge of the New York FBI office. "They'll make a mistake. Sometimes we create the mistake through pressure. Sooner or later, there will be a witness that sees a license plate number, or we'll get an informant. These are tedious, time-consuming investigations. Then there's a break."[93] The mistakes had not yet come.

Meanwhile, the cadre faced the same problem as others underground: how to sustain themselves. Betty Ann Duke and Linda Evans had gotten some support when they were in Austin from LSD manufacturers, but now the underground cadre had rules and "principles that will govern you."[94] Given these rules, with few members able to work, and paltry assistance from above ground, supporting themselves proved daunting.[95] "Expropriations" became necessary. The government would claim that the group's members would "plot to support their operations, in part, through theft and armed robbery . . . conduct studies and surveillances at banks, stores and other areas which were potential robbery targets."[96]

There was only one robbery that the government ever tried to prove. It took place in the small central Connecticut town of Cromwell. Despite Alan's admonition about nonviolence toward civilians, a robbery required guns as a threat. And with guns, something could always go wrong. Alan and Tim Blunk, the former Hampshire College student and May 19th member who was part of the cadre, appeared in brown suits, with wigs and glued-on mustaches. They entered the small town's Stop and Shop grocery store pharmacy at 3:30 p.m. on September 2, 1984, and asked for the manager. They had fake credentials that identified them as federal Drug Enforcement Administration (DEA) agents with false names (Alan was DEA Agent Fusco and Blunk was DEA Agent Cleary) and a fake warrant Laura Whitehorn had created that purported to show that a U.S. magistrate in nearby Hartford gave the agents permission to investigate violations of 21 USC 841 (A) 1 and 21 USC 846 dealing with a conspiracy to distribute drugs. Alan and his comrades had done their homework. The papers looked real, and Whitehorn was a talented artist and printer.

With the fake badges and credentials they entered the pharmacy area of the store. Even though it was September, they kept their gloves on so as not to leave fingerprints. They also carried loaded guns; the one Alan had in his briefcase had a silencer. According to the local police, once they convinced Donald Corrigan, the assistant store manager, to take them into what was known as the "cash room," they "handcuffed, bound and gagged [him] with surgical tape and held him with weapons drawn. They then departed with approximately 30,000 U.S. dollars." They drove away separately, the police claimed, in a stolen "white Volvo and a bright red Datsun 280Z."[97] Later reports noted they only got $21,480, but they also told Corrigan they would "blow a hole in him" with the gun Tim Blunk had, and even "a bigger one," Alan purportedly said, with the gun that had the silencer, which he had taken out of the briefcase.[98]

While the robbery was nominally a success, Alan had broken one of the cadre's rules. The night before he apparently showed the fake search warrant to one of his comrades, picking it up with his bare hands. In his anxiety, he accidently left it behind at the Stop and Shop. It would provide his fingerprints to the authorities, and prove useful later to building a criminal case.[99] No one in the cadre expected that Alan would be this slipshod. It was the kind of error he would excoriate others for making, and the kind the FBI had been waiting for.[100]

MISTAKES, AND MORE MISTAKES

Bomb-making was dangerous business. The underground cadre knew this from their comrades' experiences in the 1970s, when explosions sometimes claimed the bomb-makers themselves, not to mention what happened to William Morales. Alan and his comrades never made clear where they put together the bombs they used, but they were very careful to make sure nothing explosive was stored in their apartments.[101] Nevertheless, the bombing equipment they stole, borrowed from others, or bought had to be stored, could become unstable as it aged, and had to be moved on occasion, as when they shared it with other clandestine groups.

The complexity of transporting matériel inevitably led to small mistakes and broken rules, which, combined with their unwillingness to kill, ultimately led to their captures. In November 1984, just after Thanksgiving, Susan Rosenberg and Tim Blunk were driving an Oldsmobile down the New Jersey Turnpike, pulling a 20-foot U-Haul filled with fourteen guns, fake identifications cards, and 650 pounds of bombing matériel for other clandestine groups. They were headed to a self-storage facility in Cherry Hill, just across the Delaware River from Philadelphia. The storage shed had been rented under a false name and actual address Rosenberg later claimed she "had found in a wallet left mistakenly in a phone booth," although the wallet's owner told the police it had been stolen.[102] If Rosenberg had just used the name and had a false phone number and address added to a faked license there would not have been a problem. Because of some mix-ups at the storage facility, the real license owner as the supposed renter of record had been contacted at her listed address. She explained the license theft, and the police then were notified. When Rosenberg and Blunk arrived, the storage manager called the police, and a lone officer arrived thinking he was just looking at individuals with stolen identifications. While Blunk tried to cover the matériel that had already been moved into the shed, the officer noticed that Blunk and Rosenberg were wearing sunglasses and cheap wigs.[103]

What happened next changed everything that followed. As Rosenberg tells the story, she asked the officer to allow her to go back to the car to get her identification. She obviously did not tell him there were guns in bags on the front seats. She could have shot the officer, or she might have tried to divert his attention so that Tim Blunk could have escaped. Instead, she did not pick up a weapon and came back to the shed. What they had, and were doing, became obvious quickly, especially after a backup officer arrived. When he lit a cigarette, Rosenberg said, "Put that cigarette out or we'll all blow up."[104] By then some of the blasting equipment was visible.

The police, however, claimed in their story the officer never let her go back to the car because, as the Cherry Hill police chief told reporters, "I would suspect that she was trying to get a gun . . . but the alertness of the officer prevented it."[105] More police backup arrived, and Blunk and Rosenberg were thrown on the ground, beaten, and spat on, she recollected, and then placed under arrest. In the shed and U-Haul, the police would find an Uzi semiautomatic rifle, a sawed-off shotgun, more guns and ammunition, the bombing supplies, and boxes of more than "10,000 false Social Security cards and identification cards for several government agencies, including the FBI and the New Jersey State Police."[106] With Rosenberg loaded into a squad car, the officer told reporters he had thanked her for not shooting him. "I guess this is your lucky day," she is purported to have replied.[107]

It would take some time to identify Blunk and Rosenberg, since they refused to give their names, and the police confused at least Blunk with other left bombers.[108] Their prints had to be flown to Washington, D.C., and back (it took fourteen hours). Then the state troopers, FBI agents, and other government officials along with the local police knew who they had. As Rosenberg recalled in her memoir, an FBI agent referred to her as "a Terrorist Kike."[109]

By the next day, Rosenberg's and Blunk's capture was in the local and national news. The others in the underground cadre were now vulnerable as the government tracked the rented U-Haul back to New Haven and Blunk's false name, and the Oldsmobile they had been driving to an address. A mechanic who had worked on their cars recognized Marilyn Buck's photograph.[110] Other pictures were shown around in apartments in New Haven and Hamden. The store manager who had been robbed in Cromwell recognized Alan and Tim Blunk from newspaper photos.

The underground cadre had to act quickly. On Saturday night, right after the New Jersey bust, Linda Evans went to her work print shop, then closed, to make false Puerto Rican driver's licenses as they planned to leave the mainland. In her rush, she left the negatives in the camera. The FBI knew she was a printer and canvassed all the New Haven print shops with her photo. Finding her workplace and the negatives, the FBI kept watch over the shop.

As the police and FBI waited for another mistake, Blunk's and Rosenberg's trial happened quickly, between April and May 1985. The government's precautions mirrored those in the other Brink's cases: defendants in forty pounds of chains, helicopters, a closed tunnel between New York City (where they were imprisoned) and the Newark federal courthouse, and motorcades with a massive show of force of police and marshals with high-powered rifles. As a U.S. marshal told the press, "I think the Chesimard [Assata Shakur] escape and the Nyack situation certainly would raise eyebrows in terms of security."[111] Rosenberg and Blunk tried to put on a political defense "to continue to struggle against U.S. imperialism," but it did not prove successful.[112] They were convicted of "conspiracy to possess unregistered firearms, explosives, and false identification documents," among other offenses.[113]

The sentences were the harshest ever for this kind of crime: fifty-eight years. Rosenberg, still trying to be a revolutionary, told her supporters before her presentencing statement to the court, "We were busted because we vacillated on our politics. . . . We failed. Our own principles were not strong enough to fight to win."[114] The police took this to mean she should have shot them. The only good news for Rosenberg in all of this was that while Rudy Giuliani, then the federal attorney in New York City, had indicted her for her purported roles in Brink's and Assata Shakur's escape, he never prosecuted her. Facing the expense and difficulties of another high-profile trial and questionable witnesses, he believed the fifty-eight-year sentence in this New Jersey case would keep her behind bars long enough.[115] Rosenberg and her attorney thought this meant he did not have enough evidence to try her and would have lost.[116]

The cadre suffered its next setback thanks to a guitar. Evans had been in a band before she went underground and had hauled a twelve-string with her from Austin and through all the many other moves. It was a small link to the person she had been, her "artistic outlet" to the woman she knew she was.[117] The guitar's neck had bowed, and Evans had been saving up her money to pay for the repair. She left it in a New Haven guitar repair store, telling them to call her workplace when it was fixed. After Rosenberg and Blunk were busted, Evans called the guitar store to say she would pick it up another time, and not to call her work. Trying to be really careful, the group moved to Baltimore and managed only one more bombing, of the New York Police Patrolman's Benevolent Association building in February. The police still could not find them. Mostly they were looking for Alan and Marilyn Buck. They really had very little idea who anyone else was in the group, or even how big it might be.

Between the end of the Rosenberg/Blunk trial and their sentencing, Linda Evans thought it might finally be safe to go get her guitar. The group understood her need for this connection to her basic humanity and sense of self, and agreed.[118] Evans called the store up and promised to come get it, and told them not to call her old workplace. But that was the number on the repair ticket. So the store called the New Haven print shop anyway to tell her it was ready. When the FBI were told about the call, they put a "trap and trace" on the guitar store's phone, hoping to catch Evans when she called. She made that call on May 9, about ten days before Rosenberg and Blunk were sentenced, from a pay phone near the print shop in Baltimore where she now worked. The FBI staked out the phone booth in Baltimore and identified a nearby print shop. Then they waited. That evening, Evans returned to the phone booth, made a call, and was picked up a few minutes later by a white male in a Toyota. It was Alan.

Alan drove Evans back to an apartment block called the Alameda in primarily black northeast Baltimore and parked the car. Because there were 200 apartments in this complex, the FBI could not determine which one Evans went into. They were really hoping to nab Marilyn Buck as well. They waited until the next day while they traced apartments with newly started electric and gas bills, until they found one that matched one of the aliases they thought Buck had used in Connecticut. Believing they had identified the group's apartment, the FBI sought a search warrant. Meanwhile, they kept watching the car.

It was a matter of time. On May 10, Linda Evans and Marilyn Buck emerged from the apartments, picked up the Toyota, made a few stops and started driving toward New York City. They were being tailed, although neither of them noticed it at first. They were on their way to Westchester County, just north of New York, to case a shopping mall for a possible robbery and to go pick up Evans's guitar in New Haven. They spent the night in a motel, while the FBI put a bug in their car. Buck and Evans became suspicious they might be tailed, took several evasive actions, then parked the car in Dobbs Ferry and went for coffee in a diner, to celebrate Evans's birthday.

They were nabbed as they went out to get their car. They both had guns in their handbags, but never got a chance to pull them out. "They practically strip-searched us in the parking lot," Evans recalled. "It was humiliating, but it all was humiliating." When they got to the FBI building in New York, the agent greeting them said to Evans, "Happy Birthday." "Fuck you," she replied.[119]

What they did not know until they got to the FBI offices was that Laura Whitehorn had been arrested that same day in Baltimore. Once Evans and Buck were caught, the FBI made a decision not to wait for a search warrant. Declaring "exigent circumstances," they banged on the apartment door in Baltimore and announced they had an arrest warrant for Alan Berkman. They could hear someone inside tearing up what sounded like paper. Fearful, they claimed, that, as with Morales in 1978 and Weather in 1970, there were bombs in the apartment, they broke in. The only person there was Laura Whitehorn, whom the FBI did not know or expect to find.

The agents chained Whitehorn to a chair as they did what in her case would later be determined an illegal search. While waiting for the warrant to arrive, they rummaged through the apartment and a basement storage area to discover an Uzi submachine gun hidden in a box in a closet with loaded bullet magazines nearby, as well as timing devices, electrical tape, batteries, solder-ing tools, a laminating machine, wigs, military uniforms and police department patches, and lots of documents about possible surveillance, potential places to bomb, and internal memorandums. The inventory of everything they confis-cated would be seventeen pages long. Whitehorn was immediately arrested and charged with assaulting an agent, which she claimed she never did and which seems unlikely given that she stands around five feet tall.[120] Unlike in other cases, she was not beaten or worse, but the FBI would keep her in preventive detention for months that would turn into years.[121]

Following another lead to the false names they had recovered in the Balti-more apartment, the FBI found that Betty Ann Duke had rented a van in Baltimore and was returning it to the Philadelphia area. When she got to the Philadelphia van rental office, a white man in a Nissan picked her up. It was Alan again. He recalled being very nervous as Duke was running late and they were stuck in Philadelphia rush-hour traffic. They were both "numbed and ex-hausted" from all the busts of their friends. While they worried that each car behind them might be a tail, in the end they pulled into a restaurant for food and coffee on their way to the Pocono Mountains in northeast Pennsylvania.[122] They hoped it was only paranoia that made them believe they were not alone.

When they pulled out again, they realized they were being followed. Alan made a few more turns off the main highway, but cars were behind them. He remembered reasoning, "My only other choice would be to try to speed away down the little country road, abandon the car, and try to outrun the agents and their guns. Although we also had guns, neither of us had a death wish or the desire to use them."[123] Hoping his instincts were wrong, Alan made a few extra turns, then drove into a school parking lot and stopped. Three cars pulled right behind them. The FBI had been watching since Philadelphia and tailed the car into suburban Bucks County.

The agents quickly had guns at every window and were barking orders. Betty Ann Duke got out of the car quickly. Alan could not get his seatbelt off in time to follow orders to get out with his hands up. As Alan recalled it, the FBI man "reached across my chest and groped around until he found the latch of the seatbelt. He grabbed me by the hair and went to pull me out of the car. My wig came off in his hand. The rest was handcuffs, being frisked down, being shoved into their car."[124] All he could see from the ground was what seemed like a score of agents, "armed with automatic rifles & bullet proof vests, and their fingers were on the triggers & the safeties were off."[125]

Relieved "they didn't blow us to kingdom come," he realized his life as a revolutionary in the underground was over.[126] He had been a small part of the resistance to American power, but he had not built a mass movement that would overcome it.

LIFE AND NEAR DEATH IN THE AMERICAN GULAG

PREVIEW

THE GOVERNMENT STRIKES BACK

Memo from Ronald H. Levine, assistant United States attorney, Eastern District of Pennsylvania

March 30, 1987

To William Mogulescu, Esquire, New York

RE: United States v. Alan Berkman, Criminal Number 85-00222

Dear Mr. Mogulescu:

The government is investigating the following matters:

(1) the flight and whereabouts of Elizabeth Duke;

(2) the flight and whereabouts of Donna Borup;

(3) the 12/28/82 RFG bombing of the Staten Island Federal Building;

(4) the 4/26/83 ARU bombing of Fort Lesley McNair;

(5) the 8/17/83 ARU bombing of the Washington Navy Yard computer complex;

(6) the 11/7/83 ARU bombing of U.S. Capitol;

(7) the 4/5/84 RGR bombing of the Israeli Aircraft Industry office;

(8) the 4/20/84 RGR bombing of the Washington Navy Yard Officers Club;

(9) the 11/26/84 RGR bombing of the South African consulate;

(10) the 2/23/85 RGR bombing of the Police Benevolent Association;

(11) the 11/26/84 armed robbery of a Stop and Shop in Cromwell, Connecticut and the roles of Buck, Blunk and others;

(12) the whereabouts of explosives and arms including, but not limited to, still missing Hercules Unigel dynamite with date/shift code 12/15/79 J1;

(13) the locations and activities of Buck, Evans, Whitehorn,

Rosenberg, Blunk, Borup, Duke, Shakur, Powers and others during the period 1/1/81 to the present.

(14) the locations and identities of the person(s) who stored dynamite in California, of the same date/shift code as that in this case and which was discovered in Santa Fe Springs in 8/86;

(15) the purchase of Tovex under the false identity "Melvin Kessler"; and

(16) the 10/81 Nyack-Brink's robbery during which three persons were murdered.

This letter reiterates the government's long standing request to Alan Berkman that he cooperate fully and truthfully in the government's investigations of these and other matters.

Please let me know by April 15, 1987, whether Alan Berkman is willing to cooperate fully and truthfully. You should inform Alan Berkman that should he decline to cooperate, the government will apprise the court of that fact at the time of sentencing. . . .

From Alan Berkman's "Brother Doc" on Prison Medical Care

Fear transformed itself into a scream: "Help! Help me!"

The guards' desk was right outside my room. I could hear their radio playing the late night Howard University jazz station. If I could hear them they should be able to hear me.

"Help me, goddamn it! Help me!"

Nothing. Was I so weak that my voice only sounded to me?

"Please help me! Help!" I heard one of the guards comment to the other about the "fucking yelling." The bastards could hear me after all!

"Please! I'm dying! I'm really dying!"

Nothing. Nothing. Absolute nothing. No call button — prisoners don't get call buttons. They get guards who didn't give a shit.

The side rails were up on the bed, so I couldn't get out of the bed even if I had the strength to move myself to the edge. I had to take a minute to figure this out; the act of yelling had left me exhausted.

10

BECOMING BROTHER DOC

The agents with itchy trigger fingers had roughed Alan up when he was pulled from the car and whisked into the FBI office at the Philadelphia federal courthouse in May 1985. He spent the first few hours in custody shackled to a chair, then was processed separately from Betty Ann Duke and offered some sort of trade-off of reduced imprisonment for his cooperation. "Up yours," he remembered thinking.[1] As he was being carted off to jail several hours later, an FBI man greeted him carrying a short-barreled shotgun that had been impounded from the car that Alan had been driving. "What are you planning to do with this, Berkman?" he recalled the agent asking. "I should put this barrel in your ear and squeeze the fucking trigger."[2]

That question went to the heart of Alan's dilemma as a revolutionary who abhorred killing. "I know I didn't really intend to use it," Alan wrote a decade and a half later.[3] The agent also found a Walther PPK .380 caliber pistol with ammunition in its chambers in the car. Presumably the ease of obtaining the Walther with its slim design, ability to be concealed and hold a silencer, and link in popular culture to its most famous owner — James Bond — fueled Alan's imagination when he carried it.[4] To be ready to use it, even if he never did and believed he never would, was part of his bloodless revolutionary stance. Besides the Walther and the shotgun there was a 9 mm Beretta pistol with a silencer; and Duke had a loaded 9 mm Browning automatic pistol in her handbag too.[5] Every one of his white comrades who had been arrested had also been armed or had guns nearby, and had not used them even if they were able. Only Marilyn Buck had pulled a trigger, by accident, and she was her own victim. Even though a number of Alan's white comrades had been roughed up, none was tortured the ways the BLA and FALN men had been.[6]

The FBI agents had every reason to believe that Alan and his comrades were ready to kill. They had allied themselves with black and Puerto Rican revolutionaries who had killed civilians and police — sometimes offensively rather than in self-defense, and sometimes not on trumped-up charges — and that was enough. They were known for freeing their comrades from prison. FBI agents would continually point to the bombs in storage and the guns they carried and link them, not only to the Brink's case in 1981 and then their bombings, but also to the FALN's bombs at Fraunces Tavern in 1975, the BLA killings of police and armed guards over the decades, and other radical actions.[7]

Alan's revolutionary position may have meant only destroying property and never hurting anyone, but the weaponry forced government authorities to prepare for nothing less than a blazing battle. Alan wrote a letter to his high school drama teacher, joking that the FBI agents had been "reading too many 'spy v spy' stories" from *Mad Magazine,* or believed themselves to be television actor Efrem Zimbalist Jr., the decade-long star of *The FBI.*[8] Alan was not ready to acknowledge that the FBI's precautions might be justified.

Guns were just the beginning. In the car they had been in, the FBI also found blank identification forms, cash, and a set of keys. As agents discovered, these unlocked a small garage Duke had rented in a suburban backyard in nearby Doylestown, Pennsylvania. Inside, the FBI found a gold mine for building the government's case: more guns, dynamite in various states of decay, ammunition, pistol powder, bulletproof vests, fake identifications by the hundreds, document-making equipment, thousands of dollars in cash, and pamphlets and books on how to make bombs and avoid surveillance. The FBI's inventory ran to seventy-seven items on the bombs and other weaponry and ninety-seven items on the written materials. Their find included a newspaper clipping called "How to Counterfeit Credit Cards and Get Away with It," the Army's technical manual *Unconventional Warfare Devices and Techniques: Incendiaries,* handwritten instructions on the use of firearms and ammunition, and *The Poor Man's James Bond,* by right-wing survivalist Kurt Saxon. There were also internal memos and self-criticisms about individual actions and possible future bombings or "expropriations."[9]

The federal authorities still had to build a criminal case. There was no evidence that Alan had ever been in the truck Duke used to move the matériel or in the garage. Except for the stolen dynamite and the lack of a permit to store it, much of the matériel captured was legal to own. Even the books and guides were available in bookstores, newspapers, and libraries. It is not illegal to own weapons, lots of them, an argument Alan would make later in one of his court cases. It was what was actually done with them, or might have been done, that became the subject of the legal proceedings. More difficult to explain would be the typewritten discussions of violence and the self-criticisms of the comrades' mistakes.[10]

Alan expected that the government would soon label him a terrorist, and that he would be facing a lifetime in prison. Given the charges and the fact that he had already proved himself a flight risk, there was no question of bail. He was held in preventive detention, a form of carceral control pretrial that began to be more widely used in the 1970s.[11] Arraigned on May 27, 1985, Alan announced, "I am not guilty of any crimes. I'm just trying to stop them."[12] And he made his first phone call to Susan Tipograph, the political lawyer who had worked some of the Brink's cases. "Alan," she recalled, "had no intention of being a martyr."[13]

Alan and Duke coordinated their public statements when the FBI began referring to them as terrorists. They declared, "Nothing could be further from the truth. We have never and would never consciously endanger an innocent civilian." They condemned racism and oppression and cited the City of Philadelphia's bombing and indiscriminate killing two weeks earlier of the black activists and children in the MOVE compound that destroyed a whole city block. "Many of us—many more—will have to be willing to fight—and perhaps die—to end this corrupt system and clear the way for a new one. We'll fight any way we can and it will always be on the side of the people—never against them."[14] In 1985, then, Alan was writing about fighting and dying, hinting at killing those who were not assumed to be "innocent civilians." The revolutionary posture was there at least in writing, even if he knew he was not willing to shoot or blow up anyone.

Duke's next moves made things even more difficult for Alan, even though he must have understood them. Because she had less of a record, she was awarded bail in July. The court ordered her to stay with her two sisters in San Antonio, Texas, who put their houses up to secure her return to Philadelphia for trial. The FBI continued to follow her, furious that she had been let out of custody. In response, she would take their pictures, as one agent complained.[15] A former university instructor in English, mother of two, fluent in Spanish, and a longtime political activist, especially with Linda Evans in the John Brown Anti-Klan Committee and May 19th, she was well known in Austin's political circles. When she returned to the Philadelphia area in October 1985 she was in the custody of her lawyer.[16]

Not for long. For whatever reasons, she bolted. The government responded by jailing her lawyer, but to no avail. Despite the FBI's wanted posters and its continued searches for her, she has still not been found, decades later.[17] Alan discovered that many of his old friends at the time were visited by the FBI under the "ruse" of the search for her. Alan thought this was "a façade to give some semblance of legitimacy. And the desired side effect is to intimidate people and make them think twice before having anything to do with me."[18]

The authorities became even more determined to keep Alan under the most stringent control. The government prosecutor told the media, offering no evidence, that authorities had "some indication she [Betty Ann Duke] was going to try and get him out, but nothing happened." The government's security arrangements, the prosecutor would claim, had prevented this from occurring.[19] Alan had no knowledge that Duke had ever tried this.

Right after his capture, Alan was placed in the Philadelphia lockup, and then moved to the century-old Holmesburg prison, a Quaker-inspired penitentiary that resembled a nineteenth-century dungeon.[20] In the entrance to the cell was a narrow door that forced Alan to "crouch down to get in," with no windows and "high, arched ceilings" like a "catacomb." The space was broken up only by "a metal basin, toilet without a seat, and cot." Its meaning was clear to him as a "zoo seen from the inside."[21] There was also the company of "a hellish infestation of roaches and two-inch long water bugs." Anyone who had lived in New York City had lived with roaches, mostly in their sink. "But now," he noted, "I'm living in the sink," although this one also had bloodstains on the floor from its previous occupant's being "stomped" by the guards, his cell neighbors told him.[22]

For the first few months he was isolated out of the "general population" into solitary in a twenty-three-hour-a-day lockdown and allowed only three phone calls a month. He worried continually that his isolation was a setup to leave him vulnerable to attack by prisoners egged on by the corrections officers (COs) or the guards themselves. Sleep eluded him.[23]

What struck him first was the controlled chaos that besieged all his senses: the sounds of the nearby prisoners, the commands of the COs, the continual efforts to remind him of his powerlessness, and the absolute filth and miasma everywhere. The noise seemed tremendous: inmates yelling for and at the COs, radios and TVs blaring, conversations screamed across the tiers to create some kind of human contact that went on and on. "[The sounds] start at 5 a.m. most mornings," he wrote, "when people who are going to court are awakened, and never stops until about midnight."[24]

Then there were the smells. All the carbohydrates in the food fouled the skin of his fellow prisoners. The fear and anger in their perspiration added to the odor of the mold that oozed off the prison walls, and the human waste that bubbled up from the open toilets. Every time he was moved there were handcuffs, leg irons, and a chain that connected them all and made four-point restraints. Strip searches, and the tossing of his tiny cell for contraband, were frequent. Surrounded by the sounds and presence of others, he was very alone. He was no longer a person with a name. He had become to the guards No. 85-07644.

To survive, Alan tried to make connections and to mend bridges from his past. "Communication with old friends is one of the few redeeming features of this situation," he mused.[25] Those he had been afraid to contact during the underground years for their safety, and his, could now come back into his life.

He wrote to his parents less than week after he was caught for the first time in years, assuring them that he was fine if a little banged up from the arrest, upset that they saw him as a "common criminal." He wanted them to know what he had really done, and what the government would say. "I know one of the most upsetting things must be the whole variety of charges I'm accused of," he acknowledged to them. "Some of them are true, some aren't. You should just know that I've never hurt anybody & have never compromised my own principles."[26] Half-kidding in another letter to them, he wrote, "Other than some frustration and boredom, I'm feeling well. I was thinking that one of the few advantages of being in isolation is it's hard to catch a cold from anyone else."[27] Mostly he was fearful his parents would say something to Sarah to make her think differently about him and his actions. He wanted her protected from the government views of what he had done.

He was seen as extremely dangerous. The guards told him he was the highest security-risk prisoner in Holmesburg in its 100-year history.[28] They took extra precautions and made threats while watching him, reminding him they had the power by singing "America the Beautiful" and the Vietnam War support song "The Ballad of the Green Berets" when they walked past his cell. "The humor is sophomoric," he wrote, "but the implications are anything but funny."[29]

Some of the prisoners, especially those who were Black Muslims, understood what he was supposed to have done; others thought with all the security he must just be some high-ranking mobster. Alan discovered they were passing around both a *Philadelphia Inquirer* story that linked him to Brink's and a December 1984 *Reader's Digest* that included a photo of him as part of the "Terror Network, USA," which included Mutulu Shakur and Cheri Dalton (Nehanda Abiodun) from the BLA.[30] His supposed dangerousness gave him street cred. When he was finally out of solitary months later, he used this to connect with others. A fellow prisoner called him "Brother Doc" when introducing Alan to other Black Muslims.[31] The name would stick.

After two and a half years of living with a small number of like-minded comrades, almost all of whom were women, he now had to create relationships under the most difficult of circumstances with male prisoners and guards. He had to search carefully for those who shared at least some of his worldview and admired his actions, without falling into the danger that he was talking to a snitch sent in to trap him. This was not just paranoia: sometimes his cell mates or cell neighbors would admit that the guards had set them up to spy on him.[32] He ached for company and understanding but knew he had to rely mostly on himself and friends and family outside.[33]

Part of what made Alan's survival at Holmesburg possible was his growing friendship with Mumia Abu-Jamal, the brilliant, eloquent, and deep-voiced black activist journalist then on death row for the supposed murder of a police officer. Mumia had not yet become the most nationally and internationally recognized U.S. political prisoner, known by his first name.[34] In 1985, he was another black convict who had been mostly forgotten outside his own community. Mumia recognized something in Alan. "What struck me was the anger seething within him, boiling in his eyes," Mumia recalled. "He detested how he was treated, of course, and he detested how the men around him were treated by thuggish guards, and the prison system generally. . . . When he was in his cell, however, and among guys he considered friends or comrades, his eyes softened, widened; his face loosened, and his smile warmed like sunrise. Here, he was curious, sensitive, attentive and open."[35]

Alan, in turn, had found a comrade on the deepest and most profound level. Writing to his friend Stephen Wangh, Alan told him about "this very wonderful man affiliated with MOVE who is facing execution. . . . He has a beautiful spirit that shines in his face, and he has the longest dreadlocks I've ever seen . . . I could get a vision of him bald, strapped to the electric chair. Horrifying. . . . It haunts me."[36] Mumia, in turn, watched as "2 big guys from West Philly" kept Alan from using the phones because he wouldn't pay them. Mumia intervened, explaining who Alan was to them, and what he had done. Access to the phones ceased to be a problem.

The guards had been circulating the story that Alan was really part of a "racist skin-head group." Once Alan's true story got around, Alan got the respect he needed, and Mumia another comrade.[37] It was Alan who made others in his outside support groups aware of Mumia's case, and made sure it was discussed in their pronouncements. This work then began the international campaign that at least eventually got Mumia off death row. And it made more visible the overuse of imprisonment against black militancy and the ways charges were concocted.[38]

With the exception of Mumia and a few other prisoners, however, Alan's loneliness was acute. Comforted by the letters he received from comrades and old friends, he was still trying to find a way to put his own predicament in context. His dreams and thoughts filled with warmth and love for Barbara, Sarah, and for Dana, with whom he had renewed contact.[39] Regarding Dana, he admitted to his friend Bruce Taub, "After my arrest, we began to write & then see each other, & it was pretty clear from the outset that some of the same feelings were/are there."[40] He made phone calls, and Sarah and Barbara could make regular visits.[41]

Women mattered to him. Marilyn Buck's stoicism impressed him, as it had when they were underground, and he wrote her about what he had learned about "her clarity and courage at her arraignment." A bit less romantic, she wrote him back to say that she appreciated his support "but that she had always just seen it as an ability to endure." Over and over he thought about the other revolutionaries he knew or read about, and the black and Latina women he had cared for. It was his knowledge of women's strength in the face of powerlessness that he turned to, the strength, he wrote, "to endure, not in a passive sense but to persist in struggle no matter what happens."[42]

THE LEGAL AND MEDICAL ROUND 1:
THE GOVERNMENT BY TECHNICAL KNOCKOUT

Despite his supposed dangerousness, Alan's fears he would become a schlemiel began to come true one month after his imprisonment when he suffered, of all indignities, a sports injury.[43] During an exercise hour, Alan was playing basketball alone in the cement prison yard. As he was taking a jump shot, in his imagination as basketball star Dr. J, he both "heard and felt a pop in my left ankle. Intense pain shot up my leg and I came down hard on my knees."[44] Alan had what orthopedists call a "male weekend warrior" injury.

He began his self-diagnosis immediately and begged the guard to look at the blood pooling under his skin. His Achilles tendon had torn and settled in around his ankle. Accompanied and half-dragged by four guards to the infirmary, he was at least spared the leg irons. The prison doctor knew enough to suggest an orthopedist. A caravan of U.S. marshals, hurtling down the highway at reckless speed and joined by the flashing lights on the top of state trooper cars, delivered Alan to the door of a cleared-out emergency room in a suburban hospital. It took "30 cops of all different flavors," Alan recalled, to make this possible. With the marshals wielding submachine guns and surrounding him, he was taken into an examining room. After the x-ray, the nervous young doctor taking care of him declared it merely a muscle pull. Alan was incredulous. He was given an ace bandage, aspirin, and a cane, and sent back to Holmesburg.[45]

He thought he might still be able to get the appropriate medical care; this proved a false expectation. It would take more time, and the efforts of his public defender, before the diagnosis would be made correctly by a prison orthopedist. Alan awaited what would now require surgery for a tendon graft and weeks in a hard cast. On the day in early July when he was supposed to be taken for the surgery, however, gun-wielding marshals and troopers hauled him off again. Duke had fled her bail that day, and the government was taking no chances with Alan.

"Who the fuck are you?" his fellow prisoners asked, incredulous, as he was loaded into a prison van for transport.[46] After a three-hour ride he arrived at a maximum-security federal prison in Lewisburg in central Pennsylvania.[47] Since he had been moved without notice, at that point no one except state authorities knew where he was or how to reach him.[48] He had vanished.

Instead of the required surgery, Alan was taken to lockdown in a psychiatric observation cell with white gleaming walls that engendered sensory deprivation. In the prison infirmary finally later, he received only a cast for his leg. "I asked [the young and inexperienced doctor] if he thought he was violating medical ethics by going along with second-rate treatment, but he shrugged and kept applying the plaster of Paris." He went back to his cell with a cast and crutches.

He was kept under tight control. Alan presumed the prison authorities refused to let him get the surgery because they were too afraid that his comrades might spring him if he were sent to a real hospital, even with armed guards. He had limited showers, food only when the guards deemed it appropriate, few phone calls, and a real sense that there were "no rights, only privileges." He understood that this was like living "under a dictatorship or a colonial power." Under the latter situation, he mused, when there was not direct violence, there was always "the threat [of violence] if the gratitude is insufficient or if the oppressed begin to demand rather than request. It's just more blatant in prison, the veneer very thin or not there at all."[49]

He accepted, however, that the isolation might at least give him time to think. "I feel that I am making a transition from the intense involvement with others and the world," he wrote to Stephen Waugh, ". . . to a somewhat undetermined future but one which will undoubtedly involve a number of years in a maximum security prison. Perhaps my own existential leanings make me feel quite comfortable (if a bit lonely) with solitude."[50] He began to think of prison as his equivalent of time in the military: "The impersonality, the atmosphere of violence, the all-male dynamics, the involuntary mingling of people who would never have met in the normal course of events."[51]

He had made a connection at Holmesburg that started the process to get him moved back there again. Joaquin Foy, a Black Muslim with a conspiratorial view of the world, had been next to Alan there. When Alan was moved without notice to Lewisburg the day Betty Ann Duke escaped, Foy held his legal papers and personal items for him and refused to give them up till the guard shift captain signed a document about who had them. It was Foy who called the FBI and asked for the agent on Alan's case, when he could not remember Barbara's phone number, to make sure they knew where Alan now was.[52] Alan's lawyer finally found him and called his judge.[53]

Alan at least won the judge lottery when his case landed in front of Louis H. Pollak. A liberal federal judge appointed by President Jimmy Carter, Pollak had been a civil rights attorney and the dean of Yale's Law School.[54] He understood Alan's principles, if not his tactics, and his concern for Alan's humanity would prove crucial to his survival. So just as suddenly as Alan had been moved, Judge Pollak intervened with the Bureau of Prisons and ordered him back two weeks later to Holmesburg.

It was like coming home. Alan's friend Foy had saved his toiletries and mirror, as well as kept track of his legal papers, and filled him on what he had missed. Other prisoners welcomed him, and wanted to hear the stories of what a federal prison was like. The dreariness of prison life soon resumed: "Meals, exercise, yard, writing letters, hanging out."[55] At least in Holmesburg he was getting to know people and had begun to figure out how things got done: the phone calls, the commissary, and the rules and regulations. The routine was only punctuated by the changes in prisoners in his area, and the frequent violence over slights, racial differences, misunderstandings, supplies from the commissary, or contraband that relieved the boredom and reflected the oppression of the everyday. On September 9, his fortieth birthday, he wrote his parents that his friends had given him a birthday "cake" made of "a sugar doughnut, the candles were matches, and the refreshments were a can of soda, the presents were snacks of candy, etc. that they sell in commissary."[56]

Years in the underground notwithstanding, Alan's upbringing and education had not given him all the skills he would need to survive inside. He found himself in awe of the ingenuity of the prisoners who figured out how to make a "stinger" to heat water for coffee, created conspiracies to explain why they had been caught and sentenced, imagined themselves buying expensive clothes out of the Gucci catalogs they passed around, and were continually discussing their sexual desires and supposed experiences. They taught him how to pace his day, get his exercise, and not succumb totally to boredom and the exhaustion of mindless television. He was warned about violence and given advice about always carrying a pen to stab anyone who attacked.[57] He made a decision not to use his card-shark skills, honed in medical school, so as not to give prisoners any reason to be angry with him.[58] The other prisoners taught him how to endure, and numbers of them admired what they thought he had done.

There was something else, however, that was even less routine than a birthday doughnut. While still hobbling around on his crutches because of the Achilles tendon, Alan noticed a lump under his right armpit. He hoped the crutch was the problem. Even when he gave up the right crutch to test this hypothesis, and just leaned on the left one, the lump persisted. Alan had reason to worry: he was a doctor who knew too much, and his Uncle Lou had developed Hodgkin's lymphoma in his thirties, a cancer that manifests at first as a swollen lymph node, often in the armpit, neck, or groin. Lou survived the Hodgkin's but developed other lymphomas and died from the cancers at fifty-seven in 1981. Alan knew what might be in store.[59]

Alan's struggles with the prison authorities took on a life-threatening urgency. He asked for a medical workup on the lump but was told he was "faking to attempt escape en route to the hospital."[60] In early October, while waiting to see if the lump would recede or its rubbery consistency resolve, Alan was suddenly moved again: this time to the Chester County jail, an hour outside of Philadelphia. As the guards came for him, he yelled to Foy to call Barbara and his lawyer. At least he felt supported when Foy yelled back, "Doc, where they taking you man? What kind of shit is this? What the fuck they taking you for? I can see some assholes in suits, man. Hang tough, Brother Doc. Assholes! You better not fuck with him. I'll kill you if you fuck with him."[61] The ride down the Pennsylvania country roads in early autumn past formal gardens and Saturday football games reminded Alan of what he had taken for granted, but also the life he might lose at any moment should the marshals decide he had really tried to make a move, or they would say he made a move.[62]

The lump truly worried him. He knew it had grown but that he did not have the "fevers, sweats and or weight loss" usually associated with a cancer. Like any patient, he tried to use magical thinking to wish it away, but as a doctor given to scientific thinking he knew what it might be. During the routine medical in-take exam in Chester County jail, he wrote about his concern in capital letters on the form and mentioned it to the physician. Medical care in the jail had been privatized and the older, semiretired doctor who now examined him had no idea how to treat him correctly. As Alan would remember with characteristic sarcasm, the doctors in the prison system were often "the desperate, the dumb and despicable."[63] When this in-take physician had him raise his arm, his pectoral muscles hid the node. Alan knew this and wanted to scream. Instead, he said politely, "Sir, you know I'm a doctor. As a professional courtesy, would you let me take your hand and show you where I feel the enlarged node?" Accepting their shared privilege, Alan guided the doctor's fingers over the lump. "'My goodness,' the physician said, 'this is enlarged.'"[64]

It would be another two weeks before he finally was allowed to see a surgeon who knew how to do a proper exam and agreed that he needed a biopsy. As he awaited this possibility, he felt the "sorrow and sadness seep from the concrete" that surrounded him and everyone else entombed with him.[65] Without notice, one evening he was told the biopsy would happen early the next day, and he spent a sleepless night trying to read in the dim light.

It would take six marshals with bulletproof vests and Uzis in three cars to get him to the hospital, and another twelve marshals to line the hospital corridor as he was taken into an examination room, still in a waist chain, black box covering his handcuffs, and leg irons. "That he might be sick and frightened counted for nothing," he recalled.[66] After orderlies wheeled him down the hall with at least the waist chain off, the surgeon did the procedure under local anesthesia (more painfully than Alan expected), while two armed marshals stood against the operating room wall.

It was not getting better. In the recovery room, some attention was also paid to his leg. An orthopedist cut off his cast to reveal "wasted muscle, pasty and peeling skin, and a big lump of scar tissue at the site of the rupture." He was advised to undertake physical therapy and use a whirlpool, as if this was possible.[67] Back in prison, it would be another five days before the verdict on his biopsy was in.

A prison nurse delivered the news as gently as she could. As Alan had feared, he had Hodgkin's. It was November 1985, six months after he was captured, and this was happening before he even went on trial. He was alone and frightened and wanted support from those who knew and loved him. He reached out when he could make a phone call: first to Dana curiously, not Barbara. He did not explain why, except that he always felt comforted and warmed by Dana's voice that, like her, he wrote, "was calm and competent and sensual." She was going to law school at night but could often be reached at work during the day. At a time without cell phones, this mattered, since Barbara's doctor schedule made her harder to get ahold of. Dana had told him he could call in an emergency, and he believed this counted. He caught her in her office during his ten-minute allotted phone call and at least felt "comforted and calmer."

When he had the next chance at a phone call that evening, he told Barbara about the diagnosis. They agreed to keep it from Sarah, for a time, and would arrange a visit for all three of them as soon as possible.[68] It would set the pattern of his relationship to these women and his daughter throughout the prison years: reliance on all of them for differing needs. That night he gave in to his fears. "Tears were streaming down my face," he recalled. "I felt myself convulse with sobs. I turned my face into the pillow, hoping to smother the noise. Perhaps I didn't 'know' how I felt, but I was sure feeling it."[69]

By the time Barbara arrived over the weekend, Alan was composed enough to realize that a campaign would have to be waged outside the prison to make sure he received the necessary medical staging, appropriately targeted treatment, and follow-up care that made Hodgkin's a very survivable cancer. He knew what he was up against. Even after his "humanitarian" request to the warden for a contact visit with Barbara given his diagnosis, he was allowed to see her only for half an hour and through plexiglass. All the other prisoners and their families were cleared out of the way because, Alan thought, it would give the guards "a free range of fire."[70]

Alan was worried, too, about where they might cart him off to next. The failures, and outright malfeasance, in carceral health care had been central to the prison rebellions in the 1960s and 1970s, and little had changed by the time Alan was imprisoned.[71] Really sick prisoners in the federal system were often sent to the prison medical center in Springfield, Missouri, more than 1,100 miles from New York City. In a prison medical system that was notoriously staffed by ill-prepared doctors and without the kind of cancer specialty center he needed, Alan's survival depended on timely and appropriate care that also made it possible for nearby family and friends to provide at least the modicum of support imprisonment allowed.[72]

Barbara and his friends on the outside organized. Letters, telegrams, and phone calls poured into the media and Judge Pollak's office. After Sarah was told what he had, and reassured that the word *cancer* did not equal death, she explained what was happening to her teachers and everyone else in her school. Letters from her teachers came into the court.[73] Even many of those who disagreed with what Alan had been charged with doing believed he did not deserve a death sentence from incompetent medicine.[74]

The pressures helped, but his health difficulties worsened. The day before a hearing before Judge Pollak on December 10, the government agreed he could be treated at the world-renowned Abramson Cancer Center at the University of Pennsylvania. First he needed the standard exploratory abdominal surgery that often led to the removal of the spleen in Hodgkin's cases. As Alan told Judge Pollak at the hearing, his family would probably not be told when this would be, and that he would go under anesthesia and awaken to see armed U.S. marshals.[75] In fact the only way he knew the surgery was happening is that rather than tell him not to drink water, they simply cut off the water supply to his cell one night.

Security considerations meant he was taken again to the Chester County Hospital under the conditions he predicted. The surgery revealed he had stage 2A Hodgkin's, which meant he had the cancer in more than one site, with tumors under both arms, but no organ involvement. While the marshals allowed some family and friends to visit, Alan developed a postsurgery pneumonia that left him breathless, febrile, and weak.

The constant "security concerns" interfered with his treatment and recovery. While on some level Alan was amused by the government's fears of the menace he posed, it had enormous consequences. Even Sarah and Harriet, then aged nine and five, were terrified by the strip-search guards imposed when they came to visit him in the hospital. Alan was infuriated.[76] A week after the surgery and pneumonia, with a catheter still in place to drain urine that increased the potential for infection if not evacuated properly and before it could be determined whether he could really eat solid prison food, he was sent back to the prison's infirmary and round-the-clock shackling. It bordered on medical malfeasance, and he wondered, half kidding, if he could sue for malpractice.[77] Within a few days he reported "consistent abdominal pain, nausea, and inability to eat," but no doctor came to see him for another week.[78]

He knew it had to become urgent to get their attention, and his body complied. When he started vomiting up blood and experiencing extreme pain, he was finally whisked back to the hospital in the middle of the night for emergency surgery. This time it was found the original operation had left him with "an abscess and scar tissue that cut off his small bowel." It would require a five-hour operation to drain the abscess and repair the adhesions. As he would write with some clinical objectivity, the "stormy post-operative course . . . included recurrent fevers, hepatitis, urinary obstruction, and . . . weeks of total parenteral nutrition through a catheter in the neck."[79] As he noted in an "understated way" to a friend, "I was a lot sicker than I expected to be. The second operation [was] necessitated by errors made by the surgeon during the first operation, and my body couldn't deal with two major operations in two weeks."[80] Other infections followed, but by mid-January he was nonetheless sent back to the prison. He would lose eight pounds in a week from the inedible food and require yet another hospitalization because of fever and infections.[81]

At the end of January he began the grueling ten-to-twelve-week, five-day-a-week radiotherapy at Penn's cancer center where, if he were treated appropriately, his chances of survival would be excellent. Each trip from the jail to the hospital required a ridiculous amount of security, with sirens blazing and four to six cars filled with officers from the Philadelphia Police Department and federal marshals. Once, in their hurry, the caravan caused an accident, sideswiping the vehicle of a terrified elderly couple. There was a real possibility that the government might kill him, or someone else, just driving to the hospital.[82]

The efforts to get Alan bail to support his medical care would fail, as it does often for prisoners, especially given his history of disappearing. So he had to begin to prepare for his court case, and to try to survive his cancer and its treatment under the control of the Bureau of Prisons. "I've been vacillating between lofty thoughts of death and final accountings and the more mundane concerns of where the nearest toilet is that I can vomit into," he wrote his high school drama teacher.[83] Between December 1985 and April 1986 he would lose forty pounds, and take on a green pallor.[84] Yet the letters he received, many from Puerto Rican comrades, some who were self-defined prisoners of war and others "whole families I had never directly known," were "a wonderful expression of support."[85]

Alan was now in "general population" in the prison, albeit in a high security unit.[86] Other prisoners were willing to help him. Alonzo Robinson, a friend and fellow prisoner, put him on the weight-lifting team, hilarious given his condition. But it allowed him to get more food and more exercise, and Robinson forced him to get up even when he was really sick.[87] It also gave Alan a chance to try to use his doctor skills. "A young Puerto Rican [man] came in and was down from me and across the tier," he recalled. "He was very thin, coughed a lot and sweated a lot. . . . This young man started to have seizures and we had to bang on our bars to get the guards to come one night to take him out. He never came back. We subsequently learned that he died in the hospital with PCP [pneumocystis pneumonia]. I think that was the first time in the prison that I saw a clear case of HIV. I worked with some other prisoners to set up a prisoners' council to begin to do some peer education in the prison."[88]

All of this waiting gave Alan a chance to contemplate his own political trajectory. He understood that his choice to be a "revolutionary" was made out of love and was not mere rhetoric. It had to be in some ways a form of propaganda of the deed, that is by "concrete life decisions and practices that demonstrated" the commitment to that love. As he wrote to his former May 19th comrade Bob Lederer, as a doctor he had learned "to love as well as to fight," and he was "profoundly grateful" for those who taught him to love.[89]

He was reading widely in the revolutionary memoir genre and seemed to have lost his naiveté somewhat on what a life fighting for and after a revolution could mean. At his most honest, he agreed that revolutionaries had to ask themselves "are we all crazy," while they worked either "in clandestinity, or as public organizers." The men and women he had met and worked with in the Puerto Rican movement had filled him with hope and were his "own heroes." These were the people he wanted to be. He dreamed, he wrote in great detail, of a triumphal return to a liberated Puerto Rico, with details that recalled Fidel's descent out of the Sierra Maestra at the culmination of Cuban Revolution.[90] He never regretted the choices he made.

Those supporting him argued that the conditions for his care seemed "to have more to do with taking his life than saving it."[91] But Alan recognized how much worse it was for others, and that his doctor knowledge and his connections to Barbara, Dana and lawyers, and a community, however small, on the left kept him from disappearing into the labyrinth of the prison system. He also maintained an awareness of the ridiculousness of his situation. As he told his friend Bruce Taub, "There is, after all, a somewhat pathetically funny aspect to the situation, reminiscent of jokes my father would tell about schlimazels."[92] He intended to survive, although "there were a few days when it is possible I would have died; I knew it, Barbara knew it, and the doctor & nurses knew it. All that jogging over the years produced a pretty strong heart, though, & it just kept pushing that blood around & wouldn't allow me to go into shock."[93]

POLITICAL ACTIONS / CRIMINAL OFFENSES

In between the operations and treatment regimens, Alan planned his defense. In the court case in Philadelphia alone he was facing fifteen criminal charges that ranged from conspiracy to multiple counts of unlawful possession (of dynamite, bombing components, guns, counterfeit identification cards, etc.) related to what had been found in the garage and the car he had been driving.[94] Then there were the leftover cases in New York of bail-jumping and accessory, the armed robbery in Connecticut, and possible other charges coming out of what had been found in Baltimore. As he wrote to his medical school and political buddy Dick Clapp, "Ye God's. Gone are days when a certain leader of the WUO [Weather Underground Organization] could put a thumbprint on a communiqué & not be charged with it." Dealing with all of it was exhausting, and a part of him just wanted to hide in his cell, "put my head under the pillow, & just ask for the result when the whole sequences of trials is over."[95]

For a time he had seen the trials as his last chance to "do mass work. Try to find sympathetic press. Try to build some support for anti-imperialism. At least talk to the young, etc. etc."[96] This kind of bravado was tempered by the reality of the courts. The most consequential legal decision was one that he made with Betty Ann Duke, before she jumped her bail: that there *would* be a defense of some kind. They knew what had happened with some of the FALN and Brink's defendants who had refused to participate in their own trials because doing so would mean accepting the "criminalization of political dissent." There seemed no reason at this point to do this. Tim Blunk and Susan Rosenberg had tried a "necessity defense, citing the international law that called on citizens of aggressive countries to actively resist their own governments."[97] It got them each fifty-eight years.

As Alan declared, somewhat dryly, "I balked at trying to turn my trial into a political spectacle." It was obvious to him now that this was not a period to promote armed groups and that "political statements" were difficult to make in court.[98] Balancing the need to explain his principles and raise doubts about the prosecution's evidence would prove daunting. It meant, however, that he was beginning to move away from the rhetoric and the moral stance alone.

He had originally opted for a public defender because the costs of a criminal defense attorney, especially a good one who understood his politics and the intricacies of the law, seemed beyond his means. He had no money, and Barbara was working part-time to support Sarah. His parents were retired and had to pay back his uncle after Alan jumped bail. He considered acting pro se, meaning as his own attorney. But he was facing a possible seventy-eight years, if the government asked for the maximum sentences on all his Philadelphia charges.[99]

He reluctantly asked for assistance. Unlike poor and working-class prisoners, Alan had friends and colleagues from his medical and political work who were now making good salaries.[100] Funds were raised through his family, old friends, and networks so that Bill Mogulescu, just a few years older than Alan and a seasoned political and criminal attorney from New York, could be brought in.[101] Alan would join him, now as the pro se second chair, but at least someone with legal expertise would be his guide.

Alan had both legal and political decisions to make. He would have to explain himself, which meant he had to come to terms with a position on violence that was both accurate for him and defensible in the court. He would admit in his autobiographical writings that his "materialistic" thinking made him believe real revolutionaries would not harm their prisoners, or "exploit the civilian population." He did know that revolutionaries used violence, but he thought they "must be motivated by great feelings of love." He was disappointed by some of the nonviolent left that took what he thought of as "an individualistic ideological position often accompanied by elitism, arrogance, and disdain." His anger focused on those who did not condemn the violence of the state, and supported those who understood why many people of color might think taking up arms was necessary. He could at least admit that he "believed that violence was necessary." At the same time, he would declare, "I was equally convinced that revolutionary change must be an assertion of life, optimism, and respect for humanity and not primarily an act of destruction."[102]

There was a naiveté and romanticism to this position that suggested he had read more theory than history, more novels than nonfiction. At the same time, Alan had seen that faith in the "system" had led nowhere. The New York City police who had used shotgun blasts to kill mentally-ill sixty-four-year-old Eleanor Bumpers in her home had been indicted—something that he hoped showed that "that Black people's lives do have value." But then "10,000 armed police who demonstrated against the indictment were asserting the contrary. They won. All charges were dropped."[103] Alan's attempts to parse all this made for thoughtful position papers and discussions; but it was more difficult to evolve these ideas into a criminal defense he could live with, or more important at the moment, win on.

Bill Mogulescu understood these issues, but he had to find a way to beat the charges, or at least reduce the sentence if Alan was convicted. Mogulescu knew that in the post-Watergate and post-COINTELPRO era juries would at least entertain the idea that FBI agents might lie and act outside the law.[104] The illegality of the FBI's searches, burglaries, and surveillance of Alan's circle had been known since 1969, and proved in the courts in 1980.[105] Alan and his lawyer would spend months going over the evidence the government claimed it had and how it had obtained that evidence, detail by detail. Mogulescu agreed that Alan could help make the arguments, using the third-person when he was acting as an attorney and the first-person when speaking as the defendant, in a form of syntactical gymnastics.[106] As Alan wrote in a poem to one of his comrades,

> And I?
> Perhaps you've heard from the above-mentioned friends
> That I am currently perched on the head
> Of a large imperial eagle that guards a
> cavernous courtroom
> in which I can be seen talking to a jury

about me who is sitting at the defense table
rebutting the charges made by dedicated servants of the system
about me that sounds only vaguely familiar
in the ways a mummy resembles its progenitor.[107]

After months of radiation, he was feeling at least healthy enough to be part of his own defense as the trial geared up. He had, for the moment, beaten the cancer, but he also knew that 30 percent of patients with his kind of Hodgkin's relapsed within five years. His biblical sense that he was becoming someone between "Job and Jonah" seemed based on this reality.[108] They were all set to begin his trial on September 15, 1986, when they got the news that Judge Pollak had had a heart attack. The trial was postponed to October. He faced not only the possibility of a more hostile judge but also the sudden death of one of his favorite aunts and the discovery of enlarged lymph node in his neck. He could no longer truthfully tell his friends he was never depressed.[109]

The lump would turn out to be nothing — but his emotional life would still get worse. As he wrote his buddy Bruce Taub, now a defense attorney in Boston, "Barbara told me that she was in a relationship with someone else; she assured me that it was totally separate from our relationship and part of her need to get on with her own life. All of which I believe & agree with but it did make me come to grips one more time with my own situation." Barbara had become partners with Jackie Haught, a former May 19th member and JBAKC organizer who worked as an acupuncturist in Portland, Oregon, then at BAAANA in Harlem with Mutulu Shakur, until it dissolved after the Brink's actions and the arrests. After BAAANA, she moved to another New York acupuncture collective.[110]

Barbara never divorced Alan nor ever stopped loving him or being the key to his support. As Alan admitted to a friend, "While I occasionally have flashes of anger toward Barbara, her unfailing commitment, warmth, & love has made it pretty easy to accept what is possible and not worry too much about what is not. I still find her a wonderful lover, comrade and friend."[111] His equanimity was tied to his sense of the reality of those facing long prison sentences, and his political beliefs. "I try to be rational," he wrote a friend. "No use waging any battles I can't win — says the man who tries to be a revolutionary in Reagan's America."[112]

He also had to come to terms with his own experiences and decide what he could and could not do to make a life. He admitted to Bruce Taub that he was depressed for a while when his "discipline went all to hell. I'm in an environment where there is little to do, minimal stimulation, and a lot of noise. . . . My spontaneous tendency is to just read endlessly." He read whatever he could: "Camus, Foucault, Whitman, Gordimer, Arendt, Baldwin, Wideman."[113] Escape then was only in his mind, but it was the kind of self-comfort he was used to.

As he often did, he found ways to cope. "So I did my catechism of personal and political principles, invoked the spirit of Che Guevara, did more physical exercise, meditated a bit and some sunshine began to enter the grayness."

He held on to his political beliefs, which kept him from accepting the views of those who held power over him. "While all prisoners have to deal with institutionalization," he concluded, "I identify myself as a political prisoner and encourage myself by affixing myself to a proud tradition of unrepentant political prisoners here and around the world."[114] His own principles had gotten him to this point, he knew. As he wrote to his parents, "I didn't make these choices for anyone else—not for Black People or Puerto Ricans—but for myself. I had to do what I thought was right. . . . I can live with whatever happens—I hope you can, too."[115]

He also had to learn to contain his rage and his sense of the unfairness and arbitrariness of the power over him. Once Barbara came to visit and was turned away at the gate, told that Alan's quota of visits that week were used up, even though this was not true. She had made the trip from New York and had arranged childcare for Sarah. Alan was furious when he found out and confronted the warden, demanding that he reprimand the guards for their errors. The warden just turned to him and "told me to leave," Alan recalled. "No answer, no apology, and no 'I'll talk to them.' Leave. I wanted to smash his fat face. It would have been the most human—the most dignified—thing to do. You are left with nothing but violence to assert your selfness in this situation. It's like that every day, and the rage grows."[116]

Alan had to come to terms with his physical and emotional life, check his anger, and develop a legal defense. He could have just ignored the court, but he chose not to. Instead, he understood that he had "to experience the contradictions of being a revolutionary in the enemy's court playing by their rules."[117] It fit everything else going on politically in these years, Alan thought. Discussing the arrest of President Manuel Noriega of Panama on drug trafficking charges and his connection to the CIA, Alan thought all the politics of the period felt a bit like *Alice in Wonderland*, where nothing made sense and everything was topsy-turvy.[118]

The trial finally started in February 1987, nearly a year and a half after his arrest. It went on for nine weeks, requiring him to get up every morning at 4:45 a.m. and not return to his cell until 8 every evening.[119] His opening argument, which he presented in the third-person, acknowledged that "Alan" was a revolutionary but tied this to being a doctor who loved and preserved life. He gave himself a political history that made him more of a student activist in college than he had been, noting that his consciousness had been raised with the killing of the young black girls at Sixteenth Street Baptist Church in Birmingham in September 1963 when he arrived at Cornell, and fueled by Stokely Carmichael's black power speech in his last semester four years later. The statement went on to trace his community medical care and willingness to treat patients who were ignored. He admitted some of the work he did in May 19th, but cast it as protected First Amendment political speech. Alan's statement acknowledged that he did not report Marilyn Buck's gunshot wound, a minor offense. But it was the government, he pointed out, that changed the charge to accessory to bank robbery and murder when he would not cooperate, and claimed he was "armed and dangerous" when he jumped bail.

The statement had to make an argument about why he had gone underground, and what he had been doing. Alan's claim was clear: he did it so that he could be a doctor for people "who for one reason, or another, could not just walk into a hospital or a clinic. [And] . . . he developed a training guide for first aid and how to develop a plan for basic medical care." Carefully, he noted that the number of weapons and amount of ammunition that had been found in the garage and in Baltimore were not unusual, and that the books on how to handle explosives suggested that the group took safety and responsibility seriously. In contrast to the Philadelphia police's bombing of the black liberation group MOVE that destroyed 61 houses and a whole city block, killing eleven people, five of whom were children, Alan pointed out, none of the people he was closely associated with had killed anyone.

In the end, his case was clearest when he talked about why he had not harmed anyone. He maintained there was no evidence that he personally possessed any of the documents about what revolutionaries should do that had been found in the garage. Rather, he argued, they were part of "a process of revolutionaries trying to figure out how to stop our government's violence while minimizing its use." Then came the clearest assertion: that those who wrote these documents may have been his comrades, but they were not his co-conspirators. Instead, he had "engaged in political discussion and debate with groupings of people he had contact with."

When he wrote to his lawyer friend Bruce, Alan was clearer about the dilemma he was caught in. "I was captured with a lot of political materials," he admitted, "and there is admissible evidence linking me to other people underground. So, it wouldn't do to play me as a hitchhiker or complete innocent. And politically, I don't want to portray myself as misguided." But there was also the matter of his comrades. "I won't proclaim anything about membership in a clandestine group, although I do admit contacts & some shared resources. A lot of stuff linked to me is medical, & that's good."[120]

Alan and his lawyer were drawing a fine line within the criminal law and conspiracy doctrine. They had to acknowledge that he was with those who defined themselves as revolutionaries who discussed and perpetuated violence and did military-like action, but they also had to claim that Alan never did anything that harmed anyone. They had to avoid naming any names, while trying to say what Alan had really done and whether he had been in proximity to others who had already been tried or for whom the FBI was still searching. Alan attempted to explain how discussions went on within the clandestine movement, without giving anything else away. And finally he averred that he "did not own the car, did not rent the garage, did not rent a truck, did not have any way to know what was packed in the trunk of the car." Betty Ann Duke and Alan were together, instead, because of the arrests of others and Alan's need to "scramble" to avoid capture, he asserted. It was the government that had made Alan part of a conspiracy.

Alan's position struck a difficult balance. He was willing, for example, to tell his lawyer where more explosives might be left unattended, but not the FBI. He agreed that the matériel found in the suburban garage should not have been stored there, but he distanced himself from knowing it was there. He differentiated between what he labeled "a stance of non-collaboration" from "a commitment to engage in armed struggle." And he was furious that the government implied he was no better than Nazi doctors, when he had spent his entire life refusing to be a good German and opposing various forms of genocide. He condemned the government's effort to paint him and other revolutionaries as "inhuman, genocidal and committed to mindless violence." Rather, he declared again and again, his motivations came from "love, concern, or a sense of social justice."[121]

It was a masterful defense of actions that were difficult to defend. At Alan's side, Mogulescu did the best he could to undermine the FBI's evidence taken from the storage garage and in the search in Baltimore, questioning the legality of the Baltimore searches in particular.[122] When he could distance himself from the experience, Alan told one of his friends, "It's actually been fun to see this parade of high level agents lying their heads off and occasionally catching them up in them. The judge knows they're lying but the play must go on, & he must make oh-so agonizing decisions to admit the evidence."[123]

A strange sideshow played out involving stethoscopes. The weekend after the beginning of the trial, one of the U.S. attorneys prosecuting Alan found a stethoscope on the driver's seat of his car, then a few days later another one in his driveway. The government claimed that Alan and his "associates" were trying to "terrorize the prosecutor."[124] The FBI became involved, and the U.S. attorney wrote the judge to say he would "never back down in the face of terrorism, and [would] redouble the vigor of his prosecution." Alan told the judge this was a "stupid dirty trick" that he thought the FBI had perpetuated. "These bastards are vindictive," Alan wrote Bruce.[125] In his press statement Alan declared, "This is a lie and a provocation, designed to serve as a rationale to send me to a maximum security prison if I am convicted."[126] The identity of who had left the stethoscopes was never determined.

The jury took the various claims made by the prosecution and the defense seriously, and deliberated for five long days, giving Alan hope. But on day four they asked the judge again about how to understand the law on what is called joint constructive possession, which meant Alan could be held responsible for the materials Betty Ann Duke had held. That did it.

Even though many on the jury told Mogulescu later they liked and were sympathetic to Alan, the law and the judge seemed to give them no choice. He was convicted on all counts.[127] The government suggested yet again if he told them more, they would ask for lighter sentencing. If he did not do this, he could possibly have faced seventy-eight years. When he once again refused to cooperate, prosecutors compromised and only asked the judge for a more realistic sentence they thought they could obtain — forty-eight years — making it clear they wanted Alan off the streets and "warehoused" for the rest of his life.[128] Alan knew that others facing similar charges in nonpolitical cases were given forty- to fifty-two-*month* sentences.[129] His Hodgkin's also militated in favor of a shorter sentence and release from the prison medical system, since in case of relapse his chance of survival would depend on quick detection (primarily by commuted tomography [CAT] scan) and treatment with a special kind of chemotherapy.

The conviction was expected, but nonetheless Alan had been "guardedly optimistic." After the decision he wrote a friend, "There I was, completely powerless, sitting with massive irresolvable anxiety about my placement and about the other potential charges the government, which appeared to be anything but powerless, could bring." His anger was palpable. "God, I hate the government. No, it was not surprising, but man was I disappointed nevertheless."[130] As he had written a year earlier to Bruce in an effort at humor, "HELP! I am being held prisoner by a hostile government."[131]

The next step was then to try to convince Judge Pollak not to follow the government's sentencing proposal. In a ten-page, single-spaced typed document Alan made his case as to why the government's claims were, as he put it, "so full of illogic, invective, and ignorance that I feel compelled to respond." He argued that no one had been harmed by the bombings, and that much of the material on which he'd left fingerprints was never used. He accepted the label of revolutionary but said he did not believe a small group conspiracy could overthrow the government, which would require a "mass social phenomenon." Responding to the government's claim that if freed he would be a danger, he professed he would "rejoin my family and resume my medical practice as well as public political involvement."

His family and friends, outside his political orbit, backed him up. Even his uncle Abe Osit, his mother's brother, who had put up his house for the bail Alan had jumped, sent a heart-rending handwritten letter to the judge. Remarking on Alan's "compassion, consideration and thoughtfulness for other human beings," he ended his letter by calling him "beautiful," while pleading to the judge to lighten the sentence.[132] Others wrote in support, and backed up Alan's claims over and over that he was being sentenced for his politics, not his "crimes."[133]

They won the judge's sympathies. Pollak could not accept the government's demand that Alan be given what would amount to a life sentence, which could amount to a death sentence, given the potential for the cancer to reappear. Instead he sentenced him on five of the fifteen counts against him, giving him ten years, making him eligible for parole in seven and a half years.[134] It was a victory of sorts, given the long sentences Alan's other comrades had received.

Closing his heart to his emotions, Alan had to come to terms with his immediate future. Being emotionless proved difficult. The hardest part, he admitted, was calling Sarah and having to tell her he had lost. The powerlessness of not knowing where he might be and what other charges he might face led to what he was willing to call "irresolvable anxiety."[135] He both wanted the comfort of his friends and family and needed to separate himself from them. He desperately missed "sex, love, tenderness, companionship" and found little comfort in the pornography and R-rated movies that prison had in abundance. He wanted to imagine that having another child was possible, and he recalled with great pleasure the sense of transcendence and connection that lovemaking had given him.[136] In his mind, he thought he needed to spend time in the kind of "self-analysis" prison made possible, a chance, as he put it, "to figure out a bit about my own personality, and how it helped account for some of the decisions I'd made over the years."[137] Now forty-one, he had to survive the next decade and find ways to continue the political life that gave him a sense of meaning.

ISOLATION AND RETHINKING

Alan did not expect to do penance or be corrected in the penitentiaries and correctional institutions to which he was confined. As he wrote early in his imprisonment, "I haven't done anything I'm ashamed of or regret."[1] Still, he knew that surviving the experience without "bitterness and self-recrimination" would require a kind of intellectual and emotional quest into his beliefs and actions.[2] As he wrote Stephen Wangh, "Realism, not heroism, has recently been prodding me into an assessment of my mental and physical resources."[3] Over the next years he would write long letters, keep journals, and attempt to compose a memoir to parse out his actions.

At the mercy of the government's power as never before, he had no way of escaping the emotional and physical costs to him and those he loved, however much his revolutionary bravado and sardonic humor sustained him. His prison years coincided with his forties, and he realized that he was reflecting on his past at a time when he had virtually no control of his future.[4] He never lost his deeply politicized mind, humanistic views, and his efforts to make sense of world events. Part of this, he knew, required "understanding [that] how people experience our shared reality and aspirations for a dignified and humane life, is the foundation for any hope of a mass politic."[5] He was forever trying to figure this out. He was never humorless about it, balancing the quotidian tragedy and absurdity of his own prison experience with what he understood of the world.

Never one to shy away from difficulties, he used his letter-writing and visits with his family and friends to try to come to terms with his life's choices on an emotional, not just intellectual, level. His deep caring that made him both an excellent doctor and committed revolutionary in a reactionary time was exactly what prison was designed to leach out of him. This stripping of his humanity would be, in the end, what he fought hardest to resist.

First Alan had to deal with his remaining legal cases, and all the uncertainty that came with them. "Where are they going to send me next?" he worried in a letter to a friend. "What's going to happen in Connecticut? Will there be more federal charges? If I had just the ten-year sentence, I could mentally adjust & settle down to doing it. But I'm afraid it's going to be a harder road than that."[6] He wasn't wrong. He described it as "the latest installment of the ongoing saga of Alan Berkman: I call this chapter 'The Empire Strikes Back—Again. And again. And again."[7]

After the sentencing in Philadelphia on May 29, 1987, troopers with heavy weapons watched as he boarded a helicopter to the Metropolitan Correctional Center (MCC) in New York. There he would have to face the charges related to his failure to report Marilyn Buck's gunshot wound, jumping bail, and then his presumed accessory-to-murder-after-the-fact for the Brink's action. In a weird acknowledgement that Alan's charges were political, rather than just criminal, he was housed in a cell with Joe Doherty. A fighter from the Irish Republican Army (IRA), Doherty had been arrested in New York in 1983 for fleeing Northern Ireland after his conviction for killing a British soldier. Doherty claimed his act was "political" because of the war between the IRA and British authorities, and thus should make him "immune from extradition."[8]

Alan and Doherty had much to discuss about questions of retaliatory violence, in the United States and Northern Ireland.[9] Alan found fascinating, if difficult, Doherty's justification for the need for the killings that shaped the Irish struggle. They often disagreed.[10] Yet in Doherty, Alan found a revolutionary brother who had a sense of humor, tied to his working-class bravado, writing skill, and brashness, as well as endless discussions of sex that helped pass the time.[11]

Other political prisoners joined them.[12] "It was almost like coming home: 7 or 8 old friends, a Palestinian, Libyan, IRA member, 2 Sikhs and a dozen Mafia dons," Alan wrote with bemusement.[13] Mutulu Shakur, whom the government would charge as the mastermind of Brink's, had been captured in California on February 12, 1986, and brought back to New York to stand trial. He and Alan had time that summer to support one another, despite Alan's criticism of the Brink's operation.[14] And since Alan was now in New York City, visits with Barbara, Sarah, Dana, and his other friends became logistically easier; although when their own lives kept them busy and made visits less frequent, the proximity increased his resentment.[15]

Just because he was with fellow political prisoners did not mean the discussions were always easy. Some thought that during his trial in Philadelphia he had not been "confrontational enough and too respectful toward the judge."

Alan disagreed. As he wrote his friend Ann Morris, "I am a militant, but I reject shrill militancy . . . [and] don't believe violence ever becomes an end. So, I'm not only in disagreement with my comrades, but somewhat disappointed with what I consider both an immature and potentially destructive strain in their politics."[16] His concern about violence would resurface again and again.

If Alan had been lucky with the judge in Philadelphia, he scored again in New York City when he come up against Rudy Giuliani, then the powerful U.S. attorney for the Southern District of New York and at the height of his prosecutorial fame. Giuliani was known for his fast arrests and "perp walks" that brought wide media coverage and induced considerable fear. But they also frequently led to the dismissal of charges when his probable cause could not be backed up by evidence.[17] By the time Alan was brought to New York, several of the major federal Brink's trials were over, with a mix of wins and losses for the government. Giuliani's office was gearing up to prosecute Marilyn Buck and Mutulu Shakur on conspiracy charges relating to Brink's, other robberies, and Assata Shakur's escape. This would prove to be the federal government's big case.[18]

Alan was somewhat less important to Giuliani, who already had used his prosecutorial discretion and declined to go after Susan Rosenberg in the Brink's case, claiming she already had a long sentence.[19] Now Giuliani's office also failed to prosecute Alan. According to one of Alan's lawyers, given that Brink's witnesses had cut deals and the evidence against Alan was less than convincing, they probably could not have convicted him.[20] Making this refusal to prosecute even more political, Marilyn Buck claimed that Giuliani declined to prosecute Rosenberg or Alan and two others "to strengthen their media lie that I was 'the sole white member of the BLA [Black Liberation Army],' and thus presumably the danger of white/black alliance less threatening."[21]

For whatever reason, this meant that Alan was only charged and convicted of jumping bail. In his sentencing, the judge added two years *concurrent* to the ten years that Alan was already serving. Thus, while Alan might have been the second doctor in American history to be *charged* with accessory to murder after the fact for caring for a patient, he was in the end never prosecuted or convicted for it.

Once he had been sentenced, the Bureau of Prisons moved him again. Put on a bus with about twenty other men in early October 1987, he was driven first to Danbury, Connecticut, where several prisoners were dropped off. Then it was back to New York to the federal prison in Otisville, "ten miles and ten thousand years away from Middletown," as he put it.[22] This was the closest to his hometown that he would get while incarcerated. "All the guards know who I am," he told Barbara. "They've all seen the stories in the Middletown paper over the years. No strong reactions—just comments." And he was greeted by a prison counselor who had been in school with one of his brothers.[23] He had vivid dreams, he told a friend, of his childhood friends: one involved "me on the verge of going out with Diane Gillman again (in other words, going straight), but I had second thoughts about it and retreated from her door. Saved by my subconscious."[24] At least he knew what he did not want.

He shared his eleven-by-seven-foot cinder block space this time with an Ecuadorian immigrant who had been caught up in the drug trade. With a lilting voice and a generous heart, he gave Alan the things he needed: from potato chips to toothpaste. Within a few days the man was moved out and Alan, having spent the summer able to talk to comrades at MCC, found himself sometimes alone, other times packed in with as many as three others. He was allowed out of his cell for an hour a day for five of the seven days of the week, able to get one book from the library every two days, and a pencil to write with, which could only be sharpened every other day. "Stupid rules," he said as his writing got harder to read as the pencil wore down and smudged the page. "I feel like a second grader," he told his daughter.[25] But he understood it was all part of the process to remind him he had no control. Or as he put it more directly to another friend, "I've hated pencils as long as I can remember. I regard the time the school system let me switch from pencil to pen as much of a rite of passage as the first time I masturbated. So far, they've only taken one of the two away."[26]

At least the cell had a window that opened, so he smelled the air for a change, and heard the hooting of what he guessed was an owl. He could see the vibrant colors of autumn on the tree leaves in the Shawangunk Mountains that ringed the prison.[27] "I sat for hours," he told a friend, "on the edge of the bed with my nose right up against the screen" that let him enjoy the pleasures of the air and escape the incessant smoking of his cellmates.[28] If he stared through the bars, he could see into the distance and "let the present blur." Despite this, he never intended to escape the present, as he deeply believed "that life and people should be experienced as much as possible and not just blurred."[29]

Moving from prison to prison was difficult every time. He had to reconstruct his universe again and again, learn to accept the ups and downs, and be patient, something that didn't come easily to him.[30] The guards often tossed out his journals rather than let him carry them. "You don't bring anything with you from one world to the next," he explained to Barbara. "Literally stripped naked and redressed in their clothes." He had to learn the routines over and over, "figuring out how to get a pillow, or a change of socks, or a book ... but most importantly, how to construct a day—a life—in an 11 × 7 cell that doesn't even have a mirror to give you feedback."

None of his health records followed him either. For much of that summer he spent "yelling pleading, pounding against the wall of bureaucratic indifference to get my health situation dealt with," when he discovered more swollen nodes in his groin that terrified him.[31] He had no idea if they were a return of his cancer or "just morbid imaginings." A new biopsy that took months to arrange proved it was only benign cysts.[32]

Then without warning in December he was driven out of Otisville and put on "con air" at a nearby small airport with other prisoners who needed to be dropped off. Because each man's designation was different, everyone went along for the ride. Over the following two weeks, he was treated to a tour of American prison hotspots: West Virginia, Alabama, Florida, Louisiana, Texas, Oklahoma, and finally Springfield, Missouri. At least he was in the air some of the time, here he could appreciate the "clear and turquoise" sky that made him feel he was flying through glaciers not clouds, and made him remember that "natural colors are breath taking." Other times he waited for days in different prisons.

The beauty was countered by the fact that, as a "designated maximum security prisoner," he flew in "leg irons, a waist chain & handcuffs . . . covered with a 'black box' attached over the cuffs that held the hands totally fixed & caused some great swelling."[33] He told his family about an unexplained ten days in an Oklahoma federal prison where he shared a tiny cell with a man, clearly in psychiatric distress, who did "sit-ups and push-ups hour after hour without stopping except for a few puffs from a cigarette. He reminds me of a bear in the zoo that paced his cage in the same exact path, using the same exact number of steps, turning in such a way that his fur wears away in one certain place."[34] But most of the time he was "in the hole," alone twenty-three hours a day in differing prisons as slowly the plane stopped to disgorge its men in state after state. He was shuffled along in what his comrade Tim Blunk labeled the new version of slavery's Middle Passage, given the crowding, the racial makeup of the prisoners, and the chains.[35]

Alan was on his way to be evaluated at the federal prison medical center in Springfield, Missouri. "I don't know what I'm doing here," he complained, since his cancer was in remission and he did not need medical follow-up at that time. It turned out that his judge in Philadelphia had gotten the Bureau of Prisons to agree to have him evaluated first before his final designation. At least in Springfield, he graduated from writing in pencil to a felt tip pen. He was desperate for something to read that was meaningful since all the moving about meant he could only read "whatever junk is lying around."[36]

Springfield proved awful. He was only allowed out of his "hole" for five hours a week. Alan considered the chief of medicine to be thoroughly incompetent, as he saw overwhelming neglect and bungling that would have triggered malpractice suits anywhere else. Over and over in his letters, he returned to the medical needs of those near him on his tier. He was horrified by what he saw: illnesses misdiagnosed, prisoners misinformed about what they had or asked to sign informed-consent forms in a language they could not read, forced feedings, or prisoners dying alone in a cell able to see only a wall or bars. Even though many of the men sent there were sick and dying, there were no doctors on staff after 4 p.m., when the labs and x-ray closed down as well. It made him understand that staying there would be a death sentence should he ever need serious medical care again while imprisoned.[37]

ISOLATION AND SURVIVAL

Without warning on December 22, 1987, his situation got worse. He was moved to southern Illinois and the control unit prison at Marion Penitentiary, which at the time was on permanent lockdown.[38] Then the highest-security lockup in the federal system, since the 1970s it had also been used to contain those who saw themselves as political prisoners. "The purpose of the Marion Control Unit is to control revolutionary attitudes in the U.S. prison and in society at large," its first superintendent claimed.[39] As one guard who processed Alan in explained, "Someone must have wanted you salted away."[40] With his characteristic self-deprecating humor, Alan told his parents, "So I'm as salty as regular lox."[41]

The prison, begun under psychological behavior modification techniques developed by Edward Schein, a professor from the Massachusetts Institute of Technology who modified Chinese "brainwashing" and Skinnerian con-ditioning theory that kept the men in isolation to make them dependent on the guards for everything. Above all Marion was set up to break the prisoners' spirits. Amnesty International and the American Civil Liberties Union (ACLU) had condemned it. Marion would be the site of a fifteen-year struggle in the prison movement to try to stop such forms of control, and the beginning of a major assault on the political uses of mass incarceration.[42]

Alan's isolation came in many forms. The staff physician who oversaw his medical care at Marion had not been able to pass licensing exams in any state.[43] Just graduating from medical school got a doctor a position at Marion. Indeed, Alan was the only licensed physician in the institution. The physician admitted, too, that he had never followed a Hodgkin's case, and he had to ask Alan, when he was examined, what tests and x-rays to order.[44] Alan had to be more self-reliant than ever and mourned the loss of contact with his friends and family that being imprisoned nearer them had made possible. Barbara and Sarah, who had plane reservations to visit him in Springfield, were able to come for a Christmas visit only because Alan had a fellow prisoner use his phone-call time to call them to explain his sudden move from Missouri to Illinois. At the last minute they were able to change their flight plans.[45]

Mostly he was deeply alone in the deprivation the prison was set up to create. "People are moved only one at a time," he observed, "so you go down long gleaming corridors and the steel gates slide open silently before you get there, and you never see another person besides the guards with you."[46] His comrade Tim Blunk had also been sequestered in Marion but had been transferred before Alan arrived, leaving at least "a residue of good feeling" that helped introduce Alan to the prisoners he did get to meet.[47] His tier mates included a psychotic man called "G.E." because he had ingested light bulbs and seemed to Alan "directly out of Faulkner." Then there was a thirty-five-year-old white man with a "bushy beard and shaved head who paces 24 hours a day, talking constantly, and occasionally goes off into a screaming, banging rage . . . and an absolutely beautiful 20 year old ebony Black man who orates like a Black preacher about the incomparable beauty of white women." Sometimes, he noted, the "whole echogenic cement block will just shake with screams like howler monkeys. . . . It is frightening if you're sleeping."[48]

The letters he received from his friends served to remind him that he still existed. Sometimes he felt otherwise, living "in a world of the disappeared."[49] He also knew that "every bit of outside contact makes them watch themselves & be more careful before doing anything to me."[50] Friends sent him a subscription to the *New York Times* that arrived two days late. It made possible his return to doing the crossword puzzles, and helped him keep up with the world's news so that he could be conversant in letters.[51] It kept alive his sense of himself as a knowledgeable political person. But he was somewhat humble about his experience. "I'm learning how much I can live without and still remain intact," he told Barbara, "and there's some value to that, but it doesn't give my reality any greater ethical value than anyone else's."[52]

Lifting his eyes from his reading, letter-writing, TV-watching, and exercise brought the barrenness of his existence into view. The only windows were on the tier, not in his cell, and faced west. Between the lack of direct sunlight and the shielded neon bulbs everywhere, he realized it diffused "shadows almost into nothingness. So a world without shadows," he mused. "Does that mean I am a person without substance? No, but perhaps that's what the goal is."[53] At least his sense of what the prison was supposed to mean gave him a way to resist it, if mostly intellectually.

Everything was about containment. He only exercised outside the cell for an hour in a small area, mostly alone, or indoors in another cage. For someone who had run four to five miles a day, four times a week, it was excruciating to be this controlled.[54] Once a week he was allowed into a gym for basketball or handball, and an occasional two hours outside. Even though he was alone, the "degrading and infuriating" strip search was a constant; a way, he began to understand, to make sure he understood the guards had "arbitrary and irrational" power over his life. They were constantly armed with "metal-balled riot batons," even though Alan was moved in waist chains and a metal brace that tightly held his handcuffs in place.[55]

"CONFORM OR DIE," as one prisoner described the Marion system.[56] Many prisoners barely managed to even get dressed most days, and the rage that built up just burbled inside individuals, sometimes breaking out, Alan realized, in many misdirected ways. While he did not want to be one of those who banged on the bars and added to the clamor, he found himself having to do it time and time again. At the other extreme, he feared becoming what was called a "mushroom" in prison lingo, a person who just lay in the dark in his cell.[57]

Calls, mail, and visits were all monitored. Arranging the calls was difficult in an age before cell phones or even call-waiting, and the arbitrary decisions about when he could and could not get to the phone. "I tried twice tonight on the phone, but it was busy both times," he wrote Barbara. "*Qué lastima* [what a pity]. I'll try again on the 19th."[58] The prison was in the middle of nowhere, and most of the men there had far less contact with their families than Alan. That Christmas, when Sarah and Barbara were able to come, he was 1 of 3 men in a population of 400 who had any visitors.[59]

The cold of the Illinois winter seeped through the concrete slabs that surrounded him, making the dreariness of his condition even more obvious.[60] His body responded to his emotional lockdown, and he found even defecating harder.[61] It did not help, of course, that all of his bodily functions could be watched at all times by the surveillance cameras, in what was clearly an American panopticon. He still had to be as stoic as he could: "Can't even give a good sob if I wanted to—it would echo like a thunderclap in these tall, narrow concrete tiers. It's bad enough the guards can see you shit, piss, and masturbate if they are so inclined, but it just wouldn't do to have them see you cry, to boot."[62]

He was trying to understand what staying strong would really mean. "I never totally relax, I won't allow myself to be vulnerable, I am always aware," he declared.[63] He was also working on self-restraint. He had given up smoking years earlier, but now was not eating meat either. He did not allow himself the candy or ice cream that could be bought in the commissary, in part because they weren't very good ("ain't Haagen Dazs," he noted) and because he wanted the discipline that gave him a modicum of humanity.

It was an ongoing struggle. "To avoid rage &/or depression, I have to constrain all my emotions," Alan wrote, while also admitting, "I would love to be able to really let go of this constant self control."[64] While waiting in Springfield to be warehoused in Marion, he admitted to Barbara that he had rolled over one morning, "and I got a sudden jolt of the horror of the whole thing. The adrenalin flowed, the nausea started, and I knew I had to stop this particular flow of emotions right away. And I did, but the sense of unease and emptiness lingers."[65]

It also gave him time to think, about how his childhood of play had become tracked increasingly with the demands of school and the friendships with the more upwardly mobile. He thought more about why his cell was a cage, not a room, with the remnants of any personality drained by its blandness. His connections to others made his survival possible. "I feel much more at peace when my love & attention go toward others," he told his friend Ann Morris. "I get more anxious when I begin to worry about myself, my relationships, the things I'd like to do. . . . the more I try to hang on to things, the worse I feel."[66]

Only two months into his stay at Marion, he wrote that it felt like it had been forever. While he tried to appreciate the time that prison gave him to philosophize about his actions and life, "I'm ready to go home."[67]

MAKING A LIFE

Like all prisoners, Alan had to determine *how* he would do his time. During the period when he was not totally in isolation, he learned early on to seek out friends among his fellow prisoners. His upbringing and his years in the underground had brought him into contact with the working class, and he had practiced medicine among the poor. "I learned a lot from 10 years of community medicine," he wrote to Dick Clapp, "but I didn't go home with people. Now we're roommates, as it were."[68] When he was not in isolation, he filled his days seeking his fellow prisoners' tales and hopes. In return he offered an open ear, a political explanation for their life stories, and whenever necessary a medical opinion on their ailments and treatment.[69]

His reputation and politics helped Alan buffer the racial divides of prison for the most part. Once knowledge of why he was incarcerated spread, many of the black and Latino prisoners gave him respect. He had some trouble with a Serbo-Croatian bomber who thought the Holocaust was a myth, but he played handball with an abortion clinic bomber whom he regarded as more of a troubled Vietnam vet with a passion for "guns, explosives and gory violence" than anything else.[70] He came to understand the importance of the pecking order: "The officers boss the guards, the guards treat the prisoners as subhumans, the prisoners have a pecking order, and the 'faggots' (pardon the expression) come hindmost. Some combination of my education, my politics & political affiliations, my heavy charges, and my personality allow me to avoid the internecine warfare."[71]

Incarceration gave Alan the time to understand his own past. Early in his imprisonment, Alan acknowledged to Hank Newman that he had been "a perfect product of that system . . . a nice, competent, test-taking machine. Never had to try hard at anything and never had to fight to push and change myself."[72] His political life had changed that. The difficulties of becoming a different kind of person and tests of a kind he had never imagined transformed his sense of self. He knew he had an "absoluteness of my convictions and my orientation to action."[73] This is what he had to rethink, or at least understand where it had taken him. Half-remembering lines from *King Lear*, he argued for the importance of speaking feelings, not just thinking; but, the issue of how to balance emotions and politics continued to confront him.[74] He refused to see himself as a tragic hero, filled with what Aristotle had called *hamartia*, meaning he had tempted the gods and failed to learn and practice their teachings.[75]

In his correspondence with Ann Morris, a Quaker, Alan was willing to muse about spirituality and mindfulness. He moaned, "I wish I could achieve some level of Blakian ecstasy, but I always feel that I run up against the psychic blunders of years of 'objective' scientific training and Marxism Leninism. I need to cultivate my own ability to experience the world & myself more fully."[76] At the same time, he tried to absorb her comments about the importance of believing in a greater being and the moments of revelation that could come from self-examination. His response was decidedly more secular, although its biblical acceptance of suffering reflected his Old Testament upbringing married to his revolutionary beliefs. "I am sustained by my sense of commitment to a human struggle for justice," he told her. "And I probably believe that through suffering . . . I will hopefully become a fuller and better person. I would balk only at the word sanctified, I guess."[77]

"I've been thinking about pain a good deal," he told another correspondent. In this case he did not mean "incision-in-the-belly, tubes-down-throat kind of pain, but emotional pain." He meant the loneliness he allowed himself to feel after he spent more than an hour with Sarah and Barbara for the first time in nearly two years. Alan began to deeply understand the words of Puerto Rican nationalist prisoner and artist Elizam Escobar, who called the problem "coldness of the heart." He did not think Escobar meant coldness in the English sense of the word, but in the Spanish sense of *frialdad*, which translated more as a change in character as an individual withdraws from those who are affectionate or kind to him.[78] In order to keep control, he felt his heart was "incased in cotton. Swaddled like a baby." He hoped that once he was no longer entombed his heart would grow and expand again. In the presence of Sarah and Barbara, he was able for a short while to again feel human and trusting. Accepting the pain of being human, he imagined socialism as a way to gain trust in a collective, a solidarity that would hold that pain at bay. Ever a romantic, such beliefs provided him with hope.

He still felt the need to repress his emotions to survive. "To avoid rage &/or depression," he told his friend Bruce Taub, "I have to constrain all my emotions; I described it to Barbara recently as a Lamaze-type technique for emotions — I effleurage through the waves of pain, trying to stay on top & not allow myself to get sucked under." But "I could really use a hug and a shoulder to cry on. I would love to be able to really let go of this constant self-control. Some day."[79] To his daughter, he was willing to admit that sometimes, especially when he was in such isolation, "I can get quite emotional at the littlest things, so I find myself feeling so bad when someone falls in the Olympics or when some animal dies on a 'Nature' show. I'm getting to be a real softie in my old age—and the government says I'm such a tough guy. Could both things be true?" There was a difference, he told Sarah, between sentiment and sentimentalism.[80]

As lonely as the solitude of prison could be, he found comfort in routine.[81] He described to Sarah the routine that shaped his days: "eat, exercise, read, eat, exercise, shower/laundry, eat, read/write, nap, read/write/phone/TV-lock in. That pattern, which changes only on the weekends, is so consistent that days blur together." Only when he could have visitors did this routine vary.[82] He continued to read as much as possible: science, philosophy, existentialism, and liberation theology. He was having trouble getting medical journals, but longed to keep up. He imagined himself writing fiction someday, attempted poetry, and even tried to learn from the "how to be a writer" books.[83] Because his day-to-day life was characterized by doing very little, he realized that his communication with correspondents would have to revolve around what he was feeling and what his concerns were. As someone who had spent years doing and being enthralled to revolutionary actions, it was a deep change.[84]

POLITICAL CHANGES, PERSONAL THOUGHTS

He never doubted his principles and values, but he was willing to question the strategies and tactics that had made him an enemy of the state. By 1987, he came to believe clearly that May 19th's vanguardism had been a mistake. "Taking the most 'advanced' positions outside of the material realities of what will advance a struggle is not really leading," he confessed to Barbara. He remembered those who had raised questions about what it meant to lead when no was behind you, and he recognized that they should not have been criticized and dismissed.[85] Over and over his letters would engage differing political questions: What could be learned from the solidarity movements for Central America, or how should the state's power be analyzed when, under attack, it lets down what he called its "democratic façade?" He carefully differentiated between an issue-oriented protest movement and the creation of political resistance. Mostly he seemed increasingly impatient with long-winded analysis that did not make a clear argument and chart a strategic way forward. He wanted those on the outside who shared his politics to focus on what he labeled "the contradictions about democratic rights and the role of the government."[86]

He reconsidered, too, his own and his comrades' assumption that armed propaganda was necessary to respond to U.S. aggression at home and abroad. Alan tried to think about why he had shared this belief. He continued to believe that principles were critical. He admitted that sometimes "an action is taken as much as an act of self-expression as it is an action in the world designed to produce effects. My goal remains to fuse the two."[87] On some level, the strategist in him understood the limits of moral positions based on principles. But the moralist in him wanted to be principled. He was caught between the two.

At the same time Alan continued to hold that on both a "macro/strategic" level and a "tactical/practical" level the "value of human life [must be] a primary consideration in any decision." This view seemed to allow him to take a gun into a robbery, as he had in Connecticut, perhaps knowing he would never use it. But of course there are always accidents, and the terrified store manager could not have known any of this as he faced down the barrel of Alan's weapon and heard his threat to blow a hole in him.

Alan's beliefs also allowed him to support those who had taken lives and yet hold that he himself would not do this. That he supported, aided, and abetted those who did was not part of his self-criticism in prison. In 1985, as the African National Congress in South Africa was beginning to consolidate its power and push for an end to apartheid, he still thought that the "Azanian masses" would want armed struggle along with others in "Namibia, the Philippines, Chile and El Salvador," but he admitted that, "perhaps, for the nth time in my life, . . . I may be overoptimistic."[88]

On some level, Alan's self-contradiction on this point was stunning. He never accepted a strategy where the ends justified the means, yet he had an amazingly naive understanding of how past revolutionaries had used violence. He knew other revolutions had "gone backwards after one generation." But he seemed to be able to justify his views: "I remain politically convinced that violence is necessary," he told Stephen Wangh, yet he continued to argue for the "assertion of life." His anger was focused on those, on the left in particular, who proclaimed their pacifism while ignoring the "violence perpetuated by this system."[89]

His experiences, and what he took from them, shaped his beliefs. Wounded Knee had been definitive for him. The lessons he had learned in Lowndes County from the old civil rights workers, who knew that Martin Luther King Jr.'s civil disobedience had to be backed up with their guns, and a willingness to use them, resonated too. His criticism of those who had failed to support the American Indian Movement in its violent, armed takeover seemed based on his belief in the need for force in the face of state intransigence. His discussions with Doherty on the IRA clearly had their effect as well. His position was deepened by the powerlessness and invisibility that prison inflicted and the concomitant building rage. He understood the psychological costs of invisibility, and accepted the human reasons for the anger that seemed a correct response to it.

He knew that holding both love and anger together was not easy. To his friend Ann Morris he admitted, "It's easy to speak rhetorically about love — about identification with the oppressed and vehement denunciations of injustices, but the trick is to not use the rhetoric to justify actions that are really based in hatred & not in love." He even thought this extended to how you treated your enemy. Fascists, he reasoned, "dehumanize their enemy & so can brutalize them." But as a revolutionary he thought he could not do this. As he was willing to admit, "People killed by love are as objectively dead as those killed with hatred."[90]

He and his comrades had been willing to accept that "political commitment was the *only* important part of our lives" and "that revolutionary struggle was going to be *the* defining part of our lives when we decided to go underground. We accepted the overwhelming possibility that we would die or spend long years in prison — that is the almost invariable history of urban guerrillas. I and I'm sure, they, stand by that." But he admitted that he was troubled by the facts that explosives had been stored in a garage next to a house in Doylestown and dynamite in a neighborhood in New Haven. He knew his need to be a revolutionary, and his emotional ties to his comrades, had shaped what he was willing to do. "Subjective ties — not just to people but positions — can be a strength but also a terrible weakness. On a microscopic level I think such ties directly contributed to my arrest, for example."[91]

His views were clearly changing. "The world isn't as simple to me now as it once was — too many revolutions have gone backwards after one generation — but the principles still seem right and worth fighting for," he admitted.[92] "I gradually am moving away from the dogma of 'scientific socialism' to a more diffuse humanism," he told Ann Morris, especially after he debated religion with her and his rereading of Fyodor Dostoyevsky's *The Brothers Karamazov*. "Principles yes," he declared, "dogma no."

Some of his political romanticism was fading. "No conscious adult is a pure victim of his/her environment," he wrote. "It's one of the reasons I believe any society will need some kind of prison system."[93] He was rereading Albert Camus for the first time in years, "thinking about his critique of socialism and dogma," he reported to Hank Newman, who was not in his political circles, "but also the whole existential crisis on the personal level."[94] To Newman he was the most clear that his values had never shifted, but he needed to explain to himself why he had become so "ideologically rigid."

Alan had an understanding of his political trajectory that built somewhat upon journalist Michael Tabor's examination of guerrilla tactics in his 1965 *The War of the Flea*.[95] "It probably isn't mysterious: people, myself included, like answers rather than questions; a version of the future that promises to give meaning to sacrifices in the present, a sense of belonging to some world historical process (especially during a time of deep social stagnation)." When the social movements were gone, he reasoned, "I think I substituted the idea of them (or an idea of what should be) for the not-very-appealing reality." But then he probed himself a bit more: "I guess that's only partially true — a lot of my actions were more of a grand refusal precipitated by actions of the government that I felt were intolerable than some grandiose strategy for social change. In some periods you can't hope to solve the problems — you can only hope to be of them, the mosquito that annoys the giant. And you have to expect to be swatted."[96] Alan chose a different insect from Tabor's but made a similar point.

He still held on to the necessity of doing real political work. He told Barbara he thought they should "make a contribution to real social justice issues now, do work you can feel good about, trust your instincts." His rigid Leninist principles were waning, and he began to admit that the "science of dialectical materialism is [not] quite as exact a discipline as we would like it to be." He was also coming much more to terms with his own arrogance. As he admitted to Barbara, "I think overachievers like you and me feel we either have to be perfect &/or should be able to make the world conform to our wishes (the reflection of political idealism on the personal level), and it doesn't seem that the world works that way."[97]

His own existential angst gave him insight to what he was reading, but also provided the way he continued to connect with those he loved. Toni Morrison's *Beloved*, a novel about slavery and individual agency, moved him enormously both for its lyricism and its analytic force. He acknowledged the novel's ambiguity around "a memory, a ghost, or an incarnation" that really mattered only because of its affect. Rather romantically, he thought, "There is a type of redemption through both communal and personal love." Morrison's meditations on what love and trust meant in the face of horror led him to remind Barbara of the profound nature of their "feelings of trust and comfort" with one another. He supported her search to figure out what to do next with her own life and appreciated finally that some kind of personal security would be needed so that she could provide for herself and Sarah.

Alan's equanimity in the face of all his sorrows and pains was astounding to his friends. He seemed determined to avoid bitterness. His friend Stephen Wangh agreed that Alan had "a concatenation of sorrows" that would have sent Wangh into "waves of anger and despair" and then "bitterness." He imagined Alan had the "inner resources of revolutionary hopefulness" that kept that "danger" at bay.[98] The son of a psychiatrist and trained in the psychodynamics of theater, Wangh understood the rituals in the theatricality of political actions. He wanted Alan not to shut down but to be willing to give himself the space "in which to digest, to mourn, to forgive, to exorcize, to make whole again." He wanted him to consider where his principles had led.[99] Alan was not afraid to do this kind of emotional and intellectual labor, even though feeling what he was thinking was often dangerous to his survival in prison.

BATHING IN LOVE

Alan's determination not to be worn down by the prison and the state's view of him was sustained not only by his force of will and sense of connection to a worldwide revolutionary struggle but also by the love that his friends and family showered upon him. His status as a thinker and friend was reinforced through his writing as he treated his correspondents as if he were sitting with them in a crowded bar over glasses of scotch, or at the beach in the haze of weed or LSD. The drug of imprisonment heightened the thoughtfulness of these exchanges. "Tell me everything," he told Sharon Newman, the recently separated wife of his high school drama coach. "It's what I want to know; at the point I don't relate to what my friends are doing on the outside, I'll know that 'they' have won. And an axiom of my particular brand of paranoia is that you never give 'them' an inch."[100] His letters mixed political commentary, details of his health and prison conditions, and concern for others and their lives.

His friends who had known him well before he went underground continued to tell him about their lives, their children, and their hopes. Alan tried to explain to Sarah what the letters meant as a way for him to stay connected. "It's almost like planning a surprise visit—and of course you always hope it will be a welcome visit." At least prison "gives you plenty of time to think of the little things to do for the people you care about."[101]

Though trapped and mostly alone in a cage-like cell, Alan's letter-writing and ability to express love and concern kept him connected. He allowed himself a certain amount of emotion with those he "clicked" with, often those who were not his political comrades but who knew him very well.[102] On paper at least, it was safer to have those feelings. And after ending the estrangement with his parents of his underground years, his letters expressed over and over his gratitude that they had bathed him in love.[103] He appreciated the model of coupledom they had provided, however much his own politics had critiqued this kind of normative arrangement. And he thanked them for the life he could look back on. "The two of you are responsible for some lovely memories. Thank you," he wrote simply.[104] Yet keeping up relationships was extremely difficult in the context of his imprisonment. As he told one friend, "Protracted absence, I fear, does not make the heart grow fonder; rather it makes emotions more abstract—the idea/memory of the feelings and not the feelings themselves."[105]

Part of his identity among his friends and comrades had been as the go-to person for conversations about political ideas and strategies. Alan had no intention of becoming politically irrelevant, to himself or his friends. His life would have seemed meaningless without its continued political content. In letter after letter he offered running commentary on the issues of the day and insight into what was happening. Watching the Iran-contra hearings in 1987, the congressional investigation into the use of weapons sales to Iran to illegally fund counterrevolutionary guerrillas in Nicaragua, he saw an element of far right's effort to take control of foreign policy and use the privatization of the CIA to its own ends. Perceptively noting that his generation had grown up believing in the American dream, he worried about what he saw as the growing "alienated fantasy to escape from reality."

In addition to political commentary, he also expressed his continuing desire to be a father and a crucial presence in Sarah's life. Becoming a wise preteen, she told Alan "that our souls are reincarnated in newborns at the moment of death, so she doesn't have to fear dying." She regaled him with stories about her New York life: from "running into Madonna on the street" to going to "the memorial for James Baldwin," and demonstrated her karate skills whenever they visited. He in turn made up stories she adored about two mischievous monkeys named Rema and Moko.[106] On a phone call she reminded him, "Whenever you're feeling lonely, remember I love you very much."[107] But he was anguished a short time later when he called home and Sarah wept, saying that she hated the prison because it did "not allow contact visits & limit[ed] the calls to two 10 minute ones a month."[108] He tried to give her a sense of his life in the prison, sparing her his fears and being mostly chatty about using his skills to clean showers and do laundry when he was not stuck in his cell, or to play handball and yell in different languages.[109] He reminded her of their shared interests in animals and nature, and always applauded her strengths, intelligence, and kindness. He wanted, he promised her, "to see things through your eyes as well as mine . . . whenever you are ready."[110]

As she grew older he made sure she understood her parents' revolutionary principles. She went to Camp Kinderland in the summer, where many on the left had sent their children for generations.[111] He also discussed her seeing films about radicals and their children, acknowledging they "probably give a good picture of how parents can deeply love their children and yet do things that can cause them pain." He willingly accepted that it was then "natural to feel angry even with those we love." After she had seen Shawn Slovo's film *A World Apart* about Slovo's mother, African National Congress leader Ruth First, who was assassinated by the apartheid forces, he told her how much First's books on Africa had shaped his own life and "in some ways she helped make me a revolutionary."[112]

Still, he did not try to force his own views on her. "I think we should give you an understanding of our values and let you know what we think is wrong with some of the ones you're exposed to in other parts of your life," he told her. "I think we should tell you the truth about the world as we see it. What you decide to do about it—whether or not you want to be a revolutionary—is something for you to decide for yourself as you mature."[113] Sarah's values were central to Alan's concerns. Discussing his upbringing, he lamented that the endless testing at school had made it "a lot harder for me to understand how to be collective instead of competitive with people." He taught her to think about the "dignity and self respect" in all kinds of work and the necessity of dealing honestly and in a principled way with those around her.[114]

Realizing that she was growing up an atheist, he wanted her to understand her religious and cultural heritage and advised her to talk to Harriet, whose Jewish grandparents gave her more of this teaching. He explained the history of Chanukah to her as best he remembered from his Hebrew school days. In his telling, Judah (the Hammer) Maccabee and his sons were guerrilla fighters who fought and defeated the imperial Syrians.[115] Other times, he acknowledged the wonderful Christmases at the Zellers and what it meant to see the world differently but still live in a "socially accountable fashion."[116]

It was difficult, sometimes impossible, to parent when contact visits were denied, and ten-minute telephone calls came only a couple of times a month, if that. He worked hard to write to her in language she would understand. When he was in Springfield, hoping she would visit soon, he acknowledged that he felt what she had said: "Bad/mad/sad when I had to get off the phone last week. I heard what you said about the letters not working, and I only wish I had something better to offer. But they're the closest I can come to sending you my heart, which would be disgusting by the time it reached [you] if I sent it direct (a little joke . . . I can hear you say 'Gross. Oh, Daddy.')."[117] In a child's life, he was there, then gone, then there. "She understands what is going on," he told Hank Newman, "but can't help but be a little angry at me, but then feels guilty about that. . . . Oh my heart."[118]

His relationship to Harriet Clark, of whom he was the biological father, was more fraught. With Judy Clark in prison for what appeared her whole lifetime, her parents, Ruth and Joe Clark, sued her and won custody over Harriet.[119] Bitter that Alan had promised to be around for Harriet and then gone underground, while most of the women who had helped care for Harriet were now incarcerated, the Clarks took over their granddaughter's life. Barbara had tried in court to adopt Harriet herself, but Harriet's grandparents blocked this as well. Every week, Harriet got to see her mother in the Bedford Hills prison, and her grandparents finally allowed her to visit Barbara and Sarah on some weekends to give her a tie to this part of her family.[120] Harriet and Sarah considered themselves sisters and became increasingly close.

For Alan, his relationship to Harriet had to be worked out. Writing to Dick Clapp in 1988, he explained that he was able to talk to Harriet, now nine, on the weekends when she was with Barbara and Sarah, "and I write her, but her grandmother doesn't want us to see each other. I understand her concerns, but I think she's making a mistake since Harriet knows I'm her father." After Joe Clark died in December 1988, Ruth began to consider relenting on her refusal to let Alan and Harriet connect. But building that connection would take a long time.[121]

With Barbara, Alan tried to mix his needs from the prison with his love and memories, writing romantically about his memory of her body expanding during the pregnancy with Sarah.[122] He would acknowledge when their conversations were filled with his anxieties, with little time to work things out over and over.[123] On their anniversary on October 20, 1987, he imagined a wine-and-candlelight dinner he wished they could share as he waxed on about her beauty and their nearly twenty years of love.[124] "I love you dearly," he promised.[125] His deepening admiration for all she was doing suffused his letters, with rapturous metaphors as he attempted to strengthen their ties. At other times he seemed critical of some of her parenting decisions and there were tensions.

He knew, too, that she was in another loving relationship. He tried over and over to balance his rational sense that this was appropriate, even revolutionarily necessary, with, as he put it to one of his friends, "some twinges of resentment & jealousy."[126] At the same time, he acknowledged his "ego, possessiveness, sexism" but did not want "to be a fool & blow a good thing for myself." He told her over and over that his love for her was built of the beauty of the day to day, to be "experienced," not just talked about.[127]

He had no idea what he would feel when his sentence was finished, and he assumed Barbara did not either.[128] From his loneliness and solitude in Marion he told her, "I cannot imagine loving another with the depth that I love you. I cannot imagine not being with you if you want me to."[129] But at other times he knew she wrote between shifts in the emergency room, and didn't always respond to his concerns. He had the miserable luxury of time; she did not, he knew. Trying not to chide or guilt-trip her, he nevertheless reminded her that "you have lots of kinds of communication; the letters are pretty much my only way."[130] Over and over when he wrote her, he reminded her of their deep connections and that she often appeared in his dreams.[131] What he was telling Dana at the same time remains in her keeping.

To his friend Bruce Taub, he explained that he and Barbara had "been through so much together, & I feel that we're soul mates, if you'll excuse the romanticism." He knew too that she was "quite seriously involved with her current lover & is probably making longer term plans." There was also still Dana, and both women knew that he cared for them both. "And I figure I'll see what Dana & I can build, even under these circumstances," he contemplated. But more realistically he acknowledged, "Who the fuck knows anything about the future? First, I have to get out of prison."[132] In his fantasies, what he wanted was to hold them all. "I must say," he mused, "I'd love one free day together with both my children — something that's never happened — and one day to make love."[133]

CONNECTICUT AND BEYOND

Alan was supposed to be "salted away" in Marion for years, but he had no control over where he might be sent and when. Despite trying in both New York and Philadelphia to have the charges in Connecticut come to trial after he was indicted there on the pharmacy robbery, it would take months and months to make this happen. He was finally extradited from Marion to face them in late 1987. Sent to a federal prison facility in Hartford, he found himself in the company of Filiberto Ojeda Rios, a Puerto Rican musician-turned-revolutionary who had been part of the Cuban intelligence service. A founder of the FALN and part of the clandestine independence group Los Macheteros, he was being prosecuted for a $7 million Wells Fargo "expropriation" that the FBI never recovered.[134] As one of Alan's lawyers quipped, it was if "Lenin met Che."[135] After years in the underground, Rios was unwell, and it did not take Alan long to realize that he had a serious heart condition. Ever the crusading doctor, after much agitating and connecting with Rios's lawyers, he was able to get Rios to have the open-heart surgery he would need to save his life.[136]

This prison was closer to New York, indeed it was in Barbara's old hometown, which made visiting much easier. When Alan first went to court in Connecticut to plead not guilty, no one was told when his case would come up, and only three reporters were in the room with the court personnel.[137] In subsequent hearings, his friends from New York drove up and filled the room to overflowing. It cheered him up enormously.[138] While his lawyer buddy Bruce Taub suggested he plead guilty by reason of insanity, Bruce's wife, Lynne Karsten, more sensibly noted that Alan was "too principled" to cop such a plea.[139]

Alan faced overwhelming fingerprint and eyewitness evidence that he had in fact taken the fake FDA badge and a gun into the pharmacy when he entered it with Tim Blunk. Blunk, already serving fifty-eight years on the New Jersey charges, was not being prosecuted because he had not been identified. Alan was more exposed because of his fingerprints. It was going to be very difficult for his lawyer to prove he had not done it.

The state had a problem, however: security. As a highly visible and presumed dangerous political prisoner, Alan required the state pay for thousands of extra hours of police and trooper time to watch over him, transport him the twenty miles or so from the jail to the court, and figure out where to imprison him.[140] Federal special weapons and tactics (SWAT) teams appeared in the courtroom, and there were continued fears that his comrades would try to spring him. In turn, his defense attorney thought Alan might need a bulletproof vest for "protection" from the troopers themselves.[141] As the sheriff in Connecticut told a reporter, we "placed sandbags within the judge's bench and hid automatic weapons in the courtroom. There were even rooftop sharpshooters and an airplane flying over the area. . . . 'We were definitely fearful of an armed attack on the courthouse.'"[142] Alan thought they merely wanted to play with their "toys."[143]

For once, the state's fear worked in Alan's favor. Not willing to incur such expense on a mere robbery and kidnapping charge (for holding the store's pharmacist against his will), the state prosecutor compromised. The judge, too, seemed annoyed by the ridiculous show of force that seemed to be taking over his town as he discussed his experiences as an Eagle Scout with Alan.[144] After spending a few months as a "guest" of the state of Connecticut as the trial geared up, on March 17, Alan agreed to plead no contest, accepting conviction without pleading guilty.

On May 18, 1988, with all the armaments, extra metal detectors, and the spectators who had to explain their relationship to Alan to get into the courtroom, he was quite uneventfully sentenced to the mandatory minimum of five years *concurrent* with his federal time to be served in a federal penitentiary. While the newspapers tried to paint him as a dangerous terrorist, Barbara spoke to the reporters and insisted that Alan was an "'anti-imperialist' who believe[d] that 'people who are oppressed and of color have the right to fight for liberation by any means necessary.'" She passed out a statement in which Alan claimed that all the military hardware was "a show of unbridled governmental power, designed to intimate not just me but the public.'" He asked if he could have a chance to visit with then eleven-year-old Sarah as the court proceedings ended. The prosecutor had no objections, but the state police chief would not allow it.[145] Alan expected then to be shipped back to Marion and to perhaps be out in five years. But the government was not yet finished with him.

On May 11, the week before his sentencing, came potentially devastating news: the U.S. District Court in Washington, D.C., had unsealed a federal grand jury's five-count indictment that had been handed down in mid-April against seven individuals in a conspiracy "to influence, change and protest policies and practices of the United States government concerning various international and domestic matters through the use of violent and illegal means."[146] The government's charges covered numerous bombings, from the U.S. Capitol, to other institutions in the District of Columbia, to New York City. The news stories on the front page of the *Washington Post*, quoting the government, reported that "members of the group, operating out of Connecticut, New Jersey,

Pennsylvania, and Maryland, commonly had on hand hundreds of pounds of explosives, including blasting caps, dynamite, detonating cords and ammunition, plus bulletproof body armor and high-powered handguns and semiautomatic weapons."[147]

The political nature of the charges was clear when the U.S. attorney told the press, in words that would trickle down to other "terrorism" trials in the future, "Let this be a warning to those who seek to influence the policies of the United States government through violence or terrorism that we will seek unrelentingly to bring them to justice. Those who attack our sacred institutions of government and seek to destroy the symbols of our democratic system ultimately will have to pay the price."[148]

The government did not have to search for most of those they charged. Only one member of the government-declared conspiracy [Betty Ann Duke] was at large; everyone else named in the indictment was already in federal prisons: Laura Whitehorn, Linda Evans, Marilyn Buck, Susan Rosenberg, Timothy Blunk, and Alan. The U.S. attorney had waited till Marilyn Buck's conviction in the Brink's trial with Mutulu Shakur, completed the day before, and presumably till Alan's Connecticut trial was done as well. As an unnamed official source revealed, the U.S. attorney's office had feared that, "if unsealed earlier, [the indictment] might have interfered with Ms. Buck's trial."[149]

Instead of heading west to Marion to finish serving his time, Alan was flown south immediately after the sentencing in Connecticut to the District of Columbia jail. He was no longer alone. Reunited in the government's eyes in a conspiracy, he and his comrades now faced a set of much more serious charges. Over all of them hung the possibility of spending the rest of their lives in prison.

RESISTANCE IS NOT A CRIME

This new indictment was no surprise to Alan and his comrades, however much they hoped it would not happen.[1] Once brought to Washington, D.C., they were put in isolation cells in its Central Detention Facility. Driven to the federal courthouse arraignment from the jail on May 24, 1988, their purported dangerousness meant, as usual, an armored truck convoy flanked by SWAT teams as helicopters flew over.

The defendants shuffled into the arraignment in handcuffs, leg irons, and chains to discover a floor-to-ceiling, plexiglass bulletproof wall between them and their supporters and spectators. Cameras monitored everything, and no one remembered seeing such a setup in a U.S. courtroom before.[2] Alan described the scene as "the state giving a demonstration of the force it can bring to bear against its enemies." Such measures looked to Alan as if the government were preparing for what used to be called a "show trial" in the Soviet Union where the purpose was propaganda, rather than determination of innocence or guilt.[3]

Angered by the symbolism that made them seem the "embodiment of evil," Alan told the judge that the courtroom reflected the ways the Israelis had contained Adolf Eichmann during his Nazi war crimes trial in 1961.[4] Judge Harold H. Greene was a Holocaust survivor, however, and not sympathetic to Alan's analogy.[5] The judge believed he knew how to manage a "so-called terrorist case," as he put it to a fellow jurist, and to apply the law equally, as he had in other big cases he had handled.[6]

The defendants' conditions in the jail were draconian. Alan reported, "The guards had hung a bed sheet in front of his cell on which the words 'off-limits' were printed."[7] The defendants were told to take showers with their handcuffs on, making washing nearly impossible.[8] Every time they were out of their cells they were shackled and in leg irons.[9] Only one of them at a time was allowed to visit with a lawyer, making planning a joint defense difficult.[10] There were no

Codefendants in the Resistance Conspiracy Case, Washington, D.C., 1988. *Left to right, seated*: Marilyn Buck, Tim Blunk, and Alan Berkman. *Left to right, standing*: Linda Evans, Susan Rosenberg, and Laura Whitehorn. *Courtesy of Barbara Zeller.*

contact visits with their families.[11] "We're in a lair," Alan contended. "The cell is dirty and dingy with a fair number of bugs.... No natural light and no time out-side."[12] Judge Greene was unmoved by their protests about their conditions.[13] Commenting on the judge, Alan reflected, somewhat jokingly, "Revolution-aries are [not] popular with liberals."[14]

Stories circulated about the dangerous defendants. The U.S. marshals told the guards that the six of them were all on the "radical right." According to this story, they were captured as part of a plot to assassinate civil rights leader Jesse Jackson.[15] Alan realized with great understatement "that kind of a rumor, of course, doesn't just stay among the guards & could set up a bad situation in a prison with a 90% Black population."[16] As one of their supporters put it more bluntly, "Rumors like that could get them killed."[17]

The government had effectively entombed them. They were in lockdown twenty-three hours a day and saw the sky or whiffed fresh air only as they moved between the jail and the courthouse. Even exercise was conducted inside. "Two hours a week at Marion & Springfield [prisons] was bad enough, but no time out is intolerable," Alan complained to Barbara in one of his few moments of self-pity.[18] The most sensuous experience available was being alone in the "warm, moist and dark" showers — and even that required handcuffs.[19] It would take almost a year, and many legal arguments, before the defendants were put into the prison's general population.

The ills the defendants had developed in their other prisons were left unattended. Alan was months behind in the screening for possible cancer remissions. Susan Rosenberg, who had been locked in the experimental control unit in Lexington, Kentucky, before this, was suffering from the violence and sensory deprivation imposed there.[20] Laura Whitehorn, Linda Evans, and Marilyn Buck needed medical follow-up for various conditions that were ignored. Tim Blunk recalled that Alan had turned to him at one of their first joint meetings and asked him what he hoped the trial outcome might be. Blunk truly believed he had already explained himself, but it turned out he had imagined it. He was so used to being in solitary that it would take time before he could differentiate between his own internal conversations and what he could articulate out loud.[21] Both Alan and Blunk felt their eyesight deteriorating, since they never looked at distances. Color, too, seemed to vanish. My world is "nicotine-stained tan, institutional washed-out yellows, & muddy gray-browns," Alan reported after thanking a correspondent for the colorful stamp on her envelope.[22]

MOUNTING A DEFENSE: BUT ARE THEY INNOCENT?

After agreeing that they *would* mount a real defense, the defendants now needed to develop one. They saw this defense as their last chance to make their political views public before they faced what might be decades of incarceration. They needed lawyers who would make the necessary detailed legal arguments, while understanding their political motivations: not an easy combination. Such a stance made relationships with lawyers difficult. Laura Whitehorn admitted, "Alan was an exacting client who would get angry if you didn't do exactly what he wanted." None of the others was willing to follow their lawyers' advice exactly either.[23] Well-known New York radical lawyers appeared for them at first, but each defendant needed their own attorney, who had to be a member of the Washington, D.C., bar.

The government postulated a wide-ranging conspiracy to bomb various sites. The five-count indictment charged that the defendants had all been involved in stockpiling weapons and explosives, using false identifications, taking photographs of potential bombing sites, and conspiring to make the bombings happen.[24] From the beginning Alan was critical of their prosecution: "I think this indictment itself is overtly political as well as vindictive—for 3+ years they prosecuted each of us in piecemeal fashion, pyramiding sentences, & now they put it all together under an umbrella conspiracy & go through it all again."[25] Susan Rosenberg saw this too and told her family, "They are in many respects trying us on our past convictions."[26] Moreover, there were neither fingerprints nor eyewitness identifications nor links of precise matériel captured to tie individuals to particular bombings. Rosenberg and Blunk had even been in prison when one of the alleged bombings happened.[27]

Much of the government's case was indeed built on evidence used in some of the defendants' previous trials, raising the question of how double jeopardy applied in a conspiracy trial. Under conspiracy doctrines, it was not at all clear what was double jeopardy and what might also just be guilt by association. Some of the evidence came from what the FBI had seized when agents captured Laura Whitehorn in Baltimore under improperly executed search warrants. All of these legal issues would be raised.[28]

The problem was that the defendants *had* individually and collectively done the various bombings. Arguing in a press release cobbled together after their arraignment, they acknowledged resisting the "U.S. support of the Contra-war against Nicaragua, the racist apartheid regime of South Africa, Israel, and the promotion of racism and racist violence," although they did not address the violence they had deployed.[29] Alan suggested that they use the words "We are charged with these criminal acts, but it is the policy and practices of the government that are violent and illegal." They had to figure out how to explain why they had done these actions, yet the word "innocent" did not cover it.[30] As radical attorney Ron Kuby, who would later become Alan's lawyer, noted, a defendant saying they were not guilty was not the same as saying they were innocent.[31]

"We are not terrorists nor [sic] criminals; we are anti-imperialist political prisoners and we are guilty of no crimes," the defendants declared.[32] Laura Whitehorn told the press, raising the question of every political group that uses violence, "Who says what's illegal, and who says what's violent?"[33] The defendants' mantras became, "Our charges are criminal, but the case is political" and "Resistance is not a crime."[34] The government, in turn, would argue that the defendants were all criminal terrorists who had been harboring bombing equipment, false identifications and guns, and had documents describing the actions that they did.

Terrorism was not a term used lightly. Modern American familiarity with the term *terrorism* started with nineteenth-century anarchists and bombers, but by the mid-twentieth century it was associated primarily with conflicts in the Middle East. *Terrorist* as a domestic label in the United States was still rare in 1988 (before the Oklahoma City bombing in 1995), except of course for those who understood the history of racial violence.[35] In fact, the first Joint Terrorism Task Force, which enabled local police to link with the FBI, only formed in 1980 after the BLA and FALN actions.

Alan and his codefendants refused to be labeled terrorists and understood the political and theatrical nature of their nonlethal bombings. They had no intention of harming anyone innocent (though their actions risked it). They had worked hard after the murders during Brink's to make sure no was killed in their bombings. Even though they did not use guns to maim or kill anyone, all of them had carried or stockpiled weapons and Alan and Tim Blunk had brought them to threaten the store manager during the Connecticut robbery.

The defendants claimed that the term *terrorist* allows the "denial of rights" and the "criminalization of people fighting for change" to seem necessary, even normative. "Terrorism tends to be a status crime," radical lawyers William Kunstler and Eleanor Stein argued in an overview article. "Once labeled, it is a status next to impossible to shed."[36] More directly, Alan and his codefendants declared that under the umbrella term of *terrorism* the government would use "massive and obtrusive surveillance, illegal break-ins, abuse of the subpoena power of the federal grand jury, and abuse of the indictment process itself."[37] Laura Whitehorn labeled the government's actions as a form of "domestic counterinsurgency" that saw "resistance as 'terrorist. . . . ' Anti-terrorism is the McCarthyism of the 1980s, sweeping a wide spectrum of groups and positions into one category of evil."[38] She was referring not just to their case but also to the long FBI surveillance into the very public Committee in Solidarity with the People of El Salvador, which opposed the Reagan administration's violent counterinsurgency against legitimate governments in Central America.[39]

The government, however, did not differentiate between what the defendants did do and what they *might* have done. "Don't freak out," Susan Rosenberg told her parents as the government's case evolved in the fall of 1988. "Alan, Marilyn, Mutulu and I are being accused by the government of helping William Morales escape from Bellevue Hospital."[40] All the violence associated rightly or wrongly with the defendants or their other comrades would continue to hover over their trial, whether they had been charged or convicted in such actions or not, and even when the government either had no evidence or had obtained it illegally.

Alan and his comrades believed their own case (along with others) was a testing ground for removing the controls put on law enforcement and the FBI in the 1960s and 1970s after scandals proved government illegal break-ins and surveillance. The government actions in their case, the defendants contended, was an attempt to portray all resistance—from protected speech to bombings—as "terrorism."

There was a flaw in this argument, however. First Amendment rights to protest or resist had never covered the right to bomb a government into changing its policies, at least from the left. Racial terrorism, from the state, white supremacy groups, and individuals, has been a part of the American landscape for generations.[41] However, Alan and his codefendants' belief in "armed propaganda" easily fit the "terrorist" label, even when the lethal weapons they used or amassed did not have deadly effects. The politics of making these positions clear to a range of would-be supporters, not to mention convincing a judge and jury, was daunting.

No longer a tight-knit cadre, the defendants still had a shared political perspective, despite their separate journeys while imprisoned. Alan had spent prison time thinking through what he had done and why. As he told Barbara, "I feel that I was learning some things about myself over the past year, & I resent having to channel my energy into such mundane endeavors as motions, discovery, affidavits." He found it "boring" and "a waste of time."[42] Many of his codefendants felt the same way.

Nevertheless, decisions had to be made together on how to mount a political defense and use the law to their advantage.[43] Several key principles were clear: the defendants wanted the trial to be as political as possible, would not "snitch" either on one another or on others in their political circles, and would participate in a defense.[44] "Some aspects of the case (and the conditions) will be fought as a group, but each of us will also clarify our individual relationship to the core conspiracy that is charged," Alan asserted. "We know there will be conflicts, but we'll work them out."[45] Solidarity mattered.

Alan and his codefendants wanted desperately for their actions to be seen motivated by love and as resistance to government policies. We need "to move beyond a political definition of the case that got defined by either the government's charges, the conditions/human rights violations/ or resistance in the abstract," Alan asserted to Barbara. He tried to think about what he wanted the outside world to know about them "as people."[46] He struggled to find a way to explain himself and his comrades "to avoid the most turgid of political rhetoric but remain at the level of analytic dialogue. Because politics for me went beyond a formal analysis or even the issue of a life spent in 'movement activities'; the caring part of—the humanism, the international—at the best points became the axis of my life."[47]

His concerns reflected how far his political journey had brought him from the rhetoric-inflamed statements of his Prairie Fire days, or even his statements several years earlier about refusing to speak before the grand jury. All his thinking while imprisoned allowed him to acknowledge, at least to himself and his friends, that mistakes had been made but that motivations mattered. "I no longer claim to know how to change the power structures of the world," he admitted, "but I know some fundamental change has to go on at the level of how people feel about themselves and each other, about identifying with other human beings across race/sex/class lines. Learning that all our lives are valuable but no one's intrinsically more so than any other's." He had come to feeling "all right about myself & also think I made some pretty stupid decisions."[48]

Yet Alan acknowledged personal motivations were difficult to explain. He knew Barbara understood his intentions and those of his codefendants, and that their situation reflected an "aspect of classical tragedy that comes from flawed people trying their hardest to transcend their own limitations & change the world / challenge the Gods. . . . It's one of the reasons I can accept my own situation with some semblance of equanimity." Without overstating their predicament, Alan paraphrased both the New Testament and Shakespeare in concluding we are "our own little prophets without honor."[49]

Everything they had done had been in support of anti-imperialist and antiracist actions on political grounds. After the 1960s, the growing "criminalization of urban spaces," the unequally applied drug busts and sentences, and the expanding "school to prison pipelines" all increased the racialized mass incarceration that was expanding as they were prosecuted.[50] They indeed had been "co-conspirators" in many ways in the most militant antiracist actions and opposition of the late 1970s and early 1980s, actions that attempted to fight back against state violence and criminalization of urban people of color. Yet the defendants were all white and middle class, and the majority of them were women, and that provided them with resources and a kind of individualization that privilege allowed.

Their whiteness, however, had afforded them very little protection so far precisely because in many ways they had chosen to ally themselves against white supremacy. And in trying to seem understandable and human, Alan and his codefendants ran up against the formulation of "political prisoners." As Alan attempted to get support for their case from the Physicians for Human Rights organization, he argued that "just because the U.S. denies it has political prisoners doesn't make it so, and that conditions that would be condemned in other countries are no less deplorable when done by one's own government."[51]

Applying that framework to the United States of the 1980s was difficult. In the 1960s and early 1970s, many had understood what it meant to yell "Free Huey!" when the Black Panther leader was charged with murder, or to see activist Angela Davis's prosecution for supposedly supplying guns to a black militant as totally political, or wonder whether the murders pinned on other black activists were setups.[52] When Andrew Young, President Jimmy Carter's UN ambassador, briefly mentioned the existence of American political prisoners in the 1970s, however, he was reviled by Republicans in Congress and almost relieved of his position for what Carter would call his "unfortunate statement."[53]

The Reagan and Bush administrations used the term *political prisoners* but only about dissidents in such countries as Cuba, China, and the Soviet Union. They never acknowledged human rights violations on our own soil.[54] The reigning assumption held that American democracy allowed opposition and did not criminalize political action. Americans who took their politics on the left into any form of violence were labeled criminals and terrorists, not political actors, and dealt with out of proportion to their actual crimes.[55] As defense attorneys Ronald Kuby and William Kunstler claimed in a 1990 editorial, "All of the world's political prisoners have been convicted of acts that the authorities *pro tem* [for the time being] deem criminal."[56]

THE RESISTANCE CONSPIRACY CASE

To make their politics more visible and appealing, the defendants needed a catchy name for their case. After some discussion they decided on the Resistance Conspiracy Case (RCC).[57] The defendants saw themselves as linked to all others "whose ideas, beliefs, and conscious actions have led them into opposition/conflict with the U.S. government who are imprisoned, either awaiting trial, serving a sentence, or are in any other status."[58] In contrast, the newspapers referred to the defendants as the "Capitol bombers," and the government's formal legal title remained the *U.S. v. Laura Whitehorn et al.*

If Alan had expected to be "salted away," as he put it, to ponder his own political trajectory, he was now very much caught up with the government's claims and the defense. "Going through this stuff for the first time in a while is depressing, personally, politically & legally," he admitted to Barbara. "But there's no getting around it, so we're each reluctantly digging in."[59] It had stopped him from things he thought more important to his own life, as he wanted "to write to relieve the pressure of my thoughts & pent-up feelings. . . . I need to turn inward for a while to consolidate & be able to move ahead in my own development."[60]

In the fall of 1988, the codefendants finally won the right to meet together to plan their defense.[61] "Things are bit better for us," Susan Rosenberg wrote her parents. "Now we can meet together without shackles, and every day, [this] means we are out at least 6 hours 5 days a week and then we are out more in the day [time]."[62] This gave them a kind of "freedom" that had not had for months and months. Alan was really glad to be back among his comrades.[63]

Levity and at least some joy sustained the defendants after so many years of isolation.[64] A supporter made them stationery: "RESISTANCE IS NO CRIME" the banner on the letterhead read with their names and prison numbers, as if they were attorneys at a law firm, listed on the left and the D.C. Central Detention Facility given as their address.[65] "We thought we'd use this stationery to communicate with the prison administration . . . no, no, just kidding," Susan Rosenberg wrote on her new "letterhead."[66] Laura Whitehorn devised a poem for Rosenberg's thirty-fourth birthday in the fall that included the lines:

We've all grown wiser in this year,
So if our trial ever grows near, we'll be glad we finally learned,
To keep all our bridges from being burned.

We won't say "yes," we won't say "no" when people clamor, "Is it so?"
Some lawyers find it quite distressing
That our defense is "keep them guessing."[67]

There were other moments that reinforced their humanity. Once someone on the legal team was able to bring in hummus and Alan tasted garlic for the first time in years.[68] Since the inspection of the bags of visitors was hit or miss, one of their legal supporters brought them decent coffee, barbeque, even lesbian novels, with "Defense Material" written on the packages. Or supporters put themselves between the guards looking in and the codefendants so they could steal a hug or kiss from lovers or family when contact visits were finally allowed.[69] Once friends made a seder at Passover with enough wine in the haroseth to give them a buzz, a privilege of "religious freedom" that three of them were accorded, even if they argued over whether or not to adhere to any of the ceremonial aspects of the holiday.[70] Rosenberg's mother and father, who were endlessly supportive of their only child, became the group's "spiritual parents."[71] Alan enjoyed visits from his parents and all his brothers, and even managed to reconcile with his oldest brother despite their political differences.[72]

All of the codefendants knew that they would need as much outside support as possible. As the national left was then focused elsewhere — on the growing HIV/AIDS pandemic, the purported drug crisis, the wars in Central America, the backlash against feminism, and antiapartheid divestment of college endowments — the RCC almost seemed like a holdover from another political time.[73] Groups like the Washington Area Committee for Political Prisoners' Rights and the New York–based Committee to Fight Repression were organized to support them, and each of the defendants reached out to whomever they could.[74] Since four of the six of them were women, Laura Whitehorn and Linda Evans had long been out as lesbians, and three of them had worked in various left feminist organizations, they sought first to find allies in the lesbian and feminist communities. "We think that fighting the government and being lesbians are really intrinsic to each other ... and that's the only way we're ever going to win liberation for ourselves and for other women and for other lesbians," Evans declared.[75] Famed lesbian cartoonist Alison Bechdel, whom one of the supporters knew, featured the defendants' arguments about their status as political prisoners in her *Dykes to Watch Out For* cartoon strip.[76] But some in those communities, angered by the codefendants' tough and judgmental stances in the past, or horrified by the bombings, stayed away.[77]

The defendants knew they needed a mass campaign to explain what it meant to be a political prisoner in a national and international context.[78]After many discussions and drafts, Barbara with Susan Rosenberg's father, Manny, sent out a heartfelt "Dear Friends" letter in August 1988. Describing the co-

Alison Bechdel, "Free Lunch," *Dykes to Watch Out For*, no. 79.
Courtesy of Alison Bechdel.

defendants' motives in ways designed to garner broad support, they claimed, "They couldn't see injustice and oppression and just walk away; perhaps they have less tolerance for hypocrisy than many of us do, perhaps their inner vision of a better world is brighter than ours. . . . Whether or not we agree with their politics, we know they are political prisoners."[79] In an era before social media, it was constant work to create a media strategy and produce varying kinds of information in the form of printed booklets, newsletters, leaflets, videos, press statements, posters, and rallies.

Alan continued to get needed emotional sustenance from his visits, letters, and phone calls as he contemplated his losses. "Too many years of having to deal with this stuff on their terms," he told Barbara. "It's too painful to see a future of freedom & as much togetherness as we choose appear to be receding in the darkness."[80] His letters still reflected his sexual ache for her as he tried to keep their love alive. He knew full well that Barbara was making a life with Jackie Haught, and that he was connected more and more to Dana Biberman through visits, calls, letters, and her work on his defense.

He seemed genuinely torn between these women. In one poignant letter to Barbara, Alan described a recurring dream in which he was still in prison and she was visiting. There was the possibility of escape in his imagination and they kept discussing it. He kept telling her, he recalled, that they had "made decisions that created our past—we can create our future. . . . If we're going to try new things together, we've got to make a commitment—we've got to engage. We can do it for each other better than we can with other people—that's just the way it is. We'll create a new life."

With uncertainty, Alan wished Barbara a good trip and vacation with Jackie Haught. In his letter he acknowledged sending these wishes with "some of the same ambivalence you probably have when you tell me to have a good weekend sometimes when Dana is visiting. True, but not wholeheartedly."[81] In another letter he was clearer, "I wish I could hug you, make love with you, and hold you while you fell asleep. Peace."[82] When she clearly was making decisions about how much she could do on the case, he reminded her that he accepted her need to make changes. "You are more important to me than this case," he announced with unlikely bravado.[83] A few months later he told her, "The depths and beauty of your spirit, which I had the good intuition to sense in 1970, I know and appreciate more than ever. You will always be an anchor of my life."[84]

He was also well aware that the government was still watching his friends and family. When Alan was in the D.C. jail, Barbara and Sarah had gone on a brief vacation to New Hampshire and found themselves followed by the FBI. Mary O'Melveny, Susan Rosenberg's lawyer, had her office broken into and her address book taken. Referring back to when a stethoscope had shown up in the car of his Philadelphia prosecutor, probably planted by the government itself, Alan commented, "I half expect a stethoscope to show up somewhere. . . . The bastards never give up, do they?"[85]

Alan's correspondence with his friends provided differing kinds of sustenance for him. With Stephen Wangh, his theater friend, he was open in exploring his motives and mistakes. With Ann, the older religious comrade whom he sometimes thought of as his psychic anima, he had wide-ranging discussions of differing ways of doing politics, accepting spirituality, and expressing love. With Sarah, he was a sensitive father trying desperately to parent in a situation where everything thwarted that effort. With numerous others who had known him before he had gone underground, he constantly sought to remind them of who he was and why it mattered.

SELF/COLLECTIVE

Conspiracy trials create complicated legal questions about due process and consistency of evidence among defendants.[86] They also raise a particular problem for each defendant: How will they stand together when their interests might be protected better as individuals? The codefendants in the RCC had done years of political work together, above and underground, but they had since spent three years in separate prisons with differing sentences. Each of them had her or his own journey, varying resources, and diverse contacts despite the similarities and alleged conspiracy.

Alan was aware of what they were up against legally. He explained, "The government basically has to prove only association & general agreement—they have no obligation to show any direct participation in any of the specific bombings." The prosecution could also try to pit the codefendants against one another. For their part, the defendants could try the difficult "necessity" defense (because the government acted this way our actions were necessary) as Susan Rosenberg and Tim Blunk had done in their previous trial. To do so, the defendants would have to admit to the acts themselves, "thus essentially pleading guilty to 40 years in prison," as Alan put it.[87] In Blunk and Rosenberg's case, this defense led to sentences of more than half century.

Alan had a bigger problem to consider: To what extent should he rely upon his own thinking and to what degree on his comrades' decisions? He came to realize he had what his friend Stephen Wangh called "some trouble with the I/we distinction." By this Stephen meant Alan could not listen to his own instincts and feelings, as he subjugated them to his sense of the politically demanded "we." Willing to ponder his friend's insights, Alan reconsidered his past. When he was in May 19th, he admitted, "I allowed ideology-dogma to alienate myself from the impulses that gave rise to the search for the ideology."[88] What he meant was that his own "pain," about what he saw around him and in his own heart, made him join a group where this pain could be fought through "rigid ideological constructs [that] played a greater & greater role in keeping the group together and me in the group." Given the "rectification" he had been through and the demand for collective discipline, he realized that "I increasingly substituted the collective ideology—the 'we'—for my own judgment, & once having convinced myself, would work hard to convince others." He saw his past as a constant struggle between his ego's needs to be right and in leadership, and his sense of the necessity of helping others and "being nice" that had been his doctor role for decades, and was part of his attempt to shed his male supremacy.[89]

Alan had spent the last three years in prison before the RCC as "not part of any 'we,'" while surviving his near death from the cancer treatments. With this new indictment, he had to reconstruct the reasoning that had led to the collective actions in the first place. "None of us are the same people anymore; I, for one, have a lot of questions about aspects of the past." They had each become an "I" that made it "hard to capture a 'we' locked in the past."

When he reached for an analogy to explain their situation, his sensual and romantic mind emerged. "Try to think of being forced back into a once serious love affair," he cautioned Stephen Wangh, "that you had since moved beyond; it's all familiar, but the magic's gone & it's not really a living process any more. Unless you succeed in building a new relationship based on the present — & that's what my co-defs. & I are trying to do. Not so easy when each person is drained by years in isolation & the emotional burden of heavy sentences."[90]

Alan was also deepening his understanding of what had pulled him into becoming an active revolutionary. In thinking this through he harkened back to the decision to take the risks at Wounded Knee, not to the seemingly transformative moment at Cornell when Stokely Carmichael spoke (his reference point in his usual radicalization tale). Recalling the angry American Indian Movement father who insisted that Alan do his wife's difficult delivery rather than allow the FBI to move her to a hospital, Alan told Barbara that "being closer to death from the .357 in the hand of our erstwhile allies than from the APCS [armed personnel carriers] or the guns of the vigilante ranchers [was] probably the most valuable part of the experience for me." It was the struggle that mattered to him, even "if it ended in an ignominious & even ludicrous death (and would they have made me a martyr?). It is right to struggle," he was certain, because of "the love & satisfaction is in the struggle, the commitment, & not in the outcome. No guarantees of either success or heroic failure."

Alan sought the honor of an American patriot in a war against a system he saw as dehumanizing, unfair, and corrupt, not unlike those who became radical abolitionists, or went to Spain during its civil war, or risked their lives in the civil rights and civil liberties battles at home. He sought solidarity to wage this fight, and did not turn back. He was clear about what mattered: not becoming "anesthetized and insensitive to the casual cruelty of this society." Others had of course faltered at a point, but he and his comrades did not. In their lives he truly believed that motives mattered "to contribute to an overall resistance," even when "any particular decision may, in retrospect, have been right or wrong, but the fact that we chose, and that our choices were often those that others would be most reluctant to take on."

Alan knew he wanted to be on the right side of history. He recalled that "people were changing the world, & I wanted to be part of it." He acknowledged that he and his comrades had made tactical mistakes and failed to have "a clear strategy about how to change this society . . . [but] I know nothing will work if there aren't more people like us."[91] He admitted, too, that he "wanted to be a big fish in a little pond & taste a little power. And somehow the revolutionary commitment that had led me to Africa was diverted into a small sectarian group here."[92] He was in a sense trying to fulfill the promise of his own intellect and commitments, yet caught in the demands of collectivity.

LEGAL LAND

After seemingly endless legal discussions, the defendants were ready to make a constitutional argument.[93] As their lawyers had argued in their first statements, much of the first charge of the indictment was based on the evidence the government had already used against Alan, Tim Blunk, and Susan Rosenberg in their other cases.[94] Rosenberg's lawyer Mary O'Melveny and Alan thought they should raise the issue of whether reusing the evidence that three of them had already been convicted on counted as double jeopardy in cases of conspiracy, not just in individual cases, and would therefore be disallowed under the Fifth Amendment to the Constitution.[95] Did the amendment apply only to individuals, or did it also apply to the group in the conspiracy as a whole? The lawyers and codefendants argued back and forth.[96] If it were double jeopardy for some in the conspiracy, didn't that extend to them all since they were liable for all the "joint" actions? The lawyers briefed the double jeopardy argument and hoped to persuade the judge.

They proved partially right. In May 1989, a year after they had first been indicted, Judge Greene determined that Alan, Susan Rosenberg, and Tim Blunk could not be part of the conspiracy because of the double jeopardy doctrine. Their charges were dismissed. The government prosecutors, however, were not willing to accept this finding and immediately appealed.[97] It was not over.

Alan's response demonstrated his continued I/we dilemma. "For a few days," he told Steven, "it seemed like great news, a real end to the incessant trials, and as close of a guarantee as I'm going to get that I'll walk out in four years."[98] Yet as often happens when there are multiple defendants and differing consequences for each, Alan's initial joy turned into what he called "a real emotional roller coaster." As he realized, "It was still a disappointment that only 3 of us had gained directly from it; there couldn't help but be a little jealousy mixed in with the joy for those who remain and a little guilt mixed with the joy for those who were saved." He would admit the sense that his prison years might be finite meant his "heart pounded, my breathing quickened, and my whole body trembled. . . . But then the adrenalin faded away and I found myself in touch with the real sadness I feel for my friends/co-defendants who face so many years inside."

Realistically, he also knew that the government's confidence in its ability to win on appeal meant he would not be immediately shipped back to the penitentiary at Marion. Rather, he was kept in D.C. for what the government thought would be an inevitable trial. There was still another small victory: after nearly a year the judge finally ordered that the prisoners had to receive the federal minimum of two hours a week outside. When he finally got out into the air, "it was the first time in 50 weeks, and even though it was rainy, windy, & cold, it felt great."[99]

The possibility of getting out of incarceration fueled his imagination. Besides the hopes that he would be engulfed in sexuality, tenderness, and the company of women he loved, he also fanaticized about walks. He wrote that the walks came in different forms and places: mountains, beaches, New York neighborhoods, and above all "being able to walk in a straight line without coming up against bars & a wall; then there's a sense of peering intently at everyone & everything, of trying to see & capture every detail before it all disappears again."[100]

Fantasy life, however, was tempered by the continuing legal work. The government's appeal wended its way up to another court. Once again, the defendants had to go over and over the arguments to be made with lawyers, have them write the brief that was filed in July and argued in the court in September 1989. Because the case involved both conspiracy and double jeopardy, it was legally fascinating to Alan's lawyer, who also appreciated that Alan was "a lovely man, gracious and appreciative, with a sense of humor throughout his ordeal."[101] He in turn thought she was doing a good job, but as he humorously put it, "I figure it never hurts to have 2 great legal minds working on it instead of just one. So, my days are filled with reading legal cases & my nights are often filled with whirling thoughts about how to respond to this or that argument."[102]

In November 1989 the appeals court handed down a ruling that was good and bad news for the defendants.[103] The case was reversed and remanded, meaning the justices did not accept that double jeopardy applied in a conspiracy and required the original court to reconsider the case. In that sense, the government "won." But the prosecutors were also required to show that the evidence against the defendants was not the same as what they had used in the previous cases—a considerable problem since the prosecution had no new evidence.[104]

Nevertheless, the various arguments continued for months into 1990 and the government appealed again, this time to the Supreme Court.

Alan in the meantime tried to use his time for something worthwhile and distracting from the endless legal concerns. He and his public health friend Dick Clapp were asked to do a paper for the annual meeting of the American Public Health Association on the carcinogens in the water at the prison in Marion. The two men went back and forth on the various scientific questions.[105] The process also allowed Alan to come up with a thoughtful differentiation between what he called "prisoner's health" and "prison health care.[106] He spent more time on other articles about political prisoners and submitted them to various left journals.[107]

While Alan was busy, there was no hiding from one of the worst things about prison life: being unable to comfort loved ones when misfortune struck. Alan was deeply troubled when Barbara's mother was killed in a car accident on January 23, 1990. "It was the biggest personal loss I've suffered while in prison," he told Dick Clapp. "Everybody's dealing as best we can. . . . It's been a hard week." But this hardly covered what this sudden tragedy meant for Barbara, and Alan's inability to be with her.[108]

In the face of this emotional loss, Alan tried to see if his time served might be limited now given his excellent prison record of no infractions or violence, and the ever-present possibility that his cancer might return. Despite his record and the pleas of friends and family, including a heartfelt handwritten letter from his father, the parole commission refused.[109] Even though the charges that he had been an accessory to murder after the fact for treating Marilyn Buck after Brink's had been dropped in New York, the federal parole board wrongly held these untried charges against him.[110] Now, if he weren't given more time if they lost the RCC, he would have to stay in prison for his full term of ninety-two months—longer, he noted, than 95 percent of those given the same time to serve.[111]

There was one way out: if Alan were willing to become an informant, the U.S. Attorney's Office would not object to his release. The government was making the same demand as the FBI and police who had confronted him in his Lincoln Hospital office and the New York courthouse's bathroom in 1982. He did not think he had anything of forensic value but believed the government wanted to separate him from his comrades with this demand. There was no way that Alan would comply.

Then it all became moot. What had begun as a case about conspiracy and resistance became a political battle to keep him from dying. His cancer was back.

13

A CONSPIRACY FOR LIFE

Even though there had always been the possibility Alan's cancer could return, the Bureau of Prisons' operating assumption was, as his codefendant Susan Rosenberg explained, "that cancer in remission is not really cancer or a problem and therefore on-going conditions are not relevant."[1] To acknowledge a prisoner's medical concerns undermined the rationale for incarceration. Alan understood it well: "If the doctors see us as human beings, then the guards might have to do that too."[2]

His class position, his white privilege (or what was left of it), his connections outside the prison, the sympathetic judge from his Philadelphia case, and his medical knowledge at least had gotten some things done. After leaving him in the D.C. jail for months without follow-up monitoring scans, his former judge tried to get them scheduled. Through Alan and Barbara's connection, a cancer specialist saw him in May 1989 and declared that the conditions in jails and prisons would heighten the possibility of the cancer's return.[3]

When he finally saw the D.C. jail oncologist in October 1989, a scan was ordered for three months later. The scheduled appointment came and went, despite Alan's pleas. In early March 1990, he palpated his own abdomen and found a mass that felt very much like the original cancerous lymph node that led to the Hodgkin's diagnosis. He was getting worried, very worried. Finally the new scan happened on March 19. Alan saw what he thought was a mass on the scan but was told "there was no problem."[4] The next visit to an oncologist was not allowed for three more weeks. The wait was interminable.

The tragicomedy of prison medical care played itself over the following month. One doctor read the wrong scan and pronounced Alan was fine, until Alan noticed the date on the report and explained there had been a more recent scan. Another examination led a physician to agree with Alan that the lymph node and latest scan were troubling, but he never contacted an oncologist as he promised for the follow-up. Even after he got to the jail's oncologist, she asserted that nothing was wrong, just enlarged iliac nodes in his pelvis, and scheduled an appointment months later. His lawyers finally were able to get him a second opinion from a Hodgkin's specialist at Georgetown Hospital, who insisted a biopsy should be done then and there. Alan's lawyer then called the federal attorneys to insist on the biopsy. It was a month since the scan had found the mass.[5]

Alan's supporters and family were frantic. Even without the biopsy, it was obvious to Alan, Barbara, and the Georgetown specialist that his cancer had metastasized. Waiting this long in any other setting would be grounds for a malpractice suit. The government then began to wrangle with Alan and his lawyers for several more weeks, arguing that he should be sent to Springfield for the biopsy because of his "security" risk.

Everyone in Alan's world was mobilized. Hundreds of letters poured into the Bureau of Prisons from fellow doctors, former patients, and major health organizations. Even those who neither knew him nor shared his politics were horrified by what was obviously a bureaucratic way to keep him from surviving.[6] Barbara wrote to her congressman, while another friend worked connections to get through to Anthony Lewis, the crusading New York Times columnist.[7]

On April 25, Alan's lawyers were able to get a judge in D.C. to sign an emergency order to have the tests and treatment done either in Washington with the Georgetown Hospital physicians or at the federal prison medical facility in Rochester, Minnesota, where medical service was run by staff from the Mayo Clinic, and which had a reputation for providing the best medical care in the federal system.[8] Yet delays continued. It took until May 3 for the biopsy to be scheduled, as more than a dozen guards accompanied him from the jail, not to Georgetown Hospital but to the Howard University Hospital, where two guards stationed themselves in the operating room suite. Alan's feet were shackled and he was chained to a hospital bed even as he went under general anesthesia. "This reduces me totally to an object," he wrote. "My last, heart-felt words as I conked out were, 'Animals . . . you people are animals.'" The U.S. marshals returned him to the D.C. jail only half an hour after he came out of the anesthesia, groggy and worried.[9]

Alan's fear proved right: a prison nurse a few days later came to his cell to tell him as kindly as she could that the cancer had returned. It was Hodgkin's again.

Even with the positive diagnosis, it seemed that nothing was happening. Then the connections to Anthony Lewis at the New York Times paid off: "Death by Delay" made it into the paper's op-ed pages on May 15, 1990. Lewis went over the details of what would be seen as cruelty and malpractice anywhere else. "It is eight weeks since his CT scan, 10 days since the biopsy, and still nothing is being done to fight the disease," Lewis wrote.[10] When Alan had been on trial in Philadelphia the government attorneys had argued he should be put in prison for his entire life. It was beginning to look as if the government might have won. If he did not receive the medically complicated treatment in a decent place under the right circumstances, his chances of survival were slim.

SECURITY AND DELAYS

The delays continued as the Bureau of Prisons' security concerns trumped Alan's medical needs. Even though his cancer's recurrence was confirmed, the prison officials kept insisting he should receive his chemotherapy treatment in Springfield as the designated secure medical facility for prisoners from or bound for Marion.[11] Alan's worries about going there were based on his own experiences, and backed up later by newspaper exposés, Amnesty International, and ACLU Prison Project legal charges about how inexperienced, inappropriately trained, dangerous, and neglectful the physicians at the facility were.[12] Judge Pollak tried to intervene again. The prison officials told Pollak there was an appropriate oncologist in Springfield, but Alan's legal team reported back to the judge that according to the county medical society, the purported oncologist had neither the training nor the specialist certification to treat Alan's cancer.[13]

It wasn't just the unqualified physician that frightened Alan about Springfield. It was the danger that he would die from rapidly spreading infections brought on by chemotherapy, a common side effect in a patient's compromised immune system, given that the doctors at that prison left after 4 p.m., and the x-ray and lab offices closed then too. Even if he had to be moved to a community hospital because the infections could cause serious sepsis, by the time the guards arrived and the arrangements were made he knew he could be dead. Only a sophisticated patient or a health professional would have known to be concerned about these possibilities.

After the Lewis article appeared, accompanied by much organizing and legal maneuvers, his transfer to Springfield was stopped. The prison officials finally determined he could be treated at D.C. General Hospital, which had a locked ward for patients from the D.C. jail. Staffed by Howard University medical personnel, it meant oncologist Dr. Laviza Mahmood, the physician who had misread his scans and delayed his treatment months earlier, would supervise Alan's care.[14] At least the Georgetown Hospital's oncologist who had seen him would be allowed to consult.[15]

Alan felt some sense of relief once the decisions to start the treatment were made. "For a while," he wrote Stephen Wangh, "I was the only doctor [in the prison system] who thought I had cancer and I felt extremely responsible (and nervous about) for the mobilization I had initiated." He was ready to take on what he knew might be really difficult. "So, much of my current sense of inner peace is a reaction to some of the pressures being lifted," he admitted. "Or perhaps having survived that period, I know I'm strong enough to deal with this period of chemotherapy. Or, my skeptical side warns, it's a false sense of well-being induced by high-dose steroids. Yea for steroids, then."[16]

CHEMOTHERAPY, COMPLICATIONS, AND *60 MINUTES*

After all the legal maneuvering and delays about where and when he would be treated, he began his first round of the powerful anticancer drugs on May 31, 1990. The regimen consisted of administrations of infusions and oral medications over nearly six months of an on/off treatment schedule, with only a week between the multiple rounds. Alan had every reason to expect very severe side effects, including the possibility of sepsis and nerve damage. Even if he survived all the various complications, he knew one loss was inevitable: chemically induced sterility from the drugs. Whatever hopes he had entertained of ever having another child when he finally got out of prison were now dashed. Banking his sperm before treatment was not exactly something the prison system allowed.[17]

For nonincarcerated cancer patients, support from experienced medical and nursing personnel, buzzers for the nurses and aides, and family members nearby as advocates would be expected. All of this was thwarted by his incarceration. Above all there was the ongoing assumption in prison medicine that the inmate patient was often lying and could not be trusted.[18]

As could have been predicted, commonplace complications were exacerbated by incompetence and delays as Alan was shuttled back and forth between the locked ward at the hospital and the jail's infirmary on his off weeks. To make the delivery of the drugs easier without the constant need to insert IVs, a Mediport and catheter were surgically implanted in his chest wall. This is a normal procedure for patients undergoing this kind of chemotherapy, but it is not supposed to go into the heart.

While it was being placed Alan was sure he was having palpitations, or what he described as feeling as if "there were a worm wriggling in my heart, a flutter in my upper chest, a slight feeling of nausea."[19] Barbara reported that the surgeon told him, "It didn't matter." As his concerns continued, Alan finally was able to demand an electrocardiogram, which showed that he was in atrial fibrillation, a form of heart arrhythmia that can be life-threatening. The port had to be replaced, but just a few weeks later it stopped working and had to be removed again because he was hemorrhaging into his chest wall. It was replaced again. This was only the first round.[20]

Had Alan not been a physician with all the knowledge and class privilege this entailed, and had Barbara not been coming down from New York regularly to monitor what was happening, and had his legal team of supporters not been nearby, the crises after crises could have proved really serious: he experienced twelve hours of hiccups one day, and then a manic and depressive episode.[21] During one of the early chemo cycles, when one of the drugs was withdrawn, Alan felt severe muscle pain, weakness, excessive sweating, and dangerously low blood pressure. Even when he was given IVs of fluids to bring his pressure up, he and Barbara both worried that he might have kidney damage or sepsis. Dr. Mahmood agreed he was in danger and ordered antibiotics, but it would take almost another nine hours before they arrived from the pharmacy. In cases of possible sepsis, such a delay was extremely dangerous.

After this, Alan went back in the jail infirmary to await the next chemo round. His fever spiked and he thought he might be septic again from infections (the drugs to prevent a white cell count drop in chemo patients did not exist yet). The physician's assistant who monitored the jail's infirmary patients agreed to call a doctor, but Alan knew he was in real danger. It would take another five hours for the doctor to arrive. He was taken back to the hospital for more antibiotics delivered by IVs.

For most patients and their families, hospital horror stories are not uncommon, even in the best institutions. Medical mistakes can prove fatal, nursing and medical personnel can be indifferent, and it can take hours before the right drugs are administered. Alan experienced all of these same risks, but he did so as a prisoner in a locked hospital ward or jail infirmary, where he could only shout in the hope that someone would take him seriously.

During Alan's third cycle a drug called Vincristine had the serious side effects it was known for: autonomic neuropathies that meant he was developing serious, possibly irreversible nerve damage.[22] When the fourth cycle started, the Georgetown doctor consulted and substituted a different drug. Alan's white cell count began to drop precipitously; he could not stand up without danger of fainting, and his fevers returned. His body was not strong enough to continue the chemotherapy. Given Alan's constant medical challenges after each chemo round, the prison officials finally agreed to let him stay in the hospital, and not be moved back to the jail infirmary, till the treatment was over.[23] At least in this kind of space, in an institution he was familiar with as a physician, he might have more access to care in an emergency.[24]

If the government let him stay in the hospital, it was not just out of concern for his health. Alan had become increasingly visible, and corrections officials knew they were being watched. Producers from the CBS news show *60 Minutes* had read about his situation in the *New York Times*. They were working on

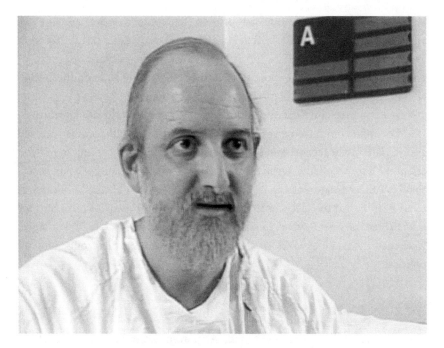

Alan during chemotherapy for his second round of cancer in prison.
Still from Alan's *60 Minutes* interview at the Howard University
Hospital Prison Ward, Washington, D.C., November 1990. The "That's
the Law" episode aired March 17, 1991. *Courtesy of CBS News.*

a story on medical care in prisons, and wanted to feature Alan. Newsman Steve
Kroft showed up to interview him on September 16, 1990, although the show
did not air until the following March. After Alan described the incompetence
of the doctors who were supposed to be monitoring his progress after his first
cancer, Kroft asked him, "What do you think your condition would be if you
weren't a doctor?" Alan replied, "I think I'd be dead."

On television, Alan looked like a very sick cancer patient in chemotherapy.
His stringy hair hung from an increasingly bald pate, his face was pale and hag-
gard, his eyes sunken, and his hospital clothes drooped from a thinning frame.
It was a shocking sight. When Alan argued that going to either to Marion or
Springfield would have killed him, the *60 Minutes* segment shifted to the head
of health services at Springfield Prison Hospital, who said he was wrong. Kroft
pointed out that a federal judge had agreed with Alan, to which the prison doctor and bureaucrat shot back, "Where did the federal judge get his medical degree?"[25]

Kroft had done his homework. After citing several cases of dangerous sur-
geries done by incompetent prison doctors, and the ways inmate patients were

shipped about, he said, "We had lawyers that have come to us, and, and inmates who have come to us and said that . . . and show us cases that said that what they amount to is torture." The Bureau of Prisons' medical official disagreed, of course, but Kroft pressed on, quoting another official who had admitted, "Balancing security and medical care is a difficult problem."

The prison doctor's callous response made clear the authorities' priorities: "Dr. Berkman committed a very serious offense to start with, but he received appropriate medical care. And obviously, he's still alive and kicking to tell you about it." Kroft replied, "Because of his court battle, Dr. Alan Berkman is getting his cancer treatment at a public hospital outside the Federal Prison System." Alan got in the last word: "I have gotten decent medical care, but not *from* the federal prison system, *in spite of* the federal prison system."[26] His voice, weakened by his illness and treatment, was nevertheless still strong, and still political.

NEAR DEATH AND NEEDING "TWO BIG-LEGGED WOMEN"

The next cycles of the treatment made Alan even sicker. His white cell count dropped again and, after his inability to stand worsened, the chemo was stopped. He knew something was really wrong. He had difficulty making Dr. Mahmood understand how terrified and dangerously sick he was. His rage at her had to be contained if he was to get anywhere, he knew, but this too had its costs in stress.[27]

He was right again: he was in trouble. He was certain the port and catheter in his chest had become infected, as his skin around it was getting redder and warm to the touch. It "felt like a lump of coal left burning inside the surgically created pocket carved in the flesh of my chest," he wrote. Despite the IVs of antibiotics he was being given, he had all the signs of a raging infection: high fevers with his lips and ears tingling, drenching sweats, muscle shivers, and goose bumps. He was getting weaker as his leg muscles were shrinking, a process called fasciculation and another sign of possibly irreversible nerve damage. He had to shuffle to make it from the bed to the bathroom, hanging on to whatever he could find. "Dizzy and drunk with effort," he wrote, "I would grab the sink and then slide down onto the nearest toilet, hoping it was not again plugged up. . . . Even brushing my teeth made me short of breath and dizzy."

He felt himself getting still worse. Even stumbling to a bathroom became impossible. Because changing the drug cocktail might mean he would never beat the cancer, his choices, as he put it, "were dying or becoming progressively paralyzed. I had opted for the possible paralysis." As things got still worse, he thought about just letting go rather than remaining dependent on prison care in a state of paralysis. But that feeling did not last very long.[28]

Then over the weekend of October 14, his bladder suddenly stopped working. He worried that the distended organ would then harbor more infections his body could not fight off. Dr. Mahmood came to see him and suggested they have the port in his chest removed, but Alan feared that the surgeon who had botched it before would do so again. He was assured that doctor was not on that day. The resident who looked in on him did the normal neurological tests, which showed he was losing muscular and neurological control. He said he'd come back later, yet Alan kept waiting. He was in increasing pain as his bladder filled but could not be emptied.

The Georgetown oncologist returned to check on him and determined the port was indeed infected. Alan recalled that he said, "My god, that's going to kill you. I can't believe you've had that in all this past week. You have no neutrophils [white blood cells]. It could kill you." As he went out to find the other doctors, Alan realized that his bladder was reaching a state of crisis, as his medical personnel seemed to be waiting for it to empty on its own. While other arrangements were being made, a new and barely experienced resident put a Foley catheter into Alan's urethra. From his distended bladder the catheter drained almost a quart and a half of urine, which had been backed up for nearly a day. Finally the steps were taken to have the port in his chest removed, and as Alan spoke to the surgeons who would do this, he felt for the first time that he did not have to be, as he put it, "both patient and doctor."

His turn playing both roles was not quite over, as his condition was about to become as life-threatening as ever. Although the surgeons had ordered a different set of antibiotics, he again had to play doctor to insist the nurses bring the right ones. It took hours more for them to arrive. He awoke, determining he had passed out hours before. In the dark, he realized that paralysis was taking over most of his body. He feared it would reach his lungs, causing him to "suffocate silently while fully awake." He knew he needed assistance, and immediately. It was then that he began to scream. His body was beginning to shut down and no one was responding.

Alan realized what was happening: not just paralysis but septic shock. "I couldn't move because my blood pressure was too low and there wasn't enough oxygen getting to my muscles. . . . I had to take advantage of the time I had to get some help before I passed out again and possibly died." He knew that when a bacterium overwhelms a body the toxins could cause the cardiovascular system to fail. He recalled sobbing, tears pouring down his face, "totally dependent . . . as a baby with only my tears and screams as tools."

No one was responding to his screams. He focused on the infusion pump controlling the IV fluid that was delivering the antibiotics into his arm. An alarm would sound if it was interrupted, but he could not move to reach it. "It suddenly came to me: gravity could help! I concentrated all my energy on my neck. I began to turn my head to the right. With an assist from gravity, I was able to turn it all the way, getting my jaw cradled into my right shoulder. The IV tubing was right in front of my face. I bit it. I bit it hard."

In his weakened state, he was woozy and confused by the noise the pump set off, but his gambit worked. A nurse came in, angry that Alan had been yelling and set off the alarm. She agreed to take his blood pressure, which turned out to be a dangerously low 65 over 30 (normal is 110 over 70). An intern was called and then finally Dr. Mahmood. She thought he might just be anemic, but Alan was sure he was in septic shock. As arrangements to get him blood for the anemia went on, he grew more desperate. Conversing with a nurse who had taken a liking to him, Alan convinced him to try increasing the rate of fluids coming into his body through the IV. It was a worthy try, but it did not change his situation. In his stupor he kept hearing the roar of the crowd at the Redskins-Giants game at nearby Robert F. Kennedy Stadium. He "started to laugh. Could anything have been more All-American? I was going to die on an NFL Sunday with the crowd cheering all around. My laughter mixed with my sobs."

Finally enough doctors arrived who agreed that he was in septic shock and needed different drugs. They knew it was serious. One of them told Alan, "If you believe in a God, now's the time to start praying." They had to continue to titrate between the drug that would increase his blood pressure, but not so much as to risk a heart attack, and six different antibiotics on a revolving IV carousel to deal with all the infections in his body, including a new one introduced by the Foley catheter now removing his urine. The sweats continued. He remained in what one consultant later characterized as "florid shock" for another sixteen hours.[29]

Meanwhile, word had gotten to a member of his legal and support team who reached Barbara at home, about to leave to celebrate her birthday at the Metropolitan Opera House.[30] Instead, she jumped into her car and drove the four hours to Washington. She barged into the hospital in the middle of the night, headed straight to the locked ward even though it was not visiting hours, and announced, "I'm Dr. Zeller, and I have to see him." The guards let her through, although she is not sure why.[31] More needs to be done, she insisted, as she made the staff call another doctor. Just as important, she wrapped her arms around Alan as the raging sweats continued.[32]

A very tough nurse from the oncology unit realized that morning that the complicated titration of so many antibiotics and drugs could not be handled by the prison ward nursing staff. She worked her magic, and Alan was moved to an isolation room in her unit, as he put it, with his "paralyzed legs . . . shackled to a hospital bed in a real hospital room, complete with a bathroom I couldn't get to and a buzzer that I could. . . . A guard sat outside my room and periodically came to check my shackles." After a few days some of the medicines were stopped as his various infections receded. "I felt a little stronger," he recalled, "but my legs and bladder were still totally paralyzed, my shoulders and hands were partially paralyzed, and my left arm was still hung straight up in the air. I was a mess, but at least I was alive."[33]

His sense of humor and ability to connect with others, even those who guarded him, returned. A young corrections officer who had befriended him marched into his room after hearing about all the drama of the weekend. As Alan recalled, the young officer put everything in perspective: "Al. Al man. I'm so sorry, man. I was off over the weekend. When I got back, they told me you had almost gone out the back door. I couldn't believe it, man. I didn't know what to do. The only thing I could think of was to get you two big-legged women. They'd bring you back from the dead if anything would. You want me to get them in?"

Alan remembered his response: "I gaped at him. Two big-legged women? I laughed until I cried. Life went on and I was glad to be part of it."[34] He believed for sure that "if this episode had occurred at Springfield, I would not have survived."[35]

LEGAL BARGAINING FOR ALAN'S LIFE

Alan was through the worst of it, but he still had to deal with continuing medical difficulties: more protracted shaking chills, fevers above 103 degrees, more neurological deterioration, and a catheter put into his abdominal wall to drain his bladder because the nerve damage left it dysfunctional. Even when he was recommended for physical therapy, Alan dictated a letter to Judge Pollak that according to D.C. jail officials "it would require two correctional officers to escort me (even though only one officer ever escorts me for x-rays or other tests)" and that more delays were happening. No physical therapy was being arranged.[36] Judge Pollak was worried enough about his condition to call the hospital and try to speak to Alan's doctor. Dana was visiting Alan at the time and was able to convey to the judge more of the difficulties, especially the jail officials' refusal to get him physical therapy. She explained that conditions at Springfield, now that Alan was confined to a wheelchair, would make his rehabilitation impossible.[37] His supporters were so worried about him that a "Save Alan Berkman" vigil was held outside the hospital in mid-November, sponsored by a dozen Washington groups from Women Strike for Peace to the National Conference of Black Lawyers.[38]

Alan's codefendants were desperate to help. News of his condition came back to them from other prisoners who worked in the jail's infirmary.[39] Barbara shared with them her fears about what might happen to him, even if he survived, if he was sent back to the prisons in Springfield or Marion. Trying to keep in contact, Laura Whitehorn sent him cards every day filled with her mother's bad Jewish jokes.[40] "We missed him at the legal meetings," Whitehorn recollected, "and we were really afraid he was going to die."[41]

As his comrades met, they discussed what it might mean to settle the case *before* it got to the Supreme Court, and whether this might save Alan's life. It really mattered to them to be seen as not giving in to the government's view of them as terrorists. At the same time, as Linda Evans put it, that "our main goal was to get a deal for Alan so that he had a chance to get parole based on the other cases with lesser sentences. Every minute we thought about how we could get him better medical care."[42]

Alan's comrades had extraordinarily difficult decisions to make. They had wanted a trial to demonstrate their political commitments and to expose what they saw as the government's criminality, not their own. They hoped that the questions about the legality of the searches, and the lack of evidence on individual culpability for the bombings, might mitigate their own sentences, or even lead to a verdict in their favor. Their lawyers made it clear that the government would have to stretch to find evidence that had not been used in their other trials. In addition, at one point some of the evidence of the actual dynamite and instructions on bombing had been sent to Massachusetts to be used by the government in another conspiracy case to show linkages between underground groups. There were breaks in the chain of custody over the materials that the codefendants could use to bolster their case.[43]

Over and over his codefendants worried that Alan might not survive much longer unless they did something. "The idea [to negotiate with the government] arose out of our attempt to assert some power over his situation," they explained in a letter to supporters.[44] Alan, in turn, did not want to influence their possibly momentous decision. He sent instead his "love and appreciation" as he put it mildly.[45] Alan, the healer and caregiver, had to accept that his comrades might have to take on years and years in prison to save him.

After many discussions, the codefendants worked out the elements of what they would or would not agree to, and their lawyers took their proposals to the government attorneys. After the negotiations, the case was settled with guilty pleas and dropping of some of the charges. Alan would be spared the pressures of a trial.

The sentencing was harsh. The judge gave Laura Whitehorn (who had been in preventive detention for more than five years by then) twenty more years, and Linda Evans another five years on top of the thirty five she was already serving for the illegal gun purchases. Susan Rosenberg and Tim Blunk were left to serve their half-century from their other charges. The government also agreed to make a "good faith effort" to coordinate with New Jersey any charges still outstanding against Marilyn Buck that referred to the freeing of Assata Shakur but left her with an aggregate of a life sentence of eighty years.[46]

Then it was over. Within a few weeks before the end of 1990 all the co-defendants, except Alan, were scattered to federal prisons across the country to serve out their very long sentences. Their decision to settle meant there would be no lengthy trial. The government finally agreed that Alan could continue his medical care in Washington and that his charges as part of this case would be dismissed after he finished his treatment. What the codefendants could not do was force the government to send Alan somewhere decent after that, as the Bureau of Prisons would make the decision. Still, his legal team at least had time to pressure the government to send him somewhere where he could recover, if he survived.

The government obtained most of what it wanted from this deal. There were admissions of guilt, long sentences, and no exposure of the problematic chain of custody and searches, possible exposure of the illegal break-ins in the 1980s, and more publicity about Alan's worsening condition. In a similar trial the year before in Massachusetts, the federal government had spent millions of dollars and heard testimony from 200 witnesses in nine-month proceedings that ended primarily as a mistrial. In that case too, there were defendants who had long sentences for other actions before the conspiracy was alleged.[47] There was every reason for the government attorneys to worry that the same might happen with this case. But Alan's codefendants did not want to take the gamble.

Judge Greene had been anything but lenient, and the contrast between the sentencing of defendants on the left and the right could not have been starker. The headline of a James Ridgeway article in New York's *Village Voice* newspaper summed up the problem: "Hard Time: Why the Left Goes to Jail and the Right Goes Home."[48] Ridgeway contrasted the case of Oliver North, who received a light sentence that was later thrown out on appeal. North had orchestrated the Iran-contra deal that moved weapons to Nicaragua for an illegally funded war against those fighting the contras, a conflict that left thousands dead. North had thwarted the will of Congress, and when caught lied about it. John Poindexter, also convicted in Iran-contra illegalities and sentenced by Judge Greene a few months earlier, received only six months, and was expected to only serve three or four, even though he could have been sentenced to twenty-five years and a $1.25 million fine.[49] In contrast, Evans's initial sentence of thirty-five years for buying guns under a false name, was, Ridgeway claimed, longer than that received by anyone else charged with a similar offense. As he concluded ominously, "So if the government were to decide that *you* were an enemy of the people, you could be arrested and charged on a whole host of relatively minor felony charges, and an unelected official could put you away for life. Like Linda Evans."[50]

In explaining their guilty pleas to their political supporters, the codefendants placed Alan's needs front and center: "We felt it [pleading guilty] was the only way to ensure that he would not be subjected to the stress of a trial and the possibility of a longer sentence. . . . Alan has a much better chance [now] of winning parole and getting out of prison to recuperate from his chemotherapy. We also believe that doing anything we can to save Alan's life is an expression of our revolutionary politics—a commitment to comradeship, to love and to life."

They did not want to be seen as martyrs: "That others of us had the charges dismissed and that sentence exposure is limited for the other three is also important." The effort to politicize the criminalization of their actions, they argued, had been achieved by all the organizing that already had been done. They asked for continued support for themselves, and all other political prisoners and prisoners of war, but especially for Alan and for Mumia Abu-Jamal, still struggling to get off death row. "*Venceremos*," they signed their statement, using the Spanish word meaning "we will overcome" or "we will win."[51]

In a still longer statement to other supporters, both in the United States and in Europe, they explained they were not providing the government with any information or collaborating in any way. By saying they were "guilty," they argued, they were not accepting the *terrorism* label since they had been exposing the real reasons for the government's use of this terminology ever since their arrests. They believed the trial would consume resources that could be used for more political work, and they were not certain what issues they might have been able to bring up in their defense. Realizing that many of their comrades in the "New Afrikan, Puerto Rican and white anti-imperialist movements" had been arrested, they had understood that "tactics are flexible." In applying this understanding, they had not violated any of their essential principles. "We are endeavoring to be as accountable as we can be in the course of making some very difficult choices," they concluded. Their sense of being part of an international struggle and their willingness to take responsibility for principled stands shone through in their statement.[52] "Don't let the walls go back up between us," Laura Whitehorn pleaded at her sentencing, as she asked those who supported the defendants to keep up the political work.[53]

ORGANIZING FOR RECOVERY

And then Alan was alone in Washington, D.C. His comrades were now gone, and he could not write to them as no contact was allowed among federal prisoners. "They've been the core of my life for the past two and [a] half years," he explained to his correspondent Ann, "& my friends for longer than that. It could be a long time until I see them again. . . . I miss them." He realized what his comrades had done to save him but said very little about it. He must have been overwhelmed.

Slowly he was recovering from the infections and septic shock. His bladder still wasn't working, either, and the catheter that drained to a bag was a constant companion. He was in a wheelchair now because of the paralysis in his legs and unable to use his hands to write to anyone. In a dictated and typed form letter to his friends, he reminded them, "I enjoy hearing from each of you and appreciate the love and support I've received. Please don't misinterpret any prolonged periods of silence on my part. It'll be because I can't write, not because I don't want to."[54]

As 1990 ended, his chemo had finished and the staging studies showed the Hodgkin's to be in remission. Even so, he was still partly paralyzed and unable to walk very far even with assistance. Despite numerous neurological workups, his multiple doctors were not sure whether the paralysis was due to one of the chemo drugs or to some other cause. Magnetic resonance imaging (MRI) and a spinal tap, which might help identify what was causing the paralysis, had never been ordered, much to the horror of an outside specialist who saw him.[55] This specialist recommended that he be transferred to a rehabilitation facility capable of dealing with his "neuromuscular compromise," as well as that he receive regular special blood checkups. A second specialist insisted that he needed water therapy and specific kinds of muscle splinting if he were to ever walk again and regain use of his arms.[56]

"Timely access" to care was considered essential given his now "lifelong defect in the immune system." This meant, one of the specialists argued, that "any infection must be regarded as a medical emergency and be dealt with far more aggressively than similar infections occurring in non-immunocompromised patients."[57]

The specialists clearly identified with him as a physician, whatever he had done, and were horrified by the medical failures. The list they wrote of Alan's needs ran for three pages.[58] They made clear that only very specific kinds of rehabilitation and specially trained physicians monitoring Alan regularly would enable him to survive. As one specialist explained, "The cost he has paid physically from his therapy is unparalleled in the experience of this consultant. Indeed, it is truly a major miracle that Dr. Berkman is alive today."[59] With chemotherapy and initial antibiotics treatments complete by January 1991, Dr. Mahmood discharged him back to the Bureau of Prisons. The question was, to where?[60]

Ron Kuby, now Alan's key lawyer, worked with Barbara, Dana, and other lawyers to draft what he called jokingly his "Dr. Berkperson strategy" to keep the prison officials from sending Alan back to Springfield and on to Marion. He was trying instead to get Alan sent to the Federal Correctional Institution in Rochester, Minnesota, with its connection to the renowned Mayo Clinic. In his affidavit Kuby listed all of Alan's ills: his paralysis, his inability to walk, his in-dwelling catheter, as well as his persistent tachycardia and other heart problems that meant his heart was working at only 50–55 percent efficiency, the excess fluid buildup in his lungs, and adrenal problems that affected his potassium and calcium levels.[61] He was still a very sick man.

The negotiations continued into February when Alan was in the D.C. jail infirmary. As he feared, the monitoring of simple things—like his temperature—was already being ignored. But, although he still had his heart, renal, lung, and neuromuscular difficulties, and could do very little, being frequently winded, he was feeling better. As he waited for a decision he was getting bored, passing time watching the roaches and mice that scurried about.[62]

Finally, it was settled. The National Rehabilitation Hospital in Washington was nixed; Alan reported that prison officials told the hospital that "I'm a terrorist with presumed links to pro-Iraqi groups. [This was right after the U.S. invasion of Kuwait to push the Iraqis back across their border.] For some reason the hospital then decided they weren't interested in taking me as a patient."[63] So as a "compromise," Alan would be sent to the medical center at the Federal Correctional Institution in Rochester, Minnesota. Alan thought this was indeed a victory since his blood chemistries were still off and he still feared being put in the "hole" at Springfield. In the letters he could now write with less shakiness, his old political self emerged. His friends now received commentaries on the Iraq war, the Clarence Thomas Supreme Court confirmation hearings, the electoral defeat of the Sandinistas in Nicaragua, and other news of the day.[64]

He was beginning to sound alive again. He had gained twenty pounds and grown back most of his hair ("not my bald spot, alas") and looked forward to recovery, even if he would be half a country away from his friends and family.[65] That he had survived this far was, if not a medical miracle, the result of a formidable combination of his medical skills, family, medical and legal support, a selfless act of solidarity by his codefendants, and a sympathetic judge who thought he should not die at the hands of the Bureau of Prisons.

"A MAJOR IN MEDICINE, AND A MINOR IN PRISON"

Opened just six years before Alan transferred there, the Federal Medical Center at Rochester housed more than 500 male prisoners of varying security risks in need of intensive or long-term medical or mental health care. A standard federal prison was also attached. With the renowned Mayo Clinic just ten minutes down the road, it gave prison doctors a way to further their training and Mayo Clinic doctors very sick patients to learn from. Ironically, it turned out the retired physician who came back to run the prison hospital had been a friend of Barbara's doctor father in Connecticut.[66] Alan was now in the best medical facility in the federal system instead of the worst.

At Rochester, he entered the general population. The prison officials had given up on separating him for now. Barely able to push his wheelchair and with his arms still somewhat paralyzed, he hardly seemed a flight risk. He was in a cell with another prisoner but spent much of his day in physical and occupational therapy or at the gym. He even had a Sony Walkman, which allowed him to listen to an oldies radio station.[67] He also had a bit of a view "of the recreation yard & a city park beyond the fence. After the first snowfall," he reported, "it looked like a Xmas card scene."[68]

It was still a prison, however. A month after he arrived he had another high fever, and the chills began again. He found the prison's physician assistant and asked if he would take his temperature. The man refused but suggested Alan take an aspirin and check with the nurse in the morning. Alan was too exhausted to do more and went back to bed, but another prisoner tracked down a nurse on another floor. She checked his temperature, which was 103 degrees, and called the doctor. An x-ray and blood tests were ordered and Alan was started on antibiotic IVs. He was sure that anywhere else in the prison system, none of this would have happened as quickly.[69]

He began to see the medical difficulties of his neighbors. His first cellmate, a twenty-seven-year-old man with a tumor that did not respond to chemo, was waiting for his mother to arrive, but he was brain dead by the time she was let in. She stayed holding his hand but was forced to leave at 4 p.m. when the count of the prisoners by the guards happened. The man died an hour later.[70] His next cellmate was blind and gave Alan a sense of what it was like to navigate the prison world without sight. The man also tested his patience, however, as he stayed up late at night typing.[71]

Alan was coming back to life. As his walking improved he was ecstatic to be outside, "breathe the fresh clean air, look at the sky, & even see moon and stars at night." In March, the long-awaited 60 Minutes episode aired, giving him a bit of notoriety in the prison. "My fellow prisoners seem to appreciate it. Many have thanked me for speaking out, and a number now call me 'the 60 minute man.'" His focus on his own "corpus" and surviving made him "weary with my self-preoccupation." He knew he had to process his multiple near-death experiences and to consider what would come next.

With his strength returning, and inmates around him sicker than himself, he was happy that his "healer/comforter instincts" were returning.[72] By June, he would write his oncologist friend Tom Garrett, "I just had a CAT scan, & it was read as normal. My marrow seems to slowly be coming back, and my neuromuscular and cardiac damage is improving. So, for now, I can quote Coué: every day in every way, things are getting better and better. Of course, they couldn't have gotten much worse."[73] He was hardly out of the medical woods just yet. Abnormal blood chemistries kept appearing, along with two abscessed teeth within a few months. But having had "death on his shoulder" for so long, as he put it, he preferred to focus on just living.[74]

He was beginning to imagine a work life outside of prison. He had Barbara send him a number of medical journals and began to study for a review course in internal medicine. His license to practice had never been revoked, but he knew the New York medical licensing board had the power to stop its renewal.[75] He was making inquiries as to work, ahead of a presumptive release the following year: possibly with a friend who did alternative treatments for AIDS patients, or monitoring prison health care in New York State for a nonprofit.[76] His science brain was clicking in as he considered what he thought about mainstream medicine (which in many ways had both saved and nearly killed him). Curious about non-Western modalities, he was nevertheless doubtful about unproved alternative medicines and the early assumptions of acupuncturists like Jackie Haught, Barbara's partner, who thought that acupuncture might have saved her AIDS patients.[77] Other times he imagined himself either in obstetrics or with dying patients, as he mulled the extremes of life.[78]

He was also thinking more and more about HIV/AIDS. The first reports of the disease had appeared four months before the Brink's action in 1981. As Alan cycled in and out of various prisons, the difficulties of incarcerated patients with HIV had attracted both his and his comrades' concern. Each of them had seen how isolated and terrified many HIV-positive prisoners had become, and how little was being done for them. They faced fear and stigma from fellow prisoners and correctional officers alike.[79]

When the codefendants had been in the D.C. jail and before Alan had his recurrence, Laura Whitehorn recalled, he had talked to them extensively about the biology of HIV and what was known and not known about how to treat it. In the women's prison in Bedford Hills, New York, Alan's friends Judy Clark and Kathy Boudin had been part of the beginning of a peer counseling and education program to provide support, teach prevention, and provide help for women in prison, including those about to be released.[80] While he was not allowed to write to his codefendants, he did know that both Susan Rosenberg and Linda Evans also were working on HIV/AIDS peer programs in their respective prisons.[81] Barbara, who had been working in emergency medicine at a Bronx hospital, was increasingly volunteering with an organization for AIDS patients and would eventually become a physician and then medical director for the group. The combination of the epidemic's political nature and the difficulties of caring for AIDS patients, especially in black and Puerto Rican communities, just as the first antiretrovirals were coming on the market, appealed to Alan. But first he had to finish his time.

For so much of his prison experience Alan had been either really sick, in solitary, or preparing for a trial. The year and a half he spent in Rochester gave him a chance not only to breathe in the outside air and recover but also to communicate more broadly with the world outside, including about his concerns with prison medicine. He wrote on Wounded Knee for a left journal, and more on prison health for other publications. He corresponded with a South African activist physician who had written about prisons, health, and political prisoners in her country.[82] Although he never let his guard down, Rochester felt different, he wrote in his journal. Here the "chaos" and sense of a "veneer of civilization over the heart of darkness" was less omnipresent. The mechanisms of control seemed to be not so much the bars and officers as the "prisoners' subliminal awareness that once yielded to, the madness would engulf and destroy all of us."[83]

Continuing to write and think staved off that madness, although survival required that he contain his anger. He knew that an articulate and political doctor in the prison system was an anomaly, and that he could at least make use of some of his talents and experiences. After the *New York Times* and *60 Minutes* coverage he was becoming something of a household name in the criminal justice arena. A lawyer with the People's Law Office in Chicago wrote him that the CBS program had influenced the judge of one of her sick clients to let the man out on bail.[84]

His experience would reach the halls of Congress. Having seen the *60 Minutes* program, in June 1991 the staff counsel of the House Judiciary Committee wrote to ask if he would testify at a subcommittee hearing on prison medical care. A subpoena had been drawn up to get him to Washington, but the Bureau of Prisons' leadership intervened and "vehemently objected" to his appearance. The chair of the committee backed down and the subpoena was withdrawn, although Alan was allowed to provide testimony. He spent a good deal of July 1991 writing a twenty-five-page document that summed up both his own experiences and those he had witnessed.[85]

It was a tour de force. As the *New York Times'* Anthony Lewis noted when he read the copy Dana had sent him, "Dr. Berkman's statement ... I found chilling and impressive. To maintain the professional tone he did was remarkable."[86] Alan began by describing his own medical training and then the trail of disasters and incompetence that had plagued his own ills. His calm explanations belied the anger beneath the words as he detailed the endless examples of how close he came to dying again and again, and the inadequacy of the doctors hired by the prison system. He was certain that if he had been sent to Springfield he would be dead, and he was equally certain that other prisoners died because they were sent there.

He interwove his own experiences with those of patients he had observed. He named men at Springfield who were lied to about their options and side effects, or told their recurring liver problems were caused by "winter weather and depression" rather than hepatitis. He described infected surgical wounds that were left uncared for, and a brutal force-feeding. The context of lockdowns, exercise in what he described as barely a dog kennel, and being shackled into showers three days a week made for bone-chilling reading. Having come so close to death himself, he was particularly horrified that others had been left to die. He described a man in the final stages of lung cancer, alone on his bunk as his "hacking cough and increasingly-labored respirations echoed down the tier at night."

His stories documented the prison officials' refusal to require their doctors be licensed, or to participate in continuing education to keep up their skills. Sympathetic doctors, who did know what they were doing, should not be belittled if they were decent to the prisoners, and they should be taught not to ignore patient concerns, he argued. The physicians assistants, the first to determine what kind of care the prisoner needed, were equally inadequate to the tasks. What he saw above all was that the triage system of medicine, which often sends the sickest to the appropriate tertiary facility, never worked for prisoners: security was the basis for the triage, not the level of needed care. In the end he thought the courts, or in his case a concerned judge and his own medical knowledge, had made the difference, but this was no solution, even in his own unique case. He suggested detailed policy changes at the highest level, including letting dying patients out, better accreditation, and outside physicians monitoring illnesses and deaths. Alas, his recommendations made little headway.[87]

Given that he was now in the general population, he had the chance to meet and talk with more prisoners as he moved from physical therapy, to the gym, to the outside field, to the chow line. He was not the only "celebrity" in Rochester: evangelical pastor Jim Bakker and political sect leader Lyndon LaRouche were each other's cellmates for a time. Alan found Bakker, in particular, mildly amusing. He recalled discussing American society with "His Holiness," as he called Bakker, who opined, "One thing you have to remember about the American people is that 99% of them are sheep. When Christ called us sheep it wasn't a compliment. Sheep are so dumb they'll drown in a puddle if you let them." LaRouche was less talkative, and Alan was just as happy to ignore him, remembering when his sect undertook a "Smash the Left" campaign that harmed many. It was at least entertaining when Alan could look over in the visiting room when his parents came to see him, and watch his mother's amazement at seeing Bakker's wife, Tammie Faye, in all the false eyelashes, thick makeup, and teased up blond hair for which she had become notorious.[88]

It was the other prisoners, however, whose stories really touched him. There was the young tattooed punk who met his father for the first time in the prison. There was a flamboyantly gay prisoner who had his picture taken, with Alan on one side and the wincing Jim Bakker on the other, who made Alan confront his own discomfort with what felt like an "unmanly" image. There were the prisoners who volunteered to be in a prisoner-to-prisoner hospice program. There was the robber facing more than four decades in prison who said he might do it again if he ever got out. Or the crack addict who was grateful the guards supplied his drugs, and who told Alan, after Alan warned him about AIDS, "Doc, this is my life, man. It's what I do. What else am I gonna do? Work in McDonalds? I did that. I'm gonna die of something. I just don't wanna die before my Mom. She'd be hurt."[89]

Alan bemoaned the lack of education that made the simplest political ideas inaccessible to other incarcerated men. It was not that he was making fun of them, or blamed them. It was just another reminder of the kind of political work that needed to be done to reach them. One prisoner asked him to explain the difference between right and left wings in politics and where Alan stood. Alan thought he had gotten through, but when they were in the chow line, the man asked him, "Hey, Doc, were you well paid for being a winger?" And during a discussion of the Gulf War, one of Alan's pals commented, "Yeah, wasn't it wild to see all those Arabs with those things on their heads? What are they called? Doo-rags?" Or another man who thought a good example of American racism was the existence of a movie star named "Arnold Schwartznigger."[90] Having paid the cost of being in a "search for purity" political group, Alan was now rethinking what needed to be done politically, and for whom.

He returned to reflecting on what he had done, and what he hoped to do in the future. He began asking his correspondents to send back his letters so he could try to recreate his own thinking in a prison journal he had been trying to keep. While he wasn't yet sure he had a book, he was trying to make meaning of his life and to contemplate writing about it.[91]And he wanted to rethink his politics, he told Ann Morris: "I, after years of being in small political groups where we discussed/argued/did criticism-self-criticism until we agreed or understood every nuance of every difference, real or imagined, no longer want to engage in that kind of dialogue. Increasingly in my life, I've grown to recognize & respect difference & don't feel compelled to argue about it." He was realizing how hurtful and critical he had been of others, and struggling to understand the difference between "polemicizing and debating," on the one hand, and discussing, on the other. He was considering how to respect the limits others put on what they willing to do in a struggle, even if he was making what he saw as greater sacrifices.[92]

Even his dreams had changed to reflect his shifting politics. He read Peter Matthiessen's *In the Spirit of Crazy Horse* on what had happened during the siege at Wounded Knee and its aftermath, when the corrupt tribal leadership killed those who had protested. Alan was infuriated. But then he dreamed he was there to obtain justice . . . with his gun. He rounded up some obvious suspects but just pointed "the gun at their chests" and began to "growl & make threatening noises . . . "but I couldn't fire because I kept worrying that I'd made a mistake, or that some were more guilty than others." He tried to figure out who was most guilty, "but, as I did, it dawned on me that this was all having less & less to do with my original passion for justice & more & more with an abstract need to show I could do it. But really I had no need to do it, so I let everyone go & felt greatly relieved." It was a remarkable subconscious statement of his political principles.[93]

He had not stopped being an anti-imperialist, nor had he changed his political values. In interviews with two supporters who visited him, he argued that the rest of the left should understand how much he and those like him were taking responsibility for trying to stop U.S. aggression at home and abroad. Like Che, he thought, they were part of what he called a "self-less struggle for a people." He clearly thought resistance in solidarity with other international struggles was needed. He was willing to admit tactical mistakes, but not mistakes of values.[94] Commenting on a Citizens' Conference in North Carolina on pollution that his friend Dick Clapp had attended, Alan declared that "grassroots empowerment is the only hope for the future," a far cry from his purist days.[95] He wanted to continue to be political, but he was beginning to imagine what this would look like now.

Alan never stopped feeling that he was a political prisoner. His visibility even made it into art on the other side of the country. Miranda Bergman, a famed San Francisco muralist who would become one of the artists who covered the walls of that city's Women's Building, and who was the sister of Lincoln Bergman, a key figure in Prairie Fire and in the support groups for the Resistance Conspiracy Case, was asked to do a mural about political prisoners and freedom struggles in 1991. Working with Chicano poet and political activist Raul Salinas at his Resistencia Bookstore in Austin, Texas, Bergman designed a mural called *Raices de libertad / The Roots of Freedom* that centered on a bird in flight, with images of gas masks from the first Gulf War, chalk outlines of police murders, children near an olive tree that had been uprooted in Palestine when Bergman visited there, and a woman releasing freedom symbols from differing cultures. But in the left-hand corner were four U.S. political prisoners behind bars: Leonard Peltier (American Indian Movement), Dylcia

Raices de libertad / Roots of Freedom mural by Miranda Bergman, Raul Valdez, and Ambray Gonzalez, painted in 1990 at the Resistencia Bookstore in Austin, Texas, and now housed in the student union at San Francisco State University, California. Political prisoners, *left to right*: Leonard Peltier (American Indian Movement), Dylcia Pagan (FALN, Fuerzas Armadas de Liberación Nacional), Alan Berkman (May 19th), and Geronimo Pratt (Black Panthers). *Courtesy of the photographer, Laura Mamo.*

Pagan (FALN), Geronimo Pratt (Black Panthers), and Alan. The mural then moved from Austin to San Francisco, where it still hangs in the San Francisco State University student union. Although neither Miranda Bergman nor Raul Salinas ever met Alan, they knew he was important.[96]

A LIFE AFTER

Despite his years in prison, Alan bemoaned that his friends were in for so much longer. He knew he was in some ways "lucky."[97] Once his release date of July 10, 1992, was firm, Alan began to consider much more seriously what he would do with his freedom.

His lawyer, Ron Kuby, prepared a long memorandum sent to the Board of Professional Medical Conduct in New York in October 1991 to get Alan's license renewed.[98] It claimed, "Dr. Berkman forthrightly acknowledges his criminal convictions and admits his mistakes," although Kuby admitted this "minor masterpiece of vagary" only meant that Alan agreed he had criminal convictions, "not that he acknowledges that he ever did anything criminal."[99] The memo detailed his commitment to community medicine, and then quoted from the letters of nine well-known doctors, three lawyers, his judges, an Episcopal bishop, and six Democratic congressmen, who all supported his parole on humanitarian grounds, reminding the board in part that the government had never prosecuted him for the treatment of Marilyn Buck after Brink's. It detailed all his community work, his humanity and skills as a physician, and included the 1990 letter from a nationally known prison reform and prisoner support group that offered Alan a position in its substance abuse treatment facility in the Bronx.

Unlike many doctors who lose their licenses because of drug and alcohol abuse, prescribing illegal drugs, or serious malpractice, Alan had never been accused of abusing his medical skills. When the medical board's investigator told Kuby, "Wow, that Dr. Berkman certainly has had an interesting life," Kuby thought they had won.[100] The board agreed Alan could have his license restored as long as he agreed to some supervision and to work with the poor.[101] It was a real victory.

As the months passed toward his release, Alan checked off time with an advent-like calendar his family had made for him. He wrote to old friends in New York about possible other jobs, as he was not sure what he wanted to be doing. He told Dick Clapp that his experience as a prisoner had done more than give him insight into his own experience; he also had "spent the time living with & among those who make up the prison class. By & large, they're the same people who are getting AIDS, tuberculosis, etc." He also reflected on the problem of HIV among the homeless, a medical situation that had not existed when he went to prison.[102]

His concern for Sarah dominated much of his thinking. He desperately wanted to contribute financially to her upbringing but was not sure what he would be able to do. He knew he needed time to adjust to being out and really wanted to make her key to his life. He had tried to stay a part of her life, sharing parenting responsibilities with Barbara, writing to her, telling her stories, and watching as Sarah changed from a young girl of six when he went underground to a teenager in New York. He wanted to take more direct responsibility for her needs, and to be able to make a home for her before she left for college.[103]

The biggest question he faced was what would happen to his love life. Dana and Barbara sustained him, showering him with love. Their respective professional skills, as a lawyer and a doctor, had saved him in different ways over the prison years, with Dana often spending up to eight hours a day with him on "legal" issues.[104] Now that the desperate struggle to save his life had passed, and the months were counting down to when he would get out, the decisions he had been able to postpone for the last decade had to be faced. He knew he did not want to "decide anything until I'm out," he confessed to Dick Clapp, "but I guess I don't know if I *want* to be intensely in love with anyone for a while." He knew neither woman, nor he, thought he could sustain "two simultaneous relationships" on the outside.[105] He realized that he and Barbara knew one another very well and were in a "deep, but . . . comfortable" relationship. He also understood that she had moved on with her life and that he would have to adapt to that, if he fit into it at all.

Eight months before he got out, he and Dana were already having fights. She had waited long enough and wanted him to make a decision about how they would go forward, but she also needed him to assure her that his relationship with Barbara was now what Alan called "platonic." The pregnant pauses in their phone calls meant he was feeling "guilty & miserable" and she "hurt and demeaned," he thought.[106] He knew that her argument had "merit," but he was unable to decide. "I sometimes feel that I've grown so solitary that no relationship can work until I've been out a good while & have done some internal thawing," he admitted to Dick.

He felt he was in what he called "the emotional marshlands."[107] As he had realized several years earlier, he needed to be out from what he labeled "the thumb of the state" and wanted "to be left alone. But not completely—I also want love & companionship after years of not having it." He knew this was contradictory, and even "selfish," telling his friend Ann Morris, "I want love & companionship when I want it, & I want to be able to walk away & be by myself when I want to."[108] His position sounded like the male behavior contemporary feminists critiqued, despite all his efforts to understand women's lives.

Barbara helped him make the decision. She came out to see him in early December 1991, with more clarity about what might happen than he had, and they "decided it was best to try *not* to being lovers & see how it goes," he told Dick. "I'm not so sure it's the right decision," he admitted, "but we know the current situation isn't viable, & I think Barbara really does believe I need space. She also isn't into competing." He knew this made it somewhat easier for him to sort things out. "So," he concluded, "that took some of the pressure off my relationship to Dana, & she was happier when she visited this past weekend. And I hope I'm mature enough to not translate my ambivalence about Barbara into resentment of Dana & instead evaluate that relationship on its own merits. Mostly, I feel tired & want some time off from thinking about it, which is what I think BZ has done for me."[109]

Yet he knew his ties to Barbara had not ended.[110] In a short card to her after her visit he quoted from *The Four Loves*, a book by of all people C. S. Lewis, the Christian apologist and novelist best known for his *Chronicles of Narnia*.

> The coexistence of Friendship & Eros may also help some moderns to realize that Friendship is in reality a love, and even as great a love as Eros. Suppose you are fortunate enough to have "fallen in love with" and married your "Friend." And now suppose it is possible that you are

offered two futures: "Either you two will cease to be lovers but remain forever joint seekers of the same God, the same truth, the same beauty, or else losing all that, you will retain as long as you live the raptures & ardour, all the wonder and the wild desire of Eros. Choose which you please. Which should we choose? Which choice should we not regret after we had made it?"

"I love you," he said simply at the conclusion to the quote.

As 1992 became his last year in custody, he began to make decisions. He knew, that he was "hold[ing] something back" from Dana out of a sense of "Barbara & Sarah being my family & somehow immutable," even though he knew Barbara had been involved with someone else "for years." Even to his analytic brain, he could admit, "emotions . . . are not often rational." His I/we analysis was at work again, as he told his friend Hank Newman, "I know I'm most comfortable by myself. Most comfortable, but not necessarily happy, & it wouldn't be a bad thing to make Dana and her daughter happy."[111] What he would tell his folks seemed difficult, as Dana was getting tired of being seen as "the other woman," as Alan put it. But he also knew that "I ain't wishing to get divorced & Dana wants some legitimacy for our relationship."[112]

What he would do the day he would get out now loomed. The government would provide him with a plane ticket to New York, but who would meet him at the prison door now seemed problematic. "Sarah wants to be here to greet me & so do Barbara & Dana—not a great combination," he told Hank. "I'll offend everyone from Day #1."[113]

He realized too he would have to get used to normal life again. "Choosing clothes, hassling the subway, going to work, finding time to exercise, making supper for me & Sarah, helping her with her homework, etc." He also worried about the new technologies: "I've never used a VCR, a cellular phone, a PC, a CD or lots of other things with initials." He was aware that the skills that made survival in prison possible—his ability to be alone, his jumpiness when anyone got near him, his anger when someone cut in front of him in line—would all have to be countered. And, he knew, "somewhere in the whole goulash, I need to figure out what my political commitments are and how to actualize them." He even began to consider that a therapist, what he called "a non-judgmental person," might be of help.[114]

Finally, as he neared what in prison is known as "short time," the details began to come together. A friend found him a sublet with two bedrooms in New York's West Village, which would make it easier for Sarah to get to her high school when she stayed with him. Barbara and his brother Steve agreed to loan him some money since he had none. Dana assented to have Barbara and Sarah pick him up in Rochester and bring him back to New York. She would wait.[115]

He knew he faced a series of somewhat contradictory feelings: "wanting emotional security & to be cared for / wanting to be left alone; wanting to jump back into a career / wanting plenty of time to smell the roses; wanting to make some money & live decently / wanting to keep life simple; wanting to help my friends inside / wanting to stay away from organized politics."[116]

In all the time he had been alone, and then near death, he realized how deeply he felt connected. "It was like being at the center of a spider web that allowed me to communicate with loved ones all over. I ultimately found some inner peace in that & lost, I believe, some of my own egotism," although how this merged with his complete focus on his own survival he did not admit.[117] In his own life, he now believed that the need to be connected had led him to the political groups he had chosen in the past. Now this would have to be different.[118]

He knew what was next: "Resurrection. I hope I am done with my trip to Hades & can now emerge from the underworld a changed man."[119]

PART
FOUR

SAVING LIVES

HIV/AIDS AND
GLOBAL ACTIVISM

BREAKING THE SILENCE

"SILENCE = DEATH" is a slogan that crystallized a crucial stage in the struggle against HIV/AIDS in the United States. On one level it captured the determination of the first HIV-affected generation of gay men and AIDS activists to speak with their own voice and play an active role in shaping the American response to the AIDS epidemic. On another level it was a demand that official America—the politicians, researchers and medical establishment—break their silence about HIV and address the public health emergency that was killing tens of thousands of young Americans. . . .

Silence does not just allow ignorance to continue. It can also hide policies and practices that perpetuate suffering. In the United States, activists from a number of organizations formed a coalition called Health GAP to specifically address the issue of global access to HIV-related medications. Aware of our own ignorance, we reached out in two directions: to activists in the poor and developing world to understand their needs and demands, and to progressive consumer-oriented "think tanks" that have real expertise in global trade and development issues. . . .

Health GAP and other groups broke the silence surrounding the U.S. policy and exposed the actions of some of the politicians responsible for implementing those policies. Exposure of these immoral practices has begun to create the political will necessary to change them. This process needs to be pushed forward, and every medical, public health, human rights and AIDS-related organization should pass a resolution and take actions that bring U.S. policies into line with global initiatives to broaden access to essential medications. This will coincide with global efforts to have the pharmaceutical industry, which has the highest profit margins of any industry group in the U.S., assume some of its responsibility to make essential drugs available at the cost of production in poor countries where AIDS is a national emergency. Greed still kills.

The International AIDS conference will not mark any new dramatic advances in vaccine development, prevention efforts or treatment. What it can herald is a new determination to break the silence around global AIDS and usher in an era of international activism that creates the political will needed to make those advances.

Alan Berkman, MD, 1999

14

RESURRECTION AND SOCIAL RAGE

The man who walked out of the Rochester prison gate at 8 a.m. on the morning of July 10, 1992, could not have been more physically different from the prisoner who had entered a year and a half earlier. Alan's green pallor had given way to a tanned visage, and the sunken eyes and visible cheekbones had disappeared. Most of his hair had returned as a salt-and-pepper mix. His muscles, once wasted from fevers and paralysis, were now buffed and visible beneath his short-sleeved shirt and pants. His weight was back up and he could walk again, even if his neuropathies would on occasion make him wobble and his right leg drag.[1]

Alan walked out of the prison into the arms of Barbara and the now-sixteen-year-old Sarah. As they stood by the convertible Barbara had rented for the occasion, a smile filled his face, and he hung on to them as if it were the first time. "You look beautiful," Barbara told him just before they embarked on the hour-and-a-half drive to Minneapolis, where they would take the plane home.[2] He would write in his memoir, "One minute I'm still locked up with a bunch of saints and sinners and the next minute I'm in a rented convertible cruising down the American highway on a sunny day."[3]

Alan said very little during this first drive after nearly a decade of separation.[4] A few hours later, the reunited family was at a picnic thrown by their friends Bruce Taub and Lynne Karsten, who happened to be in Minneapolis on a visit.[5] As Barbara filmed them with her camcorder, Taub asked for posterity, "So how long have you been liberated?" Alan looked at his watch, hugged Sarah and Barbara again, and said "about seven hours," and then added laughing, "What a long strange trip it has been." Sarah agreed, thinking it all seemed so normal and surreal at the same time.[6]

On the plane he looked both happy and a bit bewildered. When they landed in New York, the taxi dropped Alan and Sarah off at his newly rented apartment in Greenwich Village. Barbara headed back uptown to her home. The next day Alan went to see Dana.[7] So much was still ahead to be decided.

Barbara, Alan, and Sarah Zeller-Berkman, Minneapolis, Minnesota, on Alan's first day out of prison, July 10, 1992. *Courtesy of Lynne Karsten.*

HOMECOMING AS RESURRECTION

Two days afterward Alan was in the auditorium of the Trevor Day School on East Ninety-Fifth Street, where his friend and comrade Shelley Miller taught, for a homecoming party with hundreds of well-wishers. "It looks like a political archeological dig," Eve Rosahn, his fellow former May 19th member and grand jury resister, now a law student, quipped as master of ceremonies for the event. Representatives from the Puerto Rican independence movement, the former Black Panthers, and the still functioning Prairie Fire, as well as his lawyers all spoke as their children scampered onto the stage to interrupt their parents' emotional speeches. From prison, his codefendants sent a message of love, reminding him that his return was "a victory more precious in its rarity." Outside the frame of Barbara's camera, Dana's attendance must have been poignant and complicated.[8] For Sarah, it was the first time she had really seen her father as a public figure, as she began to comprehend anew what she called his "larger self."[9] Twelve-year-old Harriet, his comrade Judy Clark's daughter, was present too, hanging on to Shelley Miller, her "other" mother, beholding the biological father she barely knew.

Alan's survival, strength of character, and devotion to his values came through in speech after speech. "This is a miracle," a supporter told him, "in these difficult times for those who believe in liberty and freedom." Hyperbolically, his lawyer Ron Kuby likened Alan's journey to those who had endured "slavery's middle passage, the trail of tears, and the Holocaust." Others extolled his bravery and importance as a comrade. "On behalf of my community of *compañeros*, our people's revolutionary movement," a Puerto Rican *independentista* told him to cheers, "we understand very profoundly what you have given of your life. You have saved lives of comrades whose lives were much threatened . . . and our people will never forget you."

The most overtly political talk came from revered long-time activist Yuri Kochiyama, who had been Malcolm X's comrade and had held him in her arms as he lay mortally wounded.[10] Summarizing Alan's political actions, she applauded his "revolutionary love." She told Alan and his well-wishers, "You have taken the same path, the same consequences, the same punishment, the same callous brutal prison experience, and you have come through perhaps psychologically and physically scarred, but perhaps wiser, more indomitable . . . and how much we need you Alan, your courage, your love for all humanity, and your sense of justice."[11]

Over and over, this nonreligious but deeply spiritual event returned to the miracle of his resurrection. In Alan's comrades' eyes, the enemy had gone after a righteous man, thrown all it could at him, and yet he had risen. Alan seemed a bit overwhelmed, even kidding that as a "scientist and longtime dialectical materialist I'm not sure of this [miracle talk], but I am reporting this experience as lived." He knew his survival had depended on collective acts and recalled many of the friends inside and outside the prisons who had given him material and psychological support. He named his fellow codefendants, and a range of prisoners, but especially Mumia Abu-Jamal, as mentors who taught him "under the most dire circumstances, that loving people was what kept me alive, and what kept him alive. . . . I don't know if I want to be quoted, but I may have a position on miracles myself." As he stood trying to look modest, the crowd gave him a long standing ovation.

Yet hidden behind the video camera, Barbara remembers that she was "a fucking mess." What would happen next between them was still unknown. In his remarks, Alan had thanked everyone in general but made no mention of Barbara, Sarah, Harriet, or Dana for that matter. It would probably have been too complicated.

READJUSTMENT

The attention must have been overwhelming. Alas, there are no more long letters to friends and family to reveal Alan's thoughts and feelings. For now on his communication would be as it for most of us: through telephones, personal meetings, texts, and emails. For windows into his internal life after his release, we must rely on the recollections of others, a few snippets in his memoir, and the emails, reports, and letters on his computer.[12]

In his prison memoir's last sketched-out pages, he did briefly chronicle how he tried to adjust to his new life.[13] While incarcerated he had survived by focusing on the day to day, he noted. Now that he was no longer there it was his daily life that for a while seemed unnatural. "I've been aware of the sense of playacting since I got out," he wrote. "I remember many of the mechanics of daily life (but not all) and can go through them. . . . But it all lacks a context. . . . Now I've got the disruption of being on the outside . . . so, I go through the motions and mostly enjoy them, knowing that slowly *this* will become the next stage of my life."[14]

He had so much to figure out: his personal relationships, his parenting, how to make a living, and what kind of political life he would have. First there were just the basics. His new apartment was a two-bedroom railroad flat whose walls he would fill with political posters over the next months.[15] The space allowed him to share with Barbara the custody of Sarah, who moved back and forth between her parents' apartments as she began her junior year at Stuyvesant High School, New York City's most selective public school. They settled into a routine as he began to take great pride in making a life for her: cooking her dinners, asking about her friends and courses, integrating Barbara's rules for her into his own, making sure she did her homework, and always pushing her to do better. "My grades shot up that year," she recalled. "He would talk to me about what I was submitting, push me to make things better."[16]

As with many formerly incarcerated people who did long time, Alan's readjustments were both profound and mundane. When, he asked Sarah one day, had toilet paper become more than one ply? Or he would marvel at the sky as she was trying to rush him to get her to an appointment or to school. They had the usual fights between parents and teenagers, where she would sometimes think, "Who the fuck are you?" But other times she mused on how wonderful it was to have him back.[17] Sarah had been raised in "collective women's households," as Barbara labeled them, and now had to adjust to a new parent's demands.[18] Alan, in turn, wrote himself notes about what seemed weird: "cars feel fast & out of control, opening sealed mail, feeling older when seeing all the younger people, a headache from looking at people, amount of garbage I generate, can only do one thing a day, having no want-likes or wishes but no internal craving or desire."[19] In many ways, he was still numb and self-protective.

Most of that first summer out was spent organizing his daily and personal life. Barbara had made it clear she was still with Jackie, however confused her feelings, and Alan renewed his intense relationship with Dana as he had expected. As he had worried when incarcerated, he knew he still had "a thick layer of emotional scar tissue that worked in keeping the prison out but also made it difficult to allow loved ones in." He was still wary and frightened because, he wrote, "I felt that letting anyone else inside would destroy me."[20]

He did try. He and Dana made a trip a month after his release to a friend's home in the Catskill Mountains, not far from where Alan had grown up. He enjoyed the "sense of isolation" in the nearby woods filled with animals and quiet, and he loved the peace. But another time they were going to dinner at the home of Dana's close friend Jennifer Dohrn, their former Prairie Fire comrade, who was a nurse midwife, and her husband, W. Haywood Burns, a longtime civil rights activist and dean of the City University of New York's School of Law. They were dressed up, bringing wine for the occasion. As they mounted the stairs to their hosts' apartment, Alan felt unreal. As he wrote, "Here's Alan, carrying his gift of a reasonably priced wine, to these two interesting and eminently civilized people. The music will be jazz, the conversation interesting, and the dinner tasteful. Who could ask for more? It's all bullshit." He felt for an instant that the "banter in the prison" and his friends there "were all more real and more *me* than the dinner party-to-be." Then the thought passed and he was sure that "prison was behind me, and this culture was part of me too, so I kept walking up those stairs."[21]

He was still dreaming of the past too. His incarcerated friends populated his nighttime imagination.[22] That ambiguity would continue for months, even years, as his sense of what was real and what unreal kept shifting. What was clear was he was never going to forget where he had been, and why it had mattered.

How his political action would remain true to what he had experienced, and what he could do while on parole at this political moment, had to be determined. He knew he had to assess what was possible. He had gotten out a few months before Bill Clinton's election as president. No change in the presidency, he must have known, would restructure the underlying inequalities of American society. Yet the election of a centrist Democrat, after twelve years of Republican rule, might make the country different in ways no one could predict yet.

New York, in turn, was still a very racially tense city, having dealt just a few years before with the killing of a Guyanese boy by an Orthodox rabbi's motorcade, angry mobs and the subsequent stabbing of a rabbinical student, and the false charges (then believed to be true) of supposed "wilding" by a group of black teenagers against a white jogger in Central Park, who was raped, brutalized, and left to die. Murder rates were declining slowly, and the drug war was increasing the incarceration of black and brown men and women.[23] The AIDS epidemic was still expanding rapidly, and the AIDS Coalition to Unleash Power (ACT UP) was confronting the presidential nominees over the failures of federal policy.[24]

Faced with this array of needs for activism, Alan's earliest political work after prison was cautious. He kept close ties to his imprisoned comrades however he could: being at someone else's house when they called so he could talk to them, since they could not call an "ex-felon" directly, getting letters to them through others, and working on their continual support.[25] He kept arguing at the different political meetings he attended that each prisoner needed her or his own committee and that getting them out in any way possible, short of snitching, had to be the priority. He was critical of the call for total amnesty, which he thought was unrealistic and not achievable.[26]

One thing was sure, he wrote and told everyone: no more small political groups. By this he seemed to mean that whatever faith he had had in a Leninist vanguard had disappeared. As he declared poignantly in his memoir, "But how do I want to integrate the prison years? More importantly, what do I want the present and future to be?"[27]

FINDING WORK

Alan was forty-seven years old, facing a number of decisions about love, life, and work that are normal at middle age. Amplifying the difficulty were his ten years in the underground and prison, his commitment to political action, and the cancers that he knew might reappear at any time.

He was fortunate to have his doctor skills to fall back on. One possible work option stood out: a part-time physician's position at the South Bronx treatment center of the Osborne Association, a prisoner support group.[28] Two months after he got out, he had a job at a center called El Río. Set up in 1989 as a response to the crack epidemic, and today a health center, it was then a drug treatment and rehabilitation program for the formerly incarcerated in an extremely poor, primarily Puerto Rican and black Bronx neighborhood. Its first medical director had been Michael Smith, who championed the use of auricular acupuncture to relieve addiction cravings and whom Alan had known when he was at Lincoln Hospital.[29]

Alan and El Río were a good match since Alan was willing to accept the use of acupuncture and Chinese herbs, and was one of the few doctors who understood from the inside the carceral experience. "He had more empathy for our clients than anyone else," the Osborne Association president remembered.[30] This was Alan's first direct experience with treating patients with HIV/AIDS, as nearly half the men and women he saw were HIV-positive. Through caring for them, he expressed his compassion and learned about the new antiretroviral drugs and acupuncture for immune enhancement.[31]

A year and a half after he started at El Río a New York Times reporter profiled him. The article focused on how unusual it was for a doctor to be on parole. As the reporter observed, Alan never lectured his patients, who told their parolee doctor of their "sexually transmitted diseases, guns, and drugs" and prison time they had experienced. He appeared sympathetic to people other medical practitioners would have judged harshly.[32] The reporter recounted Alan's joy of seeing the sky, just as Sarah had remembered when he first got out, and the layers of self-protection that complicated emotional connection, which Alan expressed by saying, "It can be very threatening to let the people you love get close again."[33]

Alan's story seemed so unusual that, after reading the *Times* story, the actor Robert De Niro's production company got in touch with him to discuss making a film. Alan turned it down because he wanted to control how his life narrative was portrayed.[34] The newspaper story did not reflect his growing doubts over what he was doing, since no matter how much he understood his patients, he was still a doctor with authority and power over their lives. It still was not enough politics for him.[35]

The work at El Río fit Alan's multiple skills, but it was only part-time. To make enough money to contribute to Sarah's upbringing and coming college expenses, he began teaching physiology at Harlem Hospital's Physician Assistant Program.[36] Having become more and more aware of the problems of housing and care for HIV-positive men and women, he learned at El Río about a nearby HIV/AIDS residential program that had just opened called the Highbridge Woodycrest Center (HWC). As he found out more about it, the work there beckoned him.

Housed in a beaux arts limestone building, with elegant bays, arched windows, moldings, and terracing, that overlooked the Harlem River in the Bronx, Highbridge Woodycrest had been built in 1901–2 as "a home for needy and abandoned children" by the American Female Guardian Society and Home for the Friendless. Closed in 1974, it had become a neglected, hulking relic of a mansion.[37] Working with New York City, two community organizations were able to get a loan to refurbish it. It opened in 1991 as a home for families with AIDS. It also served many parolees with substance abuse and mental health problems, hepatitis, and tuberculosis infections, as well as homeless people with an AIDS diagnosis who needed housing, health care, and mostly hospice services until they died.

Alan took a full-time position as a staff physician because of the challenge of the work and its focus on AIDS.[38] Hired in January 1994, within a year and a half he had become HWC's medical director.[39] He brought to the position his knowledge of the failures of prison medical care, his own perennially precarious health, and his belief that everyone mattered. He told his colleagues in an interview about his perspective as the medical director that success was based "quite simply, ... [on] the long-term commitment to human touch, to compassionate care and to contemporary approaches to providing help to people who are often facing the end of their lives."[40] He remained focused on comprehensive care that included forms of complementary medicine, psychological services, and the best formal Western medicine obtainable.

Clearly his memory of being shackled to operating tables and ignored, and of others left to die, shaped his approach to the residents at HWC. As he said in the interview, "If you are going to die, you won't be left alone. You will experience a dignified pain-free death in a comfortable environment. No one dies at Highbridge Woodycrest without someone holding their hand." Nor did everyone he cared for die. For those patients the staff sought to help a "person, growing, rebuilding, recreating a sense of themselves, being full."[41] It was as if he was still haunted by the patient with congestive heart failure he had sent home when he was an intern, and by those who died in the Springfield prison without family or friends by their side.

The position allowed him to exercise his compassion and his leadership skills, yet in some ways it made him little different from any other responsive, liberal doctor administrator. His emails during the nearly ten years that he spent there document the carefulness with which he approached his patients and the opportunities he thought important for the staff, all of whom he held to high standards. "I was reviewing MJ's chart in order to fill out the school form," he wrote one of the center's doctors. "I couldn't locate any test for lead, the results of any audiology test, or documented Pneumovax. . . . Do you think we should follow up on any or all of these things?"[42] His letters ranged from requests for an airline refund for a sicker patient to a note to a court explaining why a patient could not meet his child support payments due to AIDS-related blindness and other disabilities. Another letter to a family expresses his condolences on the loss of their loved one.

He was a thoughtful but exacting administrator. He worried about the costs of medications and waste, taught seminars on HIV, and wrote recommendations for his staff to get further training.[43] His memos to other health care personnel, like the one to the Center doctor, clearly involved them in the decisions. "Last year, if I remember correctly, we set up a small working group to look at our policies and procedures for central lines," he reminded the nursing director. "I am circulating a recent review of the literature concerning line infections and potential interventions to reduce them. I would propose that the working group reconvene and discuss which ones are appropriate for HWC."[44]

He created hundreds of "policies and procedures" to make the institution run better.[45] He reminded the staff about the need to keep the charts up, to understand why residents tended toward violence and how to contain it, or who was coming to a prevention conference. By the late 1990s, he was getting HWC to become part of several research projects on long-term care for HIV. He was being, as he had said at his homecoming party, "both a scientist and a dialectical materialist," binding his politics and his medical skills together.

Yet his experience of incarceration marked him as different. His colleagues knew he had "street cred" and that "he'd been on the other side." If the staff were having a problem with a resident who was "acting out," they would call Alan because he could "cut through the bullshit."[46] There was also his tough side: "There was no pushing him once he made up his mind," nurse Patricia Williams recalled, and "if you screwed up," he could get really angry. When he became surer of his skills and knowledge, and felt safe with his colleagues, he told them slowly about his experiences that helped explain both his compassion toward HWC's residents and his anger at mistreatment, or any sign that others were not giving their best.[47]

He was still a medical director, with all the responsibilities this entailed. He spent more time than he liked dealing with bureaucratic rules that made it difficult to offer the best care. As the new protease inhibitors for HIV/AIDS became available in 1996, he found himself doing battle with Medicaid regulations on what would be paid for, or arguing with the HWC higher-ups about why the institution should cover these expenses till the rules changed. He had to deal with the center's being labeled a skilled nursing home, despite having a relatively young patient population for whom the extensive bureaucratic requirements for the elderly did not fit. He was constantly using scientific reports to set rules for various new drugs while looking at the literature on complementary medicine to make the best modalities and herbs or teas available for both comfort and cure.[48] It was meaningful but at times very frustrating work.

He still was not sure this was enough. "I'm living in a nice apartment, frugally buying the kind of clothes my friends wear, finding a progressive but decent-paying job. Is that it? I could have done all this without prison and without cancer." He knew something else had to happen. "To continue this way, to be comfortable and white and professional, just doesn't seem adequate. If I do that, the only challenging part of my life is that which is behind me—a rather ironic and ludicrous development. Is the inner 'me' untransformed by the prison experience?"[49]

REMAKING A FAMILY

He knew he would have to determine how to make a life with those he loved, and not just fit into the lives they had carved out in his absence.[50] As Dana perceptively noted, when he was in prison most of his life was "about him and his survival."[51] Now he had to relate in person to others who loved him, and not in the distant and crisis mode that imprisonment and his various illnesses had entailed. The terrible price that families pay when a loved one goes to prison was played out.

During the first years after his release, Alan struggled to figure out whom he could really love and trust. He had shut down most of his emotional core in prison, where authorities wanted inmates to "do their own time," that is not to get involved with others.[52] He had gotten to know fellow inmates when he could, and he had created a sense of solidarity. Many people had his back in prison, and he understood how much this had mattered.[53] Now he was out and in an apartment by himself and Sarah half the time. That part he could figure out. But what was he going to do about his still-undetermined relationships with Dana and Barbara? Barbara was not sure yet how, or if, he could fit back in her life. For the first year and a half he was out she was still living in an apartment she had bought with Jackie Haught, along with her former May 19th comrade Liz Horowitz and her infant, Dylan. Sometimes Barbara spent time in an old houseboat someone had given her docked on the Hudson River. It was a getaway that gave her a sense of the expanse of nature.[54] Sarah moved back and forth between her parents' households every few days. Dana, who at that point had her ten-year-old daughter, Abby, welcomed Alan back into the relationship although they did not live together.[55] For the next year and a half, he was working hard to find his way, unlock his frozen emotions, and rebuild a personal life with Dana.

Yet Barbara was never far from his mind, or he from hers.[56] He had to be in relatively constant contact with her over Sarah's needs and schedule. He was also talking a good deal to Liz Horowitz, who was now working as a surgical physician's assistant. Brought into the political movement as a very young woman, she had lived with Barbara more than with her natal family. She spoke to Alan often on the landline when she reached to answer it before Barbara could, creating the kind of multiple connections such a phone system made possible. In her own romantic view, as she put it, "I was desperate to get them back together. They belonged together. They loved one another." When she met with Alan to talk or just have coffee, he would ask about Barbara. "I told him you have to pursue her and not give up. I told him he could win her back." Liz Horowitz had been through the ups and downs of Barbara and Alan's relationship, but she still thought they could make it work, and it mattered to her, and many of the other women who had supported Barbara over the years.[57]

Barbara, for her part, felt conflicted.[58] Jackie Haught had understood about Barbara's connection to Alan while he was imprisoned, as everyone assumed until the last case settled and his health improved that he might either spend decades of his life in prison or die there. Haught had helped raise Sarah, attended Alan's trial in Philadelphia, and even drove Barbara to see Alan at various prisons. She was a generous and "lovely person," as Barbara put it, dedicated to her acupuncture practice. Haught had been in May 19th and the John Brown Anti-Klan Committee both in New York and in Portland, Oregon, and knew Alan through that political work as well as when she had been at BAAANA. She had lived over the years collectively with Barbara, as well as with many others in their political group, including Dana, and considered Alan a close friend held in deep respect. It was a small circle.[59]

Barbara was under enormous pressure about what to do once Alan got out. How could she possibly "fuck over" the woman she loved, as she felt the "you can't do this, you can't do that" of her divided loyalties. Throughout his years in prison, and his illnesses, she knew she had been dealing with someone who wasn't "totally depressed and lashing out." It made it easier in some ways to keep up with him, and to try to figure out what loving him might mean for their lives, even though she would acknowledge he did seem to love Dana as well. She knew that had to be settled before she could even consider whether it was possible to be back with him.

Alan and Barbara had a daughter together, more than two decades of political history, and a shared medical experience in the past, and now in the present. It was her work with AIDS patients that had drawn him to his current field. Beginning in 1991, Barbara had become the medical director of HELP/Project Samaritan Inc., described as a "66-bed integrated residential health care facility for individuals suffering from the double scourge of drugs and AIDS." Her work at the facility was very similar to what Alan was doing at HWC.

Barbara was trying to make the best and most decent care available to those people often denied a modicum of humanity. Although AIDS became less of a death sentence in the mid-1990s because of new drugs, the work was still challenging. "Our patients have been through the war of the streets in ways that I can hardly describe, their medical and psychosocial problems are vast and sometimes overwhelming," she told a reporter. The journalist noted that Barbara could always "pick up the phone" and call Alan, or "better yet, meet him for lunch."[60]

She also had continued her political work in support of Alan's codefendants and other political prisoners. In 1992, as a way to "de-celebrate the Columbus Quincentenary and affirm 500 Years of Resistance," she and longtime feminist and anti-imperialist writer Meg Starr edited a thirty-three-page booklet called *Diss'ing the Discovery*. Full of poems, short stories, and ruminations by political prisoners on the meaning of Columbus, and dedicated to both Mumia Abu-Jamal and Leonard Peltier, it proved that Barbara's political work was not limited to her medical efforts around AIDS.[61]

Despite all they had in common, Barbara was not sure if she and Alan could be together. She knew he could not have, as she put it, "two wives."[62] She had her own complicated feelings about Jackie Haught and their life together to contend with. Dana and Barbara, although they had to work together to save Alan over the years, never met to discuss what had happened between them.[63]

In addition to all this, Alan had decided to rebuild his connections to Harriet, Judy Clark's daughter. Their relationship was beyond complicated. He had donated his sperm in 1980 because Barbara had asked him to, and they kept his role in Harriet's creation a secret from most of their comrades.[64] One by one, many of Harriet's caregivers went into prison or the underground, including her mother and Alan. This meant her grandparents Ruth and Joe Clark had no idea from day to day who was taking care of their only grandchild. After Alan disappeared, Shelley Miller was convicted of criminal contempt of court for refusing to testify that she knew anything about the FALN and its bombings, and went to federal prison in West Virginia for two years in the spring of 1985.[65] When Harriet's grandparents wrested custody of her from their imprisoned daughter, it was not clear how much Judy's larger political community would be allowed to be in Harriet's life.[66] The judge in the case ruled that the others who had cared for Harriet and were still out of prison would have only the limited ability to see her every two weeks.[67]

Harriet's relationship to Alan was similarly fraught. While she considered Sarah to be her sister, and had been taken numerous times by Barbara to visit Alan in prison, or spoke to him on the phone if she was around at Barbara's when he called, Alan had not written to her while he was incarcerated. The fact that on one hospital visit she and Sarah had both been strip-searched must have upset at least her grandparents, even if Harriet did not remember it. By the time Alan was released, Harriet had been living with Ruth and Joe Clark for seven years (and most of this with Ruth, since Joe died in 1988), and she was now only eleven.

To Ruth Clark, Alan embodied all that was wrong with the political group their daughter had joined. Although the Clarks had been in the American Communist Party leadership, and had even raised their family part of the time in the Soviet Union, they had fled and rejected the Party after the Stalinist horrors were exposed. Harriet had been taught to "hate Alan the devil" because he had abandoned her when he went underground.[68] In a sense she was being told that her father had not wanted her. Only years later would she learn from her mother that Judy had never intended to have Alan in her family life. But by then "that portrayal of him as an abandoner had done harm and it could almost not be undone."

Her real memories of Alan began after he was released. During the prison years, she vaguely recalled the facilities, going in to see him with Sarah, and one or both of them singing to him when he was in a prison hospital bed. But there was little else. She remembered making the "advent" calendar with Sarah for his last months of imprisonment, but she then kept thinking of him as "my sister's father."[69] Harriet was caught: everyone else in her political and chosen family thought that Alan's going underground had been "a moral good," as she put it, but for her it was rejection. Her mother was available, even if in prison, but her father was gone after promising to be around. For her, his walking away became "the defining gestures for my life and as my grandmother used to say as proof of his values."

Alan, however, remained determined to find a way to be part of Harriet's life. After he was out, he approached Harriet's grandmother to see what could be done to repair his paternal relationship. Ruth Clark had strong terms, insisting that he see her therapist to discuss how this might be possible. Alan complied.

Slowly, he was allowed more time with Harriet. She remembered most strongly his driving her up to the Bedford Hills prison to see her mother about a year after he got out, when she was twelve. Since he was still on parole, he could not go in to visit Judy Clark, but Harriet could. Trying to be honest with her, Alan was discussing Clark's recent decision to take herself off the lists of political prisoners and to begin expressing her deep remorse for what she had done.[70] Alan tried to explain to Harriet why he saw things differently, and how "every revolution in history had to have an armed wing." She recollected, "So the first memory I have is being highly uncomfortable in a car and he was counter posing himself against my mother's [views]. So after that I asked Shelley [Miller] to not let me be left alone with him."

When Ruth Clark developed lung cancer in the mid-1990s, she began to see Alan differently. Alan, the doctor, had connections in the New York medical community, and especially with skilled oncologist Tom Garrett, his friend from his internship year, who became Ruth's physician. Slowly she came around, as Alan was more and more of a direct help as her illness grew worse, and because she believed in "blood" relations and he was her granddaughter's father. She had moved what Harriet called "180 degrees" on him, now asking Harriet to see him in a different light and "be nicer to him when he came to visit."

Their relationship slowly evolved. When Harriet was in college and having emotional difficulties, it was Alan who insisted that she see a psychopharmacologist, and Alan who helped to adjust her medicines properly to her body weight. They began to see one another as what Harriet called "whole people," and to appreciate their differing strengths. Family vacations together would follow, as Harriet made a place in her life for her biological father to become her social father.[71]

Alan's relationship with Dana also began to evolve, and in a different direction. Even when he was no longer imprisoned, Dana realized he had so much to determine and that she "needed something he could not give."[72] He still tried to make their relationship work. In addition to the therapy that Ruth Clark had insisted on to reunite him with Harriet, he was seeing a couple's therapist with Dana, and his own therapist as well. Laughingly, he wrote the therapist he picked "looks like my grandmother. I tell her my long sad story. She says she never met a more powerless egomaniac."[73]

He seemed determined to not be powerless. He needed to make decisions about his life. During the fall of 1993, Alan's connection to Dana began to fall apart, as did Barbara's relationship with Jackie Haught.[74] Barbara remembers what happened next very romantically.

It was New Year's Eve at the end of 1993, and to make extra money she was working a night shift in the emergency room at the Bronx's Our Lady of Mercy Hospital. She agreed to meet Alan in Greenwich Village after work late that night, and they walked through the streets as light snow was falling. In the quiet beauty and stillness that New York can have in the chiaroscuro of light and darkness, their old magic rekindled. Seemingly alone in city, they made the decision to try to reconcile and rebuild their lives together. It would take a lot of negotiations, promises made, and time, as they also had to reconcile their lives with their respective partners. Nine months later Barbara sold her apartment and moved with Sarah to Alan's rented place in Greenwich Village.

With the money from the apartment sale, they went looking for a house in the country as an escape on weekends from the city. In the spring of 1995 they found a late eighteenth-century rambling farmhouse with a large dining room, several bedrooms, a babbling brook, and land. It was off a country road near the small town of Dingmans Ferry in Pennsylvania, less than two hours from New York City and an hour from where Alan had grown up. It appealed to them immediately, and they bought it on the spot. The family was back together again and now had a new home where friends and relatives could gather. It gave Alan a sense of stability he had not had for years, and a way to be near trees, brooks, hills, waterfalls, and above all the sky he had missed for so long.[75]

POLITICAL PRISONERS AND SOCIAL RAGE

While still learning more and more about AIDS and sorting out his emotional life, Alan's nonwork time was mostly spent on political prisoners and prison issues. He was a thoughtful formerly incarcerated man with a powerful story to tell that linked to a broader societal critique and demand for change. In 1995 his comrade Nancy Kurshan, who had worked on prison issues for decades, brought him to Chicago to speak.[76] The occasion was the anniversary of the lockdown begun in 1985 at Marion Penitentiary, where Alan had been held for months between 1987 and 1988.

Alan told the audience about his experience as he described his concrete box of a cell, the lockdowns, and the lack of outside contact. The inane strip-searching and tossing of the cells, he recalled, were all part of the dehumanization to remind the prisoner of the senselessness of it all and his lack of control. "Marion and all the other control unit prisons are concrete and steel embodiments of the dynamics of power," he explained to his audience. "But power recognizes no rights but its own. There are no rights remaining to you as a prisoner or to anyone subjected to power. I would say that this is the same dynamic that we see in colonial situations, for instance." As a political prisoner, he continued, he knew they were trying to break him, because "if they could strip me of my sense of dignity and self they would be stripping me of my political identity . . . and . . . strik[ing] a blow against the movements."

He went on to discuss rage. He had always had some visible anger, but his politicization and then the prison years made him understand the "social rage" created by loss of "dignity, self esteem, and self determination." To rage was not to be an animal, he argued, "but to show your humanity toward those who try and disempower you." What he did not talk about was how difficult it was to direct the rage so that the prisoner did not appear to be an out of control and could remain human, and not become the thoughtless animal the prison sought to create. His audience seemed to understand and gave him a standing ovation.

A few months later he was a major speaker at a New York City rally to support Mumia Abu-Jamal. Abu-Jamal was being denied his commentaries on National Public Radio because of Republican congressional threats to shut off the network's public funding. Along with actors Ossie Davis and Mike Farrell, lawyers, and labor union leaders, Alan lent his voice to this political attack on censorship and the trumped-up charges against his prison comrade.[77] He would continue to work on Abu-Jamal's case for years.

Alan's anger about what happened to political prisoners and what should be done to pardon them played out in an extraordinary television show he participated on PBS as part of its *Debates Debates* series. In April 1998, Alan, along with his lawyer Ron Kuby and black political activist Safiya Bukhari, took the "yes" side on the question "Should we grant amnesty to America's political prisoners?"[78] Unlike the quick back-and-forth of other political shows, this format allowed for an hour of discussion by "experts in a face off on policy issues."[79] That such a debate could even take place was a reflection of the political work that had been done over the years on behalf of the still-incarcerated members of the Black Panthers and Puerto Rican independence and Native American groups.[80]

The first debater on the "no" side was an unsurprising choice. Former assistant U.S. district attorney Charles Rose had often opposed Kuby in the courtroom, prosecuting many in the FALN and in white anti-imperialist groups.[81] The other two are far better-known today than they would have been to a 1998 audience. Peter Thiel, identified as a libertarian and a representative of the In-

Alan speaking at a demonstration to support black political prisoners, New York City, 1998. *Courtesy of Barbara Zeller.*

dependent Institute in Washington, D.C., and California, has since come to fame as the founder of PayPal, a critic of college education and big government, and a prominent Donald Trump supporter. The third debater was Ted Cruz, described as "an attorney with a Washington, D.C., law firm," since this was before he worked for George W. Bush, became Texas solicitor general then U.S. senator, and ran for president.

Kuby led off for his team by arguing that the United States would not admit it had political prisoners, but that it did nonetheless and gave them the maximum punishment possible. In opposition, Rose claimed that such prisoners were killers and bombers who had been convicted of federal offenses. He named Alan as an example of someone who had been "convicted of being involved in bombing and possessing explosives," even though only the latter was true (even if he had been indicted for bombing) and Alan corrected him later in the debate. Alan, in turn, named several of his black and Puerto Rican comrades and argued they "are as committed to the freedom and dignity of their people as Nelson Mandela has been. Shouldn't people be given amnesty? Yes, we need truth and reconciliation just as South Africa has recognized."[82]

"The United States is not a fascist country," Peter Thiel countered, as he named bombers from the right and asked if they counted as political prisoners too. We have "avenues for peaceful change," he argued. The debate grew more heated over the question of who counted as a political prisoner and whether killing in the name of freedom is different than "ordinary" murder. Kuby agreed that "mistakes had been made," but Cruz, known for his debating skills, responded by asking, "Does murder count as a mistake?"[83]

Alan tried a different tack against Cruz. He spoke of his experiences at Wounded Knee and the claim for "democracy" that had led to the murder of millions of Native Americans over the centuries. Cruz ignored this and repeated that the right to free speech did not include the right to bomb and kill. Alan's team's arguments about the illegal wars in Central America did not move their opponents. Bukhari recalled the unlawful use of counterintelligence programs within the FBI that had disrupted the Black Panthers and black liberation groups, and even propelled some of them toward more violence.

Over and over, Rose, Thiel, and Cruz stood by their claim that the United States was a democracy with peaceful ways to agitate for change. In contrast, Alan and his side tried to insist on the liberation aspect of the Puerto Rican struggle, and the systematic violence against Native Americans and African Americans that justified the turn toward armed struggle. As Bukhari put it, "You don't become political activists out of a vacuum."[84]

Their differences centered on the use of violence. Alan grew angrier, especially in response to Cruz's casting of anyone who used violence as a monster. Alan insisted that "people make judgments sometimes that were marred by the reality of police and FBI repression about when to engage in armed struggle. And not because they had some lifelong commitment to violence."[85] As Kuby would say at the end, "It's certainly true that one person's terrorist in some circumstances becomes another person's freedom fighter . . . and if are ever going to resolve the problem of political violence in this country, it can only come through discussion, through dialogue, through amnesty and hopefully through freedom."[86]

None of the participants' minds were changed in this debate, and the differences between the sides would continue to rend the country for decades. Alan's arguments demonstrated how much motives and political circumstances that drove people toward political violence still mattered to him, even if he, like Kuby, could acknowledge mistakes. Alan's social rage had not receded, but where he would use it still was evolving.

LEARNING MORE ABOUT HIV/AIDS

Alan's relationship to the AIDS epidemic began to change in ways that more strongly connected his politics to his medical practice. Both he and his comrades had been sent to prison just four years after the first cases of the disease were recognized in 1981. They all saw firsthand the treatment of incarcerated people who were identified as HIV-positive or had full-blown AIDS. They were infuriated that prisoners were left to waste away and die alone from the fevers, sores, blindness, pneumonias, and continual diarrhea that the disease produced.[87]

The RCC defendants had discussed this when they were in the D.C. jail, and Alan's comrades worked on HIV/AIDS education projects in their respective prisons after they left Washington.[88] They saw the necessity for the education of inmates, but their efforts ran up against prison authorities' demands for control, isolation, and security.[89] Even after more effective drugs became available, much remained to do.[90]

Alan's concern about HIV/AIDS and the failures of prison health care surfaced in a 1995 article he wrote for the *American Journal of Public Health*, in which he incorporated his experiences and his knowledge of the disease. He expanded on the dehumanization of prison health care and reflected on the underlying problems of poverty and racism. He made suggestions for policy change that allowed the separation of health care from correctional control, and he called for peer-based education connected to policies of harm-reduction and voluntary testing.[91] He sought to make the public health community understand that what happened in prisons mattered for the rest of the country, concluding, "The chain of common humanity is only as strong as its weakest link, and for the current generation of public health planners, prisons are the breaking point."[92] It was the beginning of his foray into the world of public health that looked at populations, rather than the more individually focused clinical doctoring he had been doing.

The connections between his medical knowledge of AIDS, his political understandings of injustice, and his commitment to act would shape the rest of his life.

15

CONFRONTING GLOBAL HIV/AIDS

By the late 1990s, Alan was growing restless. His work at Highbridge Woody-crest was meaningful as he connected the best medical care and practices he could devise to his patients' lived realities. He saved lives, or eased his patients' last days. He stayed as linked as possible to his former comrades as they continued to do HIV/AIDS education in their prisons.[1] He continued working in support of their cases and those of other political prisoners.[2] His life with Barbara and Sarah and his connections to Harriet gave him stability. For someone else, all of this might have been enough. Not for Alan. He knew he needed some way to connect his politics more fully to what was becoming a worldwide struggle against AIDS. Making the largest political and humanitarian efforts of his life would take his political connections, luck, and the recognition of his strengths by sympathetic others. This time the stage he was on was much bigger.

DENIALISTS AND HIV/AIDS

Alan was drawn into debates against those who refused to believe that HIV caused AIDS, or thought its origins were man-made and that the new treatments were useless. Once considered merely a fringe, the ranks of the so-called HIV "denialists" continued to grow during the 1990s despite scientific break-throughs. Some of the beliefs were actually spread in the mid-1980s by the Soviet KGB (Committee for State Security) with claims that the United States had created the virus. Stories labeled "Link AIDS to CIA Warfare" or "AIDS/Gay Genocide" made their way into American newspapers and then across the world.[3] Sharing a deep mistrust of Western medicine, Big Pharma, and the government, the denialists, even without the KGB's help, thought in conspiratorial terms.[4] Wide swaths of people, including some cancer scientists, were suscep-tible to these beliefs for differing reasons. The conspiracy theories were powerful, and they made stopping the spread of HIV/AIDS far more difficult, as such beliefs led some people to avoid testing and treatment. In the words of one AIDS activist, "A half-truth is like a half a brick: You can throw it further."[5]

David Gilbert, the former Weather member serving a life sentence for his role as a getaway driver in the Brink's action in 1981, helped alert Alan to the prevalent denialism inside prisons. Gilbert penned an important essay in 1996 that became a pamphlet called AIDS Conspiracy? Tracking Down the Real Genocide.[6] Understanding that harmful beliefs about AIDS could seem believable alongside many perfectly reasonable fears, Gilbert tried to explain the difference between actual conspiracies (COINTELPRO, the CIA, and the spread of crack) and what he called "cockamamie theories." His mission was to "SAVE LIVES" and "take on this new trend of irrational and harmful analysis perpetrated on the oppressed."[7]

Alan's friend Bob Lederer, a comrade who had been in May 19th, worked with Puerto Rican militants, and served time in jail for resisting the 1980s grand jury investigations of various political groups, brought Alan into the work against denialists. A longtime ACT UP New York member, Lederer had stayed connected to Alan while the latter was imprisoned. By the mid-1990s, Lederer was an editor for the HIV/AIDS magazine POZ; produced a health radio show on WBAI, a New York independent station; and worked with his partner, John Riley, on these issues.[8] Alan spoke on Lederer's show to spread the word that the new combination drugs had stopped AIDS from being a death sentence, and he traveled with Lederer to SUNY-Purchase to debate denialists.[9] Alan understood what Lederer meant when he wrote, "Where does one draw the line between the healthy skepticism of dissidents and the dogma of denialists? To keep challenging and keep asking questions is not always comfortable. But as AIDS has taught us, it's the only way to survive."[10] Like David Gilbert, Alan could acknowledge the reasons for the distrust of the drug companies and fear of the government while as a doctor also providing the data from his work on why the treatments mattered.[11] It was a place where his medical expertise and politics aligned.

The struggles against the denialists came at a crucial moment in the history of AIDS. The actions of primarily gay and lesbian ACT UP members had made the critique of the stigma around the disease, and the demand for treatment, visible throughout the 1980s and early 1990s. AIDS, more than almost any other disease in the late twentieth century, had become completely entwined in race, class, gender, and homophobic politics. By 1996, after years of protests and organizing, new protease inhibitors became available. Patients rose from their deathbeds in what was called the "Lazarus effect."[12] Yet the new treatments were controlled by the big pharmaceutical companies and were very expensive.

At the same time, the political environment was changing, but not quickly enough. The Clinton administration acknowledged the crucial importance of fighting AIDS, created an AIDS policy office, and funded much more research. But it did not lift the ban on needle exchanges that reduced HIV transmission among drug users. Activist and actress Elizabeth Taylor called this failure "a measured act of premeditated murder." While some AIDS activists supported the Clinton administration, others saw impressive rhetoric but little actual action where it counted.[13] Alan knew more had to be done.

MAKING CONNECTIONS

Serendipity made it possible for Alan to dive deeper into AIDS politics and refocus his concerns. In 1994, he was still on parole and could not leave the country, even for relevant medical conferences. Barbara did not have these limitations and traveled to the Tenth International AIDS conference in Yokohama, Japan. These huge biennial conferences, held all over the world beginning in 1985, brought together thousands of health care professionals, government officials, AIDS researchers, pharmaceutical representatives, people with the disease, and their care organizations to present papers and hear the latest on available treatments and policies. Barbara was in a Japanese hotel lobby when Columbia University AIDS researcher Zena Stein overheard her speaking about Alan. Stein recalled who Alan was and remembered that she and her family had been involved in getting support for him when he was incarcerated.[14] After a conversation about Barbara's work and Alan's, they went to conference events together and made plans to see one another in New York. Stein would end up shaping the rest of Alan's life.

Zena Stein and her husband, Mervyn Susser, were South African–born physicians and renowned epidemiologists. They had become two of the founders of community-based health care in their home country but had to flee in the 1950s because of their antiapartheid political work. After a decade in England, they arrived at Columbia University's public health school in the mid-1960s. Zena Stein would go on to become one of the earliest epidemiology researchers on HIV/AIDS, working to set up Columbia's center on the disease's social and behavioral aspects in 1987, while Mervyn Susser became the editor of the *American Journal of Public Health*.[15]

Alan and Barbara could not have found a more compatible intellectual and political family. Old enough to be their parents, Zena Stein and Mervyn Susser knew firsthand the personal price paid by those who fought for revolutionary change, having been friends with the exiled, killed, or imprisoned Joe Slovo, Ruth First, Oliver Tambo, Walter Sisulu, and Nelson Mandela, who had led or supported armed struggle in apartheid South Africa. They were schooled in how political economy, class structures, gender politics, and racism determined health care systems and illnesses. They believed in health politics driven by the best scientific research possible.

When Alan met them, they had already set up a conference in Mozambique in 1990 to warn the African National Congress (ANC), just coming to power in South Africa, about the emerging AIDS crisis there. "It could be the most critical immediate contingency facing the movement, more so than Natal violence, or police riots, or unemployment, or all the chronic diseases," Stein and Susser wrote to the ANC's Oliver Tambo after the conference in a letter Alan kept a copy of in his files.[16] Their understanding of the political nature of health and medicine in an international context, and the kinds of actions that brought change, was a perfect match for Alan.

Once back in New York, Stein, true to her word, set up at meeting for Alan with her son, Ezra Susser, a psychiatrist and epidemiologist who also worked at Columbia's public health school. Ezra Susser's main research project then was examining the interrelationships among people with severe mental illness, HIV/AIDS, and homelessness, with the goal of developing strategies to reduce sexual risk in this very vulnerable population.[17]

At that point Alan was a clinician and political activist, but he had no real experience with the world of research medicine he had left behind more than two decades before. He did, however, have a great deal of respect for a politics driven by scientific knowledge and evidence, whether that was in biomedicine or Marxism. Ezra Susser, like his parents, believed in using epidemiological research to affect social policy and best practices around illness and health care. He was seven years younger than Alan, so they could have been brothers, and their political and medical concerns meshed.

Their meeting would prove life-changing for Alan. "I could tell in five minutes how smart he was," Susser remembered, "but he did not know how to write a grant proposal or do research."[18] Everyone in the Susser/Stein family decided to take a chance by advancing Alan's career. There was the problem, however, of how to explain his professional trajectory to get him accepted into a formal program at Columbia. Their family had enough influence at the HIV Center to smooth over the ten-year gap in Alan's résumé between 1982 and 1992. They had already taken in a physician who had fled Augusto Pinochet's military regime in Chile, and they understood what it meant to have a political past. Allan Rosenfield, the school's beloved and open-minded dean, who had already made a major impact on global maternal health, recognized Alan's talents, too, and was willing to downplay the relevance of at least part of his history.[19] In this case as in others, Alan's Ivy League degrees, race, and gender gave him access to support and opportunity not available to most formerly incarcerated people.

While keeping his job in the Bronx, Alan received a two-year (1995–97) postdoctoral research fellow position in HIV prevention at Columbia. As he cut back on his working hours, the Columbia training allowed him to learn what most physicians in clinical practice do not know how to do: epidemiological studies of populations, randomized control trials, and grant writing. He was getting other professional opportunities as well, including being asked to join the New York City Health Department's Institutional Review Board (IRB). For the next several years, Alan would be a stalwart defender of protections for human subjects and of their rights to proper compensation for their efforts.[20] His humanity and intelligence, and life experience, made him a valued colleague in numerous professional circles.

At Columbia, Alan became part of a research project on sexual risk in underserved populations that were sometimes known in the academic literature as "elusive" and "urban." These were euphemisms for drug users, the homeless, and the mentally ill, who might also have incarceration histories. With Ezra Susser's team, Alan worked to develop and test interventions they labeled "sex, games and videotapes" to prevent HIV's spread.[21] The researchers learned how to speak to the homeless men and women and to make a video about safe sex that could be shown at a lunchtime gathering place.

Alan's thinking is clear in one of the reports when he and the other researchers wrote, "A frequent and painful part of the lives of many homeless, mentally ill men and women is being treated as non-persons."[22] The researchers worked hard to treat their research subjects with dignity. The work, which involved a carefully set up control trial that tested in two arms the intervention and nonintervention with the same kind of population, led to Alan's first publications not about imperialism, political activism, or prison health. He, Susser, and their colleagues began to identify through research the best procedures for saving lives most thought not savable or valued.[23]

Halfway through his fellowship, Alan was already presenting papers on the project. After much bureaucratic rigmarole, he got permission from his parole officer and Canadian officials to present a paper at the next World AIDS Conference, in Vancouver in July 1996.[24] For the first time, he and Barbara could attend an international conference together. The experience started him on a global road.

AIDS IN GLOBAL AND HUMAN RIGHTS PERSPECTIVES

By 1996, as the new combination drugs against AIDS were announced, concern arose about how such expensive pharmaceuticals could ever stave off the growing pandemic in low-resource countries. Prevention was seen as the best "treatment" in the developing world. The medical and public health literature was filled with worries about countries' not being able to pay for the drugs, the lack of health system structures to distribute them, and individuals' inability to adhere to complicated dosage schedules that could lead to developing drug resistance. There were still debates, too, over whether to take a human rights approach based on tolerance and treatment for individuals or to employ traditional public health protections for whole populations that involved preaching prevention and often imposed quarantines and restrictions on individual behaviors.[25]

In Vancouver, Alan and Barbara would hear arguments on both sides of this debate. Before conference attendees numbering in the thousands, New York ACT UP activist Eric Sawyer argued passionately for making affordable treatment available to everyone. A survivor of the epidemic in New York that had taken many people he loved, Sawyer fought for worldwide equality of access to the life-saving drugs. Sawyer's critique of the pharmaceutical companies' voracious capitalism stood out at a time when other AIDS activists were loath to attack Big Pharma, which not only was producing new drugs that were saving at least some lives but also was often funding their organizations.[26]

A leading American HIV/AIDS researcher, Jonathan Mann, championed the human rights approach in soaring terms at a plenary session.[27] Mann used his international experience to argue that it was possible to protect both individuals and populations by examining the "societal root causes of vulnerability."[28] Mann was struggling to find a teaching and research path that would link health and human rights while reexamining key values in public health from the perspectives of individual rights and dignity and the social causes of disease. His approach followed the growing realization that issues including the subordination of women, illiteracy, poverty that led to sex work, forms of work that separated families, and homelessness were among a host of drivers in the spread of HIV/AIDS.[29]

Mann's speech at Vancouver is still remembered in the AIDS community for its passionate call for fairness around the world. Before an audience that included Barbara and Alan, Mann bemoaned the preaching of prevention and quarantine for underresourced countries while the new protocol of drugs, costing many thousands of dollars, was available in richer ones. This disparity had to end, he declared. "This is not charity. This is not humanitarianism. This is solidarity—which is radically different—for it is based on the knowledge that we are in some basic and clear way incomplete without the other." Mann closed with a powerful sermon on human connectedness, demanding solidarity as a "destiny! Worthy of our past, our aspirations, our commitment, our dignity, and our lives."[30] He could not have spoken more closely to Alan and Barbara's deepest values.

How to address this need in the underresourced parts of the world became a fierce debate in the new century. Bioethicists and researchers clashed over the ethics of various research trials and the costs of pharmaceuticals. The moral issue of the failure to treat, regardless of cost, when drugs were available was now a public debate that spilled out of the arcane world of medicine and public health into such newspapers as the *Wall Street Journal*.[31]

Such debates put Barbara and Alan's work on AIDS into a much larger global context. The anticolonialism and anti-imperialism they had been concerned with for so long now could be approached through a melding of science and politics. What they had known intellectually became more real when they made their first trip to South Africa two years later in the spring of 1998. Alan was finally off parole and could leave the country without government permission, even if his name kept popping up on various lists that made navigating border security a hassle.[32]

The trip was a partial realization of Alan's decades-old desire to work in an African country, even if it was not the revolutionary path he had originally wanted.[33] He went with Ezra Susser as a consultant to the South African Directorate of Mental Health and Substance Abuse to look at ways to strengthen prevention of HIV/AIDS among the mentally ill, and to help rewrite the mental health code now that the ANC was in power.[34] Alan had been made an assistant professor of clinical psychiatry at Columbia as part of this work, a position he would keep while still working at HWC. Susser had wanted the best people he could think of to advise the South African government, and Alan, he thought, fit this definition.[35] Barbara came along to do some clinical work, and to see the country.

Alan was indeed the right person for the project. Ezra Susser recalled that he found it hard to hire Alan at Columbia, given his lack of training and political past. In South Africa, however, Alan had the perfect résumé to be believed: he was a doctor who had been a political prisoner of the United States.[36] The very president of the postapartheid state had been incarcerated for decades for his activism. The South Africans, unlike their American counterparts, understood that political prisoners were tried on criminal charges and that a truth and reconciliation tribunal of some sort was needed. They accepted an individual's past political actions.

What Alan learned about AIDS in South Africa frightened him. "In the context of mental illness, I began to look at the world through an AIDS lens," he recalled a few years later. The prevention messages had not done enough, there was very little treatment going on, and the disease was growing exponentially, killing patients and health professionals alike, and leaving behind orphan after orphan.[37]

Alan and Barbara's plan was to leave South Africa after the consultation to enjoy a safari in Botswana and to go on to Europe. The contrast between the wide plains, roamed by thousands of animals, and his own carceral experience of just a few years before could not have been starker.[38] They then flew to Geneva for the June 1998 international AIDS conference, titled "Bridging the Gap" and focused on equalizing care and treatment around the world.

Despite the hopes that had been raised at Vancouver two years before, the chasm between rich and poor countries was wider than ever. UNAIDS director Peter Piot broke the news that since the Vancouver meeting another 10 million people had become HIV-positive, in what he labeled a "runaway epidemic."[39] The cost of the new antiretroviral therapies could be $36.5 billion annually.[40] The global data confirmed Alan's sense of an exploding epidemic in South Africa.

The divisions between the Global North and Global South were obvious. Just as Jonathan Mann had feared, solidarity was not the basis of connection for those trying to fight the epidemic.[41] As ACT UP members noted, no global policy or strategy appeared to be getting enough "drugs into bodies."[42] The editor of the British medical journal *The Lancet* watched researchers walk out on talks by colleagues from the Global South. He left Geneva with what he labeled, in fine English reserve, "an overall sense of disappointment," questioning why so much of the conference was funded by the very pharmaceutical companies charging outrageous prices for their drugs. His reserve faded as he argued that leaving this industry "unaccountable for its policies and priorities, [and] fail[ing] to call them to account[,] is nothing less than a betrayal of those in the developing world."[43]

Others in various ACT UP chapters around the world tried different kinds of disruptions to bring attention to the inequality. These ranged from seizing the podium to denounce the World Bank, spray-painting "GREED KILLS, STOP AIDS PROFITEERING" on the booth of the pharmaceutical giant Merck, and pulling a banner that read, "Greed Kills: AIDS Treatment for All," onto the main stage at the opening ceremony. Such actions, however, received little media coverage and seemed to be having little effect.[44] The divided AIDS activist community was loath to take on the pharmaceutical giants on behalf of unknown, impoverished individuals half a world away.

In assessing what had happened in Geneva, Alan was even more direct. The increasing "inertia manifested by people who were supposed to be providing leadership around global AIDS" horrified him. He watched as the AIDS drug cocktails sold "like hotcakes" and pharmaceutical representatives "wined and dined" doctors and scientists from high-resource countries, feeling as if there was "something . . . pornographic about it, having just come from Africa."[45] He also listened as speakers raised the fear of drug resistance in patients who failed to adhere to the complicated drug schedules, even though others showed that "adherence was not the monopoly of the rich."[46] He and Barbara left the conference with what Alan had called earlier "social rage."

The next stop in their trip was in Germany near Munich, where they made a pilgrimage to the Nazi concentration camp at Dachau.[47] Alan's thoughts on the Holocaust were troubled by watching a film at the camp's museum, and then a real-time oral history by a survivor. Despite its supposed radical content organized by German leftists, the account made no mention of the Jews. "They had a fascinating history of the rise of fascism, totally sincere," Alan would later recall, "and the effect of this elegant analysis was that they ignored the human dimension of what this museum was about."[48] On the long train ride with Barbara to Paris, Alan reviewed what they had witnessed: the terrible expansion of the epidemic in South Africa, the failure of the international conference in Geneva to do anything meaningful in the Global South, and the eclipsing at Dachau of the humanity of those murdered. His moral, medical, and political sensibilities became fused as he considered what might be done.[49]

By the time Alan and Barbara were back in New York, Alan was pondering strategies for treatment access to save lives in the Global South. He was aware it was not revolutionary in the ways he had thought about this before; but he believed there had to be action for a "politics of human solidarity."[50] Jonathan Mann's Moses-like commandments on the basis for the global fight against AIDS had gone deep into Alan's mind and heart, joining his long-standing political principles. His Joshua moments at the walls of a medical and political Jericho were at hand.

CALLING IN THE ACTIVISTS:
THE FOUNDING OF HEALTH GAP

Decades earlier, Alan had tried and failed to change the world. His vanguard of revolutionaries remained tiny. His efforts to bring the cost of racism and imperialism home led to prison time. Now, he saw an opening for another revolutionary act. He sought to read the zeitgeist to determine a way to bring together his medical, political, and organizing talents. This time grassroots activism, not a small cadre, would be needed.

Alan was realistic about where he was attempting: he was an AIDS doctor at a small treatment and nursing home facility in the Bronx. Though he had a recent connection to an academic institution, he was also just off parole and had almost no global health experience. However, he brought to the table a unique grasp of global politics, some useful contacts — especially with the Stein/Susser clan — and sheer chutzpah. He had an intimate knowledge of what the lack of treatment meant, and a commitment to the humanity of individuals that in differing ways had animated all his political and medical work. His efforts would play out the old adage from the anti–Vietnam War movement: radicals do what liberals only say they are going to do.

Alan started to develop a set of principles, a strategy, and then specific tactics to address the problem of getting treatment around the world.[51] Even though those with left politics in public health had long emphasized the importance of prevention and primary care, as well as attention to the underlying social determinants of health, Alan saw the urgency of treatment in the face of so many avoidable deaths. As a leading public health figure had put it, "Treatment is like bad money, it drives out prevention, good money. No one sees what you prevent."[52]

The prevention strategy was not stemming the pandemic, and without hopes of available treatment, Alan knew that fatalism would soon settle in. Organizations like Partners in Health, primarily working in Haiti, and the Brazil experience, where health care was declared a right by the government and the costs of the generic HIV drugs lowered, had demonstrated that it was possible, even with low-resourced health care systems, to get appropriate treatment to those who need it.[53] "Treatment is integral to rather than in opposition to prevention," would become Alan's position; anything else was immoral.[54] The major problems for treatment, he knew, were the drug costs and the laws, policies, and politics that were keeping them from being lowered.

Over the next few months Alan developed a four-page position paper, "From Geneva to Durban: Solidarity Bridges the Gap."[55] Using the fact that the next international AIDS conference, hosted by South Africa's third-largest city, would be the first one in the developing world, Alan proposed what he called a "multi-level strategy, rooted in grassroots activism." It was a demand for lower-cost drugs "as a matter of right and justice" and not just a call for "drastic bulk discounts or outright donations." Alan wanted a different kind of price-setting, expansion of distribution in countries that had and could afford the drugs, and the relinquishing of patent rights to allow poorer countries to develop generic drugs themselves, or import them from others. From there, Alan argued for "A People's Call to Action against AIDS," linking community and AIDS service organizations, while pressuring governments and the AIDS conference itself to ensure that the goals were attained.

Alan prepared an impressive proposal. He began with what he already knew about the success of AIDS activists in the United States who had forced the lowering of the cost of the first antiretroviral drugs. "The vast majority of profits on pharmaceuticals come from the countries of the North [and] voluntarily allowing regional production of these products would result in little direct loss for the drug companies." This was not just a moral statement; he was trying to devise a strategic vision for action to change the course of the global pandemic.

Alan began by contacting colleagues at Columbia he trusted: Zena Stein and anthropologist Richard Parker, who had a long history of activism with the

Brazilian AIDS movement.[56] Both Stein and Parker thought Alan's ideas were worth pursuing. Parker would add his name to Alan's initial position paper. Still, as Alan knew, an intellectual proposal like this one, however worthy, did not mean anything would happen. Next he would turn to activists.

Alan drew from his long political history with Bob Lederer, with whom he had worked to counter the AIDS denialists.[57] Lederer, and his life partner and fellow ACT UP leader John Riley, had the experiences Alan needed: they knew many in the activist community, could focus on tactics, and had the connections needed to mobilize a demonstration. ACT UP itself was a shadow of its former power, having been diminished by "death and neoliberalism," as one ACT UP leader put it.[58] But Lederer and Riley in New York, and others in the Philadelphia ACT UP chapter, which counted more people of color as members, were still very active.

After an initial dinner and discussion with Alan, the activists went to work. Lederer contacted ACT UP founder Eric Sawyer, who had spoken so passionately at the Vancouver conference, asking that he keep in confidence the "tentative draft proposal" and join the three of them (Alan, Lederer, and Riley) to discuss it further.[59] After Sawyer came on board, the proposal went out to a handful of treatment advocates in the United States and others around the world. The ideas began to come in email, still a relatively new form of communication, then slower because it relied on a modem.[60] It was, however, a far cry from Alan's experience of organizing that used landlines, public phone booths, or mimeographed pages, letters, and printed manifestos.

The proposal began to be refined in response to the feedback. Micronutrients, herbs, water purification, and testing kits were added to the protease inhibitors and other antiretrovirals that the proposal set out to make available.[61] The activists were well aware that "patient assistance programs" run by the drug companies were charitable, often ineffective efforts that could require onerous paperwork and be canceled at a corporate whim.[62] They knew that some Global South countries were producing their own generic versions of the key drugs, but they did not know much about how trade laws affected these efforts. The focus at the beginning was on Big Pharma and how to change its policies.

Over the next few months, the proposal evolved as the activists made connections with AIDS advocates in Brazil, South Africa, France, and other countries.[63] When to show the drafted proposal to the people in UNAIDS and the World Bank, where Eric Sawyer had contacts, was of concern. There was also the good news that Médecins sans Frontières (Doctors without Borders) was working on strategies to lower drug costs in Thailand, while Alan's Columbia colleague Richard Parker had connections to organizations doing the same in Brazil.

The activists debated numerous questions: Should there be a focus on other kinds of essential medicines? Would one demand fit for every low-resourced country? What about rural areas that lacked electricity, providers to monitor patients, and the dangers of some of the medications?[64] The exchanges, some playing out on the new communication platform of the LISTSERV, showed, as one activist acknowledged, "an incredible example of how we can use electronic networking to create instant and global solidarity around shared concerns."[65]

By October 1998, everyone who had been contacted agreed to the proposal's broad outlines, but the group continued to exchange information and concerns. Sometimes the process was slow, and Alan was worried about how "problematic" it all was, as much of his out of work time was being spent setting up a very successful conference on alternative and integrative treatments for HIV/AIDS, and at which both he and Barbara spoke.[66] Bob Lederer kept reaching out to ACT UP activists in other cities, as Alan and Richard Parker waited to hear back from their connections in South Africa, since the Durban conference was going to be pivotal to their demands.[67] No one wanted another "ugly American" story where the North American activists got ahead of their Global South allies on issues affecting them.[68]

In late November 1998, the focus started to become clearer as the problem of international trade agreements came into view, a subject even *Time* magazine found so boring that its opening story on the issue began, "Please — wake us when it's over."[69] Lederer sent to Alan and his closest allies an article by John S. James, the longtime editor of the *AIDS Treatment News*, called "GATT and the Gap: How to Save Lives."[70] In what could have been seen as an obscure part of global trade policy, James was pointing out that the big pharmaceutical companies were protecting their intellectual property rights more than ever by moving against the generics of the anti-AIDS drugs that were being produced in the Global South. James explained that the U.S. government, through the newly developed World Trade Organization (WTO), was also enforcing patent rules and pressuring developing countries to change their own laws to follow them.[71] Nothing could have seemed more obscure, yet been so crucial to the difficulty of producing and selling AIDS drug generics at lower costs. The new structures of globalization were affecting pharmaceuticals in a way trade policy never had before.[72]

There are times when activists need policy wonks. In "GATT and the Gap," James translated into the terms of AIDS activism information he had learned from economist Jamie Love, an expert on intellectual property and pharmaceuticals at Ralph Nader's Consumer Project on Technology. Love had become one of the world's most knowledgeable experts on the intricacies of trade and the Trade-Related Aspects of Intellectual Property (TRIPS) agreements set up by the WTO in 1995.[73] Love and his organization were already working with Doctors without Borders on the South African government's efforts to keep the United States, acting on behalf of Big Pharma, from suing it for developing generics of essential medications.[74] Love believed ways could be found within these rules to get the generics produced or imported from other countries, but he had just begun to have contact with AIDS activists.

By December 1998, the emailing comrades were moving toward having their first big meeting in person. Alan had been waiting to hear back from the chair of the Durban AIDS conference to be held in 2000, who he hoped would support their efforts. But the South African doctor could not get the Durban planning committee to agree to chastise the drug companies that were financing the conference.[75] As Alan told Bob Lederer, "It seems to me that there are plenty of initiatives around that maximize cooperation with the pharmaceutical industry and minimize grassroots solidarity, so I don't immediately see how we would work together."[76] Lederer thought it was time to move, and, after six months of planning, the HIV/AIDS Forum on Africa was held in New York on January 19, 1999.[77]

HOPE FOR POLITICAL CHANGE

Alan had once said he thought the "parrot of death" often sat on his shoulder. As he was doing his political work, his body refused to cooperate, and he began to think the parrot was back. In late December 1998, he had begun to notice that his stool was becoming bloody and dark. Anyone with his cancer history would have imagined the worst, but Alan was good at denial. "It is probably an ulcer," he told Barbara, but she was already fearful.[78] The first few tests he was given showed very little, and he was scheduled for an endoscopy and a colonoscopy to visualize both ends of his alimentary canal. At least this time there was the comfort of knowing everything was being done in a timely manner, there were no chains holding him down, and he was seeing a former medical school classmate who knew what he was doing. No more unlicensed quacks or unfeeling guards.

His tests showed a small bulge at the end of his colon. When he came out of the anesthesia from the colonoscopy, he and Barbara were told "everything looks fine," even though there was no immediate explanation for the bleeding or the lump. As is often done and just to be careful, samples from his intestine were sent for a biopsy.[79] As Alan waited for the report from the pathologists, the planning for the January meeting continued.

January 19 turned out to be a more momentous day than Alan had expected. That afternoon, his colleague doctor called with the results: there was a malignancy called T-cell lymphoma at the intersection of his large and small intestines. Unlike the Hodgkin's lymphoma he had survived twice before, this was a rare and serious cancer with a shortened survival time.[80] Only then could he admit that "denial had worked and this came as a shock, and shook me quite a bit. The parrot [of death] had gone away, and now the parrot was back."[81] He would go into the evening meeting of his newly formed coalition with this in his mind, acutely aware of how tenuous life could be and why appropriate treatment mattered.

Over the next few weeks, the new coalition would continue to meet as the activists' histories of confronting various pharmaceutical companies were evaluated and discussed. The question of how to channel moral outrage into a winnable political position underlay much of the talk. Would the old strategies work? Was there something else that had to be tried? What could be done that linked government policy and the pharmaceutical companies' intransigence on pricing?[82]

Jamie Love, the policy wonk, came to the January meeting to explain the WTO and how it affected licensing and international property law.[83] The details of parallel importing (allowing countries to import generics from another country) and compulsory licensing (allowing the production of a patented product without the consent of the patent owner under the new trade agreements in specific countries) appeared less esoteric as their importance for AIDS drugs became the focus. As Love made clear, "AIDS activists had a strong basis under international law upon which to make their demands."[84] His knowledge helped concentrate the coalition's members' attention on how to use trade agreements to change government policies and pressure drug companies. With so much political experience in the room, the attendees made plans to send people to an upcoming Geneva Conference on Compulsory Licensing and considered how to approach the Clinton administration.[85]

As the meetings continued, Alan had to step back to determine his medical options to combat the growing cancer in his abdomen. "It was a very stressful period," he would admit in an understatement.[86] Unlike when he was in prison, he could now get multiple opinions on various chemotherapy or other regimens from different physicians. But when he made a list of what he had been through to explain to yet another doctor, his last comment was "Whew!"[87] After listening to the various opinions, he did not think he could stand the anxiety of undergoing the more experimental treatments, so he opted for an older drug combination similar to what he had survived in the past, and which an important study had showed to be as effective with fewer side effects than the newer combinations.[88] While still working and attending at least some of the new coalition's meetings, he once again began a chemotherapy protocol that left him with nausea, hair loss, and weakness that increased as the treatments went on.[89]

He was also at least willing to consider alternatives. His friend Bruce Taub knew of a Peruvian healer who was visiting New York, and Taub bought Alan a session. In an apartment, Alan met a man half-naked and covered in amulets and beads. The healer chewed petals, spitting all over Alan as he chanted and blew smoke. Alan thought it all pretty hilarious.[90]

Whether it was the spittle and smoke or the chemotherapy, by the late spring of 1999 he was feeling better, but with what his doctors diagnosed as "hip arthritis with effusions [fluid leakage]" that gave him considerable pain, especially when he walked.[91] The fluids were drained, and by August a CT scan revealed only arthritic involvement, not any spread of the cancer.[92] Now taking many over-the-counter analgesics, he had survived again.

THE FIRST ACTIONS: GOING AFTER GORE

Throughout the spring of 1999, as Alan was undergoing chemotherapy, the coalition he had helped create kept meeting in person and in conference calls.[93] At a meeting that March that Alan could not attend, they had agreed to edit his document as their group's mission statement and expand it "to target the negative role of governments and the issue of patents in blocking treatment access." Turning around the title of the International AIDS conference in Geneva, "Bridging the Gap," they debated various names before settling on the Health Global Access Project Coalition, shortened to Health GAP.[94] At this point most of them were working for other organizations and volunteering their time. Slowly, efforts were also made to begin to raise some foundation funds to support more full-time work.

The antiglobalization movement that would explode in Seattle later that year at a November WTO meeting linked the Health GAP members to a broader political movement.[95] Activists from many perspectives were trying to counter the worldwide effort by industries, World Bank interests, and governments to privatize just about everything and to limit government responsibility for social needs.[96] The fighting in Seattle's streets rallied individuals and groups from differing perspectives to attack the global expansion of capitalism. Health GAP became part of this broad effort to lay bare the U.S. government's complicity with drug companies, and the enormous human cost they were willing to pay for profit and higher share prices, as well as U.S. pressure on other countries to do Big Pharma's bidding.

As a start, members of Health GAP had to debate how to think about the problem and what tactics to take, whether to focus on Big Pharma, the government, or both.[97] Alan was crucial, since, as Health GAP activist Asia Russell declared, he was "an incredible interrogator of the knowing and unknowing public health experts who agreed it was too expensive to provide the drugs, or cited broad drug resistance problems, or that other diseases matter more."[98] Alan helped them begin to concentrate on the government.

The coalition started by taking the normative stance of lobbying for a Hope for Africa bill that U.S. Representative Jesse L. Jackson Jr. of Illinois was sponsoring in the House that would have encouraged trade and helped make generic AIDS drugs more available.[99] The Clinton administration, through surrogates in Congress, was supporting a different trade bill that would have protected the drug companies' patents, although there were debates within various government agencies over how to handle trade and generic drugs.[100] While working with Jackson on the bill, Eric Sawyer and Jamie Love received a copy of what Sawyer called "the smoking gun memo." Sent by the Clinton administration to a New Jersey congressman, the memo explained how much the administration was doing to protect the patent rights of the many pharmaceutical companies headquartered in the congressman's state, and to punish the South African government if it went ahead with making and importing generic drugs.[101]

Sawyer and Love were furious. They turned their attention to Vice President Al Gore, who led the administration's focus on trade agreements that in the end supported Big Pharma.[102] Jamie Love and Ralph Nader had written to Gore about the problems of drug pricing and trade as early as 1997, but they had received no reply.[103] Although concerned by the spread of AIDS, Gore was the Clinton administration's point man on trade. He had been discussing South Africa's move on generics with that government's officials for several years. At a February 1999 meeting, he told Thabo Mbeki, then South Africa's deputy president, that his nation was being put on a "'watch list' of countries risking sanctions because they were trying to produce or import generic AIDS drugs."[104]

As the Health GAP coalition members debated what to do next, Gore's presidential ambitions gave them an opening.[105] Building on their knowledge of tactics that had worked in the past, ACT UP members from New York and Philadelphia rented a van and drove nearly sixteen hours to Carthage, Tennessee, for Gore's June 16, 1999, formal announcement that he was running for president. Wearing faked "Columbia Students for Gore" and "without tickets, they 'sweet-talked' a ticket-taker into allowing them in and assumed a camera-friendly spot close to the stage."[106] They brought with them leaflets printed with "blood money" and "medical apartheid" to symbolize the role Gore and the rest of the Clinton administration were playing in support of Big Pharma.

Halfway through Gore's speech about "America's highest ideals in governing," loud whistles startled the crowd. Leaflets began fluttering as the "Gore's Greed Kills" and "AIDS Drugs for Africa" signs the activists had hidden beneath their coats went up and their "Greed kills" chants interrupted Gore's promises. Looking disturbed, Gore added he was for "free speech" and finished his announcement.[107] The cameras captured it all. The activists had gotten what they hoped: national media attention.

Not done yet, the activists got back into their van and raced through the night up the east coast to Manchester, New Hampshire, for Gore's next campaign stop. They picked up the girlfriend of one of their members, then-AIDS activist and now-MSNBC news anchor Rachel Maddow, in western Massachusetts on the way. When they arrived, they gave fake names and paired themselves off into purported heterosexual couples. Because they were "young and cute," as Philadelphia ACT UP participant Paul Davis put it, "they put us behind the podium." Once the activists pulled out their banners, "we get escorted out." Eric Sawyer had spoken directly to Gore at the photo op before his speech. During it, after Sawyer yelled out about the need for AIDS drugs and about complicity, the Secret Service "grabbed handfuls of the flesh of my love handles and pulled me off the table to the floor, back onto my feet, and out the door."[108]

As they were leaving, Democratic Party bigwig Donna Brazille stopped them. She had recognized Davis from the funeral of a mutual friend. "What the hell do you people want?" she asked, assuming they must be a very large organization to appear in two places within twenty-four hours.[109] They exchanged contact information as the activists discussed their demands. Meanwhile, joined by others, the activists did other actions they called "zaps" at a Gore speech on Wall Street the same day, and at his wife's fund-raising luncheons, as they massed people outside the events with signs about greed and the need for drugs in Africa that forced political donors to go through police escorts to get in.[110]

Between the contact with Gore and Brazille, the negative publicity, and the internal agency debate that suggested there was sympathy for their position within the administration, things moved more quickly than they had imagined: within a week, on June 22, they were invited to a meeting in Washington to discuss their demands and meet with Brazille and others on Gore's campaign staff. There would be more "zaps" outside his offices, a thousand people marching to the D.C. office of the U.S. trade representative, Charlene Barshefky, a sit-in a month later, and more marching to the White House. We just kept "bird-dogging them," Davis said.[111]

The efforts had an impact. Images of the interruptions of his campaign undermined the compassionate internationalist image Gore was trying to project.[112] Other government officials were concerned with the security impact of a wider pandemic. Whatever the reasons, on September 17, the U.S. trade representative announced that South Africa was no longer on the "watch list."[113] As Barshefky would tell the *Washington Post*, "Largely it was the activities of ACT-UP and the AIDS activists that galvanized our attention [to the fact] that there was an absolute crisis." At the WTO meeting in Seattle that December, Clinton would tell the world the United States would use its policies to make sure "that people in the poorest countries won't have to go without medicine they so desperately need."[114] In May 2000, following more meetings between the activists and the administration, Clinton signed an executive order assuring sub-Saharan African countries that they would be able to provide access to needed HIV/AIDS pharmaceuticals without fear of American sanctions.[115]

Health GAP had begun the new century as an important actor in the movement to make HIV/AIDS drugs more widely available.[116] Increasingly the media, including a Pulitzer Prize–winning eight-part series about AIDS in Africa in the *Village Voice*, was bringing attention to the global urgency of the disease and the cost of its drugs.[117] Alan had galvanized something really big.

ON TO DURBAN

By the summer of 1999 Alan was well enough to celebrate the return of his comrade Laura Whitehorn from her fourteen years in prison, even if they could not meet in person under the terms of parole.[118] She too remained concerned about AIDS and was soon working at the HIV/AIDS magazine POZ.

When not practicing medicine or studying at Columbia, Alan focused on the upcoming July 2000 International AIDS conference in Durban, South Africa. As he had told the activist friends in the Health GAP coalition, "We need to mobilize at the grass roots level. . . . In South Africa, by the time we get there . . . more than 20% of the people [will be] infected with the virus. To let the drug companies set foot in Africa and sponsor the conference without having done something would be a moral outrage."[119] As the zaps against Gore's public outings and the private administration meetings continued, Health GAP members began to make connections to the newly formed South African Treatment Action Committee (TAC).

In South Africa, the epidemic's consequences were as dire as Alan had feared. TAC, begun by South African radicals from what was called the Marxist Workers Tendency within the African National Congress, was beginning to coalesce. The activists had experience advocating for people with AIDS and for gay and lesbian South Africans. Their first action was a December 1998 fast by ten people on the steps of a Cape Town cathedral to dramatize the need for antiretroviral drugs.[120]

Mark Heywood, one of TAC's founders, a South African self-declared "do-gooder" and a white social justice lawyer who was HIV-negative, understood that all his work with UN agencies was not making a difference. "AIDS needed a social movement," he realized, "and that movement needed to be political and mirror the demographics of the AIDS epidemic in terms of gender and race . . . led by people who had everything to lose from AIDS — people with AIDS themselves."[121] The other activists in the "AIDS Industry," as Heywood labeled it, were getting money, going to conferences around the world, and becoming comfortable with the pace of change.[122] But that pace was far too slow. The numbers of people dying or afraid to get tested for the disease gave a desperate urgency to the new activists' efforts.

Heywood, HIV-positive activist Zackie Achmat, and others were forming a social movement in January 1999, at the same time as Health GAP's first meetings. The South Africans watched the media coverage of the actions at the Gore rallies.[123] Angry and rude, they were on their way to becoming, as Heywood labeled his group, "the new punks on the block." They soon broke away from the more conservative major South African AIDS groups. The TAC organizers had a vision of what had to be done, building on South African activist history as well as what they saw in the United States and other Western countries.[124] They soon were up against some of the global health thinking on prevention and the power of Big Pharma.

The TAC organization had to contend with the South African government as well. AIDS denialists increasingly influenced Thebo Mbeki, who had succeeded Nelson Mandela as president in 1999, for a complex set of political reasons. Mbeki doubted the effectiveness of antiretroviral drugs, then thwarted their use, even for HIV-positive pregnant women, who made up a startling 25 percent of all pregnant South African women.[125] The situation in South Africa became a complex, multifront struggle against the stigma of the disease, the government's changing position on treatment, and the difficulty of getting the drugs.

Alan continued to work his South African connections, as did other members of the Health GAP coalition, in preparation for the Durban conference. TAC's Zackie Achmat had been in New York and was in contact with ACT UP members, bringing some of them and their information to South Africa.[126] In February 2000, Alan participated in a conference call with his Health GAP comrades in which they spoke to Achmat about the plans for Durban. Achmat outlined for the Health GAP members the difficulties in South Africa due to multiple language barriers, literacy rates, the government, and the complexities of what they were trying to do. Alan discussed some of the false information that circulated on the drugs as well as their actual side effects, and everyone exchanged ideas on what both sides could do.[127]

Plans were being made for a major demonstration at the Durban conference to insist on the provision of the drugs.[128] Health GAP and ACT UP member Paul Davis went to Durban two months before the June 2000 conference to help set things up. Davis, who had never been in an African country, found the experience both powerful and complicated. He went with TAC members to the townships to seek supporters for what was now planned as a march through the streets of Durban. He was moved by the times they had to wait to let mourners pass by on foot carrying the bodies of AIDS victims to their funerals.[129] TAC was distributing thousands of leaflets about AIDS in the various townships, putting up posters, and bringing in other organizations to support the march.[130] Bob Lederer and John Riley arrived in Durban a few weeks before the July 2000 conference, also to help with logistics.[131]

The Durban conference would not be like the one in Geneva. With millions sick with the disease, many too afraid to announce their status because of stigma and violence, or unable to access the drugs, the need to do something now, already too late for so many, was obvious. Alan helped draw up a People's Call manifesto. Used as an "organizing tool for the demonstration," the statement declared, "We are united with a single purpose, to ensure that everyone with HIV and AIDS has access to fundamental rights of healthcare and access to life-sustaining medicines."[132] The manifesto was sent around the world as differing groups signed on. Alan argued that pressuring for treatment at the conference meant it could "herald . . . a new determination to break the silence around global AIDS and usher in an era of international activism that creates the political will needed to make . . . advances."[133]

The difficulties magnified as Mbeki and his health minister became enthralled by the denialists. To counter the Mbeki government's endorsement of such views, what became called the Durban Declaration, separate from the manifesto Alan was working on, was published on the eve of the conference in the widely read journal *Nature*. Signed by more than 5,000 physicians, researchers, and Nobel Prize–winning scientists from around the globe, the declaration stated, "HIV causes AIDS. Curbing the spread of this virus must remain the first step towards eliminating this devastating disease."[134] In this way, science and politics were explicitly united.[135]

Despite all of this, Mbeki appeared at the opening of the Durban International AIDS Conference to interrogate the relationship between HIV and AIDS and to question the effectiveness of the antiretroviral drugs, focusing instead on "extreme poverty."[136] No one of course doubted that such poverty made the disease's spread possible and worse, but the complicated views over sexuality, Western imperialism, and drug-company mendacity made the "half-brick, half-truth" of Mbeki's claims difficult to counter. Mandela, revered but no longer in power, would object to Mbeki's view carefully at the conference, but Mbeki's control of the government would set AIDS policy for the next years, with devastating results.[137]

Alan played two roles at the conference. As an AIDS doctor and researcher, he was giving a version of the "Sex, Games and Videotapes" paper, based on the work he had done with Ezra Susser's group at Columbia.[138] As an AIDS activist, he was participating with several thousand others in the demonstration that TAC had organized, with some assistance from his Health GAP colleagues. It was one of the first major marches about AIDS in South Africa and featured

Winnie Madikizela-Mandela, ex-wife of Nelson Mandela and still a powerful ANC figure, along with Zackie Achmat and other dignitaries. The marchers (mostly women) wore bright yellow T-shirts that declared "HIV positive" and carried signs that read "One AIDS Death Every 10 Minutes: Affordable Drugs Now" or "Cheap AIDS Drugs Save Lives: Affordable Treatment Now!" with the TAC, ACT UP, and Health GAP logos on the bottom. They clogged the streets near Durban City Hall, then marched to a stadium for the speeches.[139] Amid all the others in their T-shirts, Alan stood out in his suit jacket.

The moral and medical necessity for treatment in the Global South was now impossible to ignore, even if it still met intransigence. Alan thought the demonstration was a "fantastic success" because "leaders of the conference felt pressure and were angry at us. But we became the way they were able to integrate issues of the epidemic in Africa into every aspect of the conference."[140] For him it was the biggest result of anything he had done to gain grassroots support for social justice. "It crystallized what we had been saying that treatment offers people hope and that hope is the basis for social mobilization against HIV," he wrote.[141]

The demonstration and conference were also the beginning of TAC's long and eventually successful struggle with both Big Pharma and the South African government over treatment, and a model for global solidarity that Alan and Health GAP would carry into everything else they did.[142] And, if historian Allan Brandt's declaration is correct that "AIDS invented Global Health" because of the "nature of the epidemic," then Alan, his ACT UP and Health GAP colleagues, and TAC members were inventing a postcolonial form of global health activism that linked together various localities with differing tactics and similar goals.[143]

Yet Alan had almost not made it to the conference. Just before they were supposed to leave for Durban, on a weekend when he and Barbara were at their country house in Dingmans Ferry, Pennsylvania, Alan had started to vomit blood, lots of it. He and Barbara feared he had a gastrointestinal hemorrhage, or worse. They made a midnight run back to New York and the familiarity of the hospital at Columbia. Several transfusions later their diagnosis proved correct. The bleeding was blamed on the anti-inflammatory medications he had been taking for the pain in his hips.

Alan was able to get out of bed and go to Durban, but after he got back, his abdominal pain kept getting worse. This time it felt as if it was not something simple as taking too many medications. Another CT scan showed cancer tumors that were pressing on his bowel. Alan had struggled to save others; now, he had to struggle again to save himself.

16

HIS FULL SELF

Just as Alan's politics, medical skills, and organizing of feasible tactics were coming together, his body was once again deserting him. The newest CT scan in 2000 "looked ghastly," Barbara reported, as it showed him "riddled with stomach cancer."[1] The pressure of the tumors made his abdomen bulge, as if he were pregnant, he joked. He and Barbara were told that his bowel could perforate at any time. It was enormously painful.[2] He had survived three rounds with cancer before this one, but he knew the odds were getting steep. His colleagues began to think of him as a secular Job being tested by the gods.[3]

Alan could no longer deny what the symptoms were telling him. It began to feel like a "death march" with the end in sight, as he realized he had never made a will, or considered what kind of burial he wanted. "It was pretty shocking again," he thought, "that I could be shocked again" that his life was really in jeopardy.[4] Before this latest recurrence, his daughters had gone together to Oaxaca, Mexico, for an extended trip. Sarah was hoping to take dancing lessons, and Harriet wanted to improve her Spanish. Barbara called to tell them to come home because "Alan might have just two weeks to live."[5] His other family and friends began to gather.

He and Barbara became willing to try just about anything, as most of the surgeons they consulted expressed very little hope. The chief executive officer of Highbridge Woodycrest, with interests in alternative medicine, suggested Alan see a famous naturalist physician. After Alan gave his history, the doctor, overwhelmed by all the details, suggested vitamin supplements. "You don't look like you're going to die," he assured Alan and Barbara. As soon as they were out of his office, they collapsed in peals of laughter. Still, Alan kept up with brewing herbs in a special pot as he had been prescribed years earlier. He saw nothing wrong with hedging his bets.[6]

The search began again for another allopathic medical route. He found a promising lead with a hematologist whose work was on "salvage oncology,"

Alan with his daughters, Harriet Clark, *left*, and Sarah
Zeller-Berkman, New York City, 2000. *Courtesy of Shelley Miller.*

regimens used after other chemotherapies have not worked. Alan agreed to try the new drugs, even though the doctor made no promises.[7] After the first round of chemo, his bloated abdomen went down, his bowels resumed functioning, and fears of a perforation abated. The next steps included a small surgery, continuing chemo, and then a risky therapy that would combine a high dose of drugs with a bone marrow transplant. The last step was the one he dreaded. He had rejected the transplant option two years earlier out of fear of possible deadly consequences. Now there was no choice.[8]

An immediate problem faces all those who seek such a procedure. Bone marrow transplants from a healthy donor require an extensive match between the proteins in white blood cells, or else the donated cells may attack the host. The search for a match starts usually with family members where the chance of genetic similarities is higher. All of Alan's brothers were tested, but none were a match. Neither were Sarah or Harriet, despite Harriet's hopes that with two Jewish parents she might be the one to save him. With sad irony, Sarah matched with one of Alan's brothers, but not with him.[9] Dryly Alan commented, "It threw me for a loop. . . . I liked my life. I liked staying alive. This was pretty disappointing."[10] As he knew, finding anyone else to match presented odds of "a quarter of a million to one."[11]

As when he had been ill in prison, his friends, colleagues, and comrades rallied to help. Notices about his need for a donor went out through all his networks.[12] Many were tested, but no strangers, friends, or other relatives even remotely matched. As a man of Jewish ancestry, Alan knew that "until World War II you probably could have found dozens of people with my general genetic makeup. But a lot of those genes died in the camps."[13] His chance of surviving this cancer was now limited by the horrors of a past war, not merely by the indifference and incompetence of prison health care.

There was one other possibility: his own cells. A process called autologous transplantation encouraged a patient's stem cells to grow and then harvested them from his blood stream. After several chemo rounds, the cells would be transplanted back into a patient's body. There was no certainty Alan could produce the right kind of cells, or even survive the process that killed off his immune system before building it up again. But at this point such a procedure was his only choice. Once again Alan had to save himself, this time quite literally, and he agreed to the risky procedure.

Alan hardly remembered the weeks that followed. Many of them were spent in the hospital, where his family hung hot chili lights over his bed and his friends stopped by to massage his exhausted body and express their love.[14] Then, amazingly, he had a Lazarus moment of his own. By the late spring of 2001, even though some of his blood tests were "abnormal" and the possibility of a future leukemia lurked, he was back. "I feel great," he reported in July 2001, although he knew the odds of long-term survival were not good.[15] He returned to work at Highbridge Woodycrest and Columbia, and continued to go to Health GAP meetings.

Now Alan seemed to sense, more than ever before, that his time was limited. He met with two former political comrades and continued to tell his life story on tape.[16] He returned to his "Brother Doc" manuscript and gave parts of it to his friends Bruce Taub and writer Terry Bisson, who tried to help him edit it. He contacted a fraternity brother who was now a renowned sports agent and entertainment lawyer. The friend passed the book on to a literary agent who, amazingly, pronounced Alan's voice not dramatic enough.[17] Alan had worries of his own about the story, since he could not tell the whole truth about his comrades who were still in prison or could be tried on other charges. In the end, he never finished it. He had too much else to do.[18]

More than most AIDS doctors, Alan understood what it meant to live with uncertainty yet hope. With AIDS and its treatments, he argued, medical professionals "are challenged to look inside ourselves to learn how to relate to patients and clients going through cycles of hope and despair, periods of good health and acute illness, and living day to day with profound uncertainty about long-term outcomes." With earnestness, he concluded, the epidemic "continues to offer us the opportunity to learn more about what it means to be human."[19] He could so easily describe his own ups and downs in the same terms. After giving up on reworking his old story, Alan would create a new one.

No one thought the battle to get reasonable treatment for HIV/AIDS into the Global South had been won in Durban. While Health GAP had become the first organization in the United States focused directly on the crisis in the Global South and the need for treatment, and it had succeeded in forging a worldwide network of AIDS treatment activists, this was just a start. As Alan was sidelined by chemo and stem cell treatments, the activists at Health GAP were thinking through how their actions in the United States would shape their growing global commitments. With allies, they held demonstrations at pharmaceutical companies, against the George W. Bush presidential campaign, and at Republican Party events. They wrote position papers that questioned the "deals" the drug companies were making to provide some subsidies.[20] Even if he was still too weak to put himself fully behind these efforts, Alan offered the house in Dingmans Ferry for an activist to rest up before the next planned actions.[21] He would continually argue in person and in position papers, when he could, that the fight had to be for social justice, and this meant allowing countries to either import or create their own drugs.[22] He and his Health GAP allies were trying very hard to translate this understanding into policy. They did this in the face of the South African government's continuing denunciation of the new drugs and questioning of whether HIV even caused AIDS.[23]

Health GAP's global alliances were expanding. When Alan was better, he played a part in planning a demonstration at UN headquarters in June 2001 to push Health GAP's work on AIDS. To Alan and his comrades, the deliberative nature of the United Nations was just that, deliberative, or as Health GAP's Asia Russell put it, "a weird chimera of spinelessness and compromise."[24] Forums that were going to take place outside the UN hall made it possible for global activists to discuss issues in person that had been percolating on LISTSERVs for months, and for them to raise their concerns directly with formal delegates.[25] Some activists had become formal delegates as well and were participating both in the regular UN session and the outside meetings. None of it was easy, especially when there were differences and difficulties over who could be represented and what could be done and said.[26]

The activists were up against the many government officials and health professionals who still shared the widespread belief that only prevention, not treatment, was appropriate in various African countries.[27] Drug companies were often willing to discuss subsidies, but their intellectual property rights remained sacrosanct. It seemed they would never allow WTO trade rules to be used to allow generics, even in the face of an unprecedented public health emergency.

Health GAP and its allies opted for direct action. After a press conference at the United Nations with groups such as Oxfam and people-with-AIDS organizations from across the globe, the activists, including Alan, moved into the UN hallways. This was unprecedented since the United Nations did not allow demonstrations within its walls. The global activists carried signs that read, "Pills cost pennies / Greed costs lives." As they marched, they were "chanting loudly and shaking their pill bottles [filled with pennies] in front of a phalanx of reporters and cameras."[28]

The UN security force moved quickly to take them out of the building. The guards also unexpectedly took many of the activists' formal delegate credentials, which they needed to attend the UN proceedings. Alan spoke to the press again outside the United Nations, declaring, "The pace of deliberations here does not reflect the urgency of what is happening on the ground." He went on to argue that without the pressure from the grass roots, this UN session would never have happened in the first place. Watching the video of the walkout, the viewer would never know that he had been deathly ill.[29]

Health GAP was growing quickly, but there were still fundamental questions to be resolved. A month after the UN demonstration, Alan went to a retreat where Health GAP members worked through what needed to be done and how their group would be structured.[30] Much of the discussion was strategic. They took stock of where the United States stood on various intellectual property rules in its international agreements, whether the European Union was on one side or the other, and whether Health GAP should promote an "illegal" trade in pharmaceuticals, as some groups were doing. They were planning in the context of the pressures of structural adjustments, demanded by organizations like the World Bank and the International Monetary Fund, that defunded the very public sector needed to support HIV/AIDS epidemiological surveillance and treatment. They were aware of the realpolitik. "The risk is that the poor countries are weak and will sell out public health for almost any trade benefit," as one knowledgeable participant put it. Health GAP's focus on trade and generics put the group in touch with the growing antiglobalization movements. The activists struggled to create a strategic plan that spelled out their agreed-upon priorities, tactics, and contacts. The Health GAP members made their plans based on their basic principles: "Every human life matters, available treatments" should be provided, "hope is critical to fighting the spread of HIV, and treatment offers hope."[31]

Four months later in November 2001 and just two months after the attacks on the World Trade Center and Pentagon, Alan would send out a fund-raising letter for Health GAP that listed its accomplishments, which centered on putting "treatment access ... at the forefront of public debate and concern." He acknowledged that "building global solidarity based on the sanctity of human life and respect for human rights is more important than ever."[32] Less than ten years out of prison, he was now one of the leaders of a social justice movement that was bent on accomplishing change that took on global debt, trade, and health needs. There was still so much to do.

THE BRONX, COLUMBIA, AND SOUTH AFRICA

Alan began to combine his work in the United States and across the globe, continuing to weave together his internationalist and anti-imperialist politics with his locally based health practices. He maintained his clinical work at HWC while overseeing its health care workforce and determining policies and procedures. Increasingly, he also pursued research and training with other New York medical institutions that sought various kinds of affiliations. He applied what he had learned from the Sussers' and Steins' approach and built his political principles into the best epidemiology he could get done to create evidence for a just health system.[33]

Alan's long-standing interest in South Africa had not ended with the demonstration and conference in Durban. His connection to Columbia University's Public Health School facilitated what he thought of as the approach "not to scientifically colonize Africa, but to let Africa take care of itself."[34] Well aware of the long history of what was still called in some public health schools "tropical medicine," Alan and his colleagues did not want to treat people in former European colonies as "the dangerous other," an approach where racism, imperialism, and medicine intertwined.[35] Nor did they want to fall into the tendency of *international health*, the term that had succeeded *tropical medicine*, to credit only the technologies of Western medicine and the charitable impulses and priorities of its doctors.[36] Alan and his colleagues knew that many African countries had their own biomedical practitioners, histories, and skills. They worked to build relationships where unequal power relations are disrupted and different modes of practice are accepted.[37]

After Alan's near-death experience in 2001, he came back to Columbia, still very much part-time, wanting to use the connections there to create structures that would enable meaningful change. There was a long tradition in American public health schools of training elite Global South doctors and then sending them back to their home countries to recreate the American model. Such methods often left decent care available only to a few in the urban elite. Alan and his Columbia colleagues were trying to avoid this in the training they were providing, using what were called Fogarty Grants from the National Institutes of Health's global health center to train Global South practitioners.[38]

Alan, along with others at Columbia, was focused on what was called in public health jargon "capacity-building" and the "scale-up" of services. Alan's anti-imperialism predisposed him to be attentive to models that expanded the public sector and allowed the concerns of those suffering on the ground to set agendas and develop their own expertise.³⁹ He wanted to give meaning to the term *global health*, just coming into widespread use. Its adherents sought to differentiate it from international health with a focus on "justice, not charity" and recognized global interdependence.⁴⁰ Alan knew enough about colonial and postcolonial power relationships to be wary of institutionalizing the dynamics that had strangled public health care in many Global South countries. At the same time he recognized the complicated relationship of trained professionals and even professional AIDS activists to their home countries, whose priorities might come into conflict with his.⁴¹

Alan and his colleagues at Columbia and in South Africa began to craft in 2001 what they called the Centre for the AIDS Programme of Research in South Africa (CAPRISA). They set up a model "to undertake globally relevant & locally responsive research, training to impact on the HIV and TB [tuberculosis] epidemic" with several South African universities and their communicable disease government agency.⁴² Alan returned to Durban to assess what was needed and wanted. It was his third gruelingly long trip to South Africa; he was making real his commitments. This time, he and others were particularly focused on what happened to women as the "cornerstone [for] prevention, care and treatment."⁴³

The global work that Columbia made possible fascinated him. By 2002, the Bronx and his work at Highbridge Woodycrest had become in many ways too small a venue for what he hoped to accomplish in his postprison and postcancer life. He was tiring, too, of the continual bureaucratic hassles at his job, especially whenever someone over his head raised questions about his never-hidden carceral past.⁴⁴ Still, he needed a full-time position, and the health benefits that came with it. Even though he had neither a PhD nor a master's in public health, nor even much post–med school training except for his HIV/AIDS fellowship and his part-time work, Columbia beckoned.

ON TO GLOBAL HEALTH

His Columbia colleagues had taken a chance on Alan when they gave him the fellowship and then part-time positions. His friends Ezra Susser and Richard Parker knew what Alan might be able to do for Columbia on a full-time basis, given his intellectual skills, political savvy, and global connections. They wanted him on their team. These colleagues began to work their magic with other faculty and the sympathetic dean to create a real position.⁴⁵ By January 2003 they had succeeded: Alan became an assistant professor of clinical epidemiology (the department Susser chaired) with a dual appointment in the Department of Sociomedical Sciences (where Parker was the chair). In addition to teaching, his position included managing the collaboration between Columbia and the Mandela School of Medicine at the University of Natal, as well as other global liaison work.[46]

Those at Columbia who shared his political concerns and vision for global health were inspired by Alan's compassion, commitments, actions, and willingness to think hard about building a global health practice founded on justice. He became very available to write recommendation letters, mentor students from around the world, teach courses on HIV/AIDS, read drafts of grant proposals, and think through ideas with those who knocked on his office door, or sent him a beseeching email along with an unfinished chapter or article, or even a question of how to proceed within the university's bureaucracy.[47] His self-deprecating humor made him fun to spend time with. His poor health was evident, but he never showed any self-pity. Colleagues remembered that he would go away on this or that medical travail, then reappear to keep working, perhaps limping a bit more, or taking more meds, and looking a little paler. As he joked with one colleague about someone else on the staff who never made good on threats to retire, "[This person] keeps retiring and I keep dying, but we're here."[48]

Even if most of his colleagues did not know the details of his past political life and imprisonment, enough of the information leaked out to make his character known. And then there was the strength that his multiple brushes with death gave him.[49] If you were on his side, he valued your contributions. If you opposed his concerns, he was fierce, the anger he suppressed below the surface ready to overflow if stirred.

His self-effacement and seriousness, honed by the hard work of his political life, made him good at connecting to men and women of differing backgrounds, races, and ethnicities. For the men at Columbia who were loath to speak about their emotional lives or professional aspirations, Alan proved a good friend.[50] He listened well, tried not to be too judgmental, expressed empathy, and above all knew how to keep secrets. His past refusal to give in to the FBI's offers of freedom in exchange for details about his comrades had proved that over and over. He was, as a psychiatrist colleague described him, a real leader of the wolf pack, a trait that allowed him to get closer to men.[51] His natal family of boys, and his years in the all-male environments of the prisons, enabled him to calibrate appropriate responses to those who accepted or challenged his alpha male status. Yet he also respected the political perspicacity of his women comrades and of Barbara, as well as the strength of his women patients. Among the women he worked with, he found ones to confide in, and show his vulnerabilities.

On the surface he looked like any other middle-aged white Jewish doctor or professor: bald, growing a paunch, getting slower of gait, but full of stories and knowledge, and able to go for a beer with just about anyone. Underneath was the hard seriousness of a man who had nearly died numerous times, had taken on the U.S. government in multiple ways, and exuded great comfort with his choices and commitments. Those experiences enabled him to listen, without fear, to what others had to say.

His colleague and fellow AIDS physician Waafa El-Sadr summed up Alan's being by saying, "He inspired a deep sense of trust, and people shared their dreams, fears, insecurities, irrationalities and secrets with him." He was like the subject of "Invictus," by nineteenth-century British poet William Ernest Henley. El-Sadr quoted the last stanza: "It matters not how strait the gate, / How charged with punishments the scroll, / I am the master of my fate: / I am the captain of my soul."[52] He was at the same time what his colleague the psychiatrist Stephanie LeMelle called "intense and fierce." As she described him, "When things were going well he was intense on making it happen. When things were going badly he was intense in making it right."[53]

THE TRANSFORMATIONS FOR FAMILY AND COMRADES

Outside of work, his family's circumstances were changing. Sarah had graduated from Emory University with a degree in psychology in 1998, worked a number of different positions, and entered a graduate program in social-personality psychology at the City University of New York in 2003, while Harriet was back at Stanford. By 2007, Sarah had married and given birth to Alan's grandchild, Gabriel, on whom he doted while she continued youth work in New York City. Harriet got a masters of fine arts from Iowa's famed writing program and returned to Stanford to teach.

His living situation shifted as well, as he and Barbara finally abandoned their cramped Greenwich Village flat. A friend suggested in the spring of 2002 that they look at an apartment opening up in what was known as West Harlem/ Hamilton Heights, a mainly Dominican neighborhood just a few blocks below Columbia's medical and public health school campus, where Alan both worked and was frequently treated.[54] On a huge stony rampart that looked over the wide Hudson River, they found a rent-stabilized, three-bedroom, two-bathroom corner unit on the sixth floor of an elevator building at 153rd Street and Riverside Drive. It was magnificent, overlooking the river's boat traffic and the New Jersey Palisades from its windows. These water views made the main bedroom feel like a cruise ship that was about to sail under the nearby George Washington Bridge, with its twinkling blue and white lights, and past the little red lighthouse along the shore by Columbia. Full of air and light, the apartment could not have been more different from the darkness Alan had been in before, or the cramped space in the Village flat. They filled its walls and floors with personality and warmth from their global travels: Tanzanian Masai necklaces, Zimbabwean Shona stone sculptures, South African Kuba cloth, masks from a variety of peoples, and other art that struck their fancy. Even their plants were happier, as they grew in the sunlight. Nearby Riverside Park gave Alan and Barbara a place to walk Zackie, the collie they acquired in 2001, and named after their South African comrade. They had a real city home now and still went out to Dingmans Ferry every weekend they could.

Alan also stayed closely connected to his old comrades. He wrote a support letter to the U.S. Parole Commission for Marilyn Buck, hoping against hope that she might get parole from her life sentence. He promised, "Marilyn, like myself, made serious mistakes that impacted on others in our effort to achieve a more just society. But our motivation was truly social justice and not a desire to be violent. She, as I, has rejected that path, and I have no doubt that she will be a productive member of society when released."[55] It was to no avail.[56]

Finally, some of his comrades were allowed out of their incarceration. Tim Blunk was released in 1997, after a controversial parole hearing during which he was accused of naming names, although Laura Whitehorn was certain anything he said was already known.[57] Susan Rosenberg and Linda Evans, in contrast, waged a long public appeal. Their actions led to commutation by President Bill Clinton on his last day in office in January 2001. Silvia Baraldini was sent to Italy to finish her sentence in 1999 and released in 2006. Clinton also gave twelve of Alan's FALN comrades' clemency after they renounced violence in 1999, while Oscar López Rivera and Haydée Beltrán Torres refused to sign such a statement. It took till 2009 for Beltrán Torres to be paroled, and President Barack Obama commuted López's sentence in 2016.[58] Kathy Boudin, one of the Brink's drivers, was released in 2003, while Mutulu Shakur and David Gilbert remain incarcerated. Judith Clark, after nearly two decades of campaigning, was finally granted parole in 2019. In 2004, when Laura Whitehorn was finally off parole, she and Alan celebrated by taking a trip together to Paris with Barbara and Laura's partner, Susie Day, strolling along the Seine and enjoying freedom.[59]

"BEING ABLE TO DO SO MUCH"

Alan spent his working time scaling up treatment protocols and advocacy that tackled the bigger moral questions about AIDS treatment. The global effort to ensure the provision of what came to be known as "essential medicines" (which entailed years of debates, meetings, and legal battles in South Africa and Thailand) and the political efforts of groups like Health GAP were changing the landscape for HIV/AIDS drugs.[60] Even the Bush administration shifted its position after the "war on terror" began and a feared anthrax attack put the whole country on edge. The United States, needing more global support for its battles, worked to lower prices for widespread purchase of the antibiotic Cipro as an antidote to a possible expanded anthrax occurrence. The WTO met again just two months after September 11 and called for the expanded use of generics and parallel trade in "public health emergencies," without fear of lawsuits, in what became known as the Doha Declaration.[61] The belief that medicines had to be linked to human rights was becoming more normative, if still difficult to implement.[62]

While governments were gearing up to spend more money on AIDS, NGOS around the world remained vital to the effort. In March 2002, just months before the next international AIDS conference in Barcelona, Alan was in that city representing Health GAP at what was called Ubuntu, the World Forum of Civil Society Networks. Although not focused specifically on AIDS, the organization was trying to unite various NGOS on the principle of civil society solidarity in support of humanness and against the forces of capitalist globalization. *Ubuntu*, a Zulu term for the bond that connects all humanity, became a written concept in the 1920s, then was widely used in the Zimbabwe freedom struggle and in Desmond Tutu's truth and reconciliation efforts in postapartheid South Africa.[63] The Ubuntu conference in Barcelona put Alan into conversation with people from around the world, from Advocacy for Women in Africa to the Arab Organisation for Human Rights.[64]

A few months later, he and Barbara were back in Barcelona for the International AIDS conference, where Alan chaired a session called "In the Joint: Prisons and Prisoners."[65] Health GAP and its allies held demonstrations to break what they called the "cycle of mediocrity," where not enough was done to make treatment happen even as new goals for providing the necessary drugs were established.[66] A year later in 2003, under President George W. Bush, the U.S. Congress finally authorized what came to be known as the President's Emergency Plan for AIDS Relief (PEPFAR), which provided at first $15 billion for five years to what was called "focus countries" and to UNAIDS funds.[67] It was a culmination of the work Alan and other global AIDS activists had been doing for years.

Alan's activism was recognized when a New York organization called Jews for Racial and Economic Justice presented him, along with his comrades Laura Whitehorn and Susan Rosenberg, the Meyer Risk Taker Award in 2002. Named for an American rabbi who had resisted the military dictatorship in Argentina, the award had gone to the ranks of such luminaries as poet Allan Ginsberg and lawyer Henry Schwarzchild.[68] In his speech accepting the award, Alan repeated what he had said in the letter about Marilyn Buck: "Be willing to act, even though the decision to act carries the risk of being wrong. I say that with humility knowing that some of my decisions to act were wrong." In the end he returned to the fears that had haunted his whole life about becoming a "good

German." He quoted Albert Camus's view of those who had collaborated with the Nazis: "I despised them, because being able to do so much, they dared so little." And so, he told his audience, "We, the citizens of the most powerful nation on earth, should strive to act in a way that our children will not have to echo Camus' harsh words when describing our generation."[69]

Alan's work at Columbia expanded as he was now acting as almost a utility infielder for its global public health AIDS work. Writing his sponsor and friend Ezra Susser to explain how his time was allocated, Alan detailed international collaborations with a number of Columbia's global initiatives from South Africa to the Dominican Republic. He also taught a global AIDS policy course and consulted with researchers on their projects within the HIV Center.[70] He became focused on women and children. He worked on Columbia's Maternal to Child Transmission (MTCT)–Plus Initiative, which promoted family-centered monitoring, therapy, and support for families in resource-poor countries. With his colleague Frances Cournos, he became a consultant to the United Nations Educational, Scientific, and Cultural Organization's programs for vulnerable children and orphans as the terrible cost became clear of the mortality that untreated AIDS had brought.[71] He kept on top of the funding for PEPFAR and the demands of the U.S. government regarding how the monies were allocated. He had become very busy, and essential, in the fight against HIV/AIDS.

In the summer of 2003 Alan and Barbara returned to Durban with their old comrade and nurse midwife Jennifer Dohrn to be clinicians and advisors at what Barbara called the "epicenter of the AIDS pandemic."[72] Alan already had the connections and was working directly on research with his South African colleagues at the Mandela Medical School, and Barbara had more than a decade's experience in building an integrative AIDS treatment program and managing patients who needed a multidisciplinary treatment team to manage their complex coinfections. She knew she could help with programs that were trying to "scale up" their therapies.[73] Alan hoped they might be able to make a documentary about the experience with their filmmaker friend Paul McIssac, but the funding never came through.[74]

While Alan was doing research, Barbara composed a thoughtful political and medical paper about her experiences.[75] She was horrified that she now had to ask patients whether they could afford the antiretroviral therapies. When they could not, she had to say, "I see, well let's talk about what else might help you today." What had been an HIV epidemic, she reported with great anguish, had become an AIDS epidemic, as she saw patient after patient with TB and AIDS, and other coinfections. Forced to advise parents to take their sick child to the "Dream Center," as the hospice was called, she stared into their eyes "brimming with tears." Another physician, working in the local township, told her he had lost "30% of his practice over the past three years." Jennifer Dohrn, working in antenatal clinic at a public hospital, told her, "50% of the women tested were HIV positive." As Barbara wrote with despair, "The birthing is bringing death. And the bonding of mother and child through breastfeeding is bringing death. The parents are dying. The workforce is dying." As she continued her work, her patients and the clinic workers began to call her MamZell, because her status as an elder made using her first name disrespectful.

While they were there, the disagreements between the AIDS activists and the South African government over treatment deepened into a crisis. That summer in 2003, the South African equivalent of the FDA questioned whether even Nevirapine, the drug given in one shot to pregnant women to prevent HIV transmission, was efficacious. Instead, South Africa's health minister suggested that the African potato and other vegetables could stave off the infections. Horrified, TAC, the South African activist group that Health GAP worked with, stepped up its actions to pressure the government. Finally, in 2004, as it became clear that the epidemic was primarily taking women and children, the government relented. The UN Global Fund was allowed to bring in funds for treatments to fight the epidemic.[76] Barbara and Alan's hearts were filled both with anguish at the despair and squalor they had seen and hope that treatment would make a difference.

Jennifer Dohrn, who had been Alan's comrade in Prairie Fire, found working together with him in South Africa very different from the rhetoric-fueled fights of the decades before. It gave Alan a chance to demonstrate to her the balance between what she called his "brilliance and moving from the head, his arrogance and maleness," and his ability to be a political leader and more human. He had encouraged her to speak on HIV to a South African audience, even when she felt she still knew too little and had to do it in front of him. "Isn't this the past," he asked when she expressed her fears. He both acknowledged her worry and reminded her she could do it. He had become, she called him, "a righteous full person." In the face of the epidemic, she said, Alan now knew how to use "everything he had learned, his full self, and to give back."[77]

HIS FULL SELF AS AN "ELDER"

And so it would go for the next few years. Alan in Brazil, examining what could be done there to stem the epidemic, and understanding the limitations, while visiting Sarah, who was taking capoeira lessons, and then vacationing as a family.[78] Alan at the annual meeting of Columbia's International Center for AIDS Care and Treatment Programs (ICAP) in Dar es Salaam, Tanzania, giving talks on how to provide quality care and scale up treatment in March 2006, and then in Rwanda to examine ICAP's work there and its difficulties.[79] Alan and his Columbia colleagues completing a compelling ninety-page background

Alan and Barbara on vacation, summer 2006, Harvey Cedars, New Jersey.
Courtesy of Marilyn Vasta.

paper for the United Nations Children's Fund called "Protecting the Lives of Children: Towards an AIDS-Free Generation" in August 2005.[80] By October 2006, he was an associate, not merely an assistant, clinical professor in epidemiology and sociomedical sciences at Columbia, with major grants and teaching responsibilities in the global health training programs.[81]

Ezra Susser and the dean even made him the acting chair, and then the vice chair, of the Department of Epidemiology in 2006. Without a degree in public health or epidemiology, but with his political smarts and knowledge, Alan maneuvered and supported the department's many staff, students, and faculty within the Columbia bureaucracy. Susser had been sure that once his colleagues understood what Alan could do for them, their concerns about his lack of training would dissipate. He proved right.[82] Alan's thousands of files on his computer showed how widely he was reading on the issues he confronted: from religious partnerships with health care providers around HIV, to the effect of the psychosocial interventions after the genocide in Rwanda, to the danger of HIV transmission through breastfeeding, to basic epidemiology concerns.[83]

At times the erstwhile outside agitator and activist found himself an establishment figure in global health. The tensions in his role became clear when he negotiated his work in the Dominican Republic. Because of the constant migration back and forth between the island and New York City, practitioners in the neighborhood around Columbia were seeing a rise in HIV in women, whose husbands often had other partners back home.[84]

It was a good example of how global the epidemic was in yet another way. In 2003, Columbia sent Alan to the Dominican Republic as a "care and treatment" consultant to a Clinton Foundation team, whose work there he found at first to be very disorganized. Nevertheless, he told his Health GAP colleagues he might learn "how to roll-out a national scale-up treatment plan. Hopefully that can help our work and that of our allies."[85] For the next few years, he traveled back and forth to help establish and monitor various training activities.[86]

On several trips while in the Dominican Republic he had deep discussions with Eugene Schiff, a young health activist and son of political physicians Alan knew. Schiff was there to advocate for the Agua Buena Human Rights Association, which was working on drug access and prison health care for inmates with HIV/AIDS. Schiff thought the Clinton effort was too little, too late, and too removed from what was happening on the ground. Alan agreed to meet with him as they discussed what it was possible to accomplish and in what ways. Never defensive about the limitations of the Clinton Foundation effort, Alan encouraged Schiff to hold the foundation's feet to the fire.[87] When Schiff's group wrote a critique of the UN Global Fund's actions for again doing too little, Alan congratulated him. Years later, Alan even wrote in support of Schiff when he applied to medical school.[88] Alan seemed to understand that getting treatment to needy patients also required the more government-connected work of the Clinton Foundation, alongside the kind of agitation Schiff was doing.[89]

Alan seemed comfortable becoming an "elder" in the HIV/AIDS fight. In some circumstances, as when he was with Health GAP, he was indeed the "outside agitator" trying to speak with others in the global health struggle. At Columbia, he was the learned activist and epidemiologist who imparted his understanding to another generation. In the field, he was the able researcher who examined what needed to be done, then provided pathways to make things happen. As his colleague Richard Parker noted, "He didn't have a big theory about it. [His work was] very operational." If Parker saw no grand theory, Alan seemed to have one that was in the end based on solidarity and certainly attacked what he saw as "neo-imperialism" thinking: those in the Global North speaking for others.[90] As Parker described him, "I experienced Alan as a very gentle person, very kind. Solidarity was oozing from him, not an edge."[91]

IN AND OUT OF "CANCERLAND"

As with many cancer patients, and especially those with as complex a history as Alan, there was always something else.[92] In the spring of 2003 his doctors thought he should be on Interferon, a drug used to "interfere" with cancer cells in what was called "consolidation therapy," but the side effects of severe headaches and terrible muscle pains led him to discontinue the treatment after two months. In June 2003 he developed secondary hyperparathyroidism that affected his parathyroid glands, but he managed it enough to be able to spend time in Brazil.[93] Three years later, stiff hips limited his range of motion. An MRI showed no bone death but some osteoarthritis and fluid buildup.[94] He took painkillers that helped some, but he lived with the pain, walking more slowly than in the past, and giving up hopes for long hikes in the woods and mountains. An invasive poorly differentiated squamous cell carcinoma was removed from his scalp in December 2006. Compared to everything else he had been through, it was minor.

Just before his daughter Sarah gave birth in 2007, Alan felt a lump in his neck. Not wanting to take anything away from the joy of a new child, he did not say a word. But his excitement over his first grandchild, Gabriel, was marred by more fear than he could hide. After multiple opinions, the diagnosis became clear: Alan had salivary gland adenocarcinoma, probably a consequence of the radiation he had received for his Hodgkin's lymphoma in 1987. As Alan wrote to his primary doctor, "I am definitely on an emotional rollercoaster, but I don't think there's any way to avoid that."[95] The spring of 2007 brought a surgery to remove the carcinoma, and then more radiation. Alan was not reassured by his surgeon's observation that this was an interesting case, a relatively rare tumor with between 33 to 46 percent chance of recurrence.[96] After the treatments, Alan was fine for another year, despite the continued pain.[97] He kept up his global health work and travel.

In the follow-up in the summer of 2008, the doctors grew suspicious that something else was in his neck. A needle biopsy was inconclusive: maybe tuberculosis, given where he had been in South Africa, or perhaps another cancer. Another biopsy suggested it might be another kind of T-cell lymphoma. In September, the family identified an appropriate specialist at the Fred Hutchinson Cancer Center in Seattle. Alan had an old medical school roommate out there they could stay with, and Barbara's sister Billie lived in the area as well. Alan's brother Steven joined them.

After the consultation and before they had the results, they were all driving up Mount Rainier when Alan developed a fever and became quite short of breath. They turned around and drove directly to the emergency room at Harborview Medical Center. As he was being worked up for what they thought was pneumonia, Barbara, Billie, and Steven went out to lunch. When they came back Alan looked "devastated," Barbara recalled. "My lungs are full of tumors," he told them. They took an airplane back to New York and went straight from the airport to the emergency room at Columbia's medical center.[98]

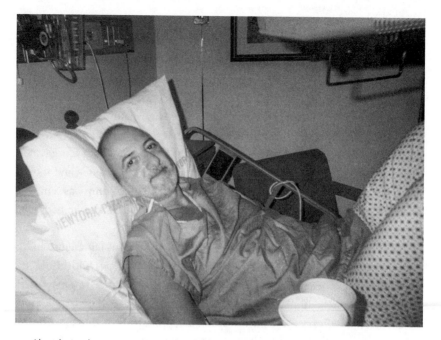

Alan during his cancer treatments, New York City, 2008. *Courtesy of Barbara Zeller.*

The latest diagnosis was myelodysplastic syndrome (MDS), in which the bone marrow does not make enough red or white blood cells or platelets. The syndrome often leads to a leukemia and is almost always fatal unless there is a stem-cell transplant from another person. MDS is sometimes linked to previous chemotherapy and radiation treatment.[99] Alan certainly had had enough of those. There was little reason to hope that an appropriate donor would be found.

For the next few months, in the fall of 2008 through the winter, Alan was in and out of Columbia's Presbyterian Hospital and then Memorial Sloan Kettering Cancer Center, trying new rounds of chemotherapy and launching another stem-cell campaign. He developed pulmonary embolisms in his lungs. Prompt treatments helped resolve them, although at least once they were missed initially, putting him in grave danger.[100] Barbara felt almost as if the hospitals had become their second home, and, unlike others not used to the medical environment, she felt safe there. He was on morphine, but Barbara knew he was still carrying much pain.

Support flooded in from his students, comrades, and friends across the globe.[101] The good wishes of his friends, and the drugs, must have helped: he began to rally in the spring of 2009. He moved about now in a wheelchair, and Barbara arranged for a private duty nurse during the day when Alan was home between treatments so she could go to work. In April, he was well enough to fly to Florida with Barbara, Sarah, and Gabriel to visit his parents and his brother Larry. His emails during this period, and Barbara's memories, are of his calm as he found his symptoms just one more challenge to experience. "He was sad," she recalled, "but not fearful."[102]

They returned from the family trip to amazing news: a donor had been found whose stem cells matched Alan's. The million-to-one odds had been beaten. Everyone was ecstatic, although the risks for his very depleted body were enormous. There was a very good chance that his body might reject the cells, that his organs might fail, or that he would develop sepsis. Still, it was his only choice, and it gave them all hope again. Alan was back in the hospital on May 18, expecting the cells right around Memorial Day. On May 21, as part of Health GAP's tenth anniversary, he and his Columbia colleague David Hoos were given the organization's Global Health Justice Award, although Alan was too sick to attend.[103]

Risky as the procedure was, Alan knew that it had to be done. He wrote two of his old fraternity brothers, "Intellectually, I know that sooner is better, but I definitely have some butterflies."[104] It was as close as he came to expressing fear, yet the existential crisis of imminent death never seemed to reach him.[105] While he waited in an isolation room as his immune system was being destroyed so a new one could be provided, he wrote one of these fraternity brothers, again promising one that they would share a bottle of Caymus cabernet (at over $100 a bottle) when he got out. He reported "doing all right so far. . . . They assure me it will get worse before it gets better."[106] When they could, his closest friends came to visit and comfort him. Laura Whitehorn arranged for Dana to come by when Barbara was not there. No one was sure this treatment would work, but then again it was Alan, and they never knew.

Always the good diagnostician, Alan proved right: it got worse. After the stem cells were transfused into his body, his various organs began to shut down. Alan became delirious, and for the first time Barbara could see fear in his eyes. He began to thrash about, and they had to restrain him. His eyes had a wild look as he fought the restraints. It was as if, Barbara thought, all his terror at being contained was being expressed. All the emotion he had shut down over the years came flying out. Although they hated to do it, the family agreed to let him be intubated and sedated.

Then Alan took one more chance at control. When the drugs began to calm him down, he pushed the nursing button, sat up, and called out a man's name the family did not recognize. Then he began a countdown: ten, nine, eight . . . When he got to zero he yelled, "Blast off!" and fell back in silence against his pillow. He slipped into a coma, and the doctors concluded that his brain functions had been compromised. Making one of her life's most difficult decisions, Barbara agreed to end life support.[107]

On the evening of June 5, 2009, surrounded by his family and close comrades, Alan died.[108] The autopsy that Barbara knew he would have wanted showed that the treatment had been his undoing: sepsis, organ failure, and a fungal pneumonia claimed him. His body showed no sign of either MDS or other cancers.[109] Treatment had killed his cancers, but his long-suffering body could do no more to absorb the new stem cells. This became the final struggle that not even Alan's intelligence, wit, strength, bravery, and capacity for love could win.

TO LOVE EACH OTHER
LIKE WARRIORS

I leave it to an impartial tribunal to decide whether the world
has been the worse or the better of my living and dying in it.

JOHN BROWN, November 28, 1859[1]

The *unusualness* of Alan Berkman's life journey should not blind us to its *usualness* as a story of action, love, and confrontation with state power. Alan's life was similar to that of Americans ranging from John Brown to Angela Davis who sought to rebuild American structures in the face of racism and inequality. Alan took his moral standards from the tenets of equality, however sugarcoated, that he learned from his parents, the Boy Scouts, and small-town America in the Cold War 1950s. He melded those beliefs to the traditions of ethical and historical Judaism to become not a schlemiel but a "tough Jew," and a warrior for universal justice.[2] A man born to the first post-Holocaust generation in the United States, he took its historical lessons of the slaughter of helpless Jews and of the normative behavior of "Good Germans" and sought desperately to become something different.[3] That he thought his righteous principles led to the correct, or his only, choices at various times had terrible consequences for him and others around him.

Alan's commitment to global solidarity and equality always worked through alliances. He taught himself to be what he thought of as a revolutionary and spent decades adjusting his strategies, though never his principles. His upbringing, political groupings, and underground and prison experiences shaped his politics, as did his medical training, intellectual abilities, and strategic acumen. The meaning he found for his life by being a doctor grew into a

Alan on vacation, summer 2006, Harvey Cedars, New Jersey.
Courtesy of Marilyn Vasta.

commitment to global public health. His caregiving on both the individual and collective levels, a reflection of his deep ability to love, was also linked with his life-long struggle to control his ego and white male privilege. Women patients, family, and comrades showed him what was politically possible and necessary, as well as new ways of doing it, bringing about an extraordinary shift from the arrogant and competitive young man he had been in his youth. His principles, strengths, and intelligence, melded with love, profoundly affected those around him. They, in turn, gave him their love, and (in the case of his comrades) even years of their lives in prison, so that he might carry on. He used their gifts to militate for policies that changed, and saved, lives around the globe.

Not many of us will ever have Alan's particular blend of personal conviction, willingness to take risks, loving and principled support, and ability to suspend fears in order to make commitments. Alan showed extraordinary physical toughness in the face of suffering, and married his intellectualism to practicality. Most of us who shared his critique of American society and politics did not join the groups and actions Alan was willing to work in. We turned away, fearful, self-protective, more aware of the government's power. Above all, we did not think this was the way to the revolution. Others were critical of the armed groups' growing sectarianism and threats of violence. They did not share these groups' views of how to move forward, and could not condone their actions. Even Alan would admit that what they had tried had not worked.

Alan may not have read certain political moments correctly, but he accepted the consequences of those experiences to support his principles. Always his own man, he was paradoxically also always caught up in the righteous needs and demands of others, and this blinded him at times. His actions reflected a belief in the power of change, equality, and global solidarity, his expression of an insufficiently taught but profoundly American political tradition.

Alan's life reflects a willingness to act on deeply held beliefs in the face of danger, if sometimes with bravado. It is not necessary, however, to experience what Alan did to be part of movements to achieve the social and medical justice that motivated his life. Those who romanticize the physician Che Guevara argue that he gave up his dream of being a "famous medical research scientist" to instead be part of revolutionary struggle.[4] In the end, Alan came to believe that his medical skills, when shared with activists and those most harmed by racist, sexist, and neoimperialist policies, might actually be more revolutionary. His shifted frame of reference never changed his priorities or principles, just the ways he accomplished them. He moved from the care of individuals to that of whole populations.

The concern with global health always includes the worry that the focus on treatment will not lead to prevention, or explicate the forms of structural violence that exacerbate biological disease.[5] Alan understood that treatment could be a form of prevention, now a watchword in the AIDS struggle, and that underlying structural inequities caused the problems. He never lost sight of this larger vision, even though he thought as many individuals should be saved as possible.

His family and his love were central to his work. One of his younger colleagues understood this when she wrote to him and Barbara in October 2008, "Yours is one of the most important lessons I have learned—to love each other like warriors, gracefully, bountifully and with principle, as you do, is the heartbeat of movement building and any good struggle for change."[6]

After Alan's death, his family held a service at the Plaza Jewish Community Chapel in New York City.[7] His brother Steven wept describing the strength, love, and knowledge they had found together, despite the differences, even angry ones, over the years. "He was always the best at whatever he did," Steven reminded everyone, "and did it with less effort than anybody." His Columbia colleague Robert Remien called Alan a "giant of a man" who became a "visionary world leader," always a "step ahead of everyone else[,] . . . who made things happen."

It would take the family another year to pull together what would be needed for a proper memorial for his larger community. Knowing that he might not survive the second stem-cell transplant, Alan spoke to both Barbara and his actor and filmmaker friend Paul McIssac about what he wanted for his memorial. They discussed having his colleagues speak, and Alan agreed his history should definitely be included.[8]

In a celebration attended by hundreds in an auditorium at Columbia's Mailman School of Public Health on April 23, 2010, a parade of Alan's colleagues, students, and friends paid tribute to what the public health school dean called his "sustained passion and outrage in the face of social injustice . . . balanced by his unfailing gentleness, generosity and moral courage." McIssac produced a professionally crafted twenty-minute video. The film traces how Alan became who he was, using a montage of stock and personal photos, his own voice from interviews, and his letters read by veteran actor Harris Yulin.[9] Never flinching from the difficult moments in Alan's life, the video acknowledged how much he hated the loss of life at Brink's but believed that his comrades were not part of a criminal act. The interviews and words used made clear Alan's belief in the need for equality of sacrifice and his desire not to privilege himself over others. The film ended with Alan walking along with South Africans at the HIV/AIDS demonstration in Durban in 2000.

For the next hours his colleagues, students, and friends spoke eloquently from the podium, often in tears, about Alan's importance to their lives, emphasizing over and over his bravery, strategic thinking, mentorship, and love. Like his colleague Waafa El-Sadr, many remembered his attentiveness, which inspired in them "a deep sense of trust . . . [as others] trusted him with their dreams and fears, their irrationality and their secrets." His colleague Fran Cournos concluded that Alan did "change the world." The memorial ended with family and friends standing on the auditorium's stage as Harris Yulin read in a voice-over Alan's last letter of thanks to all those he had worked with and loved. Many in the audience wept when Yulin emphasized Alan's last line: "So at the end of the day, Barbara, it really has been a love story."

One sentence in Alan's last letter has meaning for me in ways he could not have known: "Some of my friends [over] the years have urged me to write a book about my life, but I've enjoyed living it rather than writing about it." This statement left out his problem of being unable to say everything he wanted because so many of his comrades were still imprisoned, or could be in danger from the state if he wrote of more actions. He worried, too, about writing about his own incarceration when he knew his privileges, however attenuated, made his story different and his understanding of the men of color around him limited.

In writing this biography I met the man I never really knew, and tried to explain how he changed from the boy and adolescent I remembered. I tried to capture his multiple dimensions, mistakes, and commitments. I hope I have shown well enough his struggles and contributions, how they illuminate what he found possible, and not possible, to do politically in search of global solidarity and justice. Alan's principles may have blinded him to the limitations in the alliances he made, but he did not stop thinking and rethinking about what he did and could do. His belief in building up from the grass roots, his rejection of his former Leninist vanguard positions, his search for bridges, and his deeply rooted compassion made possible the changes for which he worked.

After Alan died and was cremated, the family took his ashes to Pennsylvania. Near the house and land he loved, his dust and bones lie in a small cemetery filled with the light and air kept from him during his prison years. The headstone has his name and dates, adding, "'DOC'—Wise, Brave and Beloved."

ACKNOWLEDGMENTS

Before I thank profusely all the individuals and institutions that made this book possible, I need to say something about what it felt like to do this work: It was hell, and I naively did not expect this. It was not as if I had not taken on difficult historical tasks before. I have, and this is not my first book. Indeed, it may be my last. This was different. The book was about someone I knew growing up, but who became a stranger to me as an adult. He was a man; I am a woman. He became a doctor, a revolutionary, a political prisoner, a global health activist, and a repeated cancer patient and survivor for decades until he was not. I became a radical and then a historian. I have never been arrested, and my chronic ills are not yet life threatening.

The book chronicles my own lifetime, not something in the distant past. It meant most of the sources I used were about events I remembered or knew how to understand, in political movements I was part of, or chose not to be. It meant I interviewed many of Alan's family members, friends, and comrades. I got to know them, stayed in their homes, went to their birthday parties, celebrated their accomplishments, and mourned their losses. I used to joke that the difference between a historian and an anthropologist is that the historian's informants are all dead, and that as my friend Harry Marks put it, we "read dead people's mail." In this case my informants were in front of me, or their letters led me to them because Alan kept their mail, or they were willing to share his writings with me. Alan's family and friends who miss him had to relive in front of me what it meant to be close to him through all his struggles.

It was weird, too, that I suddenly knew more facts about someone I did not know and would share them, if asked, with those who loved or fought with him. Some wanted every new piece of information; others did not and needed to live only with their memories. I respect those who, for a variety of personal reasons, were not willing to provide me with more materials, and I regret that I did not get the letters Alan wrote to Dana Biberman, and that I could not convince Tim Blunk to speak to me. But I do understand why.

I did what historians do who cannot just go to an archive: I created an archive. I spent the better part of one sabbatical in Barbara Zeller's apartment, using my portable scanner to make pdfs of all of Alan's letters and papers that had survived before Barbara put them in the Columbia University Medical School archives. I am also grateful to Marion Banzhaf, Diane Gillman Charney, Susie Day, Anne Nosworthy Fisher, Tom Garrett, Noelle Hanrahan, Lynne Karsten, Bob Lederer, Claude Marks, Paul McIssac, Marshall Morris, Susan Rosenberg, Jane Segal, Randy Ats Smith, Raymond Smith, James Tracy, and Laura Whitehorn, who had materials or interviews with Alan that they lent me.

I did a lot of searching and found some materials, but not others. I had people, especially Barbara Zeller, vouch for me so that others would talk to me. I tried to balance, on the one hand, sensitivity to those with painful memories that I asked them to dredge up and, on the other, my need to know so I could give a full picture. It was a delicate task because, unlike some journalists, I erred on the side of respecting people's desire to have their own past. Having taught feminist oral history for decades, I needed to act ethically toward those who knew Alan. I pushed, but only so far.

I have tried to figure out why this writing was so difficult. One former political comrade of Alan's said he thought I felt guilty that I had not done more for Alan when he was incarcerated and sick. I suspect this part is true. This comrade also accused me of being romantic about Alan's commitments and actions. I really tried hard not to be. As an historian, my work is to explain the context that led Alan to make the decisions to take what he thought of as a "revolutionary road," even if I did not and thought it was wrong.

Watching the story unfold, but knowing where it was going, was truly upsetting. I just wanted to yell at him to stop. But then I knew he and his comrades were right about the problems when they saw the racism and the international military adventurism that is so central to what makes this the United States. Writing about their efforts to be antiracists in the face of the Black Lives Matter movement, and globalists in the face of growing nationalism, is now to wonder again why they did not succeed, and what steps they did not take but should have. Historians are trained not to ask "what if" questions, but it does hang over everything we write like Clio's haint, the spirit of the dead.

Writing about political activism is always fraught. Those of us who lived through the times covered in this book, and there are many of us and many, many books and memoirs, have all tried to get a handle on the paths taken and not. Those who are younger have more distance perhaps, but there is a way my somewhat insider knowledge made some things knowable and others not. I tried really hard to make this appeal to another generation.

Going to the prisons was particularly wrenching. I am grateful to David Gilbert, Herman Bell, and Judith Clark, who saw me, and more than ecstatic that at least Bell and Clark are now out after decades of imprisonment. I got physically sick after every prison visit, as I understood viscerally what it meant to be caged. I only hope that Gilbert, and Alan's other comrades still incarcerated, will be freed before they die. It is time. In my view, justice has been served. Vengeance should never be.

My connections to the different institutions in Alan's life made learning more about him possible, and reunions were key. My Middletown High School classmates, class of 1963, have followed this journey through our fiftieth reunion, and spoke to me about their memories. I am particularly grateful to the help of Judith Pleasure Willner and Lynn Johnson Rosen. A reunion of the SDS members of the 1960s Cornell classes gave me the serendipity of meeting Alan's football coach, and his former fraternity brothers and friends filled in much information in interviews. I especially appreciate the assistance of Bruce Dancis.

The institutions I have had the good fortune to be part of gave me the support to do this research and writing. Wellesley College, where I taught in the Department of Women's and Gender Studies for thirty-four years, provided the funds to do the initial research, and its ease-into-retirement program gave me the opportunity to research and write this book in record time (for me anyway). I had the wonderful chance to be a fellow at the Charles Warren Center of the Harvard History Department in 2017–18, which gave me access to Harvard's libraries, and the camaraderie of the fellows, who were all involved in carceral studies. I am particularly grateful to Elizabeth Kai Hinton and Lisa McGirr, who ran the seminar that year, and to the fellows Donna Munch, Garrett Felber, and Heather Ann Thompson, who became friends and my guides in this new field for me. I thank Walter Johnson for accepting me into the Warren Center. I finished the book at the Project on Race and Gender in Science and Medicine at Harvard's Hutchins Center for African and African American Research, when Evelynn Hammonds agreed (big thank you) to share her office with me. I especially appreciate Krishna Lewis and Abby Wolf for their support, and Peter Hulme, Pablo D. Herrera Veita, Z. Z. Packer, Antonia Lant, Knitra Brooks, and historian Akua Naru, who shared his expertise on Weather with me.

Students at Wellesley College did much of the early work to transcribe my interviews and figure out how to index all of Alan's handwritten letters. They read the chapters as they tumbled out of my brain and computer and provided the insight I needed to make this work accessible to them. I am glad to have worked with Claudia Liss Schultz and Gabby Hartman. I could not have done this with without the enthusiasm of Cai Yoke and Shreya Thatai, who fell in love with Alan, warts and all, along the way, and were whizzes at the organizing of the materials.

I had the opportunity to try out my ideas for what became this book as lectures and talks at the American Association for the History of Medicine, the Hutchins and Warren Centers, as the Alan Berkman Memorial Lecturer at the

Mailman School of Public Health at Columbia University, the University of Western Ontario, and with the History Working Group in the History of Science Department at Harvard.

This book would not have happened if Barbara Zeller, Alan's comrade and widow, had not had faith in my ability to tell his story fairly. I promised her at the beginning it was not going to be an official biography, and that I had the final words. She read the penultimate draft, corrected factual mistakes, and raised pertinent analytic questions. In the end it is my book, but Barbara made it possible. Alan's brothers, his daughters, and grandson were magnanimous in their assistance. Dana Biberman met with me twice and was willing to discuss her viewpoints. His comrades and lawyers answered my endless questions and fact-checking both large and small, in person, in emails, and on the telephone. Their names are in the notes, but I especially want to thank Judith Clark, Linda Evans, Liz Horowitz, Ron Kuby, Shelley Miller, Mary Patten, Eve Rosahn, Susan Rosenberg, and Laura Whitehorn. Those who knew Alan at Columbia, Highbridge-Woodycrest, Health GAP, and in the HIV/AIDS activist world were also generous with their time. Alan's close friends who interviewed him — Paul McIssac, Marion Banzhaf, and Dick Clapp — provided me with their transcripts and untranscribed tapes. I could not have done this book without their generosity. Lynne Karsten, who met Alan after he got out of prison, became a wonderful friend who listened and helped me enormously.

I had the best good fortune to be part of a biography-writing group that began just as I started this book. Carla Kaplan, Nancy Cott, and Ann Braude read every chapter of the book, some chapters more than once, and were the best interlocutors, grammarians, and critics you could have. I know this book would not exist if they had not done all of this with their hard questions and loving guidance, and they set the bar for excellence really high. Dan Berger and Susan Ware, the readers for the University of North Carolina Press who outed themselves to me after their reviews were in, provided invaluable factual and analytic suggestions. I am grateful, too, that Heather Ann Thompson and Rhonda Williams accepted this book from an interloper into their series. And I had an amazing editor in Brandon Proia, who had such faith in this story and helped me to see where our generations differed. He also line-edited, a job that most editors do not do anymore. The move to shorter and more mellifluous sentences owes much to his actions, as well as to Alex Martin, who did an amazing copyediting job.

Then there is my family. Gertrude Mokotoff, my mother, died at 100 in late 2018 just as I was in the beginning of the final rewrites. She knew Alan and his family in Middletown, New York. She listened as I read her chapters out loud. I am truly sorry she did survive to read the final version, but the values she instilled in me are everywhere in this book. My daughter Mariah Sixkiller tells me this is the only one of my books she is looking forward to reading! I take these comments in the goodwill in which she offered them, and she did a wonderful job of editing the prologue. My son Micah Sieber provided his usual humorous commentary and bemusement at his mother's intellectual and political concerns. Anna, Sam, Will, and John Reuben, my grandchildren, are too young to read this, but they entertained me with the right amount of levity and distractions always.

My partner of more than two decades, and now my husband, Bill Quivers, was a part of this journey from the beginning. I could not have done all the work without his efforts, from carrying the scanner to going to prisons and traveling the country to interview Alan's friends and comrades. I am grateful that as a theoretical physicist he just needed his brain and his sheets of calculations on paper, which made it possible for him to come along with me. He made it so much less lonely a journey. I am especially grateful for the times he listened when I woke him up in the middle of the night with my fears over whether I could do this book, or when I explained how Alan's experiences entered my dreams and nightmares.

This book is about the past, but I hope it provides some guide to the future. It is dedicated to Alan's grandson Gabriel, who was two when his grandfather died, and Gabriel's sister, Amelle, who never met Alan. I write, too, for my former students, now social activists themselves, as they chart new ways to justice and equality.

Susan M. Reverby

Boston, Massachusetts, October 2019

NOTES

PROLOGUE

1. As far as I know, Alan was no direct relation to the early twentieth-century American anarchist Alexander Berkman.

2. Bruce Dancis, briefly a fraternity brother of Alan's at Cornell, and my wedding witness in 1967, served time in prison for destroying his draft card. See his *Resister: A Story of Protest and Prison during the Vietnam War* (Ithaca, NY: Cornell University Press, 2014).

3. Interview with Steven Krugman, Newton, MA, February 7, 2013; Daniel E. Bassuk, *Incarnation in Hinduism and Christianity: The Myth of the God-Man* (New York: Palgrave Macmillan, 1987), 15. All interviews cited were conducted by the author unless otherwise specified.

4. Susan M. Reverby, "The Unexpected Road: A Political Doctor Goes to Jail," *Circa 1967: 25th Reunion Yearbook Cornell University Class of 1967 June 1992* (Marceline, MO: Walsworth, 1992), 40–41. I wrote about Alan again for our fiftieth reunion in 2017 when I was working on this book. See Susan M. Reverby, "The Unexpected Journey, Part II: From Prison to World Health Activism," *Cornell Class of 1967 50th Reunion Book* (Ithaca, NY: Cornell Class of 1967), 34–37.

5. Susan M. Reverby, "'Enemy of the People / Enemy of the State': Two Great(ly

Infamous) Doctors, Passions and the Judgment of History," *Bulletin of the History of Medicine* 88 (Fall 2014): 403–30. I had moved from labor history into women's, medical, and nursing history by the 1970s.

6. Paul Heideman, "Half the Way with Mao Zedong," *Jacobin*, May 23, 2018, https://jacobinmag.com/2018/05/half-the-way-with-mao-zedong/.

7. E. Anthony Rotundo, *American Manhood: Transformations in Masculinity from the Revolution to the Modern Era* (New York: Basic Books, 1993); Gail Bederman, *Manliness and Civilization* (Chicago: University of Chicago Press, 1995).

8. Aaron Belkin, *Bring Me Men: Military Masculinity and the Benign Façade of American Empire* (New York: Columbia University Press, 2012). I am grateful to Susan Ware for her comments to me on masculinity and to Pamela Jean Maddock for her thinking on this topic. See her "Venereal Disease Control in the Progressive Era US Army" (PhD diss, University of Sydney, 2019).

9. Middletown High School, "Epilogue 1963," 103, in author's possession.

CHAPTER 1

1. Scranton Commission Report, June 1970, quoted in Clara Bingham, "When America Was on the Brink of a Second Revolution," June 2, 2016, https://lithub.com/when-america-was-on-the-brink-of-a-second-revolution; Donald Freed, *Agony in New Haven* (New York: Simon and Schuster, 1973), 71–72.

2. Writing to his girlfriend Diane Gillman in the summer of 1963, Alan noted he knew more about the pedigree of his new collie puppy than his own family. Alan Berkman to Diane Gillman, August 1963. I am grateful to Diane Gillman Charney for saving her letters from Alan and sharing them with me.

3. *Yeshiva bochers* is the Yiddish phrase for a man, usually, who spent most of his time studying at the Yeshiva (Hebrew School) rather than doing any kind of work. On the story of his grandfather, see BD, 1–2. I copied all the papers when they were in possession of Alan's widow, Barbara Zeller. They are now housed in the Columbia University Medical Center Library Archives.

4. BD, 1. See also Marion Banzhaf, "Alan Berkman Oral History," April 20, 2001, 3, in author's possession. Alan also did a shorter oral history with Marion Banzhaf in April and May that year. I am grateful to Banzhaf for sending me the transcript and the remaining untranscribed tapes, which I then transcribed.

5. Banzhaf, "Alan Berkman Oral History"; telephone interview with Steven Berkman, November 6, 2011; novelist Joseph Heller, quoted in Meredith Berkman, "A Family Gets Together," *New York Newsday*, October 3, 1994. All interviews cited were conducted by the author unless otherwise specified.

6. Morris Junk Berkman, 278 Kent St, Brooklyn, NY, *Brooklyn, New York, City Directory, 1912*, http://search.ancestry.com/cqi-bin/sse.dill?h=126272255&db=USDirectories&indiv=try.

7. Samuel Berkman, U.S. Federal Census 1940, www.ancestry.com; Berkman, Meredith, "A Family Gets Together."

8. Banzhaf, "Alan Berkman Oral History," 4.

9. Joseph Heller, *Closing Time* (New York: Simon & Schuster, 1994), 44.

10. Banzhaf, "Alan Berkman Oral History," 4.

11. Joseph Heller, *Now and Then: From Coney Island to Here* (New York: Vintage, 1999), 144. This is Heller's memoir, not a work of fiction.

12. Heller, *Closing Time*, 45.

13. Heller, *Closing Time*, 39.

14. Heller, *Closing Time*, 125. Heller fictionalized the letter. "J" was on the dog tags after 1952. Before that it was an H for Hebrew. Akiva Males, "Jewish GIs and Their Dog-Tags," www.hakirah.org/Vol15Males.pdf (accessed July 3, 2014).

15. Berkman, Meredith, "A Family Gets Together." Heller and Lou Berkman hung out together in Coney Island, went to the Caribbean islands on vacation with their wives, and then had some kind of fight that broke them apart, Meredith Berkman writes.

16. "Louis Berkman, Developer, Dies," *Middletown (NY) Times Herald-Record*, March n.d., 1981, clipping in BP.

17. Samuel Berkman, U.S. World War II Army Enlistment Records, 1938–46, www .ancestry.com (accessed February 9, 2013). Alan's mother, Mona (or Minnie Ositinsky on her birth certificate), had worked as a secretary before her marriage. Her father, Sol, or Saul, had come from Kiev and became a truck driver and seltzer bottler, while her mother, Sarah, raised the children and spoke to them primarily in Yiddish. Saul Ositinsky, Registration Card No. 171, First World War Records; U.S. Census, 1920, Brooklyn, Kings County, Sheet No. 16B.

18. Ft. Tilden was abandoned. Its beach is now a hip site, and artists use its old buildings as canvases. See Alex Williams, "No Place Like Home," *New York Times*, July 17, 2014.

19. Ricky-Dale Calhoun, "Arming David: The Haganah's Illegal Arms Procurement Network in the United States, 1945–49," *Journal of Palestine Studies* 36 (Summer 2007): 22–32. Calhoun concludes that "the Jewish Agency's U.S. arms procurement effort amounted to a highly effective criminal conspiracy" (32). Leonard Slater, *The Pledge* (New York: Pocket, 1971), outlines how the German American Jewish money helped pay for the arms, and New York junk dealers played a crucial role in procurement, storage, and shipment. I have no evidence of Moische's involvement other than the family tale.

20. Diane Gillman Charney, email to author, February 28, 2012; interview with Jerry Berkman, Stamford, CT, September 19, 2013.

21. Telephone interview with Larry Berkman, February 10, 2013.

22. Franklin B. Williams, *Middletown: A Biography* (Middletown, NY: Lawrence A. Toepp, 1928).

23. Larry Berkman interview.

24. Heller, *Closing Time*, 400. Berkman, "A Family Gets Together," reports that the stories are true according to her father, Charlie Berkman, Sam and Lou's younger brother.

25. U.S. Bureau of the Census, *Census of Population: 1950*, vol. 2, *Characteristics of Population*, pt. 32, New York, Final Report (Washington: Government Printing Office, 1952). The census found 85 percent of the population was native born, 11 percent foreign born, 3 percent black, and less than 1 percent "other races."

26. U.S. Bureau of the Census, *Census of Population: 1950*; Jerry Berkman interview.

27. I do not know when water came to the Fulton Street area, but I suspect it was in the late 1950s when urban renewal came to the area. My memory of the outhouses is strong because I was shocked to see them when we drove home a woman who worked for my family.

28. Jerry Berkman interview.

29. "Obituary Bernard 'Bernie' Polak," November 7, 2012, http://www.horancares.com /obituary?id=1131796.

30. My mother, Gertrude Mokotoff, was the first Democrat alderwoman from our ward in 1981. She went on to be the first woman city council president for four years and then

mayor from 1990 to 1993. "Former Mayor Will Head Middletown's Festivities," *Middletown (NY) Times Herald-Record*, April 16, 2013.

31. "Robeson Asks U.S. to Probe 'Terrorism,'" *Washington Post*, August 29, 1949; Steve Courtney, "The Robeson Riots of 1949," *Reporter Dispatch*, September 5, 1982, www.bencourtney.com/peeksillriots/.

32. "10,000 at Klan Gathering: Field Day and Sunset Drill Are Held at Peekskill," *New York Times*, September 2, 1930.

33. Interview with Elihu Sussman, New York City, April 10, 2013.

34. Jerry Berkman interview.

35. Telephone interview with Michael Sweeney, now a Presbyterian minister in nearby Warwick, NY, August 7, 2013.

36. Telephone interview with Marshall Morris, Alan's campaign manager, November 4, 2013; Diane Gillman Charney, email to to author, April 20, 2012.

37. As the Jewish joke goes, how does a rabbi get rid of rats in the synagogue? Give them a bar mitzvah and they never come back.

38. Banzhaf, "Alan Berkman Oral History," 1.

39. Diane Gillman Charney, email to author, April 21, 2013.

40. Banzhaf, "Alan Berkman Oral History," 2.

41. Telephone interview with Steven Berkman, July 26, 2013; Jerry Berkman interview.

42. I was the high school newspaper editor and picked Alan as sports editor.

43. Alan Berkman to Diane Gillman, March 30, 1965.

44. Banzhaf, "Alan Berkman Oral History," 1.

45. Steven Berkman interview, November 6, 2011; Dick Polman, "Tempo: Story behind the Mystery Man of the Brink's Job," *Chicago Tribune*, January 2, 1986.

46. Robbie Anderman, email to author, August 16, 2014. Anderman was in the scout troupe with Alan.

47. I asked about the drills on the Middletown, NY, Facebook page on July 6, 2014. This description fits the recollections of several of the people who responded to my query. https://www.facebook.com/groups/85763033664/, accessed July 7, 2014.

48. Bernie Gould, Associated Press, "All-Night Drill: Shelter Life Tested in School Basement," *Fredericksburg (VA) Free Lance-Star*, February 2, 1963; interviews with Lynn Johnson Rosen and Judith Pleasure Willner, New York City, April 20, 2013.

49. Middletown High School, *Twin Towers*, 1962–63, copies in my possession.

50. Benjamin and Jane Gillman were prominent lawyers in Middletown, and I worked for them for two summers as a file clerk. Ben went on to serve many years in the House of Representatives as a Republican. They invited the Little Rock students to speak.

51. Alan Berkman to Diane Gillman, April 23, 1965.

52. Interview with Barbara Zeller, New York City, July 20, 2011.

53. The Japanese garden was sold off in the late 1960s along with the land. Lou and Marion Berkman's son Jeff, who became a local Orange County politician, still manages the family's real estate. Lou served for years on the Middletown School Board, and his son Jeff on the Library Board before going into politics. Jeff's sister Marcie became the mayor of nearby Goshen, New York.

54. Interview with Diane Gillman Charney, New Haven, CT, February 22, 2015.

55. There was, of course, sexual violence in families earlier than this but most of us, unless we experienced it, learned about this only much later.

56. Diane Gillman Charney, email to author, April 20, 2012, and my memories, too; *Middletown (NY) High School Epilogue*, 1963, 58.

57. My senior year in high school my boyfriend came from the sports rival city of Port Jervis. We met at a United Synagogue Youth dance.

58. Charney, email to author, April 20, 2013.

59. Charney, email to author, April 20, 2013.

60. Charney interview.

61. Alan Berkman to Diane Gillman, August n.d., 1963.

62. See correspondence with Hank Newman and his family from prison, below.

63. Newman typed letter, BD, 54; Barry Kibrick, "Schlemiel! Schlimazel! Hasenpfeffer Incorporated!," *Huffpost*, November 9, 2015, https://www.huffpost.com/entry/schlemiel -schlimazel-hase_b_8512356.

64. Interview with Jeffrey Millman, Cambridge, MA, May 10, 2013.

65. "Tops in Test," *Middletown (NY) Times Herald-Record*, 1967, clipping in BP.

66. *Middletown (NY) High School Epilogue, 1963,* 60.

67. Middletown High School Graduation Program, June 1963.

68. Charney interview.

69. Charney interview; Millman interview; Banzhaf, "Alan Berkman Oral History," 5.

CHAPTER 2

1. There were only ten black students in our class of 2,400, and two African Americans on the faculty: one a lecturer and the other an assistant professor. See Glenn Altschuler and Isaac Kramnick, *Cornell: A History* (Ithaca, NY: Cornell University Press, 2014), digital, location 3427.

2. Only in our senior year were a few women allowed to live in apartments off campus.

3. While Alan was getting a BA in the College of Arts and Sciences, I thought I was going to be a personnel administrator and selected the School of Industrial and Labor Relations for my BS. Three out of Cornell's seven undergraduate schools were supported by the state, as was mine. My tuition was one-tenth of what Alan's parents paid for him.

4. Alan to Diane Gillman, October 3, 1963, Gillman/Berkman correspondence. I am grateful to Diane Gillman Charney for providing me with a copy of these and subsequent letters between them. All letters from Alan to Diane Gillman come from her collection.

5. Alan to Diane Gillman, April 15, 1964.

6. Marshal L. Goldstein and Kristl Bogue, "Student Government Commission Proposes Lectures, Films on Birth Control Methods," *Cornell Daily Sun* clipping, n.d., enclosed in Alan to Diane Gillman, October 31, 1963.

7. Alan to Diane Gillman, December 7, 1963.

8. Alan to Diane Gillman, October 1, 1963.

9. Alan to Diane Gillman, April 22, 1964.

10. Alan to Diane Gillman, October 3, 1963.

11. Alan to Diane Gillman, September 25, 1963.

12. Alan to Diane Gillman, April 25, 1964.

13. Alan to Diane Gillman, October 3, 1963.

14. Alan to Diane Gillman, October 16, 1963.

15. Alan to Diane Gillman, December 11, 1963.

16. Alan to Diane Gillman, October 24, 1963.

17. Alan to Diane Gillman, January 8, 1964.

18. Alan to Diane Gillman, October 24, 1983.

19. Alan to Diane Gillman, April 29, 1964.

20. Alan to Diane Gillman, November 20, 1963. He reiterated this concern in a letter a few weeks later, Alan to Diane Gillman, December 5, 1963.

21. Alan to Diane Gillman, May 8, 1964.

22. Skype interview with Dick Rothkopf, February 2, 2013.

23. As playwright Donald Freed wrote in lines that could be applied to Alan, "And many of today's revolutionaries are surprised, when they trace back their own sequence of radicalization in the 1960s, to find that the murder in Dallas was a new line drawn across this consciousness; changing them, leaving their youth on the precedent side." "Thoughts on White Suicide," *Black Panther* 8 (June 24, 1972): 1.

24. Alan to Diane Gillman, March 23, 1964. Alan gave the key for Phi Eta Sigma to Diane and asked her to wear it on her charm bracelet (Alan to Diane Gillman, September 19, 1964).

25. Alan to Diane Gillman, April 20, 1964.

26. Alan to Diane Gillman April 29, 1964.

27. Alan to Diane Gillman, April 9, 1965.

28. Alan to Diane Gillman, April 14, 1964.

29. Alan to Diane Gillman, April 29, 1964.

30. Alan to Diane Gillman, May 23, 1964.

31. Alan to Diane Gillman May 20, 1964.

32. Alan to Diane Gillman, May 22, 1964.

33. Alan to Diane Gillman, September 23, 1964.

34. Heather Booth, University of Chicago, quoted in Wendy Kline, *Bodies of Knowledge* (Chicago: University of Chicago Press, 2010), 70.

35. Glenn Altschuler and Isaac Kramnick, "Campus Confrontation, 1958," *Cornell Alumni Magazine*, September/October 2014, http://cornellalumnimagazine.com/index .php?option=com_content&task=view&id=1956&Itemid=56&ed=43; "Action Party" leaflet, 1959, box 1, folder 1957–1959, Joe Griffith Papers, Cornell University Archives, Ithaca, NY; see also Donald Alexander Downs, *Cornell '69* (Ithaca, NY: Cornell University Press, 1999), 25–45.

36. Telephone interview with John Haywood, Washington, DC, August 29, 2017. All interviews cited were conducted by the author unless otherwise specified.

37. Downs, *Cornell '69*, 13.

38. Phyllis Kaye, "Faculty Acts on Berkeley Resolution," *Cornell Daily Sun*, December 10, 1964.

39. Alan to Diane Gillman, November 3, 1964.

40. Alan to Diane Gillman, October 5, 1964.

41. Alan to Diane Gillman October 19, 1964.

42. Alan to Diane Gillman January 25, 1965.

43. Alan to Diane Gillman, October 31, 1964.

44. Alan to Diane Gillman, December 7 and 9, 1964.

45. Alan to Diane Gillman, January 17, 1965.

46. Alan to Diane Gillman, February 1, 1965.

47. Alan to Diane Gillman, February 4, 1965.

48. Alan to Diane Gillman, February 2, 1965.

49. Rothkopf interview.

50. Alan to Diane Gillman, February 25, 1965.

51. Alan to Diane Gillman, December 11, 1964.

52. Alan to Diane Gillman, January 17, 1965.

53. Alan to Diane Gillman, January 4, 1965.

54. Alan to Diane Gillman, January 6, 1965.

55. Alan to Diane Gillman, February 8, 1965.

56. Alan to Diane Gillman, March 1, 1965.

57. Alan to Diane Gillman, April 6, 1965; "Sartre," editorial, *Cornell Daily Sun*, March 25, 1965.

58. "A Meeting on Vietnam" flyer, folder Vietnam, box 2, Joe Griffith Papers, Cornell University Archives, Ithaca, NY.

59. "Group Stages 'Sit-In' after Harriman Talk," *Cornell Daily Sun*, May 12, 1965, 1. I was there and remember, too, being shocked when students started yelling at Harriman and were ushered out by the campus police. The leader of the student group, Paul Epstein, went on to become an internationally known public health physician activist around issues of climate change and health. He and Alan would also become friends, but they did not know each other at Cornell.

60. Thomas Moore, "Barton Hall Demonstrators Cited after Tense Viet Protest Sit-In," *Cornell Daily Sun*, May 18, 1965.

61. Alan to Diane Gillman, November 19, 1965.

62. Telephone interview with Alan L. Libshutz, February 26, 2013. Libshutz, along with Michael Cogan, lived with Alan in the house on Lake Cayuga. Libshutz and Cogan were my classmates in the Labor Relations School at Cornell and were also Alan's fraternity brothers.

63. Alan to Diane Gillman, November 15, 1965.

64. Alan to Diane Gillman, July 1, 1966.

65. Alan to Diane Gillman, July n.d., 1966; Alan to Diane Gillman, July 10, 1966.

66. Alan to Diane Gillman, July 10, 1966.

67. Alan to Diane Gillman, July 15, 1966.

68. For those traveling, letters were sent in care of general delivery at American Express offices and could be picked up there. Phone calls home cost hundreds of dollars, and the internet and cell phones did not yet exist.

69. Alan to Diane Gillman, July 25, 1966.

70. Alan to Diane Gillman, August 6, 1966.

71. Alan to Diane Gillman, August 6, 1966.

72. Alan to Diane Gillman, September 8, 1966.

73. Alan to Diane Gillman, September 15, 1966.

74. Alan to Diane Gillman, September 19, 1966.

75. Alan to Diane Gillman, September 19, 1966.

76. Alan to Diane Gillman, September 26, 1966.

77. Alan to Diane Gillman, October 2 and 3, 1966.

78. Alan to Diane Gillman, October 3, 1966.

79. Alan to Diane Gillman, November 10, 1966.

80. Alan to Diane Gillman, October 3, 1966. I suspect the physician said "Medicaid," but Alan at that point did not know the difference between Medicaid and Medicare. Both had just been enacted that year.

81. Alan to Diane Gillman, January 14, 1967.

82. Alan to Diane Gillman, January 25, 1967.

83. Alan to Diane Gillman, January 25, 1967.

84. Alan to Diane Gillman, January 25, 1967.

85. Alan to Diane Gillman, October 17, 1966, February 3, 1967.

86. Alan to Diane Gillman, February 25, 1967.

87. Alan to Diane Gillman, May 9, 1967.

88. Alan to Diane Gillman March 28, 1967. Diane and Alan's close friend Terry Birnbaum married in June 1967 at the end of her junior year, while I married on the same day, a week after my Cornell graduation. Alan noted that my parents did not approve of my new husband, Larry Reverby, and he also thought my marriage foolish. Larry Reverby and I split two years later.

89. Alan to Diane Gillman, April 11, 1967.

90. Alan to Diane Gillman, May 15, 1967.

91. Alan to Diane Gillman, May 15, 1967.

92. Alan to Diane Gillman, May 16, 1967.

93. For details, see Bruce Dancis, *Resister: A Story of Protest and Prison during the Vietnam War* (Ithaca, NY: Cornell University Press, 2014). My roommate Margie Holt Heins and I were one of the ten students "cited" by Cornell for organizing the burning of draft cards. Larry Reverby, working at the university and not a student, was one of the few of us with a credit card. He bought the plane tickets so the SDS leadership could go to New York City to meet with the April 15 mobilization leaders to plan the mass draft-card burning. The FBI called him in for an interview about this the following fall.

94. Interview with Bruce Dancis, San Francisco, October 26, 2012.

95. Alan to Diane Gillman, April 24, 1967.

96. Alan to Diane Gillman, April 24, 1967.

97. Marion Banzhaf, "Alan Berkman Oral History," April 20, 2001, 4, in author's possession. I am grateful to Banzhaf for providing me with the tapes and transcripts.

98. Dick Polman, "Tempo: Story behind the Mystery Man of the Brink's Job," *Chicago Tribune*, January 2, 1986. The other student he supposedly debated this with does not remember it, and it seems unlikely it would have happened as early as 1963 or 1964. She also was opposed to the war (interview with Judith Pleasure Willner, New York City, April 26, 2013). I could not find records of this at the synagogue. I suspect the debate may have been later than Alan remembered, and with someone else.

99. Stan Chess, "Carmichael Blasts War, White Supremacy, Draft," *Cornell Daily Sun*, March 1, 1967.

100. Banzhaf, "Alan Berkman Oral History," 5.

101. Libshutz interview; telephone interview with Michael Cogan, February 27, 2013; and interview with Diane Gillman Charney, New Haven, CT, February 3, 2015.

CHAPTER 3

1. Alan Berkman to Diane Gillman, October 9, 1967; in contrast, I was in London and Paris organizing antiwar actions before I returned to New York to work for Resistance, the organization that encouraged and supported resistance to the draft.

2. Leonard Dinnerstein, *Anti-Semitism in America* (New York: Oxford University Press, 1994), 158–59; Robb Burlage and Maxine Kenny, "Columbia P&S: Medical Gymnasiums?," *Health/PAC Bulletin*, no. 6, November–December 1968, 7–12; Kenneth Ludmerer, "The Forgotten Medical Student," in *Time to Heal* (New York: Oxford University Press, 1999), 196–218.

3. Marion Banzhaf, "Alan Berkman Oral History," April 20, 2001, 8, in author's possession.

4. Banzhaf, "Alan Berkman Oral History," April 20, 2001, 8.

5. Alan Berkman photograph, Alan Berkman Student File, Archives and Special Collections, Health Sciences Library, Columbia University, New York City.

6. Interview with Donna Karl, Cambridge, MA, February 4, 2015; second quote is from nurse Kathy Hubenet (telephone interview, Seattle, February 13, 2015), who was married then to Alan's close friend Franklin Apfel. All interviews cited were conducted by the author unless otherwise specified.

7. Alan to Diane Gillman, September 9, 1967.

8. Dean George Perera, "Comments by Commission on Admissions," Alan Berkman Student File, Archives and Special Collections, Health Sciences Library, Columbia University, New York City.

9. Alan Berkman, Columbia P&S Medical School Application, Alan Berkman Student File, Archives and Special Collections, Health Sciences Library, Columbia University, New York City.

10. Alan to Diane Gillman, September 9, 1967.

11. Alan to Diane Gillman, November 9, 1967. Rosen was not in the study group, and remembers breaking with Alan over his politics by the early 1970s (telephone interview with Lynn Johnson Rosen, May 13, 2019). On the history of Progressive Labor (PL), see John F. Levin and Earl Silbar, eds., *You Say You Want a Revolution: SDS, PL, and Adventures in Building a Worker-Student Alliance* (San Francisco: 1741 Press, 2019).

12. Alan to Diane Gillman, October 9, 1967.

13. On the socializing role of the dissection/anatomy laboratory, see John Harley Warner, "The Aesthetic Grounding of Modern Medicine," *Bulletin of the History of Medicine* 88 (Spring 2014): 1–47; and interview with Dick Clapp, Boston, December 14, 2014.

14. "A Statement of Concern from the First and Second Year Classes," Records of the Executive Committee of the Faculty Council, Office of the Dean Physicians & Surgeons, November 17, 1969, Archives and Special Collections, Health Sciences Library, Columbia University, New York City.

15. Alan to Diane Gillman, February 7, 1968.

16. "Student Achievement and Character Report," Alan Berkman Student File, Archives and Special Collections, Health Sciences Library, Columbia University, New York City.

17. Interview with Barbara Zeller, New York City, January 7, 2015.

18. Telephone interview with Alan's medical school classmate Ethel Siris, New York City, February 20, 2014.

19. Interview with Franklin Apfel, Brookline, MA, August 5, 2014.

20. Alan to Diane Gillman, March 3, 1968.

21. BD, 102.

22. Banzhaf, "Alan Berkman Oral History," April 20, 2001, 9. Ironically, I read Marx with Rosen in an SDS study group when we both lived in Chicago in the summer of 1966.

23. Paul McIssac, "Transcript of Interview with Alan Berkman," September 1, 1992, 1–3. I am grateful to Paul McIssac for providing me with this. Karl interview. Karl talked about Alan's coming into politics through his intellectual thoughts, not his movement experience. Karl was a graduate nurse who had been active in the Student Health Organization when she arrived in the Washington Heights neighborhood in 1970. She lived with friends of Alan's for a year and half, worked at Harlem Hospital, and was part of his political circle.

24. Comments below from Alan Berkman Student Record, Alan Berkman Student File, Archives and Special Collections, Health Sciences Library, Columbia University, New York City.

25. McIssac, "Transcript of Interview with Alan Berkman."

26. Clapp interview, December 14, 2014.

27. Clapp interview, December 14, 2014. There is, however, no record of these awards in Alan's student file (Archives and Special Collections, Health Sciences Library, Columbia University, New York City).

28. Telephone interview with Barbara Zeller, January 31, 2015. The story about this woman shows up in a number of Alan's interviews. In another interview, however, the patient is a man. See Dick Polman, "Story behind the Mystery Man of the Brink's Job," *Chicago Tribune*, January 2, 1986.

29. Paul McIssac, interview with Barbara Zeller, New York City, November 12, 1992. In her interview, Zeller remembers the patient as a man. I am grateful to Paul McIssac for sharing his Zeller interview tapes with me. I did the transcriptions.

30. McIssac, interview with Zeller.

31. McIssac, "Transcript of Interview with Alan Berkman," 1–5.

32. Clapp interview, December 14, 2014; Apfel interview.

33. Clapp interview, December 14, 2014; Apfel interview; Banzhaf, "Alan Berkman Oral History," April 20, 2001, 10; Ludmerer, *Time to Heal*, 237–59. On the control and status issues around the white coat, and its use since 1993 in a ceremony for first-year students, see Philip C. Russell, "The White Coat Ceremony: Turning Trust into Entitlement," *Teaching and Learning in Medicine: An International Journal* 14 (November 2009): 56–59.

34. *Iatrogenia* 1 (May 12, 1969), box 1, folder 2, RCP.

35. "Issues in Health," box 1, folder 2, RCP; Clapp interview, December 14, 2014.

36. Dick Clapp, "Alan Berkman's Life," June 10, 2001 (based on a conversation on April 27, 2001), unpublished manuscript, 2.

37. "Parasitology Exam," box 1, folder 1, RCP.

38. Jerry Avron, *Up against the Ivy Wall* (New York: Atheneum, 1969); "Columbia 1968 Website, Created 2008," http://www.columbia1968.com; Barbara and John Ehrenreich, *Long March, Short Spring: The Student Uprising at Home and Abroad* (New York: Monthly Review Press, 1969).

39. Banzhaf, "Alan Berkman Oral History," April 10, 2001, 14.

40. Alan Berkman, "Talk on Political Prisoners at the Marxist School," broadcast on WBAI, n.d. Paul McIssac provided the tape.

41. BD, 27.

42. Lewis Cole, "Legacy of the 1968 Columbia Student Strike," April 26, 2008, http://columbiasdsmemories.blogspot.com.

43. "Ad Hoc Committee for a Better Vanderbilt Clinic," n.d., folder 1, box 1, RCP.

44. Marion Banzhaf, "Alan Berkman Oral History," May 5, 2001, 3, in author's possession.

45. Banzhaf, "Alan Berkman Oral History," May 5, 2001, 3.

46. Franklin Apfel, email to author, April 4, 2019.

47. Telephone interview with Lynn Johnson Rosen, New York City, February 20, 2012.

48. Clapp, "Alan Berkman's Life," 2.

49. Health/PAC, *The American Medical Empire: Power, Profits and Politics*, edited by John and Barbara Ehrenreich (New York: Random House, 1970).

50. Naomi Rogers, "'Caution: The AMA May Be Dangerous to Your Health': The

Student Health Organization (SHO) and American Medicine, 1965–1970," *Radical History Review* 80 (Spring 2001): 5–34; see also copies of the various newsletters of SHO in Michael McGarvey Papers, Archives and Special Collections, Health Sciences Library, Columbia University Medical Center, New York City.

51. Merlin Chowkwanyun, "The New Left and Public Health: The Health Policy Advisory Center, Community Organizing, and the Big Business of Health, 1967–1975," *Journal of the American Public Health Association* 101 (February 2011): 238–49; Lily Hoffman, *The Politics of Knowledge: Activist Movements in Medicine and Planning* (Albany: State University of New York Press, 1989); "The Health/PAC Digital Archive," www .healthpacbulletin.org.

52. Seymour Graubard, "Press Release on ADL Report on Community Control Threat," 8, ADL of B'nai B'rith, January 24, 1971, box 4, Lincoln folder, Michael McGarvey Papers, Archives and Special Collections, Health Sciences Library, Columbia University Medical Center, New York City.

53. I was a full-time staff member at Health/PAC from October 1970 to August 1973, writing mostly on nursing, women's health, and institutional organizing.

54. The emphasis on those who took dangerous actions was quite clear when I attended a reunion of Cornell's SDS chapter in November 2015. The same issue is discussed in the reunion of those involved in the 1968 Columbia strike; see "Columbia 1968 Website."

55. Eventually Clapp would get a doctorate in public health, teach at Boston University's public health school, and become a world-renowned cancer and occupational health epidemiologist.

56. Apfel interview.

57. Annette Rubinstein, Robert Rhodes, Lili Solomon, and Janet Townsend for the Charter Group for a Pledge of Conscience, "The Black Panther Party and the Case of the New York 21," pamphlet, 1969; Murray Kempton, *The Briar Patch* (New York: E. P. Dutton, 1973).

58. Arthur M. Eckstein, *Bad Moon Rising: How the Weather Underground Beat the FBI and Lost the Revolution* (New Haven, CT: Yale University Press, 2016).

59. Thomas Barker, "The Liberal Media and the Ideology of Black Victimhood," *Counterpunch*, February 13–15, 2015, http://www.counterpunch.org/2015/02/13/the -liberal-media-and-the-ideology-of-black-victimhood.

60. Eckstein, *Bad Moon Rising*.

61. Rychetta Watkins, *Black Power, Yellow Power, and the Making of Revolutionary Identities* (Oxford: University of Mississippi Press, 2012).

62. McIssac, "Transcript of Interview with Alan Berkman," 37.

63. Interview with Dick Clapp, Boston, December 22, 2014.

64. Apfel interview. Apfel remembers that the flag was put on the George Washington Bridge. However, both Barbara Zeller and Dick Clapp recall it was at the medical school. I can find no written documentation in the student-run paper the *Columbia Spectator* or in the medical school archives about this. Alan never mentions it in his memoir or interviews.

65. Anonymous, *Medical Cadre*, pamphlet (Oakland, CA: Jellyroll, 1969).

66. Dick Clapp, email to author, March 8, 2015.

67. Interviews with Franklin Apfel, Dick Clapp (December 22, 2014), and Barbara Zeller confirm this.

68. Clapp, "Alan Berkman's Life," 3.

69. Alondra Nelson, *Body and Soul: The Black Panther Party and the Fight against Medical Discrimination* (Minneapolis: University of Minnesota Press, 2011).

70. Banzhaf, "Alan Berkman Oral History," May 5, 2001, 1.

71. Banzhaf, "Alan Berkman Oral History," May 5, 2001, 2.

72. Banzhaf, "Alan Berkman Oral History," May 5, 2001, 2.

73. Apfel interview.

74. On Jewish men and violence, see Paul Breines, *Tough Jews: Political Fantasies and the Moral Dilemma of American Jewry* (New York: Basic Books, 1990); and Warren Rosenberg, *Legacy of Rage: Jewish Masculinity, Violence, and Culture* (Amherst: University of Massachusetts Press, 2001).

75. Mark Rudd, "Why Were There So Many Jews in SDS? (Or, The Ordeal of Civility)," talk presented at New Mexico Jewish Historical Society, November 2005, http://www .markrudd.com/?about-mark-rudd/why-were-there-so-many-jews-in-sds-or-the-ordeal -of-civility.html.

76. Rosenberg, *Legacy of Rage.*

77. Betty Medsger, *The Burglary: The Discovery of J. Edgar Hoover's Secret FBI* (New York: Knopf, 2014); Nelson Blackstone, *COINTELPRO: The FBI's Secret War on Political Freedom* (New York: Pathfinder, 1975). For the FBI's position, see Mark Felt and John O'Connor, *A G-Man's Life: The FBI, Being "Deep Throat," and the Struggle for Honor in Washington* (Washington, DC: Public Affairs Press, 2006).

78. Box 1, folder 3, RCP.

79. Banzhaf, "Alan Berkman Oral History," May 5, 2001.

80. McIssac, interview with Zeller.

81. Banzhaf, "Alan Berkman Oral History," May 5, 2001.

82. Clapp interview, December 22, 2014.

83. Interview with Diane Gillman Charney, New Haven, CT, February 3, 2015. Charney would finish her PhD, become a writing and French teacher at Yale, and marry a psychiatrist who shared her talent for piano playing. She now lives part of the year in Italy.

84. Apfel email to author.

85. Interview with Barbara Zeller, New York City, January 20, 2013.

86. I am always struck by how when I tell people Barbara is not Jewish, even those who have known her for years, they are amazed.

87. McIssac, interview with Zeller.

88. McIssac, interview with Zeller.

89. Zeller interview, January 20, 2013.

90. McIssac, interview with Zeller.

91. McIssac, interview with Zeller.

92. McIssac, interview with Zeller.

93. McIssac, interview with Zeller.

94. Susan M. Reverby and Marsha Love, "The Emancipation of Lincoln: A Study in Institutional Organizing," *Health/PAC Bulletin* 4 (January 1972): 1–16.

95. L.A. Kauffman, "Ending a War, Inventing a Movement: Mayday 1971, *Radical Society* 29 (December 2002): 29–49, quote on 31.

96. Kauffman, "Ending a War," 31.

97. Alan Berkman Student File, Archives and Special Collections, Health Sciences Library, Columbia University, New York City; National Board of Medical Examiners, "Score Interpretation Guide," http://www.nbme.org/Schools/Subject-Exams/reports .html.

CHAPTER 4

1. Pauline W. Chen, "The Impossible Workload for Doctors in Training," *New York Times*, April 18, 2013, http://well.blogs.nytimes.com/2013/04/18/doing-the-math-on-resident-work-hours/?_r=0; Kenneth Ludmerer, *Time to Heal* (New York: Oxford University Press, 1999), 79–101, 190–95.

2. I have a vivid memory of a discussion with my mother after the Pentagon Papers report came out in the *Times*. "You were right, you were right," she finally admitted.

3. Betty Medsger, *The Burglary: The Discovery of J. Edgar Hoover's Secret FBI* (New York: Knopf, 2014); Brian Glick, *War at Home: Covert Action against U.S. Activists and What We Can Do about It* (Boston: South End, 1989).

4. Daniel T. Rodgers, *Age of Fracture* (Cambridge, MA: Harvard University Press, 2011); Andrew Hartman, *A War for the Soul of America: A History of the Culture Wars since the Sixties* (Chicago: University of Chicago Press, 2015).

5. Dan Berger, ed., *The Hidden 1970s* (New Brunswick, NJ: Rutgers University Press, 2010).

6. Dick Clapp remembered Alan was "pretty mixed up" about the internship, but he really wanted to learn the science. Interview with Dick Clapp, Boston, December 22, 2014. All interviews cited were conducted by the author unless otherwise specified.

7. Paul L. Montgomery, "Botulism Death in Westchester Brings Hunt for Soup," *New York Times*, July 2, 1971; Boyce Rensberger, "Grim Detective Case: Search for Vichyssoise," *New York Times*, July 18, 1971.

8. John Sibley, "Vichyssoise Alert Is Issued by State," *New York Times*, July 3, 1971; Isaac Asimov, "Profile of Botulism, Rare but Deadly," *New York Times*, July 10, 1971; Harry Schwartz, "When Death Comes in a Can: Botulism," *New York Times*, July 11, 1971.

9. AP, "Bon Vivant Files for Bankruptcy," *New York Times*, July 27, 1971.

10. Walter H. Waggoner, "A Victim Recalls Bon Vivant Soup," *New York Times*, July 18, 1973.

11. Asimov, "Profile of Botulism, Rare but Deadly."

12. Dick Polman, "Tempo: Story behind the Mystery Man of the Brink's Job," *Chicago Tribune*, January 2, 1986.

13. Jackson's younger brother Jonathan had been killed the year before in an attempt to capture a judge. Angela Davis would end up on trial for murder because the guns Jonathan Jackson had were registered in her name, but she was acquitted. See Bettina Aptheker, *The Morning Breaks: The Trials of Angela Davis*, 2nd ed. (Ithaca, NY: Cornell University Press, 1999).

14. Johnny Spain, Former Inmate, KRON-Channel 4, "Day of the Gun," https://www.youtube.com/watch?v=7XRuLlwx1sw.

15. Historian Dan Berger argues that the stories of Jackson and that day at the prison are like the film *Rashomon*; see Dan Berger, *Captive Nation: Black Prison Organizing in the Civil Rights Era* (Chapel Hill: University of North Carolina Press, 2014), 133–39.

16. Bob Dylan, "George Jackson," 1971, https://revolutionaryfrontlines.wordpress.com/2011/08/21/george-jackson-a-song-by-bob-dylan-1971/.

17. Quoted in "George Jackson, 1941–1971," in *Soledad Brother: The Prison Letters of George Jackson* (New York: Coward-McCann, 1970; rpr., Chicago: Lawrence Hill, 1994), xi.

18. Alan Berkman, "Essay on Jackson, Attica and Wounded Knee," handwritten

manuscript, ca. 1991. I am grateful to Barbara Zeller, who found this after I had been through all of Alan's papers.

19. On the impact of Jackson's murder on the left, see Asha Bandele, "After the Attica Uprising," *The Nation*, September 9, 2011, http://www.thenation.com/article/163270/after-attica-uprising.

20. Tom Wicker, *A Time to Die: The Attica Prison Revolt* (New York: Quadrangle, 1975).

21. Heather Ann Thompson, *Blood in the Water: The Attica Prison Uprising in 1971 and Its Legacy* (New York: Pantheon, 2016).

22. Jeremy Levenson, "Pouring Water on a Drowning Man: Medicine, the State of New York and the Attica Prison Uprising," honors thesis, University of Pennsylvania, 2011. I am grateful to Heather Ann Thompson for providing this to me.

23. Wicker, *A Time to Die*, 286.

24. Wicker, *A Time to Die*, 289.

25. Berger, *Captive Nation*, 148.

26. Levenson, "Pouring Water on a Drowning Man," 22.

27. New York State Special Commission on Attica, *Attica: The Official Report of the New York State Special Commission on Attica* (New York: Bantam, 1972), x.

28. Berger, *Captive Nation*, 148.

29. Attica Prison Liberation Faction, "Manifesto of Demands 1971," http://libcom.org/blog/attica-prison-liberation-faction-manifesto-demands-1971-06012012; Marcia Sollek, "Attica: Murder by Omission," *Health/PAC Bulletin* (November 1971): 7–10.

30. Interview with Donna Karl, Cambridge, MA, February 4, 2015.

31. Telephone interview with Howard Levy, Brooklyn, NY, March 11, 2015. Levy, who was then working at Health/PAC, had refused, when he was in the army in 1967, to train Green Berets to use medicine against the Vietnamese. He was court-martialed and spent twenty-six months in prison for this refusal.

32. Thompson, *Blood in the Water*, is the definitive book on what happened.

33. Berkman, "Essay on Jackson, Attica and Wounded Knee." It is hard to recapture how horrified many of us on the left were about Attica and what was done to the prisoners. When I moved to West Virginia a few years later, I named our pig Nelson, after Governor Nelson Rockefeller, who had ordered the assault, so that when we butchered him I wouldn't feel bad.

34. Berkman, "Essay on Jackson, Attica and Wounded Knee."

35. Eli Messinger, "Attica Bars MCHR Medics," *Health Right News* 4 (October 1971), 1, 4.

36. Berkman, "Essay on Jackson, Attica and Wounded Knee."

37. Susan M. Reverby, "Can There Be Acceptable Prison Health Care? Looking Back at the 1970s," *Public Health Reports* 134, no. 1 (2019): 89–93.

38. Berkman, "Essay on Jackson, Attica and Wounded Knee." For a more recent assessment of prison medicine, see Scott A. Allen et al., "Physicians in US Prisons in the Era of Mass Incarceration," *International Journal of Prison Health* 6 (December 2010): 100–106; and Homer Venters, *Life and Death in Rikers Island* (Baltimore: Johns Hopkins University Press, 2019).

39. Voice-over on DVD of Dr. Alan Berkman Memorial Service, Columbia University, Mailman School of Public Health, New York City, April 23, 2010.

40. Polman, "Tempo."

41. Quoted in Jim Groosklag, "From Middletown, USA to Holmesburg Prison: The Journey of Alan Berkman and the Life of the Movement," *Undergraduate Review* 1 (1986): 53, http://digitalcommons.iwu.edu/rev/vol1/iss1/7.

42. Quentin Young, *Everybody In, Nobody Out: Memoirs of a Rebel with a Pause* (Friday Harbor, WA: Copernicus Healthcare, 2013), 120.

43. Bruce J. Shulman, *The Seventies: The Great Shift in American Culture, Society and Politics* (New York: Da Capo, 2001), 101.

44. Karl interview.

45. Polman, "Tempo."

46. Interview with Barbara Zeller, New York City, October 10, 2011.

47. Alondra Nelson, *Body and Soul: The Black Panther Party and the Fight against Medical Discrimination* (Minneapolis: University of Minnesota Press, 2011).

48. Polman, "Tempo"; BD. For visual and aural representations of the South Bronx in the 1970s, see Gary Weis, director, *80 Blocks from Tiffany's* (New York: Above Average Productions, 1979), https://www.youtube.com/watch?v=DDb8Nr_gVcw; and Johan Kugelberg, *Born in the Bronx: A Visual Record of the Early Days of Hip Hop* (New York: Rizzoli, 2007).

49. Joshua Bloom and Waldo E. Martin Jr., *Black against Empire: The History and Politics of the Black Panther Party* (Berkeley: University of California Press, 2013), 354, on the difference between guerrilla warfare and the Panther program. See also Nelson, *Body and Soul*.

50. Barbara C. Zeller, CV 2015, emailed to author, May 25, 2015.

51. Hunter Thompson, *Fear and Loathing on the Campaign Trail '72* (New York: Simon and Schuster, 1973), 316–70; Bob Simpson, "Miami Means Fight Back: 1972," *Montgomery Spark* 2 (September 6, 1972), https://washingtonspark.wordpress.com/2014/04/26/miami-means-fight-back-1972/; *Operation Last Patrol*, directed by Frank Cavestani and Catherine Leroy (1972; New York: Cinema Libre, 2005), DVD.

52. Tim Findley, "Outside the Convention: Cops and Confusion," *Rolling Stone*, September 28, 1972.

53. On a critique of the demonstrations, see Thompson, *Fear and Loathing*, 382.

54. Robert Decherd, "A Republican Roadshow Swamps Miami," *Harvard Crimson*, September 1, 1972.

55. Interview with Franklin Apfel, Brookline, MA, August 5, 2014.

56. Zeller interview.

57. Fitzhugh Mullan, *White Coat, Clenched Fist: The Political Education of an American Physician* (Ann Arbor: University of Michigan Press, 2006); Susan M. Reverby and Marsha Love, "The Emancipation of Lincoln: A Study in Institutional Organizing," *Health/PAC Bulletin* 4 (January 1972): 1–16.

58. Samuel K. Roberts, "Radical Recovery: The People's Program and the Development of Acupuncture Detoxification at Lincoln Hospital," unpublished manuscript, April 7, 2014. I am grateful to Sam Roberts for letting me read this before publication.

59. Mullan, *White Coat*; Seymour Graubard, "Press Release on ADL Report on Community Control Threat," ADL of B'nai B'rith, January 24, 1971, box 4, Lincoln folder, Michael McGarvey Papers, Archives and Special Collections, Health Sciences Library, Columbia University, New York City.

60. Henry Palmer, "Reply to Mr. Osborn," *Iatrogenia* 1 (May 12, 1969), 4, Central Records of the Office of the Vice President for Health Services, box 220, folder Fraternities, Clubs, Archives and Special Collections, Health Sciences Library, Columbia University, New York City.

61. Paul Chatt Smith and Robert Allen Warrior, *Like a Hurricane: The Indian Movement from Alcatraz to Wounded Knee* (New York: New Press, 1997), 218–68.

62. Thomas Vernon Reed, *Art of Protest: Culture and Activism from the Civil Rights Movement to the Streets of Seattle* (Minneapolis: University of Minnesota Press, 2005), 129–55.

63. Tom Wicker, "Attica and Wounded Knee," *New York Times*, March 8, 1973.

64. Akwesasne Notes, *Voices from Wounded Knee, 1973, in the Words of the Participants* (Rooseveltown, NY: Mohawk Nation, 1974).

65. Sherry L. Smith, *Hippies, Indians and the Fight for Red Power* (New York: Oxford University Press, 2014), 187.

66. See Bill Zimmerman, *Airlift to Wounded Knee* (Chicago: Swallow, 1976), 237, for a romantic view of what happened by someone who piloted food supplies in over the FBI lines.

67. Similar meetings would take place in other big cities, and other medical and nursing teams would get in.

68. "Don't Be Afraid to Say 'Revolution?,'" October 2011, Hannah Arendt Center, Bard College, http://www.hannaharendtcenter.org/?tag=public-happiness.

69. Alan Berkman, "Wounded Knee Remembered," *Spirit of Crazy Horse*, 3, n.d., ca. 1992, clipping in BP.

70. Mary Anne McEnery, "Wounded Knee: A Doctor's View," *Middletown (NY) Times Herald-Record*, April 23, 1973.

71. Telephone interview with Phyllis Prentice, Washington, DC, September 11, 2013.

72. Berkman, "Wounded Knee Remembered."

73. BD, 155–56.

74. Dr. Alan Berkman Memorial Service DVD.

75. McEnery, "Wounded Knee," 5.

76. McEnery, "Wounded Knee," 1.

77. AP Archive, "Wounded Knee Press Conference," May 31, 1973, https://www.youtube.com/watch?v=snCT37rMGTA. This version has no sound, but I was able to purchase the sound version from the AP.

78. Rolland Dewing, ed., *The FBI Files on the American Indian Movement and Wounded Knee* (Frederick, MD: University Publications of America, 1986).

79. Akwesasne Notes, *Voices from Wounded Knee*, 260.

80. "Occupation of Wounded Knee," hearings before the Subcommittee on Indian Affairs of the Committee of the Interior and Insular Affairs, United States Senate, Ninety-Third Congress, First Session, June 16, 1973.

81. Amnesty International, "Leonard Peltier," http://www.amnestyusa.org/our-work/issues/security-and-human-rights/leonard-peltier.

82. McEnery, "Wounded Knee," 5.

CHAPTER 5

1. Interview with Barbara Zeller, New York City, October 10, 2011. In the women's health movement, we shared our addresses with women from outside New York City so they could get abortions in the municipal hospitals. Other examples are from my memory of life in New York City in the late 1960s. See also Dick Polman, "Tempo: Story behind the Mystery Man of the Brink's Job," *Chicago Tribune*, January 2, 1986. All interviews cited were conducted by the author unless otherwise specified.

2. Robert K. Summers, *The Assassin's Doctor: The Life and Letters of Samuel A. Mudd*, CreateSpace Independent Publishing Platform, January 9, 2014. Berkman and his lawyer

claimed he was only the second doctor, after Mudd, to be arrested for caring for a patient. Interview with Ron Kuby, New York City, October 10, 2011.

3. Interview with Stephanie LeMelle, New York City, January 10, 2012.

4. John Castellucci, *The Big Dance* (New York: Dodd Mead, 1986), 38.

5. BD, 5–6. Whether this was the actual conversation or not is uncertain. Alan wrote much of this several decades after the actual event, but he started his own prison memoir with it.

6. BD, 7.

7. *Clark v. U.S.*, 481 F. Supp. 1086 (1979); Mark Felt and John O'Connor, *A G-Man's Life: The FBI, Being "Deep Throat," and the Struggle for Honor in Washington* (New York: Public Affairs, 2006), 261–80, on Felt's approval of, and sentencing for, the "black bag jobs" the FBI did without warrants.

8. See Ron Jacobs, *Daydream Sunset: The Sixties Counterculture in the Seventies* (Petrolia, CA: Counterpunch, 2015), for what others were doing in this period. I left New York four months after Barbara and Alan, moved with my about-to-be second husband to West Virginia, worked on my first book and on a radical journal with other political friends, did labor education, and lived on a farm for the year. It was an escape from the intensity of New York City, but also an opportunity to do political work.

9. Interview with Barbara Zeller, New York City, May 30, 2015.

10. Zeller interview, October 10, 2011. Only years later did Alan regret that he had not allowed himself to appreciate the landscapes; Alan to Sarah Zeller-Berkman, July 7, 1987.

11. Interview with Franklin Apfel, Brookline, MA, August 5, 2014.

12. Marion Banzhaf, "Alan Berkman Oral History," May 5, 2001, 1, in author's possession.

13. Interview with David Klafter, Brookline, MA, March 24, 2015.

14. Sekou Odinga, quoted in Rick Perlstein, "Ignorant Good Will: How an Excess of Idealism and the Embrace of Violence Destroyed the American Left in the 1970s," *The Nation*, July 6–13, 2015, http://www.thenation.com/article/210161/ignorant-good-will#.

15. Zeller interview, May 30, 2015.

16. Kim Phillips-Fein, *Fear City: New York's Fiscal Crisis and the Rise of Austerity Politics* (New York: Metropolitan, 2017).

17. Rick Perlstein, *Nixonland* (New York: Scribner, 2009), rpt.; Susan Faludi, *Backlash* (New York: Broadway, 2006).

18. Oscar Guardiola-Rivera, *Story of a Death Foretold: The Coup against Salvador Allende* (New York: Bloomsbury, 2013).

19. V. I. Lenin, "What Is to Be Done: Burning Questions for Our Movement," 1901–2, https://www.marxists.org/archive/lenin/works/1901/witbd/.

20. Banzhaf, "Alan Berkman Oral History," May 5, 2001, 2.

21. Banzhaf, "Alan Berkman Oral History," May 5, 2001, 2.

22. Marion Banzhaf, "Alan Berkman Oral History," April 20, 2001, 16, in author's possession.

23. Telephone interview with Steven Berkman, July 26, 2013.

24. Banzhaf, "Alan Berkman Oral History," May 5, 2001, 2.

25. On the turn toward more sectarian or underground groups on the left, see Dan Berger, *Outlaws of America: The Weather Underground and the Politics of Solidarity* (Oakland, CA: AK Press, 2006); Max Elbaum, *Revolution in the Air: Sixties Radicals Turn to Lenin, Mao, and Che* (London: Verso, 2002); Aaron J. Leonard and Conor A. Gallagher, *Heavy Radicals* (Winchester, UK: Zero, 2014); and John F. Levin and Earl Silbar, eds., *You Say You Want a Revolution* (San Francisco: 1741 Press, 2019).

26. "Weather" changed its name several times. For simplicity's sake, and to avoid numerous initials, I am just calling it Weather.

27. Historian Arthur Eckstein, email to author, July 29, 2015. Eckstein's numbers are based on his reading of the FBI files for spring 1972 for his *Bad Moon Rising: How the Weather Underground Beat the FBI and Lost the Revolution* (New Haven, CT: Yale University Press, 2016).

28. See Eckstein, email to author; Jeremy Varon, *Bringing the War Home* (Berkeley: University of California Press, 2004); and numerous memoirs of those in Weather.

29. Banzhaf, "Alan Berkman Oral History, " May 5, 2001, 5.

30. Zeller interview, May 30, 2015.

31. Dick Clapp, email to author, June 3, 2015.

32. Prisoners got "good time (time off their sentences) for blood donations." Clapp, email to author, June 3, 2015.

33. The classic history of the busing crisis in Boston remains J. Anthony Lewis, *Common Ground: A Turbulent Decade in the Lives of Three Families* (New York: Knopf, 1985); but see also Ronald P. Formisano, *Boston against Busing: Race, Class and Ethnicity in the 1960s and 1970s* (Chapel Hill: University of North Carolina Press, 1996, 2004). My husband I moved to Boston in the fall of 1974 just as the busing crisis exploded. It felt as if we had moved South at the height of the civil rights movement.

34. Mark Rudd, *Underground: My Life with SDS and the Weathermen* (New York: Harper, 2009), 263.

35. Jonah Raskin, "Looking Backward: Personal Reflections on Language, Gesture and Mythology in the Weather Underground," in *Sing a Battle Song*, edited by Bernadine Dohrn, Bill Ayers, and Jeff Jones (New York: Seven Stories, 2006), 127; interview with Jonah Raskin, Santa Rosa, CA, March 8, 2016.

36. See Rudd, *Underground*, 262.

37. Weather Underground, "Prairie Fire: The Politics of Revolutionary Anti-imperialism," in Dohrn, Ayers, and Jones, *Sing a Battle Song*, 234.

38. Interview with Dick Clapp, Boston, December 22, 2014.

39. Interviews with Stephen Wangh (Wendell, MA, April 10, 2013), Steven Krugman (Newton, MA, February 7, 2013), and Bruce Taub (Orleans, MA, February 22, 2013).

40. Interview with Steven Krugman, Newton, MA, July 1, 2015.

41. Each one of them told separately the story about that weekend, and Alan's comments about not being depressed.

42. Krugman interview, July 1, 2015.

43. Ron Jacobs, "A Second Wind for Weather Underground? The *Prairie Fire* Statement," Verso blog, November 3, 2017, https://www.versobooks.com/blogs/3469-a-second-wind-for-weather-underground-the-prairie-fire-statement.

44. Barbara Zeller does not remember if Alan went to one of the Weather cadre meetings, but housemate Dick Clapp thinks that he did. Barbara Zeller, Dick Clapp, emails to author, June 25, 2015.

45. Rudd, *Underground*, 263.

46. Larry J. Reynolds, *Righteous Violence: Revolution, Slavery and the American Renaissance* (Athens: University of Georgia Press, 2011).

47. David Gilbert, *Love and Struggle: My Life in SDS, the Weather Underground and Beyond* (Oakland, CA: PM Press, 2011), 2, 99.

48. Berger, *Outlaws of America*, 194.

49. Alan Berkman to Stephen Wangh, October 17, 1989.

50. Alan Berkman to Stephen Wangh, October 17, 1989.

51. Krugman interview, July 1, 2015.

52. On the links between anti-imperialism and black radicals in the United States, see Robin D. G. Kelley, *Freedom Dreams: The Black Radical Imagination*, 2nd ed. (Boston: Beacon, 2003), esp. 104. On the pull of these countries on white radicals, see Stephanie Urdang, *Mapping My Way Home* (New York: Monthly Review Press, 2017).

53. Alan to Stephen Wangh, October 17, 1989.

54. Samora Machel, *Samora Machel, an African Revolutionary: Selected Speeches and Writings*, edited by Barry Munslow (London: Zed, 1985); Iain Christie, *Samora Machel: A Biography* (London: Zed, 1989).

55. Berkman to Wangh, October 17, 1989.

56. Anne-Emanuelle Birn and Theodore Brown, eds., *Comrades in Health: U.S. Health Internationalists, Abroad and at Home* (New Brunswick, NJ: Rutgers University Press, 2013); see also Lise Vogel, "Sidney Vogel: Spanish Civil War Surgeon," *American Journal of Public Health* 98 (December 2008): 2147.

57. Joshua Horn, *Away with All Pests: An English Surgeon in People's China* (New York: Monthly Review Press, 1970); Victor W. Sidel, *Serve the People: Observations on Medicine in the People's Republic of China* (Boston: Beacon, 1974).

58. Paul Epstein, a physician who had been in the Cornell class of 1965, and his wife, Andy, a nurse, would take their small children to work in 1978 in Mozambique after the revolution; see Paul R. Epstein and Dan Ferber, *Changing Planet, Changing Health* (Berkeley: University of California Press, 2011), 6–28. Epstein, who died in 2013, would go on to be an international leader in linking global warming to health concerns and would found an institute on this at Harvard's School of Public Health. Alan knew both Andy and Paul in Boston, although neither of them was in his direct political circles. Interview with Andy Epstein, Brookline, MA, April 12, 2015.

59. Barbara Zeller, CV 2015, emailed to author, May 25, 2015.

60. Alan Berkman, "Chronology," ca. 1998, edited by Barbara Zeller, 2011, BP.

61. Hasan Kwame Jeffries, *Bloody Lowndes: Civil Rights and Black Power in Alabama's Black Belt* (New York: NYU Press, 2009).

62. Jeffries, *Bloody Lowndes*, 237; J. M. McFadden, "Lowndes County Gets Pilot Project," *Washington Post*, April 6, 1967; Richard A. Couto, *Ain't Gonna Let Nobody Turn Me Around: The Pursuit of Racial Justice in the Rural South* (Philadelphia: Temple University Press, 1991), 83.

63. Jeff Hansen and Carla Crowder, "Bleak Diagnosis for Sickly Region," *Birmingham (AL) News*, November 17, 2002. By 2013, the Robert Wood Johnson Foundation claimed it was the worst county in the state for health care; "Lowndes County at Bottom in Statewide Health Rankings," *Equal Justice Initiative*, April 11, 2013, http://www.eji.org/node/761.

64. Couto, *Ain't Gonna Let Nobody Turn Me Around*, 83–118.

65. Berkman, "Chronology"; Alice Sardell, *The U.S. Experiment in Social Medicine: The Community Health Center Program, 1965–1986* (Pittsburgh: University of Pittsburgh Press, 1988), 108–17; WIC, U.S. Department of Agriculture, http://www.fns.usda.gov/wic/women-infants-and-children-wic; Couto, *Ain't Gonna Let Nobody Turn Me Around*, 112–13.

66. Couto, *Ain't Gonna Let Nobody Turn Me Around*, 280. Unfortunately, Couto does not identify the issue that led to the threat.

67. See Susan M. Reverby, *Examining Tuskegee: The Infamous Syphilis Study and Its*

Legacy (Chapel Hill: University of North Carolina Press, 2009). Alan and I discussed this in person in 1994 just as I was beginning my work on the study.

68. Joshua Newman, "Alan Berkman," unpublished paper, n.d. Newman was the son of Alan's high school theater teacher Hank Newman and his wife, Sharon. The paper was written while Alan was in prison and through correspondence and phone calls. It is one of the few places where Alan discusses his experience in Lowndes County.

69. Polman, "Tempo." See also Charles E. Cobb Jr., *This Nonviolent Stuff'll Get You Killed: How Guns Made the Civil Rights Movement Possible* (New York: Basic Books, 2014).

70. Polman, "Tempo."

71. Klafter interview; interview with Russell Neufeld, New York City, April 1, 2013; interview with Dana Biberman, New York City, April 4, 2013.

72. Berkman to Wangh, October 17, 1989.

73. Interview with Terry Bisson, San Francisco, March 7, 2016.

74. Interview with Stephanie LeMelle, New York City, January 12, 2012. See also George M. Hauser, "Meeting Africa's Challenge: The Story of the American Committee on Africa," *Issue: A Journal of Opinion* 6 (Summer–Autumn 1976): 16–26.

75. Interview with Shelley Miller, New York City, April 19, 2015.

76. Interview with Dana Biberman, New York City, April 20, 2015.

77. Biberman interview, April 20, 2015.

78. Interview with Barbara Zeller, New York City, January 20, 2013.

79. Sharon Daniel de Diaz, "Beyond Rhetoric: The NENA Health Center after One Year," *American Journal of Public Health* (January 1972): 64–68.

80. Des Callan and Oli Fein, "NENA: Community Control in a Bind," *Health/PAC Bulletin* (June 1972), 4. See also Merlin Chowkwanyun, "Biocitizenship on the Ground: Health Activism and the Medical Governance Revolution," in *Biocitizenship: The Politics of Bodies, Governance, and Power,* edited by Kelley E. Happe, Jenell Johnson, and Marina Levina (New York: NYU Press, 2018), 178–203.

81. Betances Health Unit, Inc. and Betances Health Unit Staff Association, Case 2-CA-17628, March 30, 1987, Decision and Order, *Decisions of the National Labor Relations Board,* 369–90. Alan was fired in 1980; the final decision did not come down until 1987.

82. Zeller interview, January 20, 2013.

83. Dan Berger, *Outlaws of America,* 225–43; Gilbert, *Love and Struggle,* 210–17.

84. Berger, *Outlaws of America,* 228; Eckstein, *Bad Moon Rising,* 215–16.

85. Barbara Zeller, email to author, February 28, 2019.

86. Berger, *Outlaws of America,* 229.

87. Interview with Eve Rosahn, New York City, March 14, 2014.

88. During the 2016 presidential primary season, Bernie Sanders, as a self-defined democratic socialist, running what he called a "political revolution," was confronted by women organizers of the #Black Lives Matter movement and denounced for his failure to focus on racism and their leadership. It seemed to one commentator as if this question of the "primacy of race or class in progressive politics" had gone on "forever." See Scot Nakagawa, "The Bernie Sanders Kerfuffle, #blacklives matter, and White Progressive Colorblindness," *Race Files,* August 13, 2015, http://www.racefiles.com/2015/08/13/the-bernie-sanders-kerfuffle-blacklivesmatter-and-white-progressive-colorblindess/; Toure Reed, "Why Liberals Separate Race from Class," *Jacobin Magazine,* August 22, 2015, https://www.jacobinmag.com/2015/08/bernie-sanders-black-lives-matter-civil-rights-movement.

89. Neufeld interview.

90. On the similarity to rectification in China, see David Cheng Chang, "Review: Gao Hua, How Did the Red Sun Rise over Yan'an? A History of the Rectification Movement," *China Review International* 15 (December 2008): 515–21.

91. Eckstein, *Bad Moon Rising*, 214–16. See Berger, *Outlaws of America*, 225–43, on the details of rectification.

92. Berkman to Steven Wangh, October 17, 1989.

93. Alan Berkman, "Self Criticisms from the National Committee," *PFOC: A Single Spark: Internal Newsletter of the Prairie Fire Organizing Committee*, no. 1, May 1976, 8.

94. Eve Rosahn, "Our Program: Half the Sky," in *PFOC: A Single Spark*, 37; on Laura Whitehorn's mistakes with Alan, see Rosahn, 21. Different members of the national committee for the conference, including Alan, wrote the "Our Program" article to explain their errors.

95. Penny Grillos, "New York," in *PFOC: A Single Spark*, no. 1 (May 1976), 31.

96. Rosahn, "Our Program: Half the Sky," 36.

97. Chokwe Lumumba, "Short History of the U.S. War on the R.N.A.," *Black Scholar* 12 (January/February 1981): 72–81; Donald Cunnigen, "Bringing the Revolution Down Home: The Republic of New Africa in Mississippi," *Sociological Spectrum* 19 (November 2010): 63–92.

98. Rosahn interview; Neufeld interview; interview with Nancy Ryan, Cambridge, MA, January 7, 2014.

99. Neufeld interview; interview with Jennifer Dohrn, New York City, April 22, 2015.

100. Interview with Dana Biberman, New York, April 26, 2013; Jennifer Dohrn interview.

101. Klafter interview.

102. Ryan interview.

103. Russell Neufeld, *PFOC: A Single Spark*, 16.

104. Neufeld interview. Neufeld subsequently went to law school and has become an internationally known anti–death penalty attorney. His lawyer brother, Peter Neufeld, runs the Innocence Project, which uses DNA evidence to exonerate those falsely convicted and imprisoned.

105. Interview with Barbara Zeller, New York City, April 23, 2015.

106. Interview with Laura Whitehorn, New York City, January 21, 2013.

107. For a critique of this turn, see Jesse Lemisch, "Weather Underground Rises from the Ashes: They're Baack!" *New Politics* 11 (Summer 2006): 7–13.

108. Interview with Susan Rosenberg, New York City, March 28, 2013.

109. Rosenberg interview.

110. Interview with Marion Banzhaf, Tallahassee, FL, April 2, 2016.

CHAPTER 6

1. Interview with Nancy Ryan, Cambridge, MA, October 6, 2013. All interviews cited were conducted by the author unless otherwise specified.

2. Alan Berkman, "July 4th," *PFOC: A Single Spark: Internal Newsletter of the Prairie Fire Organizing Committee*, No. 1, May 1976, 41.

3. Andrew Feffer, "Show Down in Center City: Staging Redevelopment and Citizenship in Bicentennial Philadelphia, 1974–1977," *Journal of Urban History* 30 (September 2004): 791–825, quotation on 811.

4. Feffer, "Show Down in Center City," 817.

5. Dohrn was the sister of Weather leader Bernadine Dohrn and was deeply involved in Weather and PFOC actions as well.

6. Interview with Russell Neufeld, New York City, April 1, 2013; interview with Jennifer Dohrn, New York City, April 22, 2015.

7. Interview with Shelley Miller, New York City, April 19, 2015.

8. Interview with Susan Rosenberg, New York City, March 28, 2013.

9. Interview with Barbara Zeller, New York City, April 23, 2015.

10. Mary Patten, *Revolution as an Eternal Dream: The Exemplary Failure of the Madame Binh Graphics Collective* (Chicago: Half Letter, 2011), 1. On the West Coast, the group led by Clayton Van Lydegraf continued to be called PFOC. For more details on this, see Berger, *Outlaws of America: The Weather Underground and the Politics of Solidarity* (Oakland, CA: AK Press, 2006), 238–43.

11. In his history of the George Jackson Brigade on the West Coast, Daniel Burton-Rose makes this argument about to whom such groups were speaking; see his *Guerrilla-USA: The George Jackson Brigade and the Anticapitalist Underground of the 1970s* (Berkeley: University of California Press, 2010), 38. On similar groups in the 1970s, see Dan Berger, ed., *The Hidden 1970s* (New Brunswick, NJ: Rutgers University Press, 2010); and Max Elbaum, *Revolution in the Air: Sixties Radicals Turn to Lenin, Mao, and Che* (London: Verso, 2002).

12. New York Office to Director, June 27, 1983, "May 19th Communist Organization," NW 407000, DocID: 3430241, PDF 3, 48, FBI M19, Batch 1. I filed a Freedom of Information Act (FOIA) request for these documents from the National Archives in 2013 and received the first batch in April 2019 and the second batch in October 2019.

13. Interview with Nancy Ryan, Cambridge, MA, January 7, 2014.

14. Interview with Laura Whitehorn, New York City, April 2, 2013.

15. Interview with Susan Rosenberg, New York City, January 26, 2016. See also Susan Rosenberg, *An American Radical* (New York: Citadel, 2011).

16. Alan Berkman, "Chronology," ca. 1998, edited by Barbara Zeller, 2011, BP.

17. Berkman to Wangh, October 17, 1989.

18. Ryan interview, January 7, 2014; interview with Barbara Zeller, New York City, January 20, 2013.

19. Miller interview.

20. Zeller interview, January 20, 2013.

21. Ryan interview, January 7, 2014.

22. Miller interview.

23. Ryan interview, January 7, 2014.

24. Ryan interview, January 7, 2014; interview with Dana Biberman, New York City, April 26, 2013.

25. May 19th Communist Organization, "Principles of Unity," n.d., ca. 1977.

26. May 19th, "Principles of Unity," 1.

27. Rosenberg interview, January 26, 2016; interview with Marion Banzhaf, Tallahassee, FL, April 2, 2016; "Fighting RICO: An Interview with Silvia Baraldini," *Death to the Klan! Newspaper of the John Brown Anti-Klan Committee*, July–August 1983.

28. See press releases and newsletters from Moncada Library, FA.

29. Leslie Albrecht, "Brownstone That Spurred Park Slope Gentrification for Sale for $4.8 Million," *DNAinfo*, September 19, 2013, http://www.dnainfo.com/new-york/20130919/park-slope/brownstone-that-spurred-park-slope-gentrification-for-sale-for-49-million.

30. "Koch=SCAN=KKK: Out of Park Slope!," *Moncada Library Newsletter,* February 1981.

31. Patten, *Revolution as an Eternal Dream,* 36.

32. Patten, *Revolution as an Eternal Dream,* 12.

33. Patten, *Revolution as an Eternal Dream,* 11.

34. Patten, *Revolution as an Eternal Dream,* 21.

35. Patten, *Revolution as an Eternal Dream,* 39.

36. There is no membership list. This is the number historian Dan Berger uses in *Outlaws of America,* 239, and Patten repeats in *Revolution as an Eternal Dream,* 11.

37. Ryan interview, January 7, 2014; Miller interview.

38. On the importance of prison organizing, see Dan Berger, *Captive Nation: Black Prison Organizing in the Civil Rights Era* (Chapel Hill: University of North Carolina Press, 2014).

39. Ruth Wilson Gilmore, *Golden Gulag* (Berkeley: University of California Press, 2009); Michelle Alexander, *The New Jim Crow* (New York: New Press, 2012); Heather Ann Thompson, "Why Mass Incarceration Matters: Rethinking Crisis, Decline, and Transformation in Postwar American History," *Journal of American History* 97 (December 2010): 703–34.

40. "New York KKK," *Midnight Special* (June 1973); Halia Siwatu Hodari (slave name Frank Alney), John Brown Anti-Klan Committee, "An Open Letter," June 1, 1977, in Anti-Klan Press Packet, FA.

41. For example, see Tom Wicker, "Catch 22 behind Bars," *New York Times,* May 22, 1979. The *New York Times, New York Post,* and *Daily News* covered the stories, as well as the Middletown paper; see People's Party, Napanoch, "KKK Attacks at Napanoch Fact Sheet," 1976 Press Clippings, John Brown Anti-Klan Committee, FA. See also Juanita Diaz-Cotton, *Gender, Ethnicity and the State: Latina and Latino Prison Politics* (New York: SUNY Press, 1996); and Berger, *Captive Nation.*

42. See Hilary Moore and James Tracy, *No Fascist USA: The Story of the John Brown Anti-Klan Committee* (San Francisco: City Lights / Open Media, 2019).

43. New York John Brown Anti-Klan Committee, "The Ku Klux Klan: Yesterday, Today, One Long Reign of Terror," n.d., FA.

44. May 19th Communist Organization, "War in Amerika, 1981, Fight White Supremacy, Support the Black Liberation Army," 4.

45. I am grateful to James Tracy, coauthor of a book on the JBAKC (Moore and Tracy, *No Fascist USA*), for his comments on this section.

46. Sally Avery Bermanzohn, *Through Survivors' Eyes* (Nashville: Vanderbilt University Press, 2003).

47. *Death to the Klan! Newspaper of the John Brown Anti-Klan Committee,* November 1979, 6, 11.

48. Interview with Beth Sommers, Cambridge, MA, August 5, 2015.

49. Sommers interview; Miller interview.

50. FBI, Letterhead Memorandum, "John Brown Anti-Klan Committee (JBAKC), Domestic Security," Chicago, September 29, 1982, PDF 2, 74–93, FBI M19, Batch 1.

51. FBI, Letterhead Memorandum, 82.

52. Banzhaf interview.

53. "2000 Demonstrated against Klan in Austin," *Death to the Klan! Newspaper of the John Brown Anti-Klan Committee,* April–May 1983, 1, freedomarchives.org/Documents /Finder/DOC37_scans/37.dttk.apr83.pdf.

54. Banzhaf interview.

55. Michael Ceteway Tabor, *Capitalism Plus Dope Equals Genocide* (New York: Black Panther Party, 1970), 1; see also the more scholarly Alfred McCoy, Cathleen B. Read, and Leonard P. Adams *The Politics of Heroin in Southeast Asia* (New York: Harper and Row, 1972); and the famed film *The French Connection* (1971), which tied the smuggling to the New York City narcotics detectives. This analysis comes from Samuel K. Roberts, "Radical Recovery: The People's Program and the Development of Acupuncture Detoxification at Lincoln Hospital," unpublished manuscript, April 7, 2014, 15. See also "Editorial: Who Benefits from the American Drug Culture?" *Health/PAC Bulletin* (June 1970), 1–2.

56. Alondra Nelson, *Body and Soul: The Black Panther Party and the Fight against Medical Discrimination* (Minneapolis: University of Minnesota Press, 2011); Susan Reverby and Marsha Love, "The Emancipation of Lincoln: A Study in Institutional Organizing," *Health/PAC Bulletin* 4 (January 1972): 1–16; Constance Bloomfield, "Detox: Clearing Their Heads," *Health/PAC Bulletin* 4 (January 1972): 8–9.

57. Miguel Mickey Melendez, "'The Butcher Shop': Lincoln Hospital," *We Took the Streets* (New York: St. Martin's, 2003), 162–78.

58. Melendez, "The Butcher Shop." See National Acupuncture Detoxification Association, "About NADA," http://www.acudetox.com/About-nada. There was also a pediatrics collective at Lincoln, beginning in 1970, that formed an alliance between young white doctors and the mothers of their patients; see Reverby and Love, "Emancipation of Lincoln"; Fitzhugh Mullan, *White Coat, Clenched Fist: The Political Education of an American Physician* (New York: Macmillan, 1976); and William L. Claiborne, "U.S. Methadone Role Scored," *Washington Post*, May 14, 1972; interview with Franklin Apfel, Brookline, MA, August 5, 2014; Jennifer Dohrn interview; Rosenberg interview; Mutulu Shakur, "The Politics of Drugs: A Skills for Justice Interview," August 9, 2011, http://mutulushakur.com/site/2011/08/skills-for-justice-interview/. Dohrn was then married to Mickey Melendez, one of the leaders of the Young Lords and the father of her children; see Melendez, *We Took the Streets*.

59. Jennifer Dohrn interview.

60. Taft's death was seen as either an overdose or a murder by political factions; see Michael Smith, "The Lilly Connection: Drug Abuse and the Medical Profession," *Science for the People* 10 (January–February 1979): 8–15. There never was a proper autopsy; see John Castellucci, *The Big Dance* (New York: Dodd Mead, 1986), 73. On Dohrn's statements, see Castellucci, *The Big Dance*, 74; and *Clark v. U.S.*, 481 F. Supp. 1086 (1979).

61. Apfel interview; Charlayne Hunter, "Young Doctor at Lincoln: Disillusion and Departure," *New York Times*, August 16, 1976.

62. Barbara C. Zeller, curriculum vitae.

63. Ronald Sullivan, "Leaders of Drug Unit at Lincoln Removed on Orders from Koch," *New York Times*, November 29, 1978; John L. Potash, *Drugs as Weapons against Us* (Walterville, OR: Trine Day, 2014), 265.

64. Dan Berger, "'Free the Land!' Fifty Years of the Republic of New Afrika," African American Intellectual History Society, *Black Perspectives*, April 10, 2018, https://www.aaihs.org/free-the-land-fifty-years-of-the-republic-of-new-afrika/.

65. P. Frank Williams, *American Gangster Mutulu Shakur*, Black Entertainment Television (BET), 2008, https://vimeo.com/48150647. The short film made for television is sympathetic to Shakur, despite its title.

66. See "Mutulu Shakur, New African Political Prisoner," *Can't Jail the Spirit: Political*

Prisoners in the U.S. (Chicago, El Coqui, n.d.), 93–95; Mutulu Shakur, "Code of THUG LIFE," August 23, 1992, http://mutulushakur.com/site/1992/08/code-of-thug-life/.

67. Interview with Barbara Zeller, New York City August 20, 2015.

68. "Courses in Acupuncture," *New York Amsterdam News*, May 23, 1981; http://www.mutulushakur.org.

69. Paul McIssac, interview with Barbara Zeller, New York City, November 14, 1992. I am grateful to Paul McIssac for sharing his Zeller interview tapes with me. I did the transcriptions.

70. Akinyele Omowale Umoja, "Repression Breeds Resistance: The Black Liberation Army and the Radical Legacy of the Black Panther Party," in *Liberation, Imagination and the Black Panther Party*, edited by Kathleen Cleaver and George Katsiaficas (New York: Routledge, 2001), 3–20; William Rosenau, "'Our Backs Are against the Wall': The Black Liberation Army and Domestic Terrorism in 1970s America," *Studies in Conflict and Terrorism* 36 (January 2013): 176–92.

71. Joshua Bloom and Waldo E. Martin Jr., *Black against Empire: The History and Politics of the Black Panther Party* (Berkeley: University of California Press, 2013), 159.

72. A pro-police website lists all the police supposedly killed by the BLA and the Black Panthers separately even if its headline does not differentiate; see "Meet the Police Officers Murdered by the Black Panthers," *The Professional Gunfighter: Mindset, Training and Equipment for Those Who Go in Harm's Way*, https://progunfighter.com/murdered-by-the-black-panthers/. Their list, however, runs up until 2000, when most of the BLA was finished by the early 1980s.

73. There are historical problems with all of the literature on the Black Liberation Army in terms of both facts and analysis. For a sampling, see Jalil Muntaqim, "On the Black Liberation Army" (Montreal: Guillen Press and Arm the Spirit, 1997), originally printed in the newsletter *Arm the Spirit*, September 18, 1979; Bryan Burroughs, *Days of Rage: America's Radical Underground, the FBI, and the Forgotten Age of Revolutionary Violence* (New York: Penguin, 2015); Dan Berger, *Outlaws of America: The Weather Underground and the Politics of Solidarity* (Oakland, CA: AK Press, 2006); and Umoja, "Repression Breeds Resistance." For the perspective of law enforcement, see Rosenau, "Our Backs Are against the Wall."

74. Nicky Barnes, a Harlem drug kingpin, recalls in his lurid autobiography that the police thought he was in the BLA; see *Mr. Untouchable: The Rise, Fall, and Resurrection of Heroin's Teflon Don* (New York: Rugged Land, 2007), 19.

75. Burroughs, *Days of Rage*, 457. Kersplebedeb, ed., *Kuwasi Balagoon: A Soldier's Story* (Montreal: Kersplebedeb, 2003), 54.

76. Akinyele Omowale Umoja, *We Will Shoot Back: Armed Resistance in the Mississippi Freedom Movement* (New York: NYU Press, 2014); Charles Cobb, *This Nonviolent Stuff'll Get You Killed* (Durham, NC: Duke University Press, 2015); Garrett Felber, *Those Who Know Don't Say: The Nation of Islam, the Black Freedom Movement and the Carceral State* (Chapel Hill: University of North Carolina Press, 2020).

77. Historians and participants differ on the BLA's origins, whether it came after the founding of the Black Panther Party and was part of its operations, hiding those too "hot" to stay public and willing to do armed struggles, or whether it was a loose group of militants that predated the founding of the Panthers;, see Umoja, "Repression Breeds Resistance," 7.

78. There are multiple histories and memoirs of the Black Panthers. The most recent comprehensive history is Bloom and Martin, *Black against Empire*.

79. Christian Davenport, *How Social Movements Die: Repression and Demobilization of the Republic of New Africa* (New York: Cambridge University Press, 2015).

80. M. A. Farber, "Behind the Brink's Case: Return of the Radical Left," *New York Times*, February 16, 1982.

81. Akinyele K. Umoja argues that some of the BLA anger in the late 1970s and early 1980s came from "an increase in violent acts against Black people . . . , including the murders of Black children and youth in Atlanta and Black women in Boston, and shootings of Black women in Alabama; Umoja, "Maroon: Kuwasi Balagoon and the Evolution of Revolutionary New Afrikan Anarchism," *Science & Society* 79 (April 2015), 214.

82. Sekou Odinga, quoted in Sundiata Acoli, "Brink's Trial Testimony" pamphlet (New York: Rita Squire, 1984), 50.

83. Black Liberation Army, *The Soul of the Black Liberation Army* (Chicago: Julian Richardson Associates, 1981).

84. Black Liberation Army, *The Soul of the Black Liberation Army*, iii, 22.

85. Dan Berger, "Marilyn Buck's Playlist," *Polygraph* 23/24 (2013): 111–15.

86. Burroughs, *Days of Rage*, 458. Burroughs interviewed Silvia Baraldini in Italy for his book, but many of his sources have proven to be unreliable. Buck died in 2010; see below.

87. Evelyn A. Williams, *Inadmissible Evidence* (Brooklyn, NY: Lawrence Hill, 1993); Assata Shakur, *Assata: An Autobiography* (Brooklyn, NY: Lawrence Hill, 1987).

88. Police still refer to her as a "cop killer"; see Sandy Malone, "Jet Blue Promotes FBI Most Wanted Terrorist to Celebrate Black History Month," *Blue Lives Matter*, February 22, 2019, https://defensemaven.io/bluelivesmatter/news/jetblue-promotes-fbi-most-wanted-terrorist-to-celebrate-black-history-month-wyYou-T5TEaD9IjrFaMkEw/.

89. *U.S. v. Baraldini*, 803 F. 2d 776 (2nd Cir. 1986); Margalit Fox, "Marilyn Buck, Imprisoned for Brink's Holdup, Dies at 62," *New York Times*, August 5, 2010, https://www.nytimes.com/2010/08/06/nyregion/06buck.html.

90. Mary Patten explains that the women of the Madame Binh Collective designed and distributed it; see Patten, *Revolution as an Eternal Dream*, 25. Poster at Oakland Museum of California. http://collections.museumca.org/?q=collection-item/2010547354.

91. The authorities still call her Chesmiard, while others see her as a forerunner heroine of the current Black Lives Matter movement; see Donna Murch, *Assata Taught Me* (Chicago: Haymarket, 2020).

92. Silvia Baraldini, "Fighting RICO: An Interview with Silvia Baraldini," *Death to the Klan: Newspaper of the John Brown Anti-Klan Committee*, July–August 1983.

93. Michael M. Roche, "Protest, Police and Place: The 1981 Springbok Tour and the Production and Consumption of Social Space," *New Zealand Geographer* 53 (October 1997): 50–57; Philip K. Hamlin, "The 1981 Springbok Tour of New Zealand," *Auckland University Law Review* 5 (1982): 313–25; Anti-Springbok 5 Defense Committee, "The Struggle against Apartheid Is the Struggle for World Peace," November 27, 1981, Freedom Archive, http://freedomarchives.org/Documents/Finder/DOC53_scans/53.Springbok5.StatementUN.pdf.

94. Telephone interview with Mary Patten, September 27, 2015.

95. Anti-Springbok 5 Defense Committee, "The Struggle against Apartheid," 1; "Springbok Protest Injures Policeman," *New York Times*, September 28, 1981.

96. *Bizen v. Port Authority of States of New York & N.J.*, 577 F. Supp. 1093, U.S. District Court, July 8, 1983, Nos. 82 Civ 0417, 82 CIV 0513, http://www.leagle.com/decision/19831670577FSupp1093_11477/BIZIEN%20v.%20PORT%20AUTHORITY%20OF%20STATES%20OF%20NEW YORK%20&%20N.J; Dan Collins, "The Rest of the Flight's 201

Passengers Had Already ...," *UPI*, September 28, 1981, http://www.upi.com/Archives /1981/09/28/The-rest-of-the-flights-201-passengers-had-already/9834370497600/.

97. For current instructions on how to make a stink bomb, used by others in the antiwar movement over the years, see the YouTube video, https://www.youtube.com/watch?v =18K1wQv59h8.

98. Patten interview; telephone interview with Eve Rosahn, September 15, 2015.

99. Rosahn interview.

100. Feminist activist Janis C. Kelly had gone to college and worked with Borup. Horrified when she found out in 2013 that Borup was still at large for what she had done at the airport, Kelly wrote "The Terrorist," as a public post on *Facebook*, April 4, 2013, https:// www.facebook.com/JanisCKelly/posts/581703688515535.

101. Port Authority Press Release, "The Port Authority Offers Reward of Up to $20,000 for Information Leading to the Arrest of a Fugitive Who Partially Blinded a PA Police Officer in 1981," September 26, 2013, http://www.panynj.gov/press-room/press-item .cfm?headLine_id=1832; AP, "Springboks in NEW YORK, Departure Kept Secret," *Fredericksburg (VA) Free Lance-Star*, September 28, 1981.

102. Anti-Springbok 5 Defense Committee, press statement, March 19, 1982, FA, http:// freedomarchives.org/Documents/Finder/DOC53_scans/53.antispringbok5.march .19.1982.pdf.

103. Ryan interview, January 7, 2017.

104. Mara Bovsun, "Justice Story: FALN Bomb Kills 4 at Fraunces Tavern, Where George Washington Said Farewell to Troops," *New York Daily News*, January 21, 2012, http://www.nydailynews.com/new-york/justice-story-faln-bomb-kills-4-fraunces-tavern -george-washington-farewell-troops-article-1.1008711; Neil MacFarquhar, "Clemency Opens Old Scars for Sons of Bombing Victim," *New York Times*, August 23, 1999, http:// www.nytimes.com/1999/08/23/nyregion/clemency-opens-old-scars-for-sons-of -bombing-victim.html.

105. William Morales/Ron Kuby interview on Cuba Report, *Democracy Now Global News Radio*, January 3, 1998, http://ia902307.us.archive.org/22/items/dn1998-0102 /dn1998-0102-1_64kb.mp3.

106. Marion Banzhaf, "Alan Berkman Oral History," November 2, 2001, in author's possession.

107. Banzhaf, "Alan Berkman Oral History."

108. Selwyn Rabb, "A Maimed Terrorist Flees Cell at Bellevue," *New York Times*, May 22, 1979.

109. Selwyn Rabb, "Wife of Morales Sought by Police for Questioning," *New York Times*, May 23, 1979. I measured two meters of elastic bandage wrapped around my waist, and found it stretched another meter. Whether it would hold my weight if I were hanging out a window was not an experiment I attempted. With ten feet of elastic, Morales could have lowered himself nearly fifteen feet down, adding another ten feet at most for the sheets, he would have had to drop about fifteen more feet or almost two stories of a New York building.

110. Alan Yuhas, "Cuba-US Thaw Brings Fate of Cold War–Era Fugitives on the Island into Focus," *The Guardian*, April 21, 2015, http://www.theguardian.com/world/2015/apr /21/cuba-us-thaw-fugitives-william-morales.

111. Yuhas, "Cuba-US Thaw."

112. Banzhaf, "Alan Berkman Oral History." The FBI records on May 19th repeatedly reference Alan's purported role in Morales's escape, assuming that Alan had cased the

hospital and given Morales the information. Freddie Mendez, a member of the FALN, turned and gave information to the FBI; see FBI, Teletype to Director Priority fr FBI New York, May 12, 1982, PDF 1, FBI M19, Batch 2, pp. 188–90. Present-day terrorism experts believe the FBI's claim that Alan was involved; see Hahn/Smith/Reverby email correspondence, April 11–17, 2015.

113. Robert McG. Thomas Jr., "16 in Correction Posts Accused of Negligence in Escape by Morales," *New York Times*, December 17, 1979.

114. Banzhaf, "Alan Berkman Oral History."

115. I am grateful to Susan Rosenberg for suggesting who might have actually written the letter, since Morales's lack of hands obviously would have made this impossible.

116. William Morales to Alan Berkman, April 22, 1979.

117. Alan Berkman Reminiscence of Guillermo (William) Morales, "International Campaign Supports Asylum for William Morales," *Free Puerto Rico! New Movement in Solidarity with Puerto Rican Independence and Socialism*, Summer 1996, 4–5, BL personal collection.

CHAPTER 7

1. Alan Berkman to Barbara Zeller, March 27, 1988.

2. Gil Troy, *The Reagan Revolution* (New York: Oxford University Press, 2009); Peggy Noonan, *What I Saw at the Revolution: A Political Life in the Reagan Era* (New York: Random House, 1990).

3. Marion Banzhaf, "Alan Berkman Oral History," New York City, November 2, 2001, in author's possession.

4. Mark Felt and John O'Connor, *A G-Man's Life: The FBI, Being "Deep Throat," and the Struggle for Honor in Washington* (Washington, DC: Public Affairs Press, 2006); Tim Weiner, *Enemies: A History of the FBI* (New York: Random House, 2012), 339–41.

5. Marion Banzhaf, "Alan Berkman Oral History," November 1, 2001, in author's possession.

6. Meg Starr, "Some Reflections on an Unpublished Poem," in *Kuwasi Balagoon: A Soldier's Story*, edited by Kersplebedeb (Montreal: Kersplebedeb, 2003), 17.

7. Starr, "Some Reflections."

8. I am grateful to historian Arthur Eckstein on this point.

9. Marion Banzhaf, "Alan Berkman Oral History," May 5, 2001, in author's possession.

10. Banzhaf, "Alan Berkman Oral History," May 5, 2001.

11. Interview with Dana Biberman, New York City, April 20, 2015; interview with Barbara Zeller, New York City, January 24, 2016. All interviews cited were conducted by the author unless otherwise specified.

12. Gilda Zwerman, "Mothering on the Lam," *Feminist Review* 17 (Summer 1994): 33–56. Clark's name is not given, but the internal evidence makes it clear who she is; see esp. 51. I had a copy of that poster on my office wall for decades.

13. Judith Clark, "'So Here I Am,'" in *Red Diapers: Growing up in the Communist Left*, edited by Judy Kaplan and Linn Shapiro (Urbana: University of Illinois Press, 1998), 303–7. The term refers to children of Communist Party members.

14. Affidavit of Judith Clark, December 2002, 3, www.judithclark.org (accessed April 2018, no longer available).

15. Information on Judith Clark's history came from her website, www.judithclark.org,

which is no longer available; "Targets of FBI Crimes Charge Collusion in Trial," *Black News* 4 (February 1979): 5.

16. *Clark v. United States*, 481 F. Supp. 1086 (1979); AP, "Funds from Accord on a Suit Go to Bail for Brink's Suspect," *New York Times*, December 24, 1982.

17. Interview with Judith Clark, Bedford Hills, NY, April 3, 2013.

18. Interview with Harriet Clark, San Francisco, March 5, 2016.

19. I remember a number of male friends doing this for ex-girlfriends who had become lesbians in the 1970s.

20. Zeller interview, January 24, 2016; Ralph Blumenthal, "FBI Wiretaps: An Ear on the Brink's Case," *New York Times*, August 9, 1982.

21. The story becomes even more poignant. Several years later when Clark accidently re-met the man, he was dying of AIDS. In 1979 when she was trying to get pregnant, there was no knowledge of the virus, or testing for the disease. Harriet Clark interview.

22. Zeller interview, January 24, 2016. Seventy-five dollars was probably about three-quarters of what Judy Clark would have been making a week at that time. Sperm vials are now about $790, according to the California Cryobank, email February 25, 2016. I am grateful to Rosanna Hertz for supplying this information.

23. Interview with Shelley Miller, New York City, April 19, 2015.

24. Interview with David Klafter, Brookline, MA, March 24, 2015.

25. On revolutionary Puerto Rican groups in Chicago, see Ronald Fernandez, *Prisoners of Colonialism: The Struggle for Justice in Puerto Rico* (Monroe, ME: Common Courage, 1994), 143–95. Biberman interview, April 20, 2015.

26. FBI, "May 19th Communist Organization," NW 407000, DocID: 3430241, PDF 1–3, FBI M19, Batch 1.

27. Ronald Fernandez, *Los Macheteros: The Wells Fargo Robbery and the Violent Struggle for Puerto Rican Independence* (New York: Prentice Hall, 1987), 52–65; Weiner, *Enemies*, 331–33, 346, 335, 440. The FBI files I received from the National Archives, Washington, DC, also confirm this focus on the Puerto Rican independence groups.

28. Interview with Liz Horowitz, New York City, October 15, 2015; Miller interview. The FBI tracked both Horowitz and Miller in Chicago; see FBI M19, Batches 1 and 2.

29. Zeller interview, January 24, 2016.

30. Paul McIssac, interview with Barbara Zeller, New York City, November 12, 2014. I am grateful to Paul McIssac for sharing his Zeller interview tapes with me. I did the transcriptions.

31. McIssac, interview with Zeller, November 12, 2014.

32. Michael Gonzalez-Cruz, "Puerto Rican Revolutionary Nationalism," *Latin American Perspectives* 35 (November 2008): 151–65; Carlos Gil, "Artist, Writer, and Political Prisoner: An Interview with Elizam Escobar," in *Puerto Rican Movement: Voices from the Diaspora*, edited by Andrés Torres and José E. Velázquez (Philadelphia: Temple University Press, 1998), 228–45; Oscar Lopez Rivera, *Between Torture and Resistance* (Oakland, CA: PM Press, 2013).

33. For the FBI perspective on chasing down the FALN, see Brian R. Hollstein, "Interview of Former Special Agent of the FBI Richard S. Hahn (1967–1999)," April 15, 2008, Society of Former Special Agents of the FBI, Inc., http://www.nleomf.org /museum/the-collection/oral-histories/richard-s-hahn.html; and Ronald Koziol and John O'Brien, "11 FALN Terror Suspects Seized with Arsenal Here," *Chicago Tribune*, April 5, 1980.

34. Ronald Koziol and Storer Rowley, "$22 Million FALN Terror Case Bail Set," *Chicago Tribune*, April 6, 1980.

35. Ronald Koziol and John O'Brien, "Cops Hunt FALN Bomb Factory Here," *Chicago Tribune*, April 10, 1980.

36. Jane Fritsch, "FALN Courtroom Becomes a Circus of Screams, Fights," *Chicago Tribune*, April 29, 1980.

37. For a discussion of the tensions between the white left and the Puerto Rican groups in Chicago, and the problem of unquestioning support in the face of arrests and government surveillance, see Michael Staudenmaier, *Truth and Revolution: A History of the Sojourner Truth Organization, 1969–1896* (Oakland: AK Press, 2012), 182–89.

38. Zeller interview, January 24, 2016. Jane Frish, "FALN Defendant: Six Months for Court Outburst," *Chicago Tribune*, July 8, 1980, shows demonstrators outside the courthouse in support of the FALN.

39. Barbara Zeller's name comes up many times between 1981 and 1982 in the FBI M19, Batches 1 and 2.

40. Barbara C. Zeller, MD, curriculum vitae.

41. Horowitz interview. Many of the Iranian students they worked with went back to Iran after the Shah was overthrown and then were killed when Ayatollah Khomeini came to power and the left was decimated in Iran. For divisions around support for the Iranian students in Chicago, see Staudenmaier, *Truth and Revolution*, 147–90. On the Pontiac Brothers case, see Dan Berger, *Captive Nation: Black Prison Organizing in the Civil Rights Era* (Chapel Hill: University of North Carolina Press, 2014), 253–55.

42. McIssac, interview with Zeller, November 12, 1992.

43. Banzhaf, "Alan Berkman Oral History," November 2, 2001.

44. Alan was then living with Tim Blunk, a former Hampshire College student that Alan and Susan Rosenberg had organized into May 19th.

45. Paul McIssac, interview with Dana Biberman, New York City, October 23, 1992. I am grateful to Paul McIssac for sharing his Biberman interview tapes with me. I did the transcriptions.

46. McIssac, interview with Biberman, October 23, 1992. Barbara and Alan became part of May 19th before Dana, who remained more distant until about 1980.

47. McIssac, interview with Biberman, October 23, 1992.

48. For more on Barbara's relationship to Jackie Haught, see below.

49. McIssac, interview with Biberman, October 23, 1992.

50. Alan Berkman to Bruce Taub, October 1, 1985.

51. Alan Berkman to Bruce Taub, October 1, 1985.

52. Paul McIssac, interview with Dana Biberman, October 22, 1992, New York City, 10.

53. Alan Berkman to Bruce Taub, September 29, 1985. Dana would become critical to Alan's life later.

54. Biberman interview, April 20, 2015.

55. Paul McIssac, interview with Barbara Zeller, New York City, November 14, 1992.

56. FBI M19, Batch 1, p. 209.

CHAPTER 8

1. Gil Scott-Heron, "The Revolution Will Not Be Televised," *Small Talk at 125th and Lenox* (RCA, 1970).

2. Kuwasi Balagoon, "Brink's Trial Opening Statement," 54, https://theanarchistlibrary

.org/library/kuwasi-balagoon-brink-s-trial-opening-statement; "Brief of the International Association of Democratic Lawyers as Amicus Curiae in Support of Defendant's Memorandum in the Reply to the Government's Response to the January 18, 1985 Order of the Hon. Charles S. Haight," *U.S.A. v. Mutulu Shakur*, bi, 82-CR-312-CSH, 16, who accepted there was a war between the U.S. government and the "Republic of New Afrika." See https://law.justia.com/cases/federal/appellate-courts/F2/817/189/467610.

3. Interview with Eve Rosahn, New York City, May 26, 2015; email with Barbara Zeller, May 6, 2019. All interviews cited were conducted by the author unless otherwise specified.

4. The government convicted Silvia Baraldini of assisting in the escape of Assata Shakur in September 1983; see below. On the Brink's action, see below.

5. Arnold H. Lubasch, "Federal Brink's Prosecution Nearly Completed," *New York Times* July 31, 1983. In *Days of Rage: America's Radical Underground, the FBI, and the Forgotten Age of Revolutionary Violence* (New York: Penguin, 2015), Bryan Burroughs claims Shakur used cocaine, but he gives no evidence to support this. Burroughs also discusses the police wiretaps on the drug purchases (493).

6. I specifically asked those who were around BAAANA if they knew about the drug usage, and everyone said no. Baraldini claims the same lack of knowledge; see Burroughs, *Days of Rage*, 493.

7. Baraldini spoke to reporter Bryan Burroughs in Rome, where she now lives, but he is not a reliable source on quotes from individuals. See Burroughs, *Days of Rage*, 501; see also Dan Berger, "Fictionalizing Radical Activism of the 1960s," *Socialism and Democracy* 29 (December 2015): 203–11.

8. John Castellucci, *The Big Dance* (New York: Dodd Mead, 1986), 206. Trying to trace and get accurate all the details surrounding the Brink's case is difficult. Most of the journalist accounts comes from trial transcripts, and some of the facts are acknowledged to be incorrect (see correction sheet included by the publisher in Castellucci, *The Big Dance*). Much of the government's case relied upon those who turned state's evidence or had documented mental problems. More than three decades later, people stand by their "official" or legal stories. Given the inaccuracies all around, I have tried to be as accurate as possible.

9. Paul McIssac, interview with Dana Biberman, New York City, October 23, 1992. I am grateful to Paul McIssac for sharing his Biberman interview tapes with me. I did the transcriptions.

10. David Gilbert, *Love and Struggle: My Life in SDS, the Weather Underground and Beyond* (Oakland, CA: PM Press, 2011), 273; interview with David Gilbert, Auburn Correctional Facility, Auburn, NY, November 12, 2014. Greg Yardly, "American Terrorist," *Front Page*, September 22, 2003, www.frontpage.com, provides libertarian and right-wing comments on Boudin's statements at her subsequent parole hearing as to her state of mind at the time of the Brink's event.

11. Gilbert, *Love and Struggle*, 304.

12. *Freeing Silvia Baraldini: One Country's Terrorist Is Another Country's Revolutionary*, directed by Margo Pelletier and Lisa Thomas (Thin Edge Films, 2009), DVD.

13. Burroughs, *Days of Rage*, 501.

14. On what it meant to leave her child, see Harriet Clark, "Dear Governor Paterson," April 2010; and Judy Clark statement, https://judithclark.org/.

15. The BLA men and the guards tell different stories here; see Castellucci, *The Big Dance*.

16. There are literally thousands and thousands of pages of testimony from the various

trials. The most detailed information is in Castellucci, *The Big Dance*, but those involved claim there are multiple factional errors (Gilbert interview). Burroughs takes almost all his information from Castellucci, without much attribution. There is another book to be written to analyze all of this, but that is not my purpose here. Trombino would survive Brink's only to be killed on September 11, 2001, at the World Trade Center.

17. Alan Berkman to Ann Morris, October 21, 1989.

18. Castellucci, *The Big Dance*, 220.

19. Castellucci, *The Big Dance*, 219.

20. Gilbert, *Love and Struggle*, 27.

21. Bob Feldman, "Civil Liberties and the 1981 Brink's Case," *Blogspot*, July 9, 2007, http://bfeldman68.blogspot.com/2007/07/civil-liberties-and-1981-brinks-case.html.

22. Alan Berkman, letter to the editor of *Rockland (NY) Journal News* (unpublished), June 24, 1982, BP.

23. Details are in Castellucci, *The Big Dance*, 223.

24. Gilbert, *Love and Struggle*, 278; Dan Berger, *Outlaws of America: The Weather Underground and the Politics of Solidarity* (Oakland, CA: AK Press, 2006), 248.

25. Ronald Smothers, "Man Killed in Shootout Tied to Hold Up of Brink's Truck," *New York Times*, October 27, 1981. Castellucci, *The Big Dance*, 236–37. Feldman, "Civil Liberties and the 1981 Brink's Case," argues that Castellucci gets this wrong and that Sundiata was executed. The evidence is unclear.

26. Castellucci, *Big Dance*, 235.

27. Committee to Defend New Afrikan Freedom Fighters and the Committee to Defend the October 20th Freedom Fighters, "Stop the Torture and Isolation of Freedom Fighters!" (New York, 1981), freedomarchives.org.

28. See Beverly Gage, "Terrorism and the American Experience: A State of the Field," *Journal of American History* 98 (June 2011): 73–94.

29. For a listing and copies of the media coverage, see Hands off Assata Campaign, "Assata: Exile since 1979," 2010, http://www.assatashakur.org/forum/guerrilla-warfare -tactic-technique-survival/48798-1981-1990-newspaper-articles-about-weather -underground-black-liberation-army.html.

30. Guy Hawtin, "How New Terrorists Cracked FBI's Secrets," *New York Post*, February 8, 1982.

31. Jane Lazarre, "Conversations with Kathy Boudin," *Village Voice*, February 14, 1984. See also the more negative views in Susan Braudy, *Family Circle: The Boudins and the Aristocracy of the Left* (New York: Knopf, 2003); and Ellen Frankfort, *Kathy Boudin and the Dance of Death* (New York: Stein and Day, 1983).

32. On the ways Weather's actions were not seen as political, see Arthur M. Eckstein, *Bad Moon Rising: How the Weather Underground Beat the FBI and Lost the Revolution* (New Haven, CT: Yale University Press, 2016).

33. Arnold H. Lubasch, "Brink's Suspect Released after F.B.I. Checks Alibi," *New York Times*, November 6, 1981.

34. The FBI director William Webster discusses the impact of Brink's on their planning; see Leslie Maitland Werner, "Most U.S. Cites Are Taking No Special Measures against Terrorism," *New York Times*, December 17, 1983.

35. Stanley A. Pimentel, interview with Former Special Agent of the FBI William E. Dyson Jr., January 15, 2008 (Washington, DC: Society of Former Special Agents of the FBI, 2008), 59.

36. Grace Paley, quoted in Deborah Heller, *Literary Sisterhood: Imagining Women Artists*

(Montreal: McGill-Queen's University Press, 205), 127–28. Paley's children had grown up with Kathy Boudin.

37. Murray Kempton, "Dead End Kids," in *Rebellions, Perversities, and Main Events* (New York: Times Books, 1994), 151. Far from everyone in Weather or May 19th came from an affluent family.

38. For examples, see Janis Kelly, "Grand Juries: We All Know Too Much," *off our backs* 11 (December 1981): 19; and Bruce Vail, "Park Slope Radicals Keep Talking as Fed Grand Jury Probes Connections to Nyack," *Phoenix*, March 3, 1982.

39. Susan Tipograph, quoted in Feldman, "Civil Liberties and the 1981 Brink's Case."

40. Interview with Marion Banzhaf, Tallahassee, FL, April 2, 2016. Banzhaf co-coordinated the John Brown Anti-Klan Committee in the mid-1980s. Her partner at the time, Judy Holmes, became the lawyer for Kuwasi Balagoon, one of the BLA members. Holmes shared her legal practice with Susan Tipograph.

41. BD, 8. Berkman makes clear this is what he thought at the time, not later when his critique became sharper.

42. Interview with Linda Evans, Santa Rosa, CA, March 8, 2016. Alan never mentions this in his own autobiographical memoir, "Brother Doc."

43. Alan Berkman, "Statement to the Grand Jury, May 26, 1982," in Coalition to Defend the October 20th Freedom Fighters, "Resist! Don't Collaborate! Stop Grand Jury Terrorism!," National Conference against Repression and Fascism, Denver, May 28–30, 1982, 3, BP; Peter Panych, "Minor Brink's Figure Accuses FBI of Torture," *Middletown (NY) Times Herald-Record*, ca. 1982, clipping in BP.

44. Interview with Dana Biberman, New York City, April 20, 2015.

45. Telephone interview with Shelley Miller, May 1, 2016. Chesa Boudin would later be raised by Bernadine Dohrn and Bill Ayers, former leaders of Weather, in Chicago. He became a defense lawyer and was elected as San Francisco District Attorney in 2019.

46. Paul McIssac, interview with Barbara Zeller, New York City, November 12, 1992. I am grateful to Paul McIssac for sharing his Zeller interview tapes with me. I did the transcriptions.

47. Skype interview with Judy Holmes, April 5, 2013; Banzhaf interview.

48. Dan Collins, "Eve Rosahn Today Was Formally Charged," *UPI Archives*, October 30, 1981, http://www.upi.com/Archives/1981/10/30/Eve-Rosahn-today-was-formally -charged-with-aiding-the/4381373266000.

49. Thai Jones, *A Radical Line: From the Labor Movement to the Weather Underground, One Family's Century of Conscience* (New York: Free Press, 2004), 3–14, 271–75.

50. Fulani-Ali, "Black People, My People! My Name is Fulani-Ali," *Arm the Spirit*, Fall 1982, 6, www.freedomarchives.org.

51. Rondee Gaines, "I Am a Revolutionary Black Female Nationalist: A Womanist Analysis of Fulani Sunni Ali's Role as a New African Citizen and Minister of Information in the Provisional Government of the Republic of New Africa" (PhD diss., Georgia State University, 2013), 190–220, http://scholarworks.gsu.edu/communication_diss/44; Lubasch, "Brink's Suspect Released"; Manning Marable, *How Capitalism Underdeveloped Black America* (Boston: South End, 1983), 221.

52. Kersplebedeb, ed., *Kuwasi Balagoon: A Soldier's Story* (Montreal: Kersplebedeb, 2003).

53. Ralph Blumenthal, "F.B.I. Wiretaps: An Ear on the Brink's Case," *New York Times*, August 9, 1982.

54. The legal story is complicated and depends on who tells it. See Castellucci, *The*

Big Dance; Gilbert, *Love and Struggle*; Berger, *Outlaws of America*, 245–64; and Kenneth Gribetz, D.A., and H. Paul Jeffers, *Murder along the Way: A Prosecutor's Personal Account of Fighting Violent Crime in the Suburbs* (New York: Pharos, 1989), 151–206.

55. Vail, "Park Slope Radicals Keep Talking," 8.

56. The Freedom Archives have many of these leaflets online. On the internal debate, see Alan to Cdes (Comrades), October 19, 1985, BL personal collection. The letter discusses the reasons for noncooperation with the grand jury and differences over whether to use the term *robbery*.

57. Alan Berkman, letter to the editor.

58. Arnold H. Lubasch, "Brink's Defense Derides U.S. Witnesses at Trial," *New York Times*, August 26, 1983.

59. Castellucci, *The Big Dance*, 240–55. In his autobiography, the Rockland County DA, Kenneth Gribetz, would barely mention the tensions; see *Murder along the Way*, 171–72; and interview with Judge Bill Mogulescu, New York City, March 20, 2013.

60. Appendix J, New York State Penal Law, Section 265.25, https://www.nysenate .gov/legislation/laws/PEN/265.25; A. Frampton, "Reporting of Gunshot Wounds by Doctors in Emergency Departments: A Duty or a Right? Some Legal and Ethical Issues Surrounding Breaking Patient Confidentiality," *Emergency Medicine Journal* 22 (February 2005): 84–86.

61. Alan Berkman, letter to the editor.

62. Berkman, "Statement to the Grand Jury," 2.

63. Paul McIssac, interview with Alan Berkman, New York City, WBAI, 1992; tape in author's possession.

64. Mogulescu interview.

65. BD, 8.

66. New York Committee against Grand Jury Repression, "The Political Grand Jury: An Instrument of Repression" (New York: Community Press, n.d., ca. late 1970s). See also Brian Glick, *War at Home: Covert Action against U.S. Activists and What We Can Do about It* (Boston: South End, 1987). An earlier version of this book, called *A Guide to the Grand Jury* (Boston: New England Free Press), had been coauthored with Kathy Boudin in 1969.

67. Statement from Grand Jury Resisters, *Non-collaboration: The ONLY Answer to Political Investigations* (New York: Stop the Witch Hunts, 1985).

68. Feldman, "Civil Liberties and the 1981 Brink's Case."

69. Feldman, "Civil Liberties and the 1981 Brink's Case," 3.

70. On the kind of self-respect this incurred, see Joan Didion, "Self-Respect: Its Source, Its Power," *Vogue*, 1961, http://www.vogue.com/3241115/joan-didion-self-respect-essay -1961. Harriet Clark, Alan and Judy's daughter, gave me this reference when we discussed Alan's life.

71. Berkman, "Statement to the Grand Jury," 3.

72. Alan to Cdes, October 19, 1985.

73. Alan says very little in his writing about this time period. For a brief discussion, see BD, 10–14.

74. Barbara would move back to New York in December 1982 but would go back and forth to Chicago to be with Sarah, who stayed with others in May 19th to finish her school year there. By April 1983, Sarah would be back in New York with Barbara. Telephone interview with Barbara Zeller, May 1, 2016; Miller interview.

75. Telephone interview with Eve Rosahn, April 25, 2016; Zeller interview. Alan writes almost nothing about this time period himself.

76. Panych, "Minor Brink's Figure Accuses FBI of Torture."

77. Ed Sperling, "Fugitive Life Fails to Dull Radical Doc," *Middletown (NY) Times Herald-Record*, August 4, 1985. The FBI's spokesman told the reporter that Alan's statement was "ludicrous": "The FBI does not use threats of prosecution in order to intimidate or elicit cooperation from people under arrest."

78. Alan to Sharon Newman, September 12, 1985.

79. Alan to Sharon Newman, August 26, 1985.

80. Memorandum to the Board of Professional Medical Conduct of the State of New York, "In the Matter of Dr. Alan Berkman NYS #112795, a Physician Licensed to Practice in the State of New York," New York City, October 28, 1991, 13, BP. Mudd would be pardoned for his heroic actions in saving many in the penitentiary off Key West from yellow fever. The dramatic, and extremely racist, film based on his life is *The Prisoner of Shark Island*, directed by John Ford (Twentieth Century Fox, 1936), DVD.

81. Alan shared the view his comrade Silvia Baraldini would express to the court in her opening statement in her criminal racketeering trial: "By indicting me the government is putting on trial our right to belong and organize a revolutionary movement of white people whose goals are the end to United States imperialism, the freedom of New Afrika, Puerto Rico, Native American nations, and the southwest United States which is the northern two-thirds of Mexico, occupied by this government in 1848." Silvia Baraldini, "Opening Statement—April 19, 1983," Silvia Baraldini folder, Marion Banzhaf Personal Papers, Tallahassee, FL.

82. Biberman interview, April 20, 2015.

83. "2 More Found Guilty for Refusing to Talk in F.A.L.N. Inquiry," *New York Times*, January 21, 1984. Shelley Miller, along with Silvia Baraldini, refused to speak before this grand jury in February 1983.

84. Interview with Harriet Clark, San Francisco, March 5, 2016; interview with Judith Clark, Bedford Hills, NY, April 3, 2013.

85. Interview with Laura Whitehorn, New York City, January 26, 2016.

86. *U.S. v. Alan Berkman*, U.S. District Court for the Eastern District of Philadelphia, February 18, 1997, Government Exhibit S, 75, BP.

87. Some of those I interviewed have memories of discussing this with Alan. Most do not, or do not want to talk about it.

88. *U.S. v. Alan Berkman*, 73.

89. Mogulescu interview. He thought one of the government witnesses was a consummate liar and that Alan would not have been convicted. But Mogulescu was another BLA member's attorney, not Alan's at the time, and Alan did not sense he would be acquitted.

90. Alan Berkman to Bruce Taub, September 29, 1985.

91. BD, 10.

92. Paul McIssac, interview with Barbara Zeller, New York City, November 14, 1992.

93. Alan Berkman, "Chronology," ca. 1998, edited by Barbara Zeller, 2011, 2. "1/83 Went to Chicago, desperately telling Barbara I loved her. Spent time with Sarah and returned to NYC to make plans to go underground."

94. Berkman, "Chronology," 13.

95. *United States of America v. Alan Berkman*, SSS 82 Cr. 312, Warrant for Arrest, February 3, 1983, BP.

96. BD, 13.

CHAPTER 9

1. Interview with Linda Evans, March 8, 2016, Santa Rosa, CA. All interviews cited were conducted by the author unless otherwise specified.

2. Diana Block, *Arm the Spirit: A Woman's Journey Underground and Back* (Berkeley: AR Press, 2009). Also see the fictionalized Jonah Raskin, *Underground: In Pursuit of B. Traven and Kenny Love* (New York: Bobbs-Merrill, 1978); and Marge Piercy, *Vida* (New York: Summit, 1979).

3. Alan Berkman, "Notes for 'Brother Doc,'" chap. 2, Underground, BP.

4. Evans interview.

5. Interview with Laura Whitehorn, New York City, January 26, 2016.

6. FBI, "May 19th Communist Organization," PDF 1–3, FBI M19, Batches 1 and 2, provide numerous examples of them being both watched and followed.

7. Jane M. Von Bergen, "Timothy Blunk: Idealist Turns Revolutionary," *Philadelphia Inquirer*, March 25, 1985.

8. Alan Berkman, "Undated Position Paper," ca. 1984, Government Exhibit K, *U.S. v. Alan Berkman*, "Government's Sentencing Memorandum," 1987, 1, BP.

9. Stephen Kinzer, "Federal Office Building on Staten Island Damaged by a Bomb," *New York Times*, January 30, 1983.

10. See chapter 10 for more on the bombings that the government would claim he and his comrades committed. On their actions written from a perspective sympathetic to the FBI, see William Rosenau, *Tonight We Bombed the U.S. Capitol* (New York: Atria Books, 2020).

11. Arthur M. Eckstein, *Bad Moon Rising: How the Weather Underground Beat the FBI and Lost the Revolution* (New Haven, CT: Yale University Press, 2016), 136–37.

12. See "John Brown and Beyond," twenty-seven essays and poems as part of *Let Freedom Ring: A Collection of Documents from the Movements to Free U.S. Political Prisoners*, edited by Matt Meyer (Berkeley, CA: PM Press, 2008), 463–569.

13. Alan Berkman, foreword to *Build a Revolutionary Resistance Movement* (New York: Committee to Fight Repression, 1985), iii, http://www.freedomarchives.org/Documents /Finder/DOC62_scans/62.CommuniqueBook.UFF.RGR.ARU.pdf. Alan wrote this in August 1985.

14. "Frederick Douglass and John Brown Meeting Place Informational Site, Detroit, Michigan," http://detroit1701.org/Douglas-Brown.html; David W. Blight, "Admiration and Ambivalence: Frederick Douglass and John Brown," in *The Gilder Lehrman Institute of American History*, http://www.gilderlehrman.org/history-by-era/failure-compromise /essays/admiration-and-ambivalence-frederick-douglass-and-john-brow. See an alternative history of "spectacular fiction" where former May 19th member and author Terry Bisson imagines that Brown's raid at Harpers Ferry had been successful: *Fire on the Mountain*, 2nd ed. (Berkeley: PM Press, 2009).

15. John Brown gets reinterpreted every generation, and in every new book. For a quick summary of the historiography, see Steven Mintz, "John Brown: Villain or Hero," ttp:// www.gilderlehrman.org/history-by-era/failure-compromise/essays/john-brown-villain -or-hero.

16. BD, 82.

17. Peter Panych, "Minor Brink's Figure Accuses FBI of Torture," *Middletown (NY) Times Herald-Record*, n.d., ca. 1983.

18. BD, 15.

19. Alan Berkman, "Undated Position Paper," 82–83, includes a hand-printed document that is clearly an undated political letter between the May 19th cadre and another political group (ca. November 1984 and May 1985). It discusses the sharing of internal documents, and states, "We offered you fairly extensive material aid including a quantity of materiel, offers of further military training if necessary, and giving you our internal and strategic documents."

20. I am grateful to my ongoing conversations with historian Arthur Eckstein for this view.

21. Susan Rosenberg, *An American Radical* (New York: Citadel, 2011), 8.

22. Evans interview; interview with Marion Banzhaf, Tallahassee, FL, April 2, 2016; interview with Laura Whitehorn, New York City, April 2, 2013. Former Weather leader Bernadine Dohrn spent seven months in the Metropolitan Correction Center in New York for refusing to speak to the grand jury investigating Brink's. She had managed a retail store called Broadway Baby where customers' checks were verified by the showing of licenses. Names from customers there were used by others in May 19th for their false identifications. Dohrn was never connected directly to the Brink's action and had not been involved. See M. A. Farber, "Behind the Brink's Case: Return of the Radical Left," *New York Times*, February 16, 1982.

23. See, for example, the classic from the Brazilian underground: Carlos Marighella, *Mini-manual of the Urban Guerrilla* (1969; CreateSpace Independent Publishing Platform, 2011). The book is still available and can be bought cheaply on Amazon.

24. Banzhaf interview.

25. Ed Sperling, "Fugitive Life Fails to Dull Radical Doc," *Middletown (NY) Times Herald-Record*, August 4, 1985, 3.

26. FBI, August 21, 1985, Report File No 91A-8276, 200–201, FBI AB.

27. Whitehorn interview, January 26, 2016; Rosenberg, *An American Radical*, 10.

28. Rosenberg, *An American Radical*, 10.

29. BD, 12.

30. Whitehorn interview, January 26, 2016.

31. Banzhaf interview; Evans interview. The FBI was well aware that May 19th and JBAKC members were taking evasive "counter-surveillance" actions as agents tried to follow them. See FBI, Teletype to Director Priority fr FBI New York, November 7, 1983, PDF 4, FBI M19, Batch 2, pp. 160–61. Suzy Waysdorf, Shelley Miller, Susan Tipograph, Elizabeth Horowitz, and Barbara Zeller in particular where followed on and off for years, see FBI M19, Batch 2.

32. FBI, "May 19th Communist Organization," PDF 3, 283, FBI M19, Batch 1. The FBI was also tracking her airplane trips and actions.

33. *U.S. v. Alan Berkman*, 85-00222-01, U.S. District Court for the Eastern District of Pennsylvania, February 18, 1987, Berkman testimony, 75, BP.

34. Banzhaf interview.

35. Evans interview.

36. Alan mentions Bridgeport in BD, 11, but most of his comrades do not say where they were. Interview with Susan Rosenberg, New York City, January 26, 2016.

37. See Sara Rimer, "60's Radical, Linked to a Killing, Surrenders after Hiding 23 Years," *New York Times*, September 16, 1993, on where Susan Saxe and Katherine Powers, who were involved in a robbery and murder in 1970, had hid in women's communes.

38. On the FBI's search in Northampton, see FBI, "BS91A-B8826," September 14, 1983, FBI AB.

39. For more on Weather and their underground experience, see Eckstein, *Bad Moon Rising*; and Cathy Wilkerson, *Flying Close to the Sun* (New York: Seven Stories, 2007), 349–77.

40. Rosenberg, *An American Radical*, 8.

41. Susan Bibler Coutin, *The Culture of Protest: Religious Activism and the U.S. Sanctuary Movement* (New York: Westview, 1993).

42. Janis Kelly, "Grand Juries: We All Know Too Much," *off our backs* 11 (December 1981): 19.

43. Martha Rosenfeld et al., "More on the BLA/Brinks/Grand Juries Commentary," *off our backs* 12 (April 1982): 30.

44. John Castellucci, *The Big Dance* (New York: Dodd Mead, 1986), 294.

45. Evans interview.

46. Whitehorn interview, January 26, 2016.

47. Evans interview. Evans also devised a "cancer story" to explain the wig. See FBI, Teletype to Director fr New Haven, February 23, 1985, PDF 11, FBI M19, Batch 2, pp. 76–79.

48. FBI, "Memorandum: NYRob: Major Case 37," February 21, 1984, FBI AB.

49. "To Director," May 8, 1984, FBI AB.

50. Evans interview.

51. Rosenberg interview.

52. Rosenberg, *An American Radical*, 10.

53. Interview with Harriet Clark, San Francisco, March 5, 2016; Whitehorn interview, January 26, 2016; Evans interview.

54. Rosenberg, *An American Radical*, 9.

55. Rosenberg interview.

56. Rosenberg interview; BD, 17.

57. Rosenberg interview.

58. Government Exhibit R, *U.S. v. Alan Berkman*, BP.

59. These terms are in all FBI, "May 19th Communist Organization," FBI AB files.

60. BD, 15.

61. Evans interview.

62. Whitehorn interview, April 2, 2013.

63. Rosenberg, *An American Radical*, 11. John Le Carré was known for his spy novels that were made into such films as *The Spy Who Came in from the Cold*. Diana Block, who had been underground in a similar group at the same time, wrote in her fictionalized account that it was like living in "magical realism"; see Diana Block, *Clandestine Occupations: an Imaginary History* (Berkeley, CA: PM Press, 2015), 95–96.

64. BD, 12; interview with Laura Whitehorn, New York City, January 21, 2013.

65. Interview with Jeffrey Millman, Cambridge, MA, January 23, 2013.

66. *U.S. v. Alan Berkman*, "Government's Sentencing Memorandum," 19.

67. Tipograph interview.

68. Robert Hanley, "Cost of State Brink's Case $2.5 Million So Far," *New York Times*, August 26, 1983.

69. Banzhaf interview.

70. Margot Hornblower, "Kathy Boudin Clings to Radicalism while Facing Trial in Brink's," *Washington Post*, February 21, 1984. The judge would finally allow the touch visits.

71. Affidavit of Judith Clark, *New York v. Judith Clark*, December 2002, 4, BP.

72. "Statement from David Gilbert," *Arm the Spirit*, Fall 1982, 8, FA.

73. Copies of the various leaflets on the demonstrations can be found online at FA.

74. Kenneth Gribetz, D.A., and H. Paul Jeffers, *Murder along the Way: A Prosecutor's Personal Account of Fighting Violent Crime in the Suburbs* (New York: Pharos, 1989), 181. The details of the trial are covered in both the local papers and the *New York Times*. The most detailed, if flawed, accounting is Castellucci, *The Big Dance*.

75. In April 2019, Judy Clark was finally allowed to get out on parole. Gilbert is still incarcerated and has written to the families of those killed to apologize. Balagoon died of AIDS in prison in 1986 at age thirty-nine. See Akinyele K. Umoja, "Maroon: Kuwasi Balagoon and the Evolution of Revolutionary New Afrikan Anarchism," *Science & Society* 79 (April 2015): 196–220.

76. Lisa W. Foderao, "Boudin Freed from Prison after Serving 22 Years," *New York Times*, September 17, 2003.

77. Castellucci, *The Big Dance*, mostly just follows the state trials. See also *Freeing Silvia Baraldini*, directed by Margo Pelletier and Lisa Thomas (New York: Thin Edge Films, 2009), DVD.

78. Arnold H. Lubasch, "4 of 7 are Guilty in U.S. Brink's Case," *New York Times*, September 4, 1983; Judge Bill Mogulescu interview, New York City, March 20, 2013. Mogulescu, then a defense attorney, was Jamal Joseph's lawyer in the federal trial, where he was convicted as an accessory to the Brink's action.

79. Odinga would serve more than three decades until November 25, 2014; Baraldini was sent back to her native Italy in 1999 and served a total of twenty-three years in the United States and Italy. Mutulu Shakur would not be captured until 1986, Buck in 1985 (see chapter 10). Shakur is still incarcerated; Buck died of uterine cancer less than two weeks after her release from prison in 2010. See Steve Lieberman, "Brink's Robbery Case: Who Remains of the Major Players?," *Rockland/Westchester Journal News*, April 17, 2019, https://www.lohud.com/story/news/local/rockland/nyack/2019/04/17/brinks-robbery-murders-case-who-remains-major-players/3495490002/.

80. Alan Berkman, no title, twenty-page report, ca. 1984, Government Exhibit K, *U.S. v. Alan Berkman*, "Government's Sentencing Memorandum," 6, BP. While Alan's name it is not on this, it is clearly his handwriting.

81. Berkman, no title, twenty-page report; Rosenberg interview.

82. Whitehorn interview, January 21, 2013.

83. Whitehorn interview, January 21, 2013.

84. Paul McIssac, interview with Alan Berkman, New York City, WBAI, 1992 (tape in author's possession); interview with Dick Clapp, Boston, September 24, 2011; Eckstein, *Bad Moon Rising*.

85. Berkman, no title, twenty-page report, 7.

86. Berkman, no title, twenty-page report, 7.

87. Berkman, no title, twenty-page report, 8.

88. BD, 16.

89. *U.S. v. Alan Berkman and Elizabeth Ann Duke*; *U.S. v. Alan Berkman*, "Government's Sentencing Memorandum," Criminal No. 85-222, U.S. District Court for the Eastern District of Pennsylvania, 5–6, BP, links FALN bombings to the materials in a Doylestown, Pennsylvania, garage.

90. The communiqués can all be found in Communiqués from the North American Armed Clandestine Movement, "Build a Revolutionary Resistance Movement," (New

York: Committee to Fight Repression, 1985); Nancy Lewis and Rosa Michnya, "Bomb Explodes at Fort McNair, Blowing out War College Windows," *Washington Post*, April 27, 1983.

91. Mary Thornton "Webster Tells of Concern for Bomb Threats," *Washington Post*, November 11, 1983. The FBI held several conferences to assess the evidence they did have and to share information with various units. See FBI M19, Batch 2.

92. North American Armed Clandestine Movement, "Build a Revolutionary Resistance Movement."

93. Ronald Kessler, "Capitol Bombing Fits into Pattern Familiar to FBI," *Washington Post*, November 13, 1983.

94. Evans interview.

95. Alan Berkman transcript, *U.S. v. Alan Berkman*, 85-00022-01, Government Exhibit S, *U.S. v. Alan Berkman*, "Government's Sentencing Memorandum," 1987, 10, BP.

96. U.S. Department of Justice, "Press Release, May 11, 1988," in *U.S. v. Whitehorn*, U.S. District Court for the District of Columbia, 7.

97. DEA Hartford, "GFCD-S4-3209, Impersonation of Federal Agents," September 17, 1984, FBI AB.

98. *U.S. v. Alan Berkman*, "Government's Sentencing Memorandum," 10.

99. Dave Lesher, "FBI Says Missing Fugitives Used Fake Local Addresses," undated Connecticut newspaper clipping, FBI AB files.

100. Whitehorn interview, January 21, 2013.

101. *U.S. v. Alan Berkman*, No. 85-00222-01, U.S. District Court for the Eastern District of Pennsylvania, January 5, 1987, 94; Evans interview.

102. Rosenberg, *An American Radical*, 13; Castellucci, *The Big Dance*, 296.

103. Andrew Maykuth, "An Unlikely Trail to Terror Suspects," *Philadelphia Inquirer*, December 2, 1984.

104. Jane M. Von Bergen, "3 Bags of Explosives Found in Eversham Lake," *Philadelphia Inquirer*, March 29, 1985.

105. Andrew Maykuth, "Police Arrest 2 Terror Suspects, Seize Explosives," *Philadelphia Inquirer*, December 1, 1984.

106. Jane M. Von Bergen, "Pair Found Guilty in Arms Case Avowed Radicals Assail N.J. Trial," *Philadelphia Inquirer*, March 18, 1985.

107. Henry Hurt, "The Capture of Susan Lisa Rosenberg," *Readers' Digest*, April 1985, 74.

108. "Fugitives Hunted Across the Northeast," *Philadelphia Inquirer*, June 6, 1984.

109. Rosenberg, *An American Radical*, 16–19.

110. *U.S. v. Alan Berkman*, No. 85-200222-01, U.S. District Court of Philadelphia, January 5, 1987, Transcript, 19.

111. Jane M. Von Bergern, "Two Revolutionaries to Go on Trial," *Philadelphia Inquirer*, March 4, 1985.

112. Maykuth, "Police Arrest 2 Terror Suspects."

113. *U.S. v. Rosenberg*, U.S. Court of Appeals, District of Columbia Circuit, 888 F.2d (D.C. Cir. 1989), 1.

114. Jane M. Von Bergen, "Radicals Get 58-Year Terms in Jersey Case," *Philadelphia Inquirer*, May 21, 1985.

115. "Brink's Suspect Vows Innocence," *60 Minutes*, December 14, 2000, http://www.cbsnews.com/news/brinks-suspect-vows-innocence/.

116. Mary K. O'Melveny to Susan Rosenberg, October 24, 2000, box 2, folder Mary K. O'Melveny, SRP.

117. Evans interview.

118. Telephone interview with Laura Whitehorn, June 14, 2016.

119. Evans interview.

120. *U.S. v. Alan Berkman*, No. 85-200222-01, U.S. District Court of Philadelphia, January 8, 1987, Transcript, 131–80; January 7, 1987, Transcript, 12–23, BP.

121. Whitehorn interview, June 14, 2016.

122. Selwyn Rabb, "New York Doctor Held as Fugitive in Brink's Case," *New York Times*, May 25, 1985.

123. BD, 17–18.

124. BD, 18.

125. Alan to Hank Newman, September 19, 1985.

126. Alan to Dick Clapp, August 8, 1985.

CHAPTER 10

1. BD, 25.

2. BD, 25.

3. BD, 25.

4. Chad Hunt, "The Walther PPQ: 007's Favorite Handgun Gets an Update," *Popular Mechanics*, April 5, 2012, 68; *U.S. v. Alan Berkman*, U.S. District Court for the Eastern District of Pennsylvania, No. 85-0022-01, February 18, 1987, 6, BP.

5. *U.S. v. Elizabeth Ann Duke*, No. 85-106, "Affidavit of Gregory J. Auld, FBI Special Agent," 1, BP.

6. See Susan Rosenberg, *An American Radical* (New York: Citadel, 2011), on her prison experiences. On Alan's medical care cum torture, see below.

7. Robert H. Levine to William Mogulescu, March 30, 1987, BP.

8. Alan to Hank Newman, September 19, 1985, 2. "Spy v. Spy" was actually a comic strip in *Mad Magazine* that spoofed Cold War fears.

9. Government Exhibit Q, *U.S. v. Alan Berkman*, Berkman Philadelphia Case Legal Papers, BP; see also www.KurtSaxon.com.

10. Unsigned, undated self-criticism of arrest, most probably written by Linda Evans after she and Marilyn Buck were arrested, WP-3215/1A, *U.S. v. Alan Berkman*, Berkman Philadelphia Case Legal Papers, BP; see also chapter 11.

11. *U.S. v. Alan Berkman*, No. 85–00222-01, January 8, 1987, 9, BP; Alan Berkman to "Dear Friends," November 1, 1985.

12. BD, 27.

13. Interview with Susan Tipograph, New York City, September 9, 2016.

14. Alan Berkman, Elizabeth Ann Duke, "Statement at Arraignment," May 27, 1985. See Alex Q. Arbuckle, "May 13, 1985: The Bombing of MOVE," *Mashable*, https://mashable .com/2016/01/10/1985-move-bombing/.

15. Pamela Ward, "Austinite Living Life on the Run," *Austin American Statesman*, September 5, 1995.

16. Amy Linn, "Sisters May Aid Search for Fugitive," *Philadelphia Inquirer*, October 23, 1985; Patricia Lynden, "To Jail with Love: An Interview with Linda Backiel," *OTI Online*, Spring 1992, http://www.ontheissuesmagazine.com/1992spring/lynden_spring1992.php.

17. FBI, "Most Wanted: Elizabeth Anna [*sic*] Duke," https://www.fbi.gov/wanted/dt /elizabeth-anna-duke/view. In the summer of 2014, FBI agents visited former May 19th members looking again for Duke. Personal communication from Barbara Zeller, August

12, 2014. Since 2008, conspiracy theorists on the right have posted various claims that she was actually Stanley Ann Dunham, Barack Obama's mother; see Before It's News, "Dreams from Obama's Mother: F.B.I. Most Wanted Fugitive Domestic Terrorist Elizabeth Ann Duke," July 28, 2013, http://beforeitsnews.com/politics/2013/07/dreams -from-obamas-mother-f-b-i-most-wanted-fugitive-domestic-terrorist-elizabeth-ann -duke-2537948.html.

18. Alan to Sharon Newman, September 12, 1985.

19. "Statement from Dr. Alan Berkman," December 9, 1985. I am grateful to Andy Epstein, who found this document in the papers of her late husband, Dr. Paul Epstein.

20. Although Holmesburg finally closed in 1995, ten years after Alan was there, it was used for filmmaking and photography; see "Haunting Holmesburg Prison," *Hidden City Philadelphia*, http://hiddencityphila.org/2014/10/haunting-holmesburg-prison/.

21. BD, 33.

22. BD, 35.

23. BD, 35.

24. BD, 29.

25. Alan to Stephen Wangh, November 1, 1986; Alan to Hank Newman, September 19, 1985.

26. Alan, to Mom and Dad, June 1, 1985.

27. Alan to Mom and Dad, December 21, no year.

28. Alan to Hank Newman, September 19, 1985, 2. Newman had been Alan's high school speech and theater teacher, one of the first people to recognize Alan's acting talents. Newman, his wife Sharon, and their son moved to Ithaca while Alan was at Cornell. They remained friends for decades.

29. BD, 37.

30. BD, 37. Eugene Methvin, "Terror Network, U.S.A.," *Reader's Digest*, December 1984, 111–12. On Abiodun, see Daniel E. Slotnik, "Nehanda Abiodun, 68, Black Revolutionary Who Fled to Cuba, Dies," *New York Times*, February 8, 2019.

31. BD, 38. On this page, Alan writes two different names of prisoners who gave him this moniker: Joaquin Foy is in the typescript, or another man only referred to as Alonso (probably Alonso Robinson) in Alan's handwritten notes. Alan's comrade Terry Bisson, however, thinks that the name came from Mumia Abu-Jamal; see interview with Terry Bisson, San Francisco, March 7, 2016.

32. BD, 74, 78, 80.

33. BD, 36.

34. The Mobilization to Free Mumia Abu-Jamal website, http://www.free-mumia.org/.

35. Mumia Abu-Jamal to author, August 1, 2013, BP.

36. Alan to Stephen Wangh, October 26, 1986.

37. Mumia Abu-Jamal to author.

38. See Prison Radio website, www.prisonradio.org.

39. Alan to Bruce Taub, October 1, 1985.

40. Alan to Bruce Taub, October 1, 1985.

41. Alan to Stephen Wangh, November 18, 1985.

42. BD, 29.

43. BD, 29. Alan admitted, "Most Black inmates believe that *white* and *basketball player* are actually mutually exclusive concepts." He wrote this long before the film *White Man Can't Jump* (1992) made fun of racial differences in basketball prowess.

44. BD, 39. Julius Erving, known as Dr. J, played for the NBA's Philadelphia 76ers from 1976 to 1987 and was known for his slam dunks.

45. Alan to Hank Newman, September 19, 1985.

46. BD, 53.

47. BD, 61.

48. BD, 57. In his manuscript, Alan called the chapter about Lewisburg "Disappeared."

49. BD, 61.

50. Alan to Steven Wangh, November 18, 1985.

51. Alan to Hank Newman, September 19, 1985.

52. BD, 52, 64.

53. BD, 52, 64.

54. Michael Hinkelman and John F. Morrison, "U.S. District Judge Louis H. Pollak Dies at 89," *Philly.com*, May 10, 2012, http://articles.philly.com/2012-05-10/news/31669640_1 _chief-judge-fellow-judges-judge-pollak.

55. BD, 66.

56. Alan to Mom and Dad, September 13, 1985.

57. BD, 84.

58. Alan to Hank Newman, September 19, 1985.

59. BD, 84.

60. Fran Pollner, "Political Doctors," *Medical World News*, November 28, 1988, 51.

61. BD, 70.

62. BD.

63. Susie Day, interview with Alan Berkman, New York City, summer 2003. I am grateful to Susie Day for sharing this with me.

64. BD, 72–73.

65. BD, 77.

66. Day, interview with Alan Berkman.

67. BD, 81.

68. BD, 83.

69. BD, 84.

70. Alan to Richard Clapp, November 27, 1985.

71. Susan M. Reverby, "Can There Be Acceptable Prison Health Care? Looking Back on the 1970s," *Public Health Reports* 134, no. 1 (2019): 89–93.

72. Melvin Delgado and Denise Humm-Delgado, *Health and Health Care in the Nation's Prisons* (New York: Rowman and Littlefield, 2008).

73. Alan to Richard Clapp, November 27, 1985.

74. Committee to Fight Repression, "Dear Friends," January 29, 1986, BP.

75. "Alan Berkman," *Breakthrough: Journal of the Prairie Fire Organizing Committee* 10 (Spring/Summer 1986): 14.

76. Alan Berkman, "Chronology," ca. 1998, edited by Barbara Zeller, 2011, BP.

77. Alan to Bruce Taub, April n.d., 1986.

78. Alan Berkman, "Medical History," Barbara Zeller, letter to Amnesty International, April 1990, 2, folder Alan Berkman, box 2, SRP.

79. Berkman, "Medical History," 3.

80. Alan to Bruce Taub, February 2, 1986.

81. Committee to Fight Repression, "Dear Friends." The technical medical language suggests that Alan helped write it, and that Barbara had a hand in it as well.

82. Berkman, "Chronology."

83. Alan to Hank Newman, February 18, 1986.

84. Alan Berkman, "Medical History," 3.

85. Alan to BL, March 9, 1988, BL personal collection.

86. Gillian Murphy, "In Search of Solidarity," *Body Positive* 15 (2002): 22–28.

87. BD, 47. Lawyer Ron Kuby email to author, September 30, 2019. Robinson is still in prison after 40 years and Kuby is trying to get him out.

88. Murphy, "In Search of Solidarity."

89. Alan to BL, March 9, 1988.

90. Alan to Dear Friends, February 2, 1986, BL personal collection.

91. "Alan Berkman," *Breakthrough: Journal of the Prairie Fire Organizing Committee* X (Spring/Summer 1986): 14; Committee to Fight Repression, "Dear Friends," details his medical condition.

92. Alan to Bruce Taub, November 20, 1985.

93. Alan to Bruce Taub, February 2, 1986.

94. *U.S. v. Alan Berkman*, Criminal No. 85-222, "Government's Sentencing Memorandum," 1–2, BP.

95. Alan to Richard Clapp, August 8, 1985.

96. Alan to Richard Clapp, August 8, 1985.

97. BD, 73.

98. BD, 74.

99. BD, 76; *U.S. v. Alan Berkman*, Criminal No. 85-222, "Government's Sentencing Memorandum," 2.

100. Alan to "Dear Friends," November 1, 1985.

101. Alan to Bruce Taub, May 9, 1986; interview with Judge Bill Mogulescu, New York City, March 31, 2013. Mogulescu has been a judge in various Bronx criminal courts since 1990.

102. BD, 82.

103. BD, 82.

104. Mogulescu interview.

105. Arthur M. Eckstein, *Bad Moon Rising: How the Weather Underground Beat the FBI and Lost the Revolution* (New Haven, CT: Yale University Press, 2016), 217–29.

106. Alan Berkman, "Opening Argument," BP.

107. Alan Berkman, "A Modest Supposal, 1987," BP.

108. Alan to Bruce Taub, December 7, 1986.

109. Alan to Father of the Son (Bruce Taub), November 8, 1986. Bruce Taub and his wife, Lynne Karsten, had just had their son Samuel; Alan to Stephen Wangh, October 26, 1986.

110. Telephone interview with Jackie Haught, October 25, 2015.

111. Alan to Bruce Taub, January 23, 1987.

112. Alan to Hank Newman, April 23, 1987.

113. BD, 123.

114. Alan to Bruce Taub, January 23, 1987.

115. Alan to Mom and Dad, August 18, 1985.

116. Alan to Stephen Wangh, December 26, 1986.

117. Alan to Ann Morris, January 17, 1987.

118. Alan to Bruce Taub, February 10, 1988.

119. BD, 135.

120. Alan to Bruce Taub, June 5, 1986.

121. Alan to Hon. Louis H. Pollak, May 18, 1987, 1.

122. Mogulescu cross-examination of FBI special agents, *U.S. v. Alan Berkman*, Criminal Action, 85-00222-01, Transcripts, January 5–7, 15–16, 1987, BP.

123. Alan to Ann Morris, January 17, 1987.

124. "Alan Berkman," *The Insurgent* clipping, n.d., p. 26, ca. May 1987, BP.

125. Alan to Bruce Taub, January 23, 1987.

126. Alan Berkman, "Press Statement," February 9, 1987, BP.

127. BD, 134; Linda Lloyd, "Berkman Convicted on Arms Charges," *Philadelphia Inquirer*, March 27, 1987.

128. Levine to Mogulescu; *U.S. v. Alan Berkman*, Criminal No. 85-222, "Government's Sentencing Memorandum," 1–2.

129. Alan Berkman to Jack Rosenthal, *New York Times*, August 28, 1988, box 2, folder Resistance Conspiracy Case, SRP.

130. BD, 134.

131. Alan to Bruce Taub, October 1, 1986.

132. Mr. Abe Osit to Judge Pollak, May 17, 1987, BP.

133. Douglas Colbert to Hon. Judge Pollak, April 29, 1987; and Bart Lubow to Hon. Louis H. Pollak, April 28, 1987, both BP.

134. Emile Lounsberrry, "Revolutionary Doctor Gets 10-Year Sentence," *Philadelphia Inquirer*, May 30, 1987; AP, "Berkman Sentenced to Prison," *Middletown (NY) Times Herald-Record*, May 30, 1987.

135. BD, 135.

136. Alan to Bruce Taub, June 5, 1986; Alan to Barbara Zeller, September 28, 1986.

137. BD, 136.

CHAPTER 11

1. Alan to Hank Newman, September 19, 1985.

2. Alan to Stephen Wangh, September 25, 1985.

3. Alan to Stephen Wangh, December 27, 1986.

4. Alan to Sharon Newman, October 31, 1987.

5. Alan to Stephen Wangh, September 22, 1985.

6. Alan to Sharon Newman, April 12, 1987.

7. Alan to Sharon Newman, October 31, 1987.

8. Doherty would fight the extradition for eight years but was finally deported in 1992; see James Barron, "IRA Fugitive Sent to Belfast from U.S. Jail," *New York Times*, February 20, 1992. He was released in 1998; see Corinne Purtill, "Anguish Haunts Northern Ireland's Retired Terrorists," *NBC News*, July 15, 2015, http://www.nbcnews.com/news/world/anguish-haunts-northern-irelands-retired-terrorists-n392326.

9. James T. Kelly, "The Empire Strikes Back: The Taking of Joe Doherty," *Fordham Law Review* 61 (1992): 317–99.

10. Alan to Ann Morris, July 23, 1987.

11. Alan to Hank Newman, July 8, 1987.

12. Alan to Ann Morris, December 3, 1987.

13. Alan to Hank Newman, July 8, 1987.

14. Alan to Sarah Zeller-Berkman, October n.d., 1987.

15. Alan to Hank Newman, July 8, 1987.

16. Alan to Ann Morris, July 23, 1987.

17. Joel Cohen, "No More 'Perp Walks,'" *National Law Journal*, August 5, 2002, 12.

18. Arnold H. Lubasch, "2 Ex-Fugitives Convicted of Roles in Fatal Armored-Truck Robbery," *New York Times*, May 12, 1988. The trial ran for six months, beginning in December 1987.

19. Jay Nordlinger, "Clinton's Rosenberg Case," *National Review*, March 29, 2001; Eric Lipton, "Officials Criticize Clinton's Pardon of an Ex-Terrorist," *New York Times*, January 22, 2001. Covering his tracks and by then the New York City mayor, Guiliani told the *Times* reporter he did not remember the Rosenberg case. See also chapter 9, note 115.

20. Interview with Judge Bill Mogulescu, New York City, March 20, 2013.

21. Marilyn Buck, "Carrying on the Tradition of John Brown," *Death to the Klan! Newspaper of the John Brown Anti-Klan Committee*, Summer 1986, 12.

22. Alan to Stephen Wangh, January 26, 1988.

23. Alan to Barbara, October 12, 1987.

24. Alan to Sharon Newman, October 31, 1987.

25. Alan to Sarah Zeller-Berkman, October n.d., 1987.

26. Alan to Sharon Newman, October 31, 1987.

27. Alan to Sarah Zeller-Berkman, October n.d., 1987.

28. Alan to Stephen Wangh, January 26, 1988.

29. Alan to Sarah Zeller-Berkman, October n.d., 1987.

30. Alan to Ann Morris, December 3, 1987.

31. Alan to Ann Morris, July 23, 1987.

32. Alan to Bruce Taub, October 1, 1987.

33. Alan to Stephen Wangh, January 26, 1988.

34. Alan to Stephen Wangh, January 26, 1988; Alan to Dear Folks, November 4, 1987.

35. Tim Blunk to Barbara [Zeller], February 5, 1991, BP.

36. Alan to Barbara, November 11, 1987.

37. Statement of Dr. Alan Berkman, House Committee on Intellectual Property and the Administration of Justice, Subcommittee of the House Judiciary Committee, July 1991, BP.

38. Alan to Ann Morris, November 13, 1987.

39. Ralph Aarons, quoted in Kanya D'Almeida, "*Out of Control* (Nancy Kurshan): A Review," *WIN Magazine*, Summer 2014, https://www.warresisters.org/win/win -summer-2014/out-control-nancy-kurshan.

40. Alan to Bruce Taub, January 1, 1988.

41. Alan to Mom and Dad, January 2, 1988.

42. Nancy Kurshan, *Out of Control: A Fifteen-Year Battle against Control Unit Prisons* (San Francisco: Freedom Archives, 2013); Alan Eladio Gomez, "Resisting Living Death at Marion Federal Penitentiary, 1972," *Radical History Review* (Fall 2006): 58–86; Dan Berger and Toussaint Losier, *Rethinking the American Prison Movement* (New York: Routledge, 2017), 147–53.

43. Alan to Hank Newman, December 15, 1987.

44. BD, 143.

45. Alan to Ann Morris, January 16, 1988.

46. Alan to Bruce Taub, January 7, 1988.

47. Alan to Ann Morris, January 16, 1988.

48. Alan to Sharon Newman, October 31, 1987.

49. Alan to Hank Newman, February 16, 1988.

50. Alan to Sharon Newman, October 31, 1987. Hank and Sharon Newman had separated that year, and Alan wrote to each of them.

51. Alan to Barbara Carol, January 12, 1988.

52. Alan to Barbara, January 18, 1988.

53. Alan to Ann Morris, January 16, 1988.

54. Alan to Sharon Newman, September 21, 1987, BP; Guenther, *Solitary Confinement*, p. 163.

55. BD, 147.

56. Eddie Griffin, quoted in Gomez, "Resisting Living Death," 78.

57. Interview with Alan Berkman, WBAI-Radio, March 2002, "Beyond the Pale"; tape provided by Susie Day.

58. Alan to Barbara, January 5, 1988.

59. Alan to Barbara, November 30, 1987. Flights from New York cost hundreds of dollars, took a minimum of six hours, and required at least one stop on the way. Even if his family flew to Chicago, it took another five hours to drive there. By car, the trip was nearly fourteen hours to cover the 956 miles from New York.

60. Alan to Mom and Dad, January 25, February 3, and February 11, 1988.

61. Alan to Barbara Carol, January 12, 1988.

62. Alan to Hank Newman, November 25, 1985; Alan to Mom and Dad, November 6, 1987.

63. Alan to Stacy [unknown last name], October 21, 1987.

64. Alan to Bruce Taub, February 10, 1988.

65. Alan to Barbara, November 20, 1987.

66. Alan to Ann Morris, November 2, 1988.

67. Alan to Hank Newman, February 16, 1988.

68. Alan to Richard Clapp, November 29, 1989.

69. Alan to Sarah Zeller-Berkman, July 17, 1987.

70. Alan to Ann Morris, September 2, 1987.

71. Alan to Sharon Newman, August 26, 1985.

72. Alan to Hank Newman, October 25, 1985.

73. Alan to Stephen Wangh, September 1, 1985.

74. Alan to Hank Newman, November n.d., 1985. Alan vaguely remembers the lines as "A time to remember what you think, not what you feel." The thought is in *King Lear*, but not in that exact formulation.

75. I am grateful to Mary Lefkowitz for her discussion with me of this concept in the Greek plays; see Mary Lefkowitz and James Romm, eds. and trans., *The Greek Plays* (New York: Modern Library, 2016).

76. Alan to Ann Morris, April 30, 1987.

77. Alan to Dear Friend [Ann], May 11, 1988.

78. "Spanish Dictionary," www.spanishdict.com.

79. Alan to Bruce Taub, February 10, 1988.

80. Alan to Sarah Zeller-Berkman, February 29, 1988.

81. Alan to Stephen Wangh, November 18, 1985.

82. Alan to Sarah Zeller-Berkman, November 10, 1986.

83. Alan to Tim [Blunk], January 13, 1987. Federal prisoners cannot write to one another, so the letter had to be sent through an intermediary.

84. Alan to Stacy [last name unknown], October 21, 1987.

85. Alan to B[arbara], July 7, 1987.

86. Alan to Barbara, November 30, 1987.

87. Alan to Stephen Wangh, September 22, 1985.

88. Alan to Richard Clapp, August 10, 1985. Alan's reference is to Azania, or "land of the blacks," the precolonial term used for the southeast African coast and linked to the Azanian People's Liberation Army, the military wing of the militant Pan-Africanist Congress.

89. Alan to Stephen Wangh, November 18, 1985.

90. Alan to Ann Morris, July 23, 1987.

91. Alan to Dear Comrades, n.d., 1987.

92. Alan to Hank Newman, November 25, 1985.

93. Alan to Ann Morris, January 16, 1988.

94. Alan to Hank Newman, n.d., ca. 1987.

95. Michael Tabor, *The War of the Flea* (New York: Citadel, 1965).

96. Alan to Hank Newman, n.d., ca. 1987.

97. Alan to Ann Morris, January 16, 1988.

98. Stephen Wangh to Alan, November 25, 1985.

99. Stephen Wangh to Alan, November 25, 1985.

100. Alan to Sharon Newman, September 21, 1987.

101. Alan to Sarah Zeller-Berkman, February 29, 1988.

102. Alan to Hank Newman, September 19, 1985.

103. Alan to Mom and Dad, April 9, 1987.

104. Alan to Dear Folks, November 11, 1987.

105. Alan to Stephen Wangh, January 26, 1988.

106. Alan to Sarah Zeller-Berkman, July 7, 1985.

107. Alan to Sarah Zeller-Berkman, October 7, 1987.

108. Alan to Bruce Taub, January 7, 1988.

109. Alan to Sarah Zeller-Berkman, August 7, 1987; Alan to Sarah Zeller-Berkman, August 5, 1987.

110. Alan to Sarah Zeller-Berkman, September 18, 1988.

111. On the role of these camps in left culture, see Paul C. Mishler, *Raising Reds: the Young Pioneers, Radical Summer Camps, and Communist Political Culture in the U.S.* (New York: Columbia University Press, 1999).

112. Alan to Sarah Zeller-Berkman, September 18, 1988.

113. Alan to Sarah Zeller-Berkman, October 7, 1987.

114. Alan to Sarah Zeller-Berkman, October 7, 1987.

115. Alan to Sarah Zeller-Berkman, December 30, 1986.

116. Alan to Barbara and Sarah Zeller-Berkman, December 12, 1986.

117. Alan to Sarah Zeller-Berkman, December 14, 1987.

118. Alan to Hank Newman, December 14, 1987.

119. Interview with Shelley Miller, New York City, June 28, 2017.

120. This was made more difficult for a period when Judy Clark was shipped off to a federal facility in Arizona for "security reasons" when there were renovations at Bedford Hills. Even the *New York Times* editorialized that this was a cruel punishment that visited "the sins of the mother upon the child." *New York Times* editorial, "Punish the Mother, Not the Daughter," January 11, 1988.

121. Alan to Richard Clapp, November 29, 1989; "Joseph Clark, 75, Dies; Editor at *Daily Worker*," *New York Times*, December 29, 1988.

122. Alan to B[arbara], October 12, 1987.

123. Alan to B[arbara], July 17, 1987.

124. Alan to B[arbara], October 20, 1987.

125. Alan to B[arbara], November 11, 1987.

126. Alan to Hank Newman, July 31, 1987.

127. Alan to Barbara, Sunday, ca. November 1987.

128. Alan to Hank Newman, October 1, 1987.

129. Alan to Barbara Carol, February 1, 1988.

130. Alan to Barbara Carol, January 24, 1988.

131. Alan to Barbara Carol, January 24, 1988.

132. Alan to Bruce Taub, October 1, 1987. Unfortunately I do not have access to the letters that Alan wrote to Dana.

133. Alan to Ann Morris, July 23, 1987.

134. Nancy Finlay, "Financing a Free Puerto Rico: The Great Wells Fargo Heist of 1983," https://connecticuthistory.org/financing-a-free-puerto-rico-the-great-wells-fargo-heist -of-1983/.

135. Interview with Ron Kuby, New York City, March 21, 2017.

136. Kuby interview. Rios would finally be granted bail in 1990. He fled bail and lived in the clandestine underground for the next fifteen years. In 2005, however, the FBI cornered him in Puerto Rico, shot him, and allowed him to bleed to death. There were major demonstrations over this in Puerto Rico and New York City; see "FBI Assassinates Puerto Rican Nationalist Leader Filiberto Ojeda Rios," *Democracy Now*, September 26, 2005.

137. Deborah Duffy, "Court Security High for Holdup Suspect," *Hartford Courant*, March 5, 1988.

138. BD, 172.

139. Bruce Taub to Alan, February 6, 1988, BP.

140. Matthew Kauffman, "Doctor Accused in Robbery Set to Go to Court," *Hartford Courant*, February 28, 1988.

141. BD, 161.

142. Joseph A. O'Brien Jr., "GOP Taking Over Sheriff's Office," *Hartford Courant*, May 30, 1995, http://articles.courant.com/1995-05-30/news/9505300271_1_sheriff-s-office -chief-deputy-county-sheriffs-agency.

143. Interview with Lynne Karsten, Boston, February 20, 2017.

144. Kuby interview.

145. Deborah Duffy, "Radical Doctor Sentenced to 5 Years in Robbery," *Hartford Courant*, May 19, 1988.

146. U.S. Department of Justice, United States Attorney, District of Columbia, press release, May 11, 1988, BP.

147. Lee Hockstader, "7 Indicted in 1983 Capitol Bombing; Members of Communist Group Face Charges in 7 Other Explosions," *Washington Post*, May 12, 1988.

148. Lee Hockstader, "7 Indicted in 1983 Capitol Bombing."

149. Philip Shenon, "U.S. Charges 7 in the Bombing at U.S. Capitol," *New York Times*, May 12, 1988.

CHAPTER 12

1. Interview with Laura Whitehorn, New York City, March 8, 2017. The others had already been convicted on other related charges, and only Whitehorn was in prison, in

preventive detention, for more than three years. All interviews cited were conducted by the author unless otherwise specified.

2. Lee Hockstader, "Amid Heavy Security, 6 Plead Not Guilty to Capitol Bombing," *Washington Post*, May 26, 1988.

3. Barbara Zeller and Manny Rosenberg, "Dear Friends," August 1988, BP. Barbara's political work was not just Alan's defense. She made trips to Zimbabwe and Nicaragua and continued to provide medical care to other political prisoners on the U.S. mainland and in Puerto Rico, and to go to various demonstrations in Chicago and Alderson, West Virginia. FBI, Teletype to Director fr FBI New York, June 14, 1985, PDF 8, FBI M19, Batch 2, pp. 125–26; FBI, Teletype to Director Routine fr Chicago, November 2, 1984, PDF 9, FBI M19, Batch 2, pp. 90–91.

4. Alan to Bruce Taub, June 28, 1988.

5. Robert D. Hershey Jr., "Harold H. Greene, Judge Who Oversaw the Breakup of the AT&T Colossus, Dies at 76," *New York Times*, January 30, 2000.

6. Judge Harold H. Greene to Judge George H. Revercomb, April 11, 1989, box 34, folder 1, Harold H. Greene Papers, Library of Congress, Washington, DC. In addition to overseeing the breakup of the AT&T monopoly, Greene had ordered President Reagan to testify in one of the Iran-contra cases.

7. Hockstader, "Amid Heavy Security."

8. Whitehorn interview, March 8, 2017.

9. Alan Berkman to Jack Rosenthal, *New York Times*, August 28, 1988, box 2, folder Resistance Conspiracy Case, SRP. This was an unpublished letter to the *Times* in response to a story about the penitentiary in Marion, written while Alan was in the DC Detention Center.

10. Alan to B[arbara], June n.d., 1988.

11. Alan to B[arbara], June n.d., 1988.

12. BD, 166.

13. *U.S. v. Whitehorn et al.*, Memorandum and Order, Criminal No. 88-0145, June 8, 1988, U.S. District Court of the District of Columbia, box 2, folder Resistance Conspiracy Case, SRP.

14. Alan to Bruce Taub, January 23, 1989.

15. Susie Day, "Resistance Conspiracy Trial," *Z Magazine*, n.d., ca. 1988, clipping in FA.

16. Alan to Bruce Taub, June 28, 1988.

17. Telephone interview with Judy Greenspan, March 12, 2017. Greenspan worked with the ACLU's prison project in Washington, DC, in the 1980s and would become one of the key liaisons for the codefendants to the outside world.

18. Alan to B[arbara], June n.d., 1988.

19. Alan to B[arbara], September 22, 1988.

20. Susan Rosenberg, "Reflection on Being Buried Alive," *Covert Action*, no. 3 (Winter 1989): 50.

21. Tim Blunk, "Solitary Symposium: Four Who Have Spent Time," New York University Institute for the Humanities, November 17, 2012, https://www.youtube.com /watch?v=Ub5NRBmpz3w&sns=em.

22. Alan to Ann Morris, November 2, 1988.

23. Each defendant needed his or her own lawyer, but the defense also had to be coordinated. Some hired private attorneys and others had to rely on public defenders. Whitehorn interview, March 8, 2017; telephone interview with Rosemary Herbert, New

York City, April 13, 2017. Herbert became Alan's lawyer when he appealed this case; see below.

24. U.S. District Court for the District of Columbia, *U.S. v. Whitehorn et al.*, Indictment, June 3, 1987.

25. U.S. District Court for the District of Columbia, *U.S. v. Whitehorn et al.*, Indictment, June 3, 1987.

26. Rosenberg to Dear Folks, May 25–26, 1988, box 4, folder Susan's Letters 1985–1988, SRP.

27. Susie Day, "Political Prisoners: Guilty until Proven Innocent," in *Let Freedom Ring*, edited by Matt Meyer (Oakland: PM Press, 2008), 57.

28. Day, "Political Prisoners."

29. Press release, May 25, 1988, box 2, folder Resistance Conspiracy Case, SRP.

30. Whitehorn interview, March 8, 2017.

31. Interview with Ron Kuby, New York City, March 21, 2017.

32. Statement from the Codefendants in *U.S.A. v. Whitehorn et al.*, June 24, 1988, p. 1, box 2, folder Resistance Conspiracy Case, SRP.

33. Interview with Laura Whitehorn, New York City, March 21, 2017; Whitehorn quoted on illegality and violence in Day, "Resistance Conspiracy Trial," 85.

34. Resistance Conspiracy Case Codefendants to Forum on September 30, 1988, 4, box 2, folder Resistance Conspiracy Case, SRP.

35. Beverly Gage, "Terrorism and the American Experience," *Journal of American History* 98 (June 2011): 73–94; Walter Laqueur, *A History of Terrorism* (New York: Routledge, 2001); Michael Fellman, *In the Name of God and Country: Reconsidering Terrorism in American History* (New Haven, CT: Yale University Press, 2009).

36. William Kunstler and Eleanor Stein, "The New Conspiracy Trial," in *Freedom at Risk: Secrecy, Censorship and Repression in the 1980s*, edited by Richard Curry (Philadelphia: Temple University Press, 1989), 299.

37. "Statement and Budget for Education Funds," 1998, Resistance Conspiracy Case, box 9, folder Miscellaneous, SRP.

38. Laura Whitehorn, "The 'Resistance Conspiracy Case,'" *Covert Action*, no. 31 (Winter 1989): 47.

39. Philip Shenon, "FBI's Chief Says Surveillance Was Justified," *New York Times*, February 3, 1988; CISPES, "The Hunt for Red Menace," March 10, 2008, http://www .publiceye.org/huntred/Hunt_For_Red_Menace-12.html. The FBI kept looking for links between CISPES and the clandestine groups but could not find them; see FBI M19, Batch 2. On Bush's role in the kind of counterinsurgency Alan and his codefendants opposed, see Greg Grandin, "George H. W. Bush, Icon of the WASP Establishment — and Brutal US Repression in the Third World," *The Nation*, December 4, 2018.

40. Susan Rosenberg to Dear Folks, September 19, 1988, box 4, folder Susan's Letters 1985–1988, SRP.

41. Equal Justice Institute, "Racial Terrorism," https://eji.org/history-racial-injustice -racial-terrorism; Philip Dray, *At the Hands of Persons Unknown* (New York: Random House, 2002).

42. Alan to B[arbara], August 7, 1988; Alan to Ann Morris, September 6, 1988; Alan to Dick, July 30, 1988.

43. Whitehorn interview, March 8, 2017.

44. Whitehorn interview, March 8, 2017.

45. Alan to Bruce Taub, June 28, 1988.

46. Alan to Dearest Barbara, August 31, 1988.

47. Alan to Stephen Wangh, August 28, 1988.

48. Alan to Stephen Wangh, August 28, 1988.

49. Alan to Dearest Barbara, August 31, 1988.

50. For an overview on mass incarceration, see Heather Ann Thompson, "Why Mass Incarceration Matters: Rethinking Crisis, Decline, and Transformation in Postwar American History," *Journal of American History* 97 (December 2010): 703–34. On policing as a form of counterinsurgency, see Donna Murch, "Crack in Los Angeles: Crisis, Militarization, and Black Response to the Late 20th Century War on Drugs," *Journal of American History* 102 (June 2015): 162–73; and Julilly Kohler-Hausmann, "Guns and Butter: The Welfare State, the Carceral State, and the Politics of Exclusion in Postwar United States History," *Journal of American History* 102 (June 2015): 87–99.

51. Alan to Richard Clapp, July 6, 1988.

52. Joy James, ed., *Imprisoned Intellectuals: America's Political Prisoners Write on Life, Liberation and Rebellion* (Lanham, MD: Rowman and Littlefield, 2003).

53. Andrew J. DeRoche, *Andrew Young: Civil Rights Ambassador* (Wilmington, DE: Scholarly Resources, 2003), 102–3. Two years later in 1979, when Young met with the PLO without gaining their recognition of Israel, it was the final push. He was relieved of his position at the United Nations.

54. Stuart Taylor Jr., "Political Prisoners Held by Cuba Stir U.S. Disputes," *New York Times*, January 2, 1984; Reuters, "Reagan Prods Soviets: 'Free Prisoners,'" *Los Angeles Times*, May 27, 1988.

55. There was more understanding of American political prisoners outside the United States; see Kathleen Neal Cleaver, "Mobilizing for Mumia Abu-Jamal in Paris," *Yale Journal of Law & the Humanities* 10 (Summer 1998): 327–62.

56. Ronald Kuby and William Kunstler, "Distinction without a Difference," *Los Angeles Times*, May 17, 1990, clipping in box 2, folder Resistance Conspiracy Case, SRP.

57. Interview with Susan Rosenberg, New York City, March 15, 2017.

58. Resistance Conspiracy Case Codefendants to National Human Rights Campaign, n.d., box 2, folder Resistance Conspiracy Case, SRP.

59. A to B[arbara], August 7, 1988.

60. Alan to Stephen Wangh, August 29, 1988.

61. Judy Greenspan, "Political Prisoners," *off our backs* 18 (October 1988): 20.

62. Susan Rosenberg to Dear Folks-All, September 19, 1988, box 4, folder Susan's Letters 1985–1988, SRP.

63. Alan to B[arbara], August 7, 1988.

64. Alan to Dear Friend (Ann), August 2, 1989.

65. Resistance Is No Crime stationery, BP.

66. Rosenberg to Dear Folks-All, September 19, 1988, BP.

67. Laura Whitehorn, card to Susan Rosenberg, September 1988, box 2, no name folder, SRP.

68. Alan to Dearest Barbara, August 31, 1988.

69. Greenspan interview.

70. Personal communication from Laura Whitehorn, New York City, March 22, 2017.

71. Susan Rosenberg to Dear Folks, August 23, 1988, box 4, folder Susan's Letters 1985–1988, SRP.

72. Interview with Jerry and Louise Berkman, Stamford, CT, September 19, 2013.

73. Max Elbaum, *Revolution in the Air: Sixties Radicals Turn to Lenin, Mao, and Che* (London: Verso, 2003); Susan Faludi, *Backlash* (New York: Crown, 1991); Roger Craft Peace, *A Call to Conscience: The Anti/Contra War Campaign* (Amherst: University of Massachusetts Press, 2012); Robert Kinloch Massie, *Loosing the Bonds: The United States and South Africa in the Apartheid Years* (New York: Doubleday, 1997).

74. Washington Area Committee for Political Prisoners Rights and Committee to Fight Repression, "Support the Resistance Conspiracy Defendants" poster, n.d., ca. 1988–90, BP; telephone interview with Soffiyah Elijah, New York City, March 14, 2017. Elijah was the lawyer for Marilyn Buck in many of her cases.

75. Toronto Anarchist Black Cross, "Resistance Conspiracy Case" leaflet, ca. 1988–90. I am grateful to Randy Ats Smith for posting this on his Facebook page, July 14, 2017.

76. Alison Bechdel, "Free Lunch," n.d. Lisa Roth, who had been a supporter of the RCC defendants, sent me this clip.

77. Interview with Susie Day, New York City, March 23, 2017. Day, a journalist who wrote for left and feminist newspapers, first came to Washington, DC, to cover the case for the Boston-based women's paper *Sojourner*. She fell in love with Laura Whitehorn then, and they are now married.

78. Rosenberg interview, March 15, 2017; telephone interview with Jane Segal, April 14, 2017; telephone interview with Lisa Roth, April 9, 2017.

79. Zeller and Rosenberg, "Dear Friends," August 1988, BP; Alan to Richard Clapp, July 30, 1988; interview with H. Jack Geiger, Brooklyn, NY, March 20, 2017; interview with Susan Rosenberg, New York City, March 14, 2017; A Campaign to Support the Resistance Conspiracy Codefendants, "Resistance Is Not a Crime! Stop the Political Show Trial! Drop the Charges Now!" pamphlet, ca. November 1989, BP.

80. Alan to Dearest Barbara, August 31, 1988. Unfortunately, I do not know what he was telling Dana Biberman at the same time.

81. Alan to B[arbara], ca. June 1988.

82. Alan to B[arbara], ca. June 1988, letter 2.

83. Alan to B[arbara], ca. June 1988, letter 4.

84. Alan to Barbara Carol, October 27, 1988.

85. Alan to Dearest Barbara, August 31, 1988.

86. See, for example, Milton R. Wessel, "Procedural Safeguards for the Mass Conspiracy Trial," *American Bar Association Journal* 48 (July 1962): 628–33; Chad W. Coulter, "The Unnecessary Rule of Consistency in Conspiracy Trials," *University of Pennsylvania Law Review* 135 (December 1986): 223–46.

87. Alan to Stephen Wangh, October 17, 1989.

88. Alan to Stephen Wangh, October 17, 1989.

89. Alan to Stephen Wangh, October 17, 1989.

90. Alan to Stephen Wangh, October 17, 1989.

91. Alan to Stephen Wangh, October 17, 1989.

92. Alan to Stephen Wangh, October 17, 1989.

93. *U.S. v. Rosenberg et al.*, 710 F. Supp. 803 (D.C. Cir. 1989), BP.

94. Susan W. Brenner, "Of Complicity and Enterprise Criminality: Applying *Pinkerton* Liability to RICO Actions," *Missouri Law Review* 56 (Fall 1991): 1.

95. Rosenberg interview, March 15, 2017.

96. Whitehorn interview, March 8, 2017. Mary O'Melvany, Susan Rosenberg's lawyer, does not think that she and Alan argued, but Laura Whitehorn remembers that they did. Whitehorn thought the ideas for the double jeopardy claim came from Alan, but

O'Melvany states it was from her legal work. Mary O'Melvany, email to author, September 23, 2017.

97. *U.S. v. Rosenberg et al.*, 888 F. 2d 1406 (D.C. Cir. 1989), BP.

98. Alan to Stephen Wangh, May 12, 1989.

99. Alan to Stephen Wangh, May 12, 1989.

100. Alan to Dear Friend (Ann), August 2, 1989.

101. Herbert interview.

102. Alan to Ann Morris, July 12, 1989.

103. *U.S. v. Rosenberg et al.*, 88 F. 2d 1406, U.S. Court of Appeals, District of Columbia Circuit, November 3, 1989, BP.

104. Mary O'Melvany, email to author, September 23, 2017.

105. Alan to Richard Clapp, February 17, 1990.

106. Alan Berkman and Richard Clapp, "Prisoners' Health vs. Prison Health Care," APHA Annual Meeting, 1990, BP.

107. Alan to Richard Clapp, February 17, 1990.

108. Alan to Richard Clapp, January n.d. [ca. 25], 1990.

109. Ron Kuby, "In the Matter of the Parole Application of Dr. Alan Berkman, Pre-hearing Memorandum of Dr. Alan Berkman," January 26, 1990, Exhibits I, L, and M, BP.

110. *U.S. v. Alan Berkman*, 83 CR 798, October 9, 1990, *Memorandum Opinion and Order*, BP.

111. Alan to Richard Clapp, February 17, 1990.

CHAPTER 13

1. Susan Rosenberg to Dear Folks, August 23, 1988, box 4, folder Susan's Letters 1985–1988, SRP.

2. Susie Day, interview with Alan Berkman, New York City, summer 2003. I am grateful to Susie Day for sharing this with me.

3. Fran Poller, "Political Doctors," *Medical World News*, November 28, 1988; George Freeman Solomon, "Expert Opinion of George F. Solomon, M.D. Concerning Possibility of Stress-Induced Recurrence of Hodgkin's Disease in Alan Berkman, M.D., a Defendant: *U.S. v. Laura Whitehorn et al.*," BP.

4. Anthony Lewis, "Death by Delay," *New York Times*, May 15, 1990.

5. Lewis, "Death by Delay"; Barbara Zeller to Congressman Ted Weiss, April 16, 1990. Barbara Zeller to Kenneth Morisugu, Federal Bureau of Prisons, April 16, 1990, BP.

6. Barbara Zeller, "Campaign to Free Alan Berkman, 1990," BP. I counted at least 400 letters in the files.

7. Zeller to Morisugu.

8. *U.S. v. Alan Berkman*, Crim. No. 85-222, April 25, 1990, Emergency Order, BP.

9. *U.S. v. Alan Berkman*, Emergency Order.

10. Lewis, "Death by Delay."

11. Larry Thompson, "Prisoner Demands Prompt Cancer Treatment," *Washington Post*, June 5, 1990.

12. Michael Isikoff, "Prison Hospital May Be Hazard to Inmates," *Washington Post*, June 14, 1991.

13. Interview with Ron Kuby, New York City, March 21, 2017. All interviews cited were conducted by the author unless otherwise specified.

14. See, for example, Angela Wright, Amnesty International, to Stephen Wangh, July 20, 1990; and Steve Krugman to the Honorable Barney Frank, June 21, 1990, BP.

15. Carl Ernest Freter, "Affidavit of Carl Ernest Freter, M.D., Ph.D.," *U.S. v. Alan Berkman*, Criminal No. 85-222, June 18, 1990, BP.

16. Alan to Stephen Wangh, June 26, 1990, quoted in BD, 177.

17. Barbara C. Zeller, "Clinical Course during Chemotherapy—Summary," 1990, BP.

18. Interview with Laura Whitehorn, New York City, March 8, 2017.

19. BD, 176.

20. BD, 176.

21. Alan to Tom Garrett, June 16, 1990. I am grateful to Dr. Tom Garrett for these letters.

22. B. W. Hancock and A. Naysmith, "Vincristine-Induced Autonomic Neuropathy," *British Medical Journal* 3 (July 26, 1975): 207.

23. Hancock and Naysmith, "Vincristine-Induced Autonomic Neuropathy," 207.

24. Telephone interview with Barbara Zeller, June 25, 2017.

25. CBS, "That's the Law," *60 Minutes*, March 17, 1991, video and transcript in author's possession.

26. CBS, "That's the Law."

27. Quotes and discussion of these problems are in BD, 186–99.

28. Paul McIssac, interview with Alan Berkman, August 10, 1992. I am grateful to Paul McIssac for providing me with the tape of this interview. I did the transcription.

29. Thomas L. Sacks, "Alan Berkman Medical History," December 26, 1990, BP.

30. There were no cell phones, so she had to be called on her landline.

31. Zeller interview, June 25, 2017.

32. BD, 188.

33. BD, 189.

34. BD, 199–200.

35. Alan, "Statement before the U.S. Senate Subcommittee," 9, BP.

36. Alan to Judge Louis H. Pollak, November 12, 1990.

37. Dana Biberman to Ron Kuby, "Notes from Comrade Alan," fax, November 13, 1990, BP.

38. "Save Alan Berkman," flyer, November 20, 1990, BP.

39. Laura Whitehorn, email to author, July 1, 2017.

40. Whitehorn interview.

41. RCC Codefendants, "Dear Friends," 1, not for publication, n.d., Fall 1990, box 2, folder Resistance Conspiracy Case, SRP.

42. Interview with Linda Evans, Santa Rosa, CA, March 8, 2016.

43. Laura Whitehorn, email to author, July 1, 2017.

44. RCC Codefendants, "Dear Friends," 1.

45. BD, 191.

46. *U.S. v. Whitehorn et al.*, "Plea Agreement," U.S. District Court for the District of Columbia, Criminal No. 88-0145, 1990, BP; "3 Women Plead Guilty in 1983 Bombing of Capitol," *Washington Post*, September 8, 1990. By then the story was relegated to the back pages of the *Washington Post* since the judge's bigger trial of John Poindexter in the Iran-contra case had just ended. Poindexter's trial and sentencing were regularly the subject of front-page articles in the *Post* during the first six months of 1990.

47. I attempted to get a response from the key government attorney, but he would not answer questions. On the other conspiracy case, see AP, "After 9 Months of Delay,

Sedition Trial of 3 in Revolutionary Group Opens," *New York Times*, January 12, 1989; and "Judge Declares Mistrial for 3 in Sedition Case," *New York Times*, November 30, 1989.

48. James Ridgeway, "Hard Time: Why the Left Goes to Jail and the Right Goes Home," *Village Voice*, December 11, 1990, clipping in BP.

49. David Johnston, "Iran-Contra Role Brings Poindexter 6 Months in Prison," *New York Times*, June 12, 1990.

50. Ridgeway, "Hard Time."

51. Alan Berkman, Tim Blunk, Marilyn Buck, Linda Evans, Susan Rosenberg, and Laura Whitehorn, "Statement from the Resistance Conspiracy Defendants," *Breakthrough: Political Journal of Prairie Fire Organizing Committee*, Fall 1990, 47.

52. RCC Codefendants, "Dear Friends," 6.

53. Laura Whitehorn, "Sentencing Statement," December 6, 1990, BP.

54. Alan to Dear Friends, November 1, 1990.

55. Sacks, "Alan Berkman Medical History."

56. Carl E. Freter to Ron Kuby, January 3, 1991, BP; Sacks, "Alan Berkman Medical History."

57. Freter to Kuby.

58. Follow-Up Care and Rehabilitation for Alan Berkman, December 3, 1990, BP.

59. Sacks, "Alan Berkman Medical History."

60. Ron Kuby to Dr. Herman Benson, January 6, 1991, BP; Dr. Herman Benson to Ron Kuby, January 10, 1991, BP.

61. Ron Kuby to Dr. Alan Berkperson, Dr. Barbara Zeller, Debbie Katz, Dana Biberperson, Rosemary Herbert, and Elizabeth O' Connor Tomlinson, n.d., ca. December 1990 or January 1991, BP.

62. Alan to Richard Clapp, February 8, 1991; Alan to Ann Morris, February 23, 1991.

63. Alan to Ann Morris, February 23, 1991.

64. Alan to Ann Morris, February 23, 1991.

65. Alan to Ann Morris, February 7, 1991.

66. KTTC, "Rochester Federal Medical Center Marks 30th Anniversary," September 29, 2015, http://www.kttc.com/story/30137129/2015/09/Tuesday/rochester-federal-medical -center-marks-30th-anniversary; telephone interview with Barbara Zeller, June 29, 2017.

67. Alan to Richard Clapp, April 26, 1991.

68. Alan to Richard Clapp, April 26, 1991, November 9, 1991.

69. Alan Berkman, "Statement for the U.S. House Judiciary Subcommittee," 11, BP.

70. Berkman, "Statement for the U.S. House Judiciary Subcommittee," 6.

71. BD, 216.

72. Alan to Ann Morris, March 9, 1991.

73. Alan to Tom Garrett, June 16, 1991. Alan's reference is to French psychologist and pharmacist Émile Coué (1857–1926), who developed a popular method of optimistic autosuggestion.

74. Alan to Stephen Wangh, August 5, 1991.

75. Alan to Stephen Wangh, August 5, 1991.

76. Alan to Ann Morris, May 11, 1991.

77. Alan to Ann Morris, May 11, 1991, August 21, 1991.

78. Alan to Stephen Wangh, December 28, 1991, and August 5, 1991.

79. Jim Bakker, *I Was Wrong: The Untold Story of the Shocking Journey from PTL Power to Prison and Beyond* (Nashville: Thomas Nelson, 1997), 229. For more on Bakker and Alan, see below.

80. Kathy Boudin and Judy Clark, "A Community of Women Organize Themselves to Cope with the AIDS Crisis: A Case Study from Bedford Hills Correctional Facility," *Columbia Journal of Gender and Law* 1 (1991): 47–66.

81. Alan to Stephen Wangh, August 5, 1991.

82. Alan to Richard Clapp, August 27, 1991; testimony of Judith Van Heerden, Truth and Reconciliation Commission, Special Hearings—Prisons, http://www.justice.gov.za/trc/special%5Cprison/vanheerd.htm.

83. Berkman, journal notes, June 20, 1991, in BD, 206.

84. Alan to Richard Clapp, April 6, 1991.

85. Alan to Stephen Wangh, August 5, 1991; Betty and Herman Liveright, interview with Alan Berkman, Rochester, MN, August 19, 1991. I am grateful to Noelle Hanrahan of Prison Radio for providing this tape to me. I did the transcription. The Liverights were long-standing political activists who ran the Berkshire Forum in western Massachusetts, which hosted political forums over the decades.

86. Anthony Lewis to Ms. Biberman, August 2, 1991, BP.

87. Berkman, "Statement for the U.S. House Judiciary Subcommittee." See also Susan M. Reverby, "Can There Be Acceptable Prison Health Care? Looking Back on the 1970s," *Public Health Reports* 134, no. 1 (2019): 89–93.

88. Alan to Richard Clapp, April 26, 1991; Zeller interview, June 29, 2017.

89. BD, 206–18. Alan wrote these descriptions as short vignettes, with very little commentary.

90. BD, 216–18.

91. Alan to Stephen Wangh, November 11, 1991.

92. Alan to Ann Morris, June 26, 1991.

93. Alan to Richard Clapp, December 18, 1991.

94. Betty and Herman Liveright, interview with Alan Berkman.

95. Alan to Richard Clapp, November 9, 1991.

96. Telephone interview with Miranda Bergman, San Francisco, March 2, 2014.

97. Alan to Richard Clapp, November 9, 1991.

98. Ronald Kuby and William Kunstler, "Memorandum to the Board of Professional Medical Conduct of the State of New York in the Matter of Dr. Alan Berkman, NYS #112795," New York City, October 28, 1991, BP.

99. Alan to Ron Kuby, January 24, 1990; Ron Kuby, email to author, July 13, 2017.

100. Ron Kuby email to author, July 13, 2017.

101. Alan to Richard Clapp, March 3, 1992.

102. Alan to Richard Clapp, April 26 and December 18, 1991.

103. Alan to Richard Clapp, March 3, 1992.

104. Paul McIssac, interview with Dana Biberman, New York City, October 22, 1992. I am grateful to Paul McIssac for sharing his Biberman interview tapes with me. I did the transcriptions.

105. Alan to Richard Clapp, November 9, 1991.

106. Alan to Ann Morris, November 16, 1991.

107. Alan to Richard Clapp, November 9 and 19, 1991.

108. Alan to Ann Morris, October 11, 1991.

109. Alan to Richard Clapp, December 18, 1991; see also Alan to Stephen Wangh, December 28, 1991.

110. Alan to Anne Nosworthy Fisher, February 9, 1992. I am grateful to Anne for this letter. She also went from Middletown High School to Cornell and alerted his high school

friends to his situation. It was with her encouragement that I wrote about Alan for the Cornell twenty-fifth reunion book just a month before he got out of prison. He told Anne in the same letter: "I received the article from Susan. It is very lovely, and I think the fact of her doing it, in some ways, more significant that what's written on the page."

111. Alan to Hank Newman, February 7, 1992.

112. Alan to Hank Newman, March 2, 1992.

113. Alan to Hank Newman, February 7, 1992.

114. Alan to Hank Newman, March 2, 1992.

115. Alan to Hank Newman, April 8, 1992; interview with Dana Biberman, New York City, April 26, 2013.

116. Alan to Stephen Wangh, November 11, 1991.

117. Alan to Stephen Wangh, February 10, 1992.

118. Alan to Stephen Wangh, February 10, 1992.

119. Alan to Hank Newman, March 2, 1992.

CHAPTER 14

1. On his leg problems, see Alan to Laura Foner, August 24, 1991. I am grateful to Laura Foner for this and other letters between them. The description is based on the "Alan Berkman Homecoming" DVD, 1992. Barbara took the video of Alan's first day out and then the party in his honor two days later on July 12, 1992. I have a copy of the DVD that was made from the video in 2017.

2. Alan to Laura Foner, August 24, 1991.

3. BD, 221.

4. Telephone interview with Barbara Zeller, August 27, 2017. All interviews cited were conducted by the author unless otherwise specified.

5. Interview with Lynne Karsten, Wellfleet, MA, July 29, 2017.

6. Telephone interview with Sarah Zeller-Berkman, August 25, 2017.

7. Zeller interview, August 27, 2017.

8. Telephone interview with Shelley Miller, October 22, 2017.

9. Zeller-Berkman interview, August 25, 2017.

10. Hansi Lo Wang, "Yuri Kochiyama, Activist and Former World War II Internee, Dies at 93," *All Things Considered*, June 2, 2014, http://www.npr.org/sections/codeswitch /2014/06/02/318072652/japanese-american-activist-and-malcolm-x-ally-dies-at-93.

11. All the quotes from his first day and then the party come from "Alan Berkman Homecoming" DVD; my transcription.

12. Barbara Zeller kept Alan's thumb drive of his computer files and gave them to me.

13. The memoir was built upon the letters Alan sent out during the years he was incarcerated as well as any journal notes he was able to keep. When he wrote it, circa early in 2000, he asked his correspondents to return his letters to him.

14. BD, 222.

15. Jan Hoffman, "Healing on Parole: Doctor and Ex-Prisoner, He Treats Others on Probation," *New York Times*, January 10, 1994.

16. Telephone interview with Sarah Zeller-Berkman, August 25, 2017.

17. Zeller-Berkman interview, August 25, 2017.

18. Telephone interview with Sarah Zeller-Berkman, August 27, 2017.

19. Random notes on pink sticky notes and lined notepaper by Alan, n.d., ca. 1992, BP.

20. BD, 227.

21. BD, 222.

22. Alan to Paul, "Interview," October 23, 1992.

23. John Leland, "David Dinkins Doesn't Think He Failed: He Might Be Right," *New York Times Magazine*, November 11, 2017.

24. David France, *How to Survive a Plague* (New York: Alfred Knopf, 2016).

25. Telephone interview with Laura Whitehorn, October 22, 2017.

26. Whitehorn interview, October 22, 2017.

27. BD, 222.

28. Alan had provided medical care to the Osborne's Association's head, Elizabeth Gaynes's husband, a former Attica brother, after he had a violent confrontation with the police. Sarah and Gaynes's daughter also knew one another. Telephone interview with Elizabeth Gaynes, April 12, 2017; John Kifner, "Two Policemen and Gunman Killed, Suspect Shot on Brooklyn Street," *New York Times*, April 3, 1978.

29. "The NADA Protocol," http://www.acupuncturetoday.com/Alanc/nadaprotocol.php.

30. Gaynes interview.

31. Telephone interview with Yolanda Castro, New York City, November 15, 2017. Castro was an acupuncturist at El Río who had learned her skills from Jackie Haught, then followed Alan to his next position.

32. Hoffman, "Healing on Parole."

33. Hoffman, "Healing on Parole."

34. Dick Clapp, personal communication to author, November 14, 2017.

35. Paul McIssac, interview with Dana Biberman, New York City, October 23, 1992. I am grateful to Paul McIssac for sharing his Biberman interview tapes with me. I did the transcriptions.

36. Alan Berkman, curriculum vitae, June 2006, BP.

37. Neighborhood Preservation Center, Landmarks Preservation Commission (former) American Female Guardian Society and Home for the Friendless Woody Crest Home, Designation list 312-LP-2049; Christopher Gray, "Streetscapes: Woodycrest Children's Home; A New Life — and Mission — for a Bronx Residence," *New York Times*, January 8, 1989.

38. Interview with Patricia Williams, Brooklyn, NY, March 27, 2017. Williams was a nurse and later nursing director at Highbridge-Woodycrest when Alan was there.

39. Mark Taylor to Alan Berkman, May 1, 2001, email draft of interview with "Alan Berkman, M.D., from Staff Physician to Medical Director," BP. While the interview took place in 2001, Alan became medical director in 1996.

40. Taylor to Alan, May 1, 2001.

41. Taylor to Alan, May 1, 2001.

42. Alan, memo to Dr. A. Fernandez, November 29, 1999.

43. Alan, "Letters," Woodycrest folder, BCF.

44. Alan to Pat King, Director of Nursing Services, April 12, 2000, "Memos," Woodycrest folder, BCF.

45. Alan, Woodycrest folder, BCF.

46. Williams and Castro interviews.

47. Williams interview.

48. Williams interview; Woodycrest folder, BCF.

49. BD, 222.

50. Alan to Stephen Wangh, August 29, 1988, March 6, 1988.

51. Interview with Dana Biberman, New York City, April 26, 2013.

52. Paul McIssac, interview with Alan Berkman, September 1, 1992; my transcription.

53. McIssac, interview with Alan Berkman.

54. Zeller interview, August 27, 2017.

55. I met up with Alan after we, along with 4,000 others, attended poet and activist Audre Lorde's memorial service on January 17, 1993, at St. John the Divine in New York City. I asked then about Barbara (whom I had never met), and he told me, "I'm with a woman named Dana now."

56. Zeller interview, June 25, 2017.

57. Interview with Liz Horowitz, New York City, October 28, 2015.

58. Zeller interview, August 27, 2017. All quotes in this paragraph are from this interview.

59. Telephone interview with Jackie Haught, October 25, 2015; interview with Beth Somers, Cambridge, MA, August 5, 2015. Sommers had worked with Haught in Portland.

60. Peter Wortsman, "A Small-Town Doc in the South Bronx," *P&S Journal* 18 (Winter 1998): n.p.

61. Meg Starr and Barbara Zeller, eds., *Diss'ing the Discovery* (New York: Free Puerto Rico Committee–New York Chapter, 1992), FA. Mumia Abu-Jamal, then on death row in Pennsylvania, had been in the Black Panthers; Leonard Peltier from the American Indian Movement was held by the federal government on what his supporters also thought were trumped-up murder charges.

62. Interview with Barbara Zeller, New York City, January 20, 2013.

63. Zeller interview, June 25, 2017.

64. Interview with Shelley Miller, New York City, May 19, 2015.

65. "2 More Found Guilty for Refusing to Talk in F.A.L.N. Inquiry," *New York Times*, January 21, 1984.

66. Tom Robbins, "Judith Clark's Radical Transformation," *New York Times*, January 12, 2012.

67. Miller interview, May 19, 2015.

68. Miller interview, May 19, 2015; interview with Harriet Clark, San Francisco, March 5, 2016. All quotes from Harriet that follow are from this interview.

69. Harriet Clark interview.

70. Harriet Clark interview; Robbins, "Judith Clark's Radical Transformation."

71. Harriet Clark interview. On the relationship of donor fathers to their children, see Rosanna Hertz, *Single by Chance, Mothers by Choice* (New York: Oxford University Press, 2006).

72. Biberman interview.

73. BD, 222.

74. Zeller interview, August 27, 2017.

75. Zeller interview, August 27, 2017.

76. Alan Berkman, "Speech in Chicago," late 1990s, BP; Nancy Kurshan, *Out of Control: A Fifteen-Year Battle against Control Unit Prisons* (San Francisco: Freedom Archives, 2013).

77. "Mobilize to Save Mumia Abu-Jamal," *Workers Vanguard*, no. 603 (July 8, 1984): 7. In 2011, a federal court overturned Abu-Jamal's death sentence and resentenced him to life in prison without the possibility of parole. New information about his case and lost files are now being used to contest his trial, conviction, and sentencing.

78. Laura Whitehorn, ed., *The War Before: The True Life Story of Becoming a Black Panther, Keeping the Faith in Prison, and Fighting for Those Left Behind* (New York: Feminist

Press, 2010). Kuby was asked by PBS to organize his side, and he picked Safiya Bukhari and Alan. Ron Kuby, email to author, November 25, 2017.

79. PBS, "Should We Grant Amnesty to America's Political Prisoners?," *Debates Debates*, April 1998; transcript in author's possession.

80. I am grateful to Dan Berger for his insight into this.

81. Rose died from a brain tumor a few months after the debate. See Eric Pace, "Charles Rose, 51, Ex-Prosecutor Who Pursued Reputed Mobsters," *New York Times*, December 14, 1998. Rose had also been the federal prosecutor in the case against Silvia Baraldini and Shelley Miller.

82. PBS, "Should We Grant Amnesty to America's Political Prisoners?," 3. He made a similar argument when the Liverights interviewed him in prison in 1991; see Betty and Herman Liveright, interview with Alan Berkman, Rochester, MN, August 19, 1991.

83. PBS, "Should We Grant Amnesty to America's Political Prisoners?," 8.

84. PBS, "Should We Grant Amnesty to America's Political Prisoners?," 14.

85. PBS, "Should We Grant Amnesty to America's Political Prisoners?," 17.

86. PBS, "Should We Grant Amnesty to America's Political Prisoners?," 21.

87. Craig Hemmens and James W. Marquart, "Fear and Loathing in the Joint: The Impact of Race and Age on Inmate Support for Prison AIDS Policies," *Prison Journal* 78 (June 1998): 133–51.

88. See Judy Clark and Kathy Boudin, "Community of Women Organize Themselves to Cope with the AIDS Crisis: A Case Study from Bedford Hills Correctional Facility," *Social Justice* 17 (Summer 1990): 90–109; David Gilbert, "Educating Prisoners," *Focus: A Guide to AIDS Research and Counseling* 4 (May 1989): 3; interviews with Linda Evans (Santa Rosa, CA, March 8, 2016), Susan Rosenberg (New York City, January 26, 2016), and Laura Whitehorn (New York City, March 8, 2017).

89. Kimberly Collica, *Female Prisoners, AIDS, and Peer Programs: How Female Offenders Transform Their Lives* (New York: Springer, 2013); Judy Greenspan, "HIV Infection among Prisoners," *Focus: A Guide to AIDS Research and Counseling* 4 (May 1989): 1–2; Richard Parker, "Grassroots Activism, Civil Society Mobilization, and the Politics of the Global HIV/AIDS Epidemic," *Brown Journal of World Affairs* 17 (Summer 2011): 21–37.

90. A. R. Jonsen and J. Stryker, eds., *The Social Impact of AIDS in the United States* (Washington, DC: National Academies Press, 1993), chap. 7; Carolyn Behrendt et al., "HIV Infection and AIDS among U.S. Prison Inmates," *Journal of Crime and Justice* 15, no. 1 (1992): 173–86.

91. The efforts for harm-reduction in prison required providing clean needles and condoms, which required carceral authorities to acknowledge that both drug use and sexual contact were happening in their prisons and jails.

92. Alan Berkman, "Prison Health: The Breaking Point," *American Journal of Public Health* 85 (December 1995): 1616–18, quote from 1618. Alan was making these points years before the recognition of prison as a public health problem itself came to the fore.

CHAPTER 15

1. Collica, *Female Prisoners, AIDS, and Peer Programs: How Female Offenders Transform their Lives* (New York: Springer, 2013); Greenspan, "HIV Infection among Prisoners"; Carolyn Behrendt et al., "HIV Infection and AIDS among U.S. Prison Inmates," *Journal of Crime and Justice* 15, no. 1 (1992): 173–86. Kathy Boudin and Judy Clark had started an

AIDS education project in their prison and David Gilbert in his in 1987, and his other incarcerated conspiracy case comrades would all follow suit throughout the 1990s. Interviews with Linda Evans (Santa Rosa, CA, March 8, 2016), Susan Rosenberg (New York City, January 26, 2016), Judith Clark (Bedford Hills, NY, April 3, 2013), and Laura Whitehorn (New York City, March 8, 2017). All interviews cited were conducted by the author unless otherwise specified.

2. All of Alan's white comrades are either now out or dead (Buck). Most of the BLA men are still imprisoned.

3. Jasmine Garsd, "Long before Facebook, the KGB Spread Fake News about AIDS," *NPR*, August 22, 2018, https://www.npr.org/2018/08/22/640883503/long-before -facebook-the-kgb-spread-fake-news-about-aids.

4. Seth Kalichman, *Denying AIDS* (New York: Springer Science, 2009); Nicoli Nattrass, *The AIDS Conspiracy* (New York: Columbia University Press, 2012); "Conspiracy That Attributed AIDS to the CIA," *Gizmondo*, October 25, 2013, https://io9.gizmodo.com/the -kgb-conspiracy-that-attributed-aids-to-the-cia-1451935938.

5. BL, "Dead Certain?," *POZ*, April 1, 2006; the quote appears in the longer draft version that Lederer wrote and sent to me.

6. First published in *Covert Action Quarterly*, October 1996, 55–64. It was later issued as a pamphlet by the Canadian-based Kersplebedeb in May 2002. It is also in David Gilbert, *No Surrender: Writings from an Anti-Imperialist Political Prisoner* (Oakland, CA: Arm the Spirit, 2004), 129–50.

7. Quoted in Nattrass, *The AIDS Conspiracy*, 66 and 72. Nattrass devotes an entire chapter to Gilbert's work and dedicates her book to him. Interview with David Gilbert, Auburn Correctional Facility, Auburn, NY, November 12, 2014.

8. Raymond A. Smith and Patricia A. Siplon, *Drugs into Bodies* (New York: Praeger, 2006), 36; interview with BL and John Riley, New York City, March 25, 2017; Alan to BL, October 19, 1985, BL's possession. ACT UP (AIDS Coalition to Unleash Power) was the major AIDS activist group that forced changes in drug and treatment options; see David France, *How to Survive a Plague* (New York: Knopf, 2016).

9. Alan was on Lederer's show on March 19, 1998, and went with him a few months later to the debate at SUNY-Purchase. BL and Riley interview, March 25, 2017.

10. BL and Riley interview, March 25, 2017.

11. See Berkman quotes in BL, "Dead Certain?" *POZ*, April 2, 2006, https://www.poz .com/article/Dead-Certain-2788-6789. Although this was written eight years after Alan first refuted the denialists, it reflected his longtime thinking on this problem.

12. Lance Bangs, dir., *The Lazarus Effect* (Red), HBO, May 24, 2010.

13. Quoted in Sean Strub, "Bill Clinton's LGBT Shame: Where Was He Then?," *Salon*, February 1, 2014, https://www.salon.com/2014/02/01/bill_clintons_lgbt_shame_where _was_he_then/.

14. Interview with Zena Stein and Ida Susser, Hastings-on-Hudson, NY, August 9, 2017.

15. George Davey Smith and Ezra Susser, "Zena Stein, Mervyn Susser and Epidemiology: Observation, Causation and Action," *International Journal of Epidemiology* 31 (February 2002): 34–37; interview with Ezra Susser, New York City, October 11, 2011.

16. Zena Stein and Mervyn Susser to Oliver R. Tambo, May 25, 1990, BP.

17. Ezra Susser interview.

18. Ezra Susser interview.

19. H. Roger Segelken, "Dr. Allan Rosenfield, Women's Health Advocate, Dies at 75," *New York Times*, October 16, 2008.

20. Telephone interview with Daniel Vasgird, January 22, 2018. Vasgird ran the New York City Health Department's IRB then and was impressed by Alan's commitments and knowledge.

21. Sarah Conover, Alan Berkman, et al., "Methods for Successful Follow-Up of Elusive Urban Populations: An Ethnographic Approach with Homeless Men," *Bulletin of the New York Academy of Medicine* 74 (Summer 1997): 90–108. The project started with only men but expanded to include women too.

22. Conover, Berkman, et al., "Methods for Successful Follow-Up," 100.

23. "Next Riskiest 6 Experimentals List," n.d., BCF.

24. Barbara Zeller, email to author, January 25, 2018.

25. Victoria Harden, *AIDS at 30* (Dulles, VA: Potomac, 2012).

26. Telephone interview with Eric Sawyer, January 1, 2018.

27. Elizabeth Fee and Manon Parry, "Jonathan Mann, HIV/AIDS, and Human Rights," *Journal of Public Health Policy* 29 (April 2008): 54–71.

28. Jonathan Mann, "Human Rights and AIDS: The Future of the Pandemic," in *Health and Human Rights: A Reader*, edited by Jonathan Mann et al. (New York: Routledge, 1999), 223.

29. Lara Semple, "Health and Human Rights in Today's Fight against HIV/AIDS," *AIDS* 22, supp. 2 (August 2008): S113–S121.

30. Jonathan Mann, "The Future of the Global AIDS Movement," *Harvard AIDS Review* (Spring 1999): 18–21. Mann and his wife, an AIDS immunologist, were both killed when their Swissair Flight 111 crashed on September 2, 1998, in the North Atlantic Ocean.

31. Nicole A. Szlezak, *The Making of Global Health Governance* (New York: Palgrave, Macmillan, 2012), 53–54; Mark Zimmerman and Mark Schoofs, "World AIDS Experts Debate Treatment vs. Prevention," *Wall Street Journal*, July 3, 2002.

32. Barbara Zeller, email to author, November 30, 2017.

33. "You know one thing I wish I had done is spend more time in a revolutionary TW [third world] country. I think that is an important personal & political experience." Alan to Marion [Banzhaf] and spousal equivalent, September 29, 1986. Bob Lederer had a copy of this letter.

34. Telephone interview with Pamela Collins, Seattle, February 15, 2018. Collins was in the same postdoc program as Alan and worked with him on the prevention of HIV for the homeless and in South Africa.

35. Berkman, COAP CV, June 2006, BP; telephone interview with Ezra Susser, December 17, 2017.

36. Ezra Susser, on DVD of Dr. Alan Berkman Memorial Service, Columbia University, Mailman School of Public Health, New York City, April 23, 2010.

37. Raymond Smith, interview with Alan Berkman, New York City, February 21, 2002. I am grateful to Professor Smith for sharing this interview with me.

38. Alan's photos of the animals they saw were still on his computer, BCF.

39. Lawrence K. Altman, "At AIDS Conference, a Call to Arms against 'Runaway Epidemic,'" *New York Times*, June 28, 1998.

40. Richard Horton, "The 12th World AIDS Conference: A Cautionary Tale," *Lancet* 352 (July 11, 1998): 122.

41. See Project Inform, "'Bridge the Gap?' or 'Cut the Crap!,'" *Project Inform Perspective*, no. 25, September 1998, 1–3.

42. Smith and Siplon, *Drugs into Bodies*. Alan wrote the afterword for this book.

43. Horton, "The 12th World AIDS Conference."

44. Bob Lederer, "World AIDS Conference in Geneva: Notes from Phone Conversation with Eric Sawyer," *POZ*, July 1, 1998, BL personal collection. I am grateful to Bob Lederer for providing me with this.

45. Paul McIssac, interview with Alan Berkman, July 21, 2001; my transcription. I am grateful to Paul McIssac for providing me with the transcript and tapes of this interview.

46. Zena Stein, tribute to Alan Berkman, Health GAP 10th Anniversary, May 21, 2009, BP.

47. Dachau photographs, BCF.

48. McIssac, interview with Alan Berkman.

49. Smith, interview with Alan Berkman.

50. McIssac, interview with Alan Berkman.

51. Zimmerman and Schoofs, "World AIDS Experts Debate Treatment vs. Prevention."

52. Stein, "Tribute to Alan Berkman," quoting Jamaican physician Cicely Williams.

53. Franklin List, *Global Institutions and the HIV/AIDS Epidemic: Responding to an International Crisis* (New York: Routledge, 2010).

54. Alan Berkman, "Health GAP Talking Points for HHS Consultation," February 23, 2000; notes, "HIV Center and Bronx Consortium," April 7, 2000, on various prevention strategies for high-risk populations, BCF.

55. Alan Berkman, "From Geneva to Durban: Solidarity Bridges the Gap," October 1998, BCF. All subsequent quotes from this paper. Much of this history is also in Smith and Siplon, *Drugs into Bodies*.

56. Interview with Richard Parker, New York City, March 29, 2013. Parker had also given a plenary at the international AIDS conference in Vancouver in 1996 on Brazilian community mobilization that both Barbara and Alan had heard and liked; see Richard G. Parker, "Empowerment, Community Mobilization and Social Change in the Face of HIV/AIDS," *AIDS* 10, supplement 3 (1996): S27–S31; on some of the difficulties with the Brazil experience, see João Biehl and Adriana Petryna, "Legal Remedies: Therapeutic Markets and the Judicialization of the Right to Health," in *When People Come First: Critical Studies in Global Health*, edited by João Biehl and Adriana Petryna (Princeton, NJ: Princeton University Press, 2013), 325–46.

57. Interview with BL and John Riley, New York City, March 26, 2017. Smith and Siplon, in *Drugs into Bodies*, tell the story of Alan's initiative on this issue but leave out some of the details; see 53–70.

58. Asia Russell of Philadelphia ACT UP, quoted in Richard Kim, "ACT UP Goes Global," *The Nation*, June 21, 2001, https://www.thenation.com/article/act-goes-global/. By this she meant that those with money could afford the drugs that the diminishing public sector was not providing.

59. BL, email to John Riley and Eric Sawyer, August 7, 1998. I am beyond grateful for Bob Lederer and John Riley's historical sensibilities, which led them to preserve these emails and other materials and share them with me.

60. Telephone interview with Asia Russell, December 17, 2017; see Susannah Fox, "The Internet Circa 1998," *Pew Research Center: Internet & Technology*, June 21, 2007, http://www.pewinternet.org/2007/06/21/the-internet-circa-1998/.

61. BL, email to Alan Berkman, John Riley and Eric Sawyer, August 14, 1998.

62. BL, email to Alan Berkman, John Riley and Eric Sawyer, August 14, 1998; McIssac, interview with Alan Berkman.

63. Emails provided by Bob Lederer, August 8–December 5, 1998.

64. Joshua Volle from Treatment Access Forum, email to Treatment Access@HIVnet.ch, November 20, 1998; provided by Bob Lederer.

65. Treatment Access Forum, email to Treatment Access@HIVnet.ch, October 22, 1998, moderator's note; provided by Bob Lederer. See also Patricia D. Siplon, *AIDS and the Policy Struggle in the United States* (Washington, DC: Georgetown University Press, 2002), 119.

66. Alan to BL, October 23, 1998; "Complementary Medicine: Integrated Care of Persons Living with HIV," New York Academy of Medicine, November 6–7, 1998, was cosponsored by Highbridge Woodycrest, SUNY Stony Brook Medical School, and the Balm Foundation.

67. BL to Asia Russell and Julie Davids [ACT UP activists in Philadelphia], cc: Alan Berkman, Richard Parker, Eric Sawyer, John Riley, Marie de Cenival, John James, Subject: Demands on Drug Access in Developing Countries, November 20, 1998, BP.

68. BL to Asia Russell and Julie Davids, November 23, 1998, BL personal collection.

69. Margot Hornblower, "The Battle in Seattle," *Time*, November 21, 1999.

70. BL to Alan, Richard Parker, Eric Sawyer, John Riley, and Marie de Cenival, November 20, 1998, BL personal collection. John S. James, "GATT and the Gap: How to Save Lives," *AIDS Treatment News*, no. 307, November 20, 1998, 1, 3–6.

71. The huge demonstrations in Seattle over globalization and the World Trade Organization were still a year off, taking place in November 1999.

72. Jeremy Greene, *Generics* (Baltimore: Johns Hopkins University Press, 2014), 231–60.

73. Greene, *Generics*; Smith and Siplon, *Drugs into Bodies*, 57–58; telephone interview with Jamie Love, December 17, 2017. On Love's history, see Sarah Boseley, "Big Pharma's Worst Nightmare," *The Guardian*, January 26, 2016, https://www.theguardian.com/society/2016/jan/26/big-pharmas-worst-nightmare.

74. Smith and Siplon, *Drugs into Bodies*, 57; Boseley, "Big Pharma's Worst Nightmare."

75. "Professor Hoosen Mahomed 'Jerry' Coovadia," http://www.sahistory.org.za/people/professor-hoosen-mahomed-jerry-coovadia.

76. Alan to Bob, December 5, 1998, BL personal collection.

77. BL to Alan, John Riley, Eric Sawyer, and Richard Parker, December 7, 1998, BL personal collection.

78. McIssac, interview with Alan Berkman; telephone interview with Barbara Zeller, January 21, 2018.

79. McIssac, interview with Alan Berkman.

80. "T Cell Lymphoma Survival Rate," http://www.lymphomainfo.net/articles/surviving-lymphoma/t-cell-lymphoma-survival-rate.

81. McIssac, interview with Alan Berkman.

82. The best summary of these issues and the work of the activists is in Smith and Siplon, *Drugs into Bodies*; and Siplon, *AIDS and the Policy Struggle in the United States*.

83. Keisha Franklin minutes, "HIV/AIDS Forum on Africa, 1/26/99," BL personal collection.

84. Smith and Siplon, *Drugs into Bodies*, 57.

85. Franklin minutes. NGOs concerned with this issue were being organized by Doctors without Borders, Love's Consumer Project on Technology, and Health Action International before the meeting began; see Consumer Project on Technology, "March 1999 Meeting on Compulsory Licensing of Essential Medical Technologies," http://www.cptech.org/march99-cl/.

86. McIssac, interview with Alan Berkman.

87. Alan Berkman, "History Form for Dr. Linda D. Lewis," February 2, 1999, BP.

88. R. I. Fisher et al., "Comparison of a Standard Regimen (CHOP) with Three Intensive Chemotherapy Regimens for Advanced Non-Hodgkin's Lymphoma," *New England Journal of Medicine* 328 (April 8, 1993): 1002–6.

89. McIssac, interview with Alan Berkman. Tom Garrett, a Columbia Medical School colleague and oncologist, became his physician.

90. Bruce Taub, email to author, February 15, 2018; Zeller interview.

91. Bruce Taub remembered walking with Alan and how much pain he was in. Interview with Bruce Taub, Orleans, MA, February 2, 2013.

92. Marc Brown, MD, to Dr. Tom Garrett, "Report of Radiologic Findings," August 18, 1999, BP.

93. Alan was also working with medical writer Nicholas Bakalar, the husband of one of his Columbia colleagues, on what would become a trade book, *Hepatitis A to G: The Facts You Need to Know about All the Forms of This Dangerous Disease* (New York: Warner, 2000). Bakalar wrote most of the book, but needed a doctor to front it. Bakalar, email to author, November 29, 2017.

94. John Riley and Bob Lederer, "Summary of Health GAP Coalition Meeting, March 16, 1999; Smith and Siplon, *Drugs into Bodies*, 58–68.

95. Riley and Lederer, "Summary of Health GAP Coalition Meeting"; telephone interview with Paul Davis, January 12, 2018.

96. Ronald Hayduk, "From Anti-globalization to Global Justice: A Twenty-First Century Movement," in *Teamsters and Turtles? U.S. Progressive Political Movements in the 21st Century*, edited by John C. Berg (New York: Rowman and Littlefield, 2003), 17–50, quote on 17–18.

97. Davis interview.

98. Telephone interview with Asia Russell, December 19, 2017.

99. "Health GAP Coalition—New Group for International Treatment Access," *AIDS Treatment News*, no. 314, March 18, 1999, clipping from BL.

100. Barton Gellman, "A Conflict of Health and Profit: Gore at the Center of Trade Policy," *Washington Post*, May 21, 2000.

101. Eric Sawyer, "An ACT UP Founder 'Acts Up' for Africa's Access to AIDS," in *From ACT UP to the WTO: Urban Protest and Community Building in the Era of Globalization*, edited by Benjamin Shepard and Ronald Hayduk (London: Verso, 2002), 98.

102. Sawyer, "An ACT UP Founder 'Acts Up.'"

103. Sawyer, "An ACT UP Founder 'Acts Up.'"

104. Gellman, "A Conflict of Health and Profit."

105. Sawyer, "An ACT UP Founder 'Acts Up,'" 98–99. Sawyer gets the date of the next action wrong. It was June 16, 1999, not February as he writes.

106. Mark Milano, "Persona Perspective: Zapping for Drugs," *AIDS Community Research Initiative of America* 15 (Fall 2006): 12–13, quoted in Mandisa Mbali, *South African AIDS Activism and Global Health Politics* (Houndmills, UK: Palgrave/Macmillan, 2013), 148.

107. C-Span, "Gore Announcement," https://www.c-span.org/video/?125103-1/gore-announcement (accessed January 30, 2018). The signs, whistles, and leaflets are audible and visible about halfway through.

108. Sawyer, "An ACT UP Founder 'Acts Up,'" 100.

109. Davis interview.

110. Davis interview. Groups from ACT UP New York, Fed Up Queers, and Health GAP

all were part of these actions; see ACT UP New York, "Gore Zaps," http://www.actupny.org/actions/gorezaps.html.

111. Davis interview; ACT UP New York, "Gore Zaps." I emailed former US trade representative Charlene Barshefsky about the sit-in, which she told me only that she remembered "vaguely." Barshefsky to author, January 15, 2018.

112. Szlezak, *The Making of Global Health Governance.*

113. One scholar has argued that changes in policy evolved out of U.S. and European government fears that a massive pandemic could bring security threats and unrest in many countries, coupled with other bureaucratic concerns, rather than the actions of civil society organizations like ACT UP and Health GAP, led to changes in AIDS policy. See Daniel W. Drezner, "The 'Semi-deviant' Case: TRIPS and Public Health," in *All Politics Is Global* (Princeton, NJ: Princeton University Press, 2008), 176–203. Drezner also cites other transient geopolitical factors and the interests of the United States and the European Union in improving international public health. There is an enormous international relations scholarship on this question that is beyond the scope of this book to analyze. For the counterview that gives more credit to the activists, see Raymond A. Smith, "Bridging the Gap: The Emergence of a US Activist Movement to Confront AIDS in the Developing World," paper for the American Political Science Association 2002 Annual Meeting, BP.

114. Gellman, "A Conflict of Health and Profit."

115. ACT UP New York, "Gore Zaps"; Russell interview, December 19, 2017; Davis interview; interview with BL and John Riley, New York City, March 24, 2017.

116. Smith, "Bridging the Gap." For the longer analysis, see also Smith and Siplon, *Drugs into Bodies.*

117. Mark Schoofs, "AIDS: The Agony of Africa," ran from November 3 to December 29, 1999, in the *Village Voice*; "The 2000 Pulitzer Prize Winner in International Reporting," http://www.pulitzer.org/winners/mark-schoofs.

118. Interview with Laura Whitehorn and Barbara Zeller, New York City, November 14, 2013.

119. Franklin minutes, "HIV/AIDS Forum on Africa, 1/26/99." Alan's estimate was high, and the numbers are always based on modeling and estimates, but in 2015 the number was 18 percent.

120. Treatment Action Campaign (TAC), *Fighting for Our Lives: The History of the Treatment Action Campaign, 1998–2010* (South Africa: Treatment Action Campaign, 2010), 4; Mandisa Mbali, *South African AIDS Activism and Global Health Politics* (Houndmills, UK: Palgrave/Macmillan, 2013), 107–226; Alain Vandormael, *Civil Society and Democracy in Post-Apartheid South Africa* (Saarbrucken, Germany: Dr. Muller, 2007).

121. Mark Heywood, *Get Up! Stand Up! Personal Journeys towards Social Justice* (Capetown: Talefberg, 2017), 110.

122. Heywood, *Get Up! Stand Up!*, 113.

123. Heywood, *Get Up! Stand Up!*, 111; TAC, *Fighting for Our Lives*, 7; see also Mark Heywood, "Civil Society and Uncivil Government: The Treatment Action Campaign versus Thabo Mbeki, 1998–2008," in *Mbeki and After*, edited by Daryl Glaser (Johannesburg: Wits University Press, 2010), 128–59.

124. TAC, *Fighting for Our Lives*, 8–9; Mark Gevisser, *A Legacy of Liberation: Thabo Mbeki and the Future of the South African Dream* (New York: Palgrave Macmillan, 2009), 276–96; Nathan Geffen, *Debunking Delusions: The Inside Story of the Treatment Action Campaign* (Sunnyside Auckland Park, South Africa: Jacana Media, 2010).

125. The tragic and complicated move of the ANC's leadership toward AIDS denialism has been told by multiple scholars; for examples, see Nattrass, *The AIDS Conspiracy*; Mbali, *South African AIDS Activism*; and Nicoli Nattrass, *Mortal Combat: AIDS Denialism and the Struggle for Antiretrovirals in South Africa* (Scottsville, South Africa: University of KwaZulu-Natal Press, 2007). A 2008 study estimated that because of the denialism, 35,000 babies were born with HIV that could have been prevented, and 330,000 lives were lost (Pride Chigwedere et al., "Estimating the Lost Benefits of Antiretroviral Drug Use in South Africa," *Journal of Acquired Immune Deficiency Syndromes* 49, no. 4 (December 1, 2008): 410–15.

126. Mbali, *South African AIDS Activism*, 108.

127. Health GAP/TAC Conference Call, February 5, 2000; notes provided by Karyn Kaplan from the International Gay and Lesbian Human Rights Commission, and given to me by Bob Lederer.

128. Heywood, *Get Up! Stand Up!*, 113.

129. Davis interview.

130. Geffen, *Debunking Delusions*, 54.

131. Interview with BL and Riley, New York City, March 29, 2017.

132. McIssac, interview with Alan Berkman; "Global Manifesto," Durban, South Africa, July 9, 2000, *ACT UP New York*, http://actupny.org/reports/durban-access.html.

133. Berkman, "Breaking the Silence," 2000.

134. "The Durban Declaration," *Nature* 406 (July 6, 2000): 15–16; Nattrass, *AIDS Conspiracy*.

135. Szlezak, *The Making of Global Health Governance*, 64–67.

136. Claire Laurier Decoteau, *Ancestors and Antiretrovirals: The Biopolitics of HIV/AIDS in Post-Apartheid South Africa* (Chicago: University of Chicago Press, 2013), 80; Heywood, *Get Up! Stand Up!*, 131–59.

137. Sarah Boseley, "How Nelson Mandela Changed the AIDS Agenda in South Africa," *The Guardian*, December 6, 2013, https://www.theguardian.com/world/2013/dec/06/nelson-mandela-aids-south-africa.

138. "Sex, Games and Videotapes," Durban PowerPoint, BCF.

139. "Global March for HIV/AIDS Treatment to the International AIDS Conference," July 9, 2000, Durban, South Africa, *ACT UP New York*, http://www.actupny.org/reports/durban-march.html; Geffen, *Debunking Delusions*, 54–56. Announcing one's HIV status was a courageous act in South Africa, where HIV-positive people had been murdered out of fear.

140. McIssac, interview with Alan Berkman.

141. Alan Berkman, notes for a *POZ* interview, May 21, 2002, BCF.

142. Steven Friedman and Shauna Mottiar, "A Rewarding Engagement? The Treatment Action Campaign and the Politics of HIV/AIDS," *Politics and Society* 33 (December 2005): 511–65.

143. Allan M. Brandt, "How AIDS Invented Global Health," *New England Journal of Medicine* 368 (June 6, 2013): 2149–52; Warwick Anderson, "Making Global Health History: The Postcolonial Worldliness of Biomedicine," *Social History of Medicine* 27 (2014): 372–84; Jeffrey P. Koplan et al., "Towards a Common Definition of Global Health," *Lancet* 373 (June 6, 2009): 1993–95. It can be argued that this too was pioneered by women's health activists; see Kathy Davis, *The Making of "Our Bodies, Ourselves": How Feminism Travels across Borders* (Durham, NC: Duke University Press, 2007).

Alan and others in May 19th had connections to the liberation struggles in

Mozambique, Zimbabwe, and the Congo. There was a historical link between American activists and African liberation, but most of that had not been about health; see William Minter, Gail Hovey, and Charles Cobb Jr., *No Easy Victories: African Liberation and American Activists over a Half Century, 1950–2000* (Trenton, NJ: Africa World, 2007).

CHAPTER 16

1. Telephone interview with Barbara Zeller, January 20, 2018. All interviews cited were conducted by the author unless otherwise specified.

2. Paul McIssac, interview with Alan Berkman, July 21, 2001; my transcription. I am grateful to Paul McIssac for providing me with the tape of this interview.

3. Zena Stein, "Tribute for Alan Berkman," May 21, 2009, BP; "James 5:11," http://biblehub.com/james/5-11.htm.

4. McIssac, interview with Alan Berkman.

5. Interview with Harriet Clark, San Francisco, March 5, 2016. Harriet remembered she said two weeks, but Barbara recalled saying it was just a week. Zeller interview.

6. Zeller interview.

7. McIssac, interview with Alan Berkman.

8. McIssac, interview with Alan Berkman; K. P. Papadopoulos et al., "Pilot Study of Tandem High-Dose Chemotherapy and Autologous Stem Cell Transplantation with a Novel Combination of Regimens in Patients with Poor Risk Lymphoma," *Bone Marrow Transplantation* 36 (September 2005): 491–97. Alan's doctor, David Savage, was the corresponding author on this article.

9. Harriet Clark interview; Barbara Zeller, email to author, February 26, 2018.

10. McIssac, interview with Alan Berkman.

11. McIssac, interview with Alan Berkman.

12. John S. James, "European Jewish Ancestry: Activist Doctor Needs Stem Cell Donation," *AIDS Treatment News*, December 22, 2000, clipping. I did the test, too, since we had the same broad Jewish ancestry. I was not a match.

13. James, "European Jewish Ancestry."

14. Photo of Alan in hospital bed. Interview with Lynne Karsten, Boston, February 24, 2018.

15. McIssac, interview with Alan Berkman.

16. McIssac, interview with Alan Berkman.

17. Alan's edits of the underground chapter are for April and July 2001. Interview with Bruce Taub, Orleans, MA, February 2, 2013. Terry Bisson blamed the loss of the publishing opportunity on Alan's taking the manuscript to the fraternity brother. Interview with Terry Bisson, San Francisco, March 7, 2016.

18. McIssac, interview with Alan Berkman.

19. Alan Berkman, "An Adult Infectious Disease Doctor's Encounter with HIV/AIDS," in *A History of AIDS Social Work in Hospitals*, edited by Barbara I. Willinger and Alan Rice (New York: Haworth, 2003), 3–13.

20. Timeline of Health GAP 1999–2000, "Health GAP" folder, BCF.

21. Telephone interview with Asia Russell, January 5, 2018.

22. Russell interview.

23. For more on the debate over the politics of science in South Africa and AIDS drugs, see Didier Fassin, "Adventures of African Nevirapine: The Political Biography of a Magic Bullet," in *Para-states and Medical Science: Making African Global Health*, edited

by P. Wenzel Geissler (Durham, NC: Duke University Press, 2012), 333–54; and Steven Robins, "'Long Live Zackie, Long Live': AIDS Activism, Science and Citizenship after Apartheid," *Journal of Southern African Studies* 30 (September 2004): 651–72.

24. Russell interview.

25. Alan Berkman for Health GAP, "June 23 Letter for NGOs," BCF.

26. Raymond A. Smith and Patricia A. Siplon, *Drugs into Bodies* (New York: Praeger, 2006), 105. Smith and Salon cover the actions at the United Nations in detail, 105–10.

27. Editorial, "The UN Looks at AIDS," *New York Times*, June 24, 2001.

28. Smith and Siplon, *Drugs into Bodies*, 109.

29. Jennifer Flynn Walker, "Tribute to Dr. Alan Berkman," June 5, 2009, https://www.youtube.com/watch?v=IJbDtHXSgdQ. Victoria Harden, *AIDS at 30* (Dulles, VA: Potomac, 2012), gives more credit to UN and U.S. officials than to civil society.

30. "Health GAP Retreat Notes," July 27–29, 2001, BL private collection.

31. Alan to Dear (name), HGAP fund-raising letter, November 22, 2001, BCF.

32. Alan to Dear (name), HGAP fund-raising letter, November 22, 2001, BCF.

33. Alan, "DART Overview Draft," BP.

34. Alan, "DART Overview Draft," BP.

35. See the critique in Warwick Anderson, *Colonial Pathologies: American Tropical Medicine, Race and Hygiene in the Philippines* (Durham, NC: Duke University Press, 2006).

36. Theodore Brown, Marcos Cueto, and Elizabeth Fee, "WHO and the Transition from International to Global Public Health," *American Journal of Public Health* 96 (January 2006): 62–72; Jeffrey P. Koplan et al., "Towards a Common Definition of Global Health," *Lancet* 373 (June 6, 2009): 1993–95.

37. Kavita Sivaramakrishnan, "Seeing the Invisible: Global Health History between the Lines," Global Health Lunch Panel, American Association for the History of Medicine Annual Meeting, Columbus, OH, April 26, 2019; Anna Tsing, *Friction: An Ethnography of Global Connection* (Princeton, NJ: Princeton University Press, 2005); Johanna Tayloe Crane, *Scrambling for Africa: AIDS, Expertise, and the Rise of American Global Health Science* (Ithaca, NY: Cornell University Press, 2013), gives a thoughtful analysis of how this "friction" in global health and AIDS works on the ground.

38. For example, see Karen Kruse Thomas, *Health and Humanity* (Baltimore: Johns Hopkins University Press, 2016). On the role of American foundations in setting the international/global health agenda, see Anne-Emanuelle Birn, "Philanthrocapitalism, Past and Present: The Rockefeller Foundation, the Gates Foundation, and the Setting(s) of the International/Global Health Agenda," *Hypothesis* 12, no. 1 (2014): 1–54.

39. For a critique of development theory and practices in South Africa, see Sally Matthews, "Post-development Theory and the Question of Alternatives: A View from South Africa," *Third World Quarterly* 25, no. 2 (2004): 373–84.

40. "It is justice, not charity, that is wanting in the world," wrote feminist Mary Wollstonecraft in 1792, quoted in Ilona Kickbusch, "Reflections on the U.S. Role in Global Public Health," *Health Affairs* 21 (November–December 2002): 131, 132–41.

41. Vinh-Kim Nguyen, *The Republic of Therapy: Triage and Sovereignty in West Africa's Time of AIDS* (Durham, NC: Duke University Press, 2003).

42. Salim S. Alandool Karim, "New Hope for HIV Prevention," Alan Berkman Memorial Lecture, Columbia University Epidemiology Grand Rounds, April 2012, BP.

43. Allan Rosenfield was famous for turning the world's attention to the mother in maternal and child health care; see Allan Rosenfield and Deborah Maine, "Maternal Mortality—A Neglected Tragedy, Where is the M in MCH?," *Lancet* 8446 (July 13,

1985): 83–85. See also Zena Stein to Alan Berkman and Ezra Susser, May 17, 2001, on their meeting with Rosenfield on the alliance with the Mandela Medical School, BCF.

44. Alan to Lou Santelli, HWC, October 22, 2002, BCF.

45. Richard Parker and Ezra Susser, emails to author, February 20, 2018.

46. Ezra Susser to Alan, December 13, 2002, BCF.

47. All of this is clear in the emails and files from 2001 to 2008 on Alan's computer.

48. Telephone interview with Pamela Collins, February 15, 2018. Collins worked with Alan on the prevention research with the homeless and then other global health projects at Columbia.

49. Collins interview.

50. I was struck over and over as I spoke to numerous faculty and students at Columbia by how many of the men in particular talked about his importance as a "best" friend, available, when he was not desperately sick, for support, intellectual help, and comfort.

51. Interview with Stephanie LeMelle, New York City, January 10, 2012.

52. Waafa El-Sadr, on DVD of Alan Berkman Memorial Service, Columbia University Mailman School of Public Health, New York City, April 23, 2010.

53. LeMelle interview.

54. The neighborhood is just south of Washington Heights, made famous by Lin-Mirada Manual's first musical, *In the Heights*.

55. Alan Berkman to U.S. Parole Commission, December 20, 2002, BCF. Buck was not released until 2010, ten days before she died of ovarian cancer.

56. Right after September 11th, Buck, along with other political prisoners, was sent into isolation for several weeks, even though she and the others had nothing to do with the attacks. See Marilyn Buck, "Incommunicado: Dispatches from a Political Prisoner," in *Imprisoned Intellectuals*, edited by Joy James (Lanham, MD: Rowman and Littlefield, 2003); and J. Soffiyah Elijah, "The Reality of Political Prisoners in the U.S.: What September 11 Taught Us about Defending Them," *Harvard Black Letter Law Journal* 18 (2002): 129–37.

57. Interview with Susie Day, New York City, March 23, 2017.

58. Dan Burger and Toussaint Losier, *Rethinking the American Prison Movement* (New York: Routledge, 2017), 169.

59. Paris photographs, BCF.

60. Jeremy Greene, "Vital Objects: Essential Drugs and Their Critical Legacies," in *Reimagining (Bio)medicalization, Pharmaceuticals and Genetics*, edited by Susan E. Bell and Anne Figert (New York: Routledge, 2015), 89–111.

61. James Love, "What the 2001 Doha Declaration Changed," *Knowledge Ecology International Blog*, September 16, 2011, https://www.keionline.org/21680.

62. Joanne Csete, "Several for the Price of One: Right to AIDS Treatment as Link to Other Human Rights," *Connecticut Journal of International Law* 17 (2002): 263–72.

63. Kate Torgovnick May, "I Am, Because of You: Further Reading on Ubuntu," *TED Blog*, December 9, 2013, https://blog.ted.com/further-reading-on-ubuntu.

64. Draft reference document for Ubuntu, Alan, BCF.

65. Joseph Maria Gatell and Jordi Casabona, Conference Co-Chairs, email to Alan, "Prison Session," April 2002, BCF.

66. Sharonann Lynch, Health GAP, and ACT UP, "Social Movement to Fight for Resources for AIDS, TB and Malaria," PowerPoint, March 27, 2003, BCF. Indeed by 2005 there were only a third of the target numbers in treatment even after the United Nations had set a goal labeled "3 by 5"; that is 3 million people in treatment by 2005.

67. Hayden, *AIDS at 30*, 221–44. The largest amount of funds initially were allocated to Kenya, Nigeria, South Africa, Uganda, and Zambia; see Myra Sessions, Center for Global Development, "Overview of PEPFAR," 2006, https://www.cgdev.org/page/overview-president%E2%80%99s-emergency-plan-aids-relief-pepfar.

68. Jews for Racial and Economic Justice, "Meyer Nominees and Winners List," https://jfrej.org/category/meyer.

69. Alan Berkman, "JFREJ Talk," 2002, BCF.

70. Alan, email to Ezra Susser, "My Funding and Major Areas of Responsibility," February 19, 2004, BCF.

71. Miriam Rabankin and Wafaa M. El-Sadr, *Saving Mothers, Saving Families: The MTCT-Plus Initiative* (Geneva: World Health Organization, 2003); there is an entire folder in Alan's computer files of all the work he did with Cornos on the problem of orphans.

72. Barbara Zeller, "The HIV/AIDS Epidemic in South Africa: A Personal Journey," August 29, 2003, BCF.

73. Barbara Zeller, email to Alan, April 2, 2003, BCF.

74. Alan to Slim and Quarraisha, September 9, 2002, BCF; telephone interview with Paul McIssac, February 11, 2018.

75. Barbara Zeller, "Ubuntu: Human Solidarity," August 22, 2003, BCF. All quotes that follow in this paragraph are from this document.

76. Vuyo Mkize, "How HIV Treatment Has Evolved in South Africa," *IOL*, November 28, 2017, https://www.iol.co.za/lifestyle/health/how-hiv-treatment-has-evolved-in-south-africa-12178007.

77. Interview with Jennifer Dohrn, New York City, April 22, 2015.

78. Robert Remien et al., "Adherence to Antiretroviral Therapy in a Context of Universal Access in Rio de Janeiro, Brazil," *AIDS Care* 17 (July 2007): 740–48. Alan was one of the article's eight coauthors.

79. Alan Berkman, "Quality Care: The Package" and "Scaling-Up ART in Resource-Limited Settings," Berkman PowerPoints, February 2006, BCF; Alan Berkman et al., "A Critical Analysis of the Brazilian Response to HIV/AIDS: Lessons Learned for Controlling and Mitigating the Epidemic in Developing Countries," *American Journal of Public Health* 95 (July 2005): 1162–71; Alan Berkman, "ICAP Rwanda," March 6, 2006, BCF.

80. Alan Berkman et al., ""Protecting the Lives of Children," February 26, 2006, BCF.

81. Alan Berkman, Berkman CV, October 2006, BCF.

82. Interview with Ezra Susser, New York City, October 11, 2011.

83. BCF.

84. Telephone interview with Nurys Vargas, January 28, 2014.

85. Alan Berkman, "Clinton Foundation Initiative in the Dominican Republic," report to Health GAP, March 17, 2003, BCF.

86. Alan Berkman, "Mailman Training and Technical Assistance Team, Dominican Republic HIV/AIDS Program," December 1, 2004–March 31, 2005, BCF.

87. Telephone interview with Eugene Schiff, New York City, February 16, 2018. Schiff's father, Gordon Schiff, is an expert on hospital quality care issues, and his mother, Mardge Cohen, works in Rwanda on an AIDS project for women and children, and with the Boston Coalition for the Homeless. Cohen's brother Bobby became Alan's primary care doctor at the end of his life.

88. Eugene Schiff to Alan Berkman, August 8, 2005; Eugene Schiff to Alan Berkman,

June 29, 2005; Alan Berkman to Eugene Schiff, June 28, 2005; Alan Berkman to Eugene Schiff, January 8, 2008. I am grateful to Eugene Schiff for providing these emails to me.

89. Between 2005 and 2008, Schiff became the "lead researcher and author for the Missing the Target Treatment Report Card, which is put out by the ITPC (International Treatment Preparedness Coalition)," and covered what was happening on the ground in more than a dozen countries. Eugene Schiff to Alan Berkman, January 8, 2008, BP.

90. Interview with Richard Parker, New York City, March 29, 2013.

91. Parker interview.

92. The term *Cancerland* belongs to writer Barbara Ehrenreich, from her article "Welcome to Cancerland," *Harper's Magazine*, November 2001, 43–53.

93. Dr. Thomas P. Jacobs to Dr. David Savage, July 27, 2003, BCF.

94. Dr. Ami Shah to Dr. Robert Cohen, February 1, 2006, BCF.

95. Alan to Bobby Cohen, February 14, 2007, BCF.

96. Lanny G. Close, MD, "Submandibular Gland, Left, Excision," March 14, 2007, BCF.

97. Zeller interview; Alan Berkman fax to Presbyterian Hospital Wound and Hyperbaric Oxygen Center, February 29, 2008, BCF.

98. Zeller interview.

99. American Cancer Society, "What Causes Myelodysplastic Syndromes?," https:// www.cancer.org/cancer/myelodysplastic-syndrome/causes-risks-prevention/what -causes.html.

100. Alan to David Savage, September 8, 2008, BCF.

101. Kris Kang to Dr. Berkman, October 3, 2008; Jeannie Tenuto to Alan, October 3, 2008; Ernie Drucker to Alan, October 3, 2008; Molly Delano to Daddy A, Mama B, October 3, 2008; Terry Bisson to Alan, October 10, 2008; Robert Roth to Alan and Barbara, October 10, 2008; Bernadine Dohrn and Bill Ayers to Alan and Barbara, October 4, 2008; Judy Holmes to Alan and Barbara, October 2, 2008; Caring Bridge emails. I am grateful to Bob Lederer, who saved these.

102. Zeller interview.

103. Health GAP, "Health GAP's 10th Anniversary: Global Health Justice Awards Honor Radical Drs. Alan Berkman and David Hoos," press release, May 21, 2009, BP.

104. Alan to Hi Gentlemen, Dick Rothkopf and Bob Bluestein, May 6, 2009, BCF.

105. Zeller interview.

106. Alan to Bob Bluestein, May 20, 2009, BCF.

107. Zeller interview.

108. Zeller interview.

109. "It is bittersweet," his doctor wrote to Barbara, that Alan "fought very hard and courageously against a terrible disease.... Unfortunately, despite the most advanced therapeutic measures at our disposal, it is a painful fact that cancer and its complications still defeat us all too often." James W. Young to Dr. Barbara Zeller, August 24, 2009, BP.

CODA

1. John Brown to Hon. D. R. Tilden, November 28, 1859, in *The Tribunal: Reponses to John Brown and the Harpers Ferry Raid*, edited by John Stauffer and Zoe Trodd (Cambridge, MA: Harvard University Press, 2012), 69. The letter was written four days before his hanging on December 2, 1859.

2. Paul Breines, *Tough Jews: Political Fantasies and the Moral Dilemma of American Jewry*

(New York: Basic Books, 1990); Issac Deutscher, "Message of the Non-Jewish Jew," *The Non-Jewish Jew and Other Essays* (London: Verso, 2017, rpt.); Ruth Wisse, *The Shlemiel as a Modern Hero* (Chicago: University of Chicago Press, 1971).

3. The meaning of the Holocaust to American Jews has transformed over the decades; see Shaul Magid, "The Holocaust and Jewish Identity in America: Memory, the Unique, and the Universal," *Jewish Social Studies* 18, no. 2 (2012): 100–135.

4. Ernesto "Che" Guevara, "On Revolutionary Medicine," translated by Beth Kurti, spoken on August 19, 1960, to the Cuban Militia, Che Guevara Internet Archive (marxists .org), 1999, https://www.marxists.org/archive/guevara/1960/08/19.htm.

5. João Biehl and Adriana Petryna, eds., *When People Come First: Critical Studies in Global Health* (Princeton, NJ: Princeton University Press, 2013).

6. Molly Delano to Dear Daddy A, Mama B, Sarah, Harriet, and Gabriel, October 3, 2008, Caring Bridge, BL private collection.

7. All comments in this paragraph come from the DVD of the private (family and friends) memorial for Alan at the Plaza Jewish Community Center on June 9, 2009. DVD provided to me by Barbara Zeller.

8. DVD of Dr. Alan Berkman Memorial Service, Columbia University, Mailman School of Public Health, New York City, April 23, 2010. I was on my way to this event when my father-in-law had a stroke. I had to miss the memorial.

9. On Harris Yulin, see Internet Movie Data Base (IMDB), https://www.imdb.com /name/nm0950867.

NOTE ON SOURCES

This was the first book I have written that required my working primarily outside of formal archives, whether in libraries or hospitals. Barbara Zeller's second bedroom in the last apartment she shared with Alan held boxes of his letters, legal papers, political ephemera, a draft of his prison memoir, and the thumb drives from his computer. All of this material is now in the Alan Berkman Papers in the Archives and Special Collections at the Augustus C. Long Health Sciences Library of Columbia University and can be researched there. The second major source of materials was the Freedom Archives in San Francisco that former political prisoner Claude Marks has built and maintained for more than two decades (http://freedomarchives.org). Much of this has been digitized and can be obtained online. Diane Gillman Charney, Alan's girlfriend from high school through college, kept his letters and loaned them to me.

Some materials are in formal archives. Alan's student records and political materials about his time in college and medical school are in the archives at Cornell University and Columbia University Medical School. Alan's May 19th comrade Susan Rosenberg donated her papers to the Sophia Smith College in the Archives at Smith College in Northampton, Massachusetts. They provided an additional perspective on the legal issues and the Resistance Conspiracy Case.

Through a Freedom of Information Act (FOIA) request I made in 2013 from the National Archives, I received Alan's FBI files fairly quickly. It took, alas, until early 2019 and then again right before the book went into production in late 2019 to obtain all of the May 19th Communist Organization's FBI files. FOIA requests are so backed up and then the documents have to be redacted, so it takes years to get them.

Much of the information came from interviews in person or by Skype, email, or telephone with Alan's friends, lawyers, family, and comrades. With the help of a student, at the beginning, I did almost all the transcriptions myself of the nearly 100 interviews cited in the notes.

Paul McIssac and Marion Banzhaf did long interviews with Alan, Dana Biberman, and Barbara Zeller in the early 2000s. Several of them were on discs or MP3s, and I transcribed them. In addition, Marion Banzhaf, as a leader in the John Brown Anti-Klan Committee, allowed me to see the papers she has in her Florida home on Prairie Fire, May 19th, the John Brown Committee, and support work for the Resistance Conspiracy Case. Bob Lederer's personal collection of original documents and emails, including the emails from Caring Bridge during Alan's last illness was critical in understanding the founding of Health GAP and Alan's role. Paul McIssac's video for Alan's memorial service was particularly helpful.

Barbara Zeller also made available three DVDs that documented Alan's release from prison and his welcome-home party, his funeral, and then his memorial service. His longtime friend Dick Clapp provided other interviews.

There is a growing secondary literature on the Left politics of the 1960s to 1990s, on the rise of mass incarceration and prison movements, and now on global AIDS politics. All of it was invaluable, and I cite much of it in the endnotes.

INDEX

Page numbers in italics refer to illustrations.